Cloud Native Anti-Patterns

Avoiding Common Mistakes and Driving Success
with Best Practices and Real-World Cases

Gerald Bachlmayr

Aiden Ziegelaar

Alan Blockley

Bojan Zivic

Cloud Native Anti-Patterns

Portfolio Director: Kartikey Pandey

Relationship Lead: Preet Ahuja

Project Manager: Sonam Pandey

Content Engineer: Sarada Biswas

Technical Editor: Nithik Cheruvakodan

Copy Editor: Safis Editing

Indexer: Tejal Soni

Proofreader: Sarada Biswas

Production Designer: Deepak Chavan

Growth Lead: Amit Ramadas

First published: March 2025

Production reference: 1061125

Published by Packt Publishing Ltd.

Grosvenor House

11 St Paul's Square

Birmingham

B3 1RB, UK

ISBN 978-1-83620-059-8

www.packtpub.com

Foreword

The journey of cloud native technologies—from the advent of virtualization to the rise of DevOps and serverless computing—has fundamentally reshaped the tech industry. These innovations have not only become a cornerstone of modern application development but also set the stage for building scalable, resilient, and efficient systems. Yet, despite this progress, adopting cloud native practices can feel overwhelming, requiring not just an understanding of best practices but also an awareness of potential challenges and missteps.

Many of us turn to others for guidance, whether through blog posts, Stack Overflow, ChatGPT, or even niche Slack communities. However, while these resources often explain what to do, they rarely focus on what not to do. Sure, you might encounter a snarky comment about your approach, but rarely do you get a clear explanation of why it's flawed.

When developing entire applications, steering clear of common mistakes is just as important as following the right path. That's why I'm thrilled the authors of this book have taken the time to not only highlight the best practices but also illuminate the missteps to avoid. Their insights will guide you toward implementing these ideas effectively and with confidence.

In these pages, you'll explore what it truly means to build cloud native applications, going beyond the buzzwords to understand the principles and scope of cloud native architecture. Along the way, the authors tackle some of the most common misunderstandings that can lead teams astray, offering clarity and practical advice for navigating the challenges of cloud adoption. You'll also find guidance on crafting a strategic approach to shifting your organization toward cloud native operations, including rethinking governance to match the agility and scale that modern applications demand.

The book doesn't stop at strategy—it dives into the practicalities, too. You'll learn how to manage costs effectively to avoid the dreaded bill shock that catches so many teams off guard, ensuring you get the most out of your cloud investment without unpleasant surprises. Security, often seen as at odds with rapid delivery, is treated with equal care, showing how you can deliver software rapidly and continuously while maintaining a robust security posture.

This is more than a guide—it's a blueprint for navigating the complexities of cloud native development and operations. By the time you finish the book, you'll have the tools and knowledge to not only succeed but also thrive in this ever-evolving space.

Nick Triantafillou

AWS Hero, Senior MLOps and Cloud Engineer

Contributors

About the authors

Gerald Bachlmayr is an experienced cloud strategist and DevSecOps professional with over 25 years of IT experience. Gerald spent many years as a software engineer before moving into various team lead, principal cloud architect, and chief cloud architect roles. He has designed and implemented cloud-native solutions for various industries, including financial services, tertiary education, and government organizations. As a security practitioner, he ensures that blueprints meet security, resilience, and regulatory requirements. Gerald is a passionate AWS Community Builder. As an author and public speaker, he is keen on sharing his insights and learnings with the community to make the cloud an even better place.

Aiden Ziegelaar is an experienced multidisciplinary engineer with a focus on cloud transformation, cloud native software development, and electrical engineering. With a strong background in various industries, including Telcos, Edutech, Industry 4.0, and utilities at scales from start-ups to enterprises, he has gained a wealth of knowledge and expertise in delivering innovative and practical solutions to complex problems. Transforming clients to leverage cloud technologies effectively has been a cornerstone of his career. You can often find him speaking at conferences or reading a good book (much like this one!).

Alan Blockley is a domain specialist with over 25 years of IT experience, specializing in AWS cloud technology. Based in Brisbane, he has conducted hundreds of AWS Well-Architected Framework reviews and has extensive experience in presales, cloud operations, and engineering. As a recognized leader, Alan has driven technical validations and mentored teams in DevOps practices. He holds multiple AWS certifications and was named the top AWS Ambassador for ANZ in 2023 and 2024. Alan is also an AWS Serverless Community Builder and an Associate Certification Subject Matter Expert, demonstrating his deep commitment to the AWS community and speaking at localized user groups and conferences on cloud native topics.

Bojan Zivic is an AWS Ambassador, Serverless AWS Community Builder, and principal consultant with a passion for cloud technology and a dedication to fostering community; Bojan hosts and organizes the Brisbane Serverless User Group and the Sydney GitHub User Group. With nine years of experience in IT, Bojan is an enthusiastic advocate for serverless and container computing. His expertise extends to AWS advisory work and comprehensive Kubernetes projects. He has implemented GitOps with ArgoCD, built Istio service meshes, and provided extensive support across the Kubernetes spectrum, not just serverless. His work and community efforts solidified his reputation as a leader in the cloud and DevOps communities.

About the reviewers

Shashank Tilwalli is a technology leader with over 15 years of experience, specializing in cloud solutions, application modernization, and generative AI. He has collaborated with top-notch tech companies, assisting them in designing and implementing cutting-edge solutions. His expertise spans cloud infrastructure, application modernization, and containerization, complemented by a deep understanding of generative AI and **machine learning** (ML). He excels in API management, microservices, DevOps, and security best practices. With a passion for customer collaboration, Shashank strives to understand unique challenges and deliver solutions that drive innovation and growth. He is also a strong advocate for knowledge sharing and community building within the tech industry. His credentials include a master of computer applications degree and numerous certifications in relevant areas. He is committed to continuous learning and staying ahead of the curve in the ever-evolving technological landscape.

Shanmugasundaram Sivakumar is a seasoned software engineer with over 16 years of experience in designing and optimizing large-scale enterprise and SaaS applications. His expertise spans cloud-native architectures, distributed systems, and AI-driven automation. He has a strong background in performance engineering, ensuring high availability, scalability, and resilience for mission-critical platforms. Throughout his career, he has tackled complex challenges in optimizing performance, managing cloud workload, and enhancing application reliability. Passionate about software scalability, he has worked extensively with containerized environments, microservices, and AI-driven observability to improve operational efficiency and system resilience.

Koushik Sundar is a technical architect with 17+ years of expertise in scalable financial systems and AI-driven modernization. His skill set spans algorithmic challenges, DevOps, site reliability engineering, AI, ML, deep learning, remote sensing, IoT, cybersecurity, and cloud native development. He has led application modernization by building microservice-based, cloud native solutions, leveraging multi-cloud strategies, and integrating AI to drive industry transformation. His work in engineering high-performance applications has been pivotal in solving complex algorithmic challenges, including NP-hard problems, enhancing resilience, scalability, and operational efficiency across various technology sectors.

Uman Ahmed Mohammed is a seasoned IT architect specializing in multi-hyperscalers, hybrid cloud, application modernization, platform engineering, generative AI-driven automation, and enterprise architecture. With a proven track record in designing and implementing enterprise solutions, Uman has deep expertise in optimizing efficiency, scalability, and innovation, and is a trusted advisor and subject matter expert, adept at aligning business and technology strategies to architect high-performance platforms for distributed systems, accelerating enterprise transformation.

Table of Contents

Preface | xvii

Free Benefits with Your Book | xxii

Part 1: Introduction and Overview | 1

1

Benefits of Cloud Native and Common Misunderstandings | 3

The evolution of cloud native | 4
The foundations for ML, AI, and cross-functional teams | 4
The age of virtualization | 4
The beginning of distributed applications | 5
The rise of Agile, DevOps, and the cloud | 5
Edge computing – microservices, and addressing security | 6
Containers and function as a service | 6
Cloud native and best practices | 7
Where are we now and what does the future bring? | 7

Benefits of cloud native | 8
Faster time to market | 8
Scalability and elasticity | 9
Managed services | 9
Security and compliance | 10
Reliability and availability | 10
Global deployments | 11
CI/CD – automate all the things | 11
Cost benefits and paradigm change | 12

Portability | 12

DevSecOps culture, IaC, and CI/CD | 12
The culturural aspect | 13
IaC | 15
CI/CD | 16

Observability and resilience | 18
Logging – the observability enabler | 18
Log quality | 19
Monitoring and observability | 20
Resilience | 20

Common misunderstandings | 22
The shared responsibility model | 23
Operating model confusions | 25
Missing out on cultural transformation | 25
Treating cloud like on-premises | 26
Containers solve everything | 27
Security can be an afterthought | 27
Cloud native versus microservices | 27

Summary | 28

Part 2: Setting Up Your Organization for Success 29

2

The Cost of Unclear Objectives and Strategy 31

Lack of clear objectives and strategy 32
Common anti-patterns 32
Understanding the business goals and
our current state 34
Defining technology objectives and principles 35
Defining our strategy foundations 36
Adding guardrails to our strategy 37
Enhancing our strategy 39

Lack of migration strategy 39
Common anti-pattern variations 40
A framework to navigate our migration journey 42
Transitioning into the business case 43
Kicking off the implementation and gaining
momentum 44

**Outsourcing of cloud knowledge
and governance** 46

What does it take to govern cloud
native initiatives? 46
Drivers for outsourcing 47
Common anti-patterns 48
Anti-pattern indicators 49

Lack of partnership strategy 53
Common anti-patterns 54
The value of strategic partnerships 55
General indicators for this anti-pattern 56
Considerations for selecting a partner 57
Improving our CSP partnership 59
Conclusion 60

The cloud adoption runaway train 60
CAFs 60
Common anti-patterns 63

Summary 66

3

Rethinking Governance in a Cloud Native Paradigm 67

Learning will happen miraculously 67
The cost of ignoring learning 68
Addressing the anti-pattern 69

The culture doesn't need to change 73
The cultural impact of cloud native adoption 73
The hidden costs of ignoring cultural change 74
Effective strategies for cultural change in
cloud native adoption 79

Centralized governance will scale 79
Centralized governance – navigating
challenges and crafting solutions 80

**Our business is too special for
guardrails or standards** 85
Understanding the concept and benefits of
guardrails 85
Key strengths of guardrails 86

Understanding which guardrails to use   87
RACI model   88
The necessity of endorsed GRC policies   90

Missing feedback loops   91
What are feedback loops?   91
Why we can't ignore feedback loops   92
Cost of time and effort   93

Slowed development cycle and
increased pressure   93
The role of change management in
cloud governance   95
The shift-left principle   97
Creating a proactive culture   98
Empower and uplift   99

Summary   99

4

FinOps – How to Avoid a Bill Shock   101

**Missing out on the power of good
tagging practices   102**
Common anti-patterns   103
Consequences of poor tagging practices   104
Spotting untagged resources   104
Adopting a tagging taxonomy   106
Continuous improvement   107

Not leveraging CSP FinOps services   109
Common anti-patterns   109
Impacts   111
Cost management seen through the SDLC lens   112

Ignoring non-obvious CSP cost   118
Common anti-patterns   119

Other non-obvious cost factors   122
Impacts of missing non-obvious cost   124
Indicators   125
Remediations   126

**Focusing on cost savings over
driving value   127**
Common anti-patterns   128
Impacts   130
Problem indicators   131
What does good look like, and
how do we get there?   131

Summary   133

5

Delivering Rapidly and Continuously Without Compromising Security   135

Underestimating the cultural impact   135
The siloed model – a long road to production   136
DORA – measuring the road   137
Empowered teams – increasing your speed   137
DevSecOps – the super-highway to production   138
Staying on the road   140

Drawing a new map   140

**Frequent changes to meet
business goals   141**
Pruning Git branches   141
Decoupling integration and release   142
Reversing the inevitable   144

Guardrails — 145

Keeping your developers on track — 145

Types of guardrail — 146

The case for guardrail observability — 146

Example guardrails — 147

Shifting left — 149

Development as an iterative process — 149

Test first, code later — 149

Shared ownership of output — 150

Experimenting and getting feedback early — 151

Building in security from the start — 152

Self-sufficient teams — 152

Trifecta leadership — 152

The topology of your teams — 153

Champions and the T-shaped engineer — 155

Summary — 155

6

How to Meet Your Security and Compliance Goals — 157

How to Manage Permissions Without Over-Privilege — 157

Securing High-Privilege Accounts — 158

Over Privileged Users and Services — 159

Not all logging is the same — 164

Reliance on long-term static credentials — 165

Threat modeling — 166

Importance of Continuous Compliance in Security — 167

Myth busting the One-Time Test — 167

Overnight changes — 167

The Importance of Continuous Security and Compliance — 168

The Role of Automation in Security and Compliance — 169

Building a Proactive Security Culture — 170

Wrapping compliance up — 170

Proactive Monitoring: Don't Wait for the External Audit to Spot Issues — 171

Importance of Ongoing Security Assessments — 171

Automating Security Processes — 172

Continuous Compliance Validation — 172

The Role of External Audits — 173

Building a Proactive Security Culture — 173

Misunderstanding the shared responsibility model — 174

Understanding and Addressing Misconceptions in the Shared Responsibility Model — 174

Shared Responsibility Model Across "The Big 3" — 174

Common Misunderstandings — 178

Cloud Provider Proof of Compliance — 179

Common Misconfigurations — 179

Supply chain insecurity — 180

Challenges in Supply Chain Security — 180

Avoiding Supply Chain Risks — 181

Examples of Supply Chain Insecurity — 182

Summary — 183

Part 3: Turning It into Actions   185

7

Expressing Your Business Goals in Application Code   187

Lift and shift   187
Building in the cloud versus building
for the cloud   188
The myth of "We'll build it right this time"   188
Cloud factories   189
Cloud native through the strangler fig pattern   189

Stateful applications   192
The stateless server   193
Resiliency and scalability in a stateless server
paradigm   194
State as a service   195
Application configuration as state   196

Tight coupling, low cohesion   196
The Lambdalith versus single-purpose
functions   197

Chaining serverless functions   198
Decoupling coupled services   199
Telemetry and event correlation   200

The comprehensive definition of done 200
Ignoring security   200
Ignoring observability   202
Ignoring reliability   203

Other pitfalls   206
Solving cloud native problems without cloud
native experience   206
Suffering from success – the downside
of limitless scale   207
Avoiding implicit ephemeral specification   209

Summary   209

8

Don't Get Lost in the Data Jungle   211

Picking the wrong database or storage 212
Framing the conversation   212
The right database for the right purpose   216
Manual, managed, serverless, and truly
serverless databases   218
Ignoring storage requirements   219
Ignoring the life cycle and archive policy   219

**Data replication from production
to development**   221
But we mask our production data   221
Getting started with synthetic data   221

Perfect synthetic data   222

**Backup and recovery should
theoretically work**   223
Have a plan   223
Game day   225
The real thing   226

Manual data ingestion   226
The first data ingestion pipeline   227
Failure granularity   227
Scaling the pipeline   228
Making the jump to streaming   228

No observability for data transfer errors   **228**

The data integrity dependency   229

Inverting the dependency   229

Maintaining the dependency   230

Summary   **230**

9

Connecting It All   231

Ignoring latency and bandwidth   **232**

Cloud native latency   232

Cloud native bandwidth   236

Lack of DNS strategy   **239**

Cloud native DNS management   240

Undermining traffic segregation (QoS) based on application/data criticality   242

Monolithic connectivity   244

Monolith to layered networking   246

Synchronous versus synchronous traffic   249

Ignoring cloud native networking features   **251**

SDN in the cloud – the risks from on-premises   251

Inadequate network access reviews and missing boundary guardrails   254

IaC and automation – the networking perspective   255

Zero Trust application patterns   **256**

Zero Trust in cloud native versus on-premises environments   257

Zero Trust in practice – a cloud native example   258

Network defense in depth versus flat networks – balancing security and operability   259

Summary   **260**

10

Observing Our Architecture   261

Let's Capture Everything in the Log Aggregator   **262**

Why Indiscriminate Logging Fails   262

Smart Logging: A More Effective Approach   262

The Blind Spots of Incomplete Observability and the Importance of End-to-End Distributed Tracing   264

Ignoring ML and AI capabilities   **268**

Leveraging Cloud AI/ML for Anomaly Detection   269

Improving Log Aggregation with AI Insights   270

Centralized Monitoring with Automated Intelligence   271

Reducing Operational Complexity through ML Automation   272

Neglecting Distributed Tracing   **274**

The Fragmentation Problem   275

Metrics that Matter   276

Real World Consequences   278

Best Practices for Resolving Tracing Neglect   281

Immature processes for alerts & incidents   **282**

Purpose-driven Metrics and Alerts   283

The Trap of Metric Dumping   284

Shifting Left in Observability   285

Alert Fatigue & Incident Response Maturity   287

Summary   **288**

11

Running It Without Breaking It   289

Assuming the Cloud is Just 'Business as Usual'   289
Understanding Cloud Complexity   290
Training and Upskilling   291
Collaborative learning is key   293

Inadequate Disaster Recovery & Backup Plans   293
Building a Comprehensive Backup Plan   293
RPO vs RTO   293
Disaster Recovery Strategy   294
Wrapping up Disaster Recovery and Backup   299

Out-of-Date Runbooks and Documentation   299
Maintaining Updated Documentation   299
Automating Documentation   300
Standard Operating Procedures (SOPs)   300
Documentation and Runbooks in practical terms   301

Ignoring the Cultural Shift   303
Encouraging Collaboration   303
Breaking Down Silos   304
Cross-Functional Teams   304
Knowledge Sharing   305
Promoting a DevSecOps Mindset   305
Overcoming Resistance to Change   306

Developing Around CSP SLAs   307
Building Redundancy Beyond SLAs   307
Preparing for Provider Downtime   308
Automation for Resilience   310

Summary   312

12

Migrating from Legacy Systems to Cloud Native Solutions   313

Planning for an effective migration   313
Jumping in Without a Plan: Why planning is important   314
Developing a Clear Migration Strategy   314

Minimum Stakeholder Commitment   323
Understanding the Anti-Pattern: Minimum Stakeholder Commitment   323
How Stakeholders Should Engage in Cloud Adoption   324
Technical Considerations for Stakeholders   326

Replicating On-Prem Security Controls   327
Understanding the Anti-Pattern: Replicating On-Prem Security Controls   327
How to Shift from On-Prem to Cloud Native Security   329

Underestimating Skill Gaps   331
Understanding the Anti-Pattern: Underestimating Skill Gaps   331
How to Close the Skill Gap   332
Balancing Technical and Soft Skills   333

Summary   334

13

How Do You Know It All Works?   335

General testing anti-patterns   335

Tests that have never failed   336
Coverage badge tests   336
Testing implementation details   337
Intermittently failing tests   338
Tests with side effects or coupled tests   338
Multistage tests   340

Lack of contract testing   340

Contract testing   340
Beyond the initial contract   341
Contract enforcement   343
Portability   343
Code generation   344

Manual testing   344

Typical company testing archetypes   345

The case for test automation   345
Migrating manual testing processes   347

Trying to recreate the cloud   348

The traditional testing paradigm   349
The testing honeycomb   350
Testing in the cloud versus testing for the cloud   350
Testing non-functional requirements   352

Poorly structured code   352

Key terms   353
The monolith   353
Hexagonal architecture   354
Structuring your code correctly from day one   355

Summary   356

14

How to Get Started with Your Cloud Native Improvement Journey   357

Identifying anti-patterns   357

General indicators   358
DevSecOps culture and automation   358
Strategy and cloud adoption-related anti-patterns   359
Operational and observability anti-patterns   359
Technology anti-patterns   360

Defining the best outcome and identifying gaps   361

Defining the current state   361
Defining the target state   364

Defining the best outcome and identifying gaps   366

Socializing the high-level plan with the broader group   366
Adding organization-specific details   368
Addressing external factors and technology impacts   369
Building a roadmap and keeping the stakeholders informed   371
The business case document   372
Next steps and other considerations   375

Summary   376

15

Transitioning to Cloud Native Good Habits ... 377

Stakeholder alignment ... 378
Stakeholder management considerations ... 378
Common challenges in stakeholder alignment ... 380

Your roadmap ... 384
Understanding the migration path ... 385

Continuous improvement ... 391

Establishing new or modified building blocks ... 392
Creating and modifying governance frameworks ... 392
Addressing technology dependencies ... 395

Summary ... 397

16

Unlock Your Exclusive Benefits ... 399

Index ... 403

Other Books You May Enjoy ... 420

Preface

A sound cloud native adoption approach can be a significant business enabler. It can accelerate innovation cycles, improve our time to market, increase resilience, improve security posture, and enable observability and flexible integrations for data, APIs, and connectivity. Despite all the potential that cloud native brings, the authors of this book have seen many things go wrong, were involved in the remediation steps across the software development life cycle, and had opportunities to start building new capabilities from scratch. A cloud native journey is not only about technology and tools. It starts with a cultural transformation, leveraging the right ways of working and transforming our company into a learning organization. The adoption also requires a shift in governance, security, ownership, and continuous improvement of our architecture and skills. With great power comes great responsibility. This book provides insights into where cloud initiatives tend to go wrong, how to spot those anti-patterns while they are starting to unfold, and how to remediate them to drive successful cloud adoption. By reading this book, you will learn about the following:

- How to identify common anti-patterns encountered when shifting to agile cloud native delivery
- What high-performing cloud native delivery looks like
- How to spot anti-patterns in your organization and analyze their long-term impacts
- Prescriptive guidance on how to remediate anti-patterns

Who this book is for

This book is intended for the following audience that has fundamental knowledge of information technology solutions and wants to improve their cloud native knowledge:

- Cloud platform engineers and software engineers
- Cloud or solution architects
- Quality and test engineers
- Enterprise architects
- Technical team leads
- Engineering managers

What this book covers

Chapter 1, Benefits of Cloud Native and Common Misunderstandings, explores benefits, DevOps culture and CI/CD, observability, and resilience, and clarifies some common misunderstandings.

Chapter 2, The Cost of Unclear Objectives and Strategy, discusses common strategy mistakes, such as outsourcing knowledge or lacking roadmaps and partnership strategies, and how to transition into good practice.

Chapter 3, Rethinking Governance in a Cloud Native Paradigm, steps through common governance anti-patterns, such as underestimating cultural impact and learning effort, and discusses how to develop good habits.

Chapter 4, FinOps – How to Avoid a Bill Shock, discusses mistakes including lacking tagging enforcement, focusing on cost savings instead of value optimization, and others. For each area, we will also explain what *good* looks like and how to achieve it.

Chapter 5, Delivering Rapidly and Continuously Without Compromising Security, analyzes problem spaces including cultural impacts, guardrails, and shifting left. Of course, we will also examine how to improve our organization.

Chapter 6, How to Meet Your Security and Compliance Goals, discusses pitfalls such as permission mismanagement, supply chain challenges, and reliance on penetration tests. We will step through transitioning into good habits.

Chapter 7, Expressing Your Business Goals in Application Code, explores application-related anti-patterns, such as tight coupling and stateful applications, and how to transition into good habits.

Chapter 8, Don't Get Lost in the Data Jungle, covers data-related anti-patterns, including manual data ingestion and a lack of data observability, and we will help you adopt good practices.

Chapter 9, Connecting It All, covers adopting future-proof network architectures after discussing network-related pitfalls, such as ignoring latency or bandwidth and not having a DNS strategy.

Chapter 10, Observing Our Architecture, explores observability-related anti-patterns, such as capturing everything or ignoring ML and AI capabilities, which can burden our organization, and we will explore how to improve our observability.

Chapter 11, Running It Without Breaking It, discusses operational-related pitfalls, such as underestimating the learning curve and considering **cloud service provider** (**CSP**) SLAs. We will also discuss the adoption of good operational practices.

Chapter 12, Migrating from Legacy Systems to Cloud Native Solutions, looks at migration anti-patterns, such as a lack of planning and stakeholder commitment or sticking to on-premises security controls, which will prevent successful cloud adoption, and we will discuss how to avoid these bad practices.

Chapter 13, How Do You Know It All Works?, explores test-related pitfalls, such as ignoring non-functional requirements upfront or relying on manual testing, which do not scale and will slow us down. We will explore how to avoid these anti-patterns.

Chapter 14, How to Get Started with Your Cloud Native Improvement Journey, discusses how to prepare ourselves and our organization for a successful cloud adoption journey. We will summarize how to spot anti-patterns and define the best outcome.

Chapter 15, Transitioning to Cloud Native Good Habits, dives deeper into stakeholder alignment, enhancing our roadmap, and setting our organization up for continuous improvement.

To get the most out of this book

To get the most out of this book, you will have some fundamental information technology knowledge, no matter whether your background is development, operations, testing, technical leadership, governance, security, or strategy. The book doesn't require you to install software. To follow along with some of the hands-on examples, you can optionally create a free-tier account for AWS, Azure, or GCP.

Conventions used

There are a number of text conventions used throughout this book.

`Code in text`: Indicates code words in text, database table names, folder names, filenames, file extensions, pathnames, dummy URLs, user input, and Twitter handles. Here is an example: " `WARN`: When a transient issue arises, such as a timeout during a payment request to AWS RDS, a `WARN` log is generated:"

A block of code is set as follows:

```
WARN: Payment service timeout - user_id=12345, transaction_id=txn001,
retry_attempt=1
```

When we wish to draw your attention to a particular part of a code block, the relevant lines or items are set in bold:

```
INFO: Payment initiated - user_id=12345, session_id=abc987,
transaction_id=txn001, amount=49.99
```

Any command-line input or output is written as follows:

```
gcloud services enable cloudasset.googleapis.com
```

Bold: Indicates a new term, an important word, or words that you see onscreen. For instance, words in menus or dialog boxes appear in **bold**. Here is an example: " **Aggregate and Centralize Logs**: Logs from each service are centralized using AWS CloudWatch Logs."

> **Tips or important notes**
> Appear like this.

Get in touch

Feedback from our readers is always welcome.

General feedback: If you have questions about any aspect of this book, email us at `customercare@packtpub.com` and mention the book title in the subject of your message.

Errata: Although we have taken every care to ensure the accuracy of our content, mistakes do happen. If you have found a mistake in this book, we would be grateful if you would report this to us. Please visit `www.packtpub.com/support/errata` and fill in the form.

Piracy: If you come across any illegal copies of our works in any form on the internet, we would be grateful if you would provide us with the location address or website name. Please contact us at `copyright@packt.com` with a link to the material.

If you are interested in becoming an author: If there is a topic that you have expertise in and you are interested in either writing or contributing to a book, please visit `authors.packtpub.com`.

Share Your Thoughts

Once you've read *Cloud Native Anti-Patterns*, we'd love to hear your thoughts! Scan the QR code below to go straight to the Amazon review page for this book and share your feedback.

https://packt.link/r/1836200595

Your review is important to us and the tech community and will help us make sure we're delivering excellent quality content.

Free Benefits with Your Book

This book comes with free benefits to support your learning. Activate them now for instant access (see the *"How to Unlock"* section for instructions).

Here's a quick overview of what you can instantly unlock with your purchase:

PDF and ePub Copies

Next-Gen Web-Based Reader

Access a DRM-free PDF copy of this book to read anywhere, on any device.

Use a DRM-free ePub version with your favorite e-reader.

Multi-device progress sync: Pick up where you left off, on any device.

Highlighting and notetaking: Capture ideas and turn reading into lasting knowledge.

Bookmarking: Save and revisit key sections whenever you need them.

Dark mode: Reduce eye strain by switching to dark or sepia themes

How to Unlock

Scan the QR code (or go to `packtpub.com/unlock`). Search for this book by name, confirm the edition, and then follow the steps on the page.

Note: Keep your invoice handly. Purchase made directly from packt don't require one.

Part 1: Introduction and Overview

This first part will provide an overview of cloud native concepts and their benefits. We will then explore the importance of a DevOps culture that addresses security concerns, also known as DevSecOps. We will also discuss establishing automation and observability capabilities and clarify common misunderstandings. This part will explain the foundations that are required for *Part 2* and *Part 3*.

This part has the following chapter:

- *Chapter 1, Benefits of Cloud Native and Common Misunderstandings*

1

Benefits of Cloud Native and Common Misunderstandings

Several thousand years ago, households had to dig and build wells, draw water from rivers, or set up rain barrels to collect water. They had to manage the filtration and purification to ensure water was safe for drinking and other uses, and they had to maintain that infrastructure. Water supply turned into a commodity by centralized municipal water systems. Users can now access clean water through a faucet and pay for the amount they use.

Similarly, **cloud native** commoditizes information technology aspects that we had to manage in the past. It can enable the simplification of solution architectures and operational complexity. It can also make securing our applications easier and help us meet regulatory goals. This commoditization aspect can make it easier to manage and refresh our data. The word *can* was used on purpose in the previous sentences. All four authors have worked for professional service organizations focusing on cloud technology. The cloud provides significant new opportunities, but we must understand the risks, anti-patterns, and how to mitigate them. Despite the huge potential that cloud native brings, we have seen many things going mindbogglingly wrong. That includes accidental deletion of entire environments, and leaking secrets, and the core part of the book will focus on that. Quite often, we were involved in remediating those applications or helping customers with security breaches or data losses. Of course, other times, we were working on greenfield solutions and could help to stay away from anti-patterns.

The goal of this book is to help steer away from these anti-patterns, remediate them, and move toward best practices. In this chapter, we will lay out the foundations. The following chapters will build on top of that gained knowledge. Therefore, it is important to digest the information in this chapter, which includes the following:

- The evolution of cloud native

- The benefits of cloud native

- DevSecOps culture, IaC, and CI/CD

- Observability and resilience

- Common misunderstandings

The evolution of cloud native

Cloud native did not occur overnight. Many events contributed to this paradigm change. Let's examine the history and explore key concepts that will help us understand cloud native. Why is it considered necessary today? How did we get here? Did we learn from the past? Here is a fast-forward list of the critical historical events influencing what we now know as cloud native. We are looking at it in chronological order. Therefore, we will be jumping between hardware, software, and design paradigms.

> **Free Benefits with Your Book**
>
> Your purchase includes a free PDF copy of this book along with other exclusive benefits. Check the *Free Benefits with Your Book* section in the Preface to unlock them instantly and maximize your learning experience.

The foundations for ML, AI, and cross-functional teams

Machine learning (**ML**) and **artificial intelligence** (**AI**) are nowadays often used when discussing cloud native, and various **cloud service providers** (**CSPs**) provide many prepackaged ML and AI services. The history goes a long way back.

In 1950, an English mathematician, Alan Turing, published the paper *Computing Machinery and Intelligence*, proposing the Turing test as a criterion for machine intelligence. American scientists and researchers coined the term *AI* in their proposal for the Dartmouth conference in 1956.

Many see virtualization as a major foundational step toward cloud native development. It started in the 1960s when IBM released the Control Program/Cambridge Monitor System. It enabled the division of hardware components. For example, several **virtual machines** (**VMs**) running on a physical computer can use the same physical processors and memory. VMs allow multiple users to share hardware resources.

In 1967, Melvin Edward Conway developed a theory named "Conway's Law." It describes how designers of software components that interact with each other also have to communicate with each other. Conway summarized this behavior with the following quote: *"Organizations which design systems (in the broad sense used here) are constrained to produce designs which are copies of the communication structures of these organizations."* This is a significant finding that influences how we structure teams nowadays. We use terminology such as squads, agile teams, and DevOps. We know that we have to set up cross-functional teams and excel in collaboration to deliver cloud-friendly solutions.

The age of virtualization

IBM continued developing further enhancements in 1980. However, the market was not ready yet for a wide commercial adoption of VMs. Personal computers became popular in the 1980s, slowing down the VM market. It was only in the late 1990s that VMs went mainstream. One of the market leaders was VMware.

The beginning of distributed applications

A new design paradigm, **service-oriented architecture** (**SOA**), emerged. It introduced the concept of services and promoted reusability. SOA is often seen as a precursor to micro-services. At the same time, a little bookshop called Amazon realized that they needed to change their architecture to scale it in a way that makes it future-proof. An intelligent group of Amazon engineers released the internally published *Distributed Computing Manifesto*, which explained that the architecture of our application needs to scale to manage a demand 10 times the current size of what it was back then. The paper called out that applications should not be tightly coupled. It explained a service-based model. It also proposed a three-tier architecture to separate the presentation layer (also called client or application), business logic, and data.

It also described that synchronization should be used when an immediate response is required. Asynchronous calls can be used for workflows where an immediate outcome is not required. The workflow only needs to move to the next stage. Asynchronous API calls made perfect sense for Amazon's order processes. **Amazon Web Services** (**AWS**) launched years later as a new brand. The first web services were released for public consumption. The first public launch was a message queuing service called **Simple Queue Service** (**SQS**).

The philosophy of queuing aligned perfectly with the *Distributing Computing Manifesto*. **Elastic Cloud Compute** (**EC2**), a virtualization service, and the blob storage service called **Simple Storage Service** (**S3**) were released next. S3 was a very significant milestone in the evolution of cloud native history. In 2000, Roy Fielding defined REST architectures in his PhD dissertation *Architectural Styles and the Design of Network-based Software Architectures*. REST is designed for scalable client-server applications. REST suggests that the coupling between the client and the origin server must be as loose as possible. Within the context of REST APIs, "stateless" means that each request from a client to a server must contain all the information needed to understand and process the request, without relying on any stored context on the server. This ensures that the server does not retain any session state between requests, allowing for scalability and reliability.

The rise of Agile, DevOps, and the cloud

In 2001, 17 software engineers gathered in Utah to outline values and principles for agile software development. Some of those engineers became famous software development advocates, including Alistair Cockburn, Martin Fowler, and Kent Beck. As a result of this get-together, they created the *Manifesto for Agile Software Development*, often called the *Agile Manifesto*. It highlights the importance of individuals and collaboration within software development engineering teams and with customers to deliver better software more efficiently. The collaboration aspects address some of the problems described in Conway's Law. That cross-functional team approach is still embedded in most agile delivery frameworks.

Google Cloud Platform (**GCP**) and Microsoft's Azure cloud platform were launched in 2008. In the same year, Google released App Engine, one of the first serverless computing offerings. It included HTTP functions with a 60-second timeout and a blob store and data store with timeouts.

The need for collaboration emerged even more during this decade, and software industry experts pointed out the problems that result from separating development and operations.

The term *DevOps* was coined. The first DevOpsDays conference took place in Belgium in 2009. In its early days, DevOps focused on **continuous integration/continuous delivery (CI/CD)** and infrastructure automation.

Edge computing – microservices, and addressing security

In 2010, **edge computing** gained significance, especially within the **Internet of Things (IoT)**. Edge computing is an extension of the cloud. It brings the entry points to cloud infrastructure closer to the consumer. Some of the key benefits are latency reduction and increased resilience and reliability. The use case of edge computing has evolved since then. For example, content can be cached closer to the end user. This caching approach is known as a **content distribution network (CDN)**. Well-known CDN solutions are provided by Cloudflare, Akamai, and the three major cloud platforms (AWS, GCP, and Azure).

In 2011, the term *microservices* gained popularity in the software engineering community. Microservices enhance SOA with a strong focus on continuous incremental change and lightweight communication between services and endpoints. Sometimes, people use the term microservices interchangeably with the term *cloud native*. We will talk more about that when we explore common misunderstandings.

Engineers at Heroku also developed the 12-Factor App methodology during that time. The 12-Factor App principles provide best practice guidance for building scalable and maintainable **software as a service (SaaS)** applications. They emphasize a declarative setup, a clean contract with the underlying operating system, and maximum portability between execution environments. Some key principles include managing configuration separately from code, treating backing services as attached resources, and strict separation of build, release, and run stages.

Between 2012 and 2013, the term *DevSecOps* was mentioned more and more. It was seen as an extension of DevOps. DevSecOps advocates embedding security early in the software development process, automating security testing, and embracing a culture of shared security responsibility among teams.

Containers and function as a service

In 2013, Docker containers were released. The main difference between VMs and containers is that VMs provide an abstracted version of the entire hardware of a physical machine, including the CPU, memory, and storage. On the other hand, containers are portable instances of software. Containers are unaware of other processes running on the host operating system.

Google released Kubernetes about a year later, which is a container orchestration platform. Kubernetes is still widely used for scaling containers, container management, scalability, and automated deployments.

The first **function as a service (FaaS)** capability was released in 2014. AWS released Lambda functions. Later, other CSPs adopted FaaS, such as Microsoft with Azure Functions and GCP with Google Cloud Functions. FaaS provides a fully managed runtime where we only need to manage our code. This was a fundamental shift that allowed DevSecOps practitioners to fully focus on the work that distinguishes their organization from others, including application code, and architectural design. We only pay while the function is running, and there is zero cost when the function is not being invoked.

The concept of service meshes was also introduced during that time, which are a dedicated infrastructure layer for monitoring, managing, and securing network communication between microservices in a cloud native application.

Cloud native and best practices

The **Cloud Native Computing Foundation (CNCF)** is a Linux Foundation project that started in 2015. Two years later, in 2017, Google, IBM, and Lyft open-sourced the popular service mesh implementation Istio.

In 2018, researchers at the **National Institute of Standards and Technology (NIST)** and the **National Cyber Security Center of Excellence (NCCoE)** published the **Zero Trust Architecture (ZTA)** framework. It describes a "never trust, always verify" approach. This requires strict identity verification for every device and human attempting to access resources, regardless of location within or outside the network. ZTA is now increasingly becoming more important in cloud native architectures. It is seen as a robust approach to reduce the risk of data breaches and enforce the least privileged access approach.

OpenTelemetry is an open source observability framework. It was created in 2019 when CNCF merged the two projects, OpenCensus and OpenTracing. Its purpose is to collect traces, metrics, and telemetry data. OpenTelemetry is commonly used to monitor microservices and other distributed applications.

The FinOps Foundation was established in 2019 and became a project of the Linux Foundation in 2020. It is dedicated to *"advancing people who practice the discipline of cloud financial management through best practices, education, and standards."*

Between 2020 and 2012, GitOps evolved from DevOps. It is a practice for CD using Git, a distributed version control system, as a source of truth for infrastructure and application configuration.

In 2023, **Open Policy Agent (OPA)** emerged as a security framework in the Kubernetes community. It addresses several use cases, including authorization of REST API endpoint calls, integrating custom authorization logic into applications, and a policy-as-code framework for cloud infrastructure pipelines. It had previously been a CNCF incubating project.

Also in 2023, the trend of ML and AI integration emerged. The major CSPs released their managed services, including Google's AI Platform, Amazon SageMaker, and Azure ML.

Where are we now and what does the future bring?

Many of the described frameworks and best practices continued to trend through 2024. One of the biggest trends is embedded AI services for productivity, operations, and security. Let's go through some examples before we move to the benefits of cloud native.

AI for operations (AIOps) provides predictive insights, anomaly detection, and automated responses. **Cloud native application protection platform (CNAPP)** solutions are taking the world by storm. They provide holistic protection and compliance validation throughout the **software development life cycle (SDLC)**, from development to operations. Chatbots and other generative AI services that assist developers and improve their productivity are also rapidly becoming popular.

The AI trend includes technologies such as ChatGPT by OpenAI, Microsoft's GitHub Copilot, AWS Code Whisperer, Amazon Q, and Google's Cloud AI and Vertex AI. There are legal concerns regarding generative AI services. One concern is that our sensitive data could be used to train the AI model. The main concerns are whether the data could become visible to a third party and whether the data remains within our region, which might be required for compliance reasons. Another concern is intellectual property ownership. Who owns the result if the generative AI service generates foundational parts, and a human enhances that generated outcome? Different jurisdictions have different laws, and there are often gray areas because this is a fairly new concern. Discussions about these concerns will continue for quite some time.

We now have a good understanding of significant events that contributed to what we now understand as cloud native. But what are the actual benefits of cloud native and why is it so significant for modern architectures? We will explore that in the next section.

Benefits of cloud native

What is cloud native? There are many different definitions, and for the context of this book, we will go with the definition of the CNCF:

"Cloud native technologies, also called the cloud native stack, are the technologies used to build cloud native applications. These technologies enable organizations to build and run scalable applications in modern and dynamic environments such as public, private, and hybrid clouds while fully leveraging cloud computing benefits. They are designed from the ground up to exploit the capabilities of cloud computing, and containers, service meshes, microservices, and immutable infrastructure exemplify this approach."

According to Gartner the term "cloud native" is an approach that "refers to something created to optimally leverage or implement cloud characteristics." The key phrase here is *"optimally leverage or implement cloud characteristics."* This area is exactly where we have seen many large organizations go wrong. Quite often, they treat the cloud the same as their data centers. We will dive into that in the following chapters when we go through anti-patterns in detail.

Faster time to market

Let's start with the first key benefit: *faster time to market*. It is one of the key drivers and the reason why so many start-ups have commenced using cloud native services. Those start-ups started without legacy systems and needed to show outcomes quickly to get venture capital and generate income streams for growth. Developers can leverage self-service provisioning of resources, saving them a lot of time compared to traditional mechanisms where they had to request infrastructure to be provisioned.

With a cloud native approach, they can quickly create new environments or serverless functions. Depending on the resource type, the provisioning might take seconds or minutes. Database provisioning usually takes several minutes, whereas blob storage, such as an Amazon S3 bucket or FaaS, can be deployed within seconds. This helps to achieve a quicker time-to-market goal. It also helps for quicker innovation cycles. If we want to perform a proof of concept to compare the productivity using differing programming languages, using FaaS will save a lot of time because the runtimes are already pre-provisioned by our CSP. It is easy to try out some functions in Golang, and others in Rust or Java. Provisioning and decommissioning are a minimal effort and developers can focus on the application development without any waiting times.

Scalability and elasticity

Scalability and elastic infrastructure are other benefits. Applications can easily scale up and down on demand. Cloud native architectures typically leverage horizontal scaling over vertical scaling. This is a big advantage for applications with significant peaks, such as shopping websites or payment applications. They need to scale up during day peak times or seasonal peaks. Once the traffic spike decreases, we can automatically scale back the underlying infrastructure.

This is very different from traditional on-premises deployments, where we need to permanently provision for the absolute highest traffic volume to avoid outages. The cloud infrastructure is elastic. So is the pricing model to some degree. For instance, if we dispose of a compute instance after a scaling event, we are not being charged for it anymore. However, if we store data without deleting it, we continue paying storage fees.

Managed services

Managed services are managed by the CSP. They improve the operational efficiency for customers and reliability and availability. Therefore, they are a significant advantage in cloud native architectures. The CSP manages the underlying infrastructure of managed services. Depending on the service, that may include the application itself, such as a queuing or notification application. This includes the provisioning, configuration, maintenance, and network constructs. If we use a managed relational database service such as Amazon **Relational Database Service (RDS)**, Microsoft Azure Database, or a Google Cloud database, the CSP manages the patching and upgrading of the underlying infrastructure, including the database engine. Managed database services also implement security and compliance with industry regulations up to the database layer. The customer is responsible for the security above that layer, such as the data encryption. The way our business drives business value is not impacted by how we patch our database or run a hypervisor. Managed services are abstracting away a lot of this operational overhead. This allows us to focus on the business differentiators, such as the application logic and data offering. Managed services typically provide monitoring and reporting capabilities, such as method invocation for FaaS. Managed database or data storage services usually come with out-of-the-box backup and recovery mechanisms. Managed services can scale automatically and have built-in cost management and optimization features.

Security and compliance

Further security and compliance advantages of cloud native architectures are unified access controls. **Role-based access control (RBAC)**, **attribute-based access control (ABAC)**, and **identity and access management (IAM)** services ensure we can implement the least-privilege principle. Encryption by default for data protection in transit and at rest ensures that the customer data can always be encrypted, which is a best practice and also required in many regulated industries.

There are also built-in security features, such as **DDoS (distributed denial-of-service)** protection, firewalls, **network access control lists (NACLs)**, and **security information and event management (SIEM)** tools. Most CSPs also support **multi-factor authentication (MFA)** and **single sign-on (SSO)**. Having these two controls in place is quite often an internal security requirement. MFA is also mandated by some regulatory requirements, such as the **Payment Card Industry Data Security Standard (PCI-DSS)**. SSO integration makes it easier to manage human and machine access permissions centrally. This centralized approach reduces operational effort and also helps to meet regulatory requirements.

Cloud native also provides preventive and detective guardrails, which are instrumental in protecting our teams from some human errors. Preventive guardrails ensure that specific actions, such as deleting a backup vault, can never be performed. Detective guardrails still allow specific actions, but they can send notifications if a particular event happens, and findings can be visualized on a dashboard. For example, we would like to see whether we have any unencrypted databases in a development environment. We could enforce encryption via preventive guardrails for higher environments such as testing or production. Detective guardrails can also trigger auto-remediations for existing cloud resources. If a blob storage does not have access logging enabled, an auto-remediation can perform that change. Automated vulnerability scans are another feature that many CSPs offer. They help to scan VMs, containers, FaaS code, and networks. The scanning tools typically provide a report with findings and remediation recommendations.

Reliability and availability

There are also other reliability and availability benefits of cloud native applications. Anomaly detection services help to detect suspicious user behavior or unusual system behavior due to a flaw. They help to identify incidents at an early stage. Deployment architectures can easily leverage several independent locations within one geographical region. AZs are physically isolated from each other and have separate power supply and connectivity, but highspeed interconnects within a region. A region could be Sydney or Singapore. Independent locations are called **availability zones (AZs)**. The term *AZ* has a different meaning depending on our CSP, but for now, this definition is good enough for us. It is best practice to architect our application so that it leverages several AZs, ideally all the AZs we have in our region. Multi-AZ deployments help with automated failovers from one AZ to another. In an outage in one AZ, the other AZs can absorb the load and reply to incoming requests, such as API calls. This failover is a built-in feature, but the application needs to be architected correctly to leverage those benefits. We could even deploy our application to several regions. In the unlikely event of a total region failure, the second region can take on the entire load and respond to incoming requests. A total region outage is very unlikely. Therefore, this use case is less common than the other use cases for global deployments.

Regional outages are a segway into the next advantage we want to discuss.

Global deployments

With global deployments, it becomes easy for organizations that operate in several countries or even globally to address that in their deployment architecture. With global deployments, we can reduce the latency between our customers' devices and our applications. We can leverage a CDN; this caches data closer to our customers and is helpful if customers are not located in our geographical region. For example, suppose our application is hosted in Sydney, on the east side of Australia, and our customers are 4,000 kilometers away on the west coast of Australia. In that case, we can leverage a CDN to store cacheable information in Perth, located on the west coast. Those distributed locations are called **edge locations**. We can even run certain forms of authentication on the edge location to reduce the latency for a login procedure. This additional caching layer increases the availability of content. It can also reduce the bandwidth cost because the amount of data that needs to be provided by an origin server is reduced, and therefore, we are charged less egress data. We can potentially downsize our provisioned infrastructure. CDNs can handle large traffic spikes. Hence, they protect against DDoS attacks.

Another driver for global deployments could be regulatory requirements, such as data sovereignty laws. For regulated industries such as financial services or health services, customer data must reside in the originating region. For instance, data of United States citizens must be stored within the United States, and data of European customers must be stored within the European Union. With global deployments, it becomes easier to deploy applications to different regions. The application will then store the data within that region and stay there. With a CDN, we can also use cloud native geo-restrictions. We can limit the content to particular continents or countries; usually, we can define allow and deny lists. Those geo-restrictions are why some media content is unavailable in other countries. E-commerce platforms typically deploy their applications globally as well. That way, they can have different product catalogs per region and have all the reliability and availability benefits. The reduced latency of global deployments is also why they are ubiquitous for gaming or large IoT solutions. Another use case for global deployments is **disaster recovery** (**DR**). Data can be backed up in a different region to improve business resilience.

CI/CD – automate all the things

Cloud native typically offers automation capabilities for CI/CD. They enable automated build, test, and deployment of applications.

When using CI/CD, every change goes through a controlled process that should include peer reviews of code changes. Since everything is code-based, creating new environments ad hoc is low effort. Creating environments in other regions or tearing down temporary environments is also easy. Automation helps to decrease the time to market, improve the robustness of the change management process, enable consistency between environments, improve security and reliability, and help reduce cost.

Cost benefits and paradigm change

Hosting our applications in the cloud instead of on-premises moves the cost model from an upfront **capital expenditure** (**CapEx**) investment to a pay-as-you-go model. Rather than having substantial infrastructure investments every five years, we will have an ongoing spend in the cloud.

Some of the previously described features, such as auto-scaling and automation, help with cost optimization in the cloud. But there are more native features. Each cloud resource should have tags. Tags are metadata that describe a resource. Common tags include environment, data classification, cost center, and application owner. Tags can be used for a cost breakdown or security controls. Native cost dashboards provide cost insight and give different views based on tags, regions, or resource types, such as VMs or managed API gateways. The cost dashboard solutions are AWS Cost Explorer, Google Cloud Billing Reports, and Azure Cost Management & Billing.

We can also set up budgets to ensure we are notified if the projected spending exceeds the forecasted spending. We can define budgets manually or use built-in AI capabilities to set budget values. The AI component usually takes a few days to figure out the usual peaks and lows. Most CSPs also provide rightsizing recommendation services. This service helps to reduce costs where the customer has overprovisioned resources, such as VMs or databases. CSPs also offer a committed spending plan, which grants discounts if we commit to a spending amount for longer than a year.

Portability

Cloud native also delivers a couple of portability benefits. Containers and orchestration tools such as Kubernetes promote standardized configuration and deployment processes. A container-hosted application can easily migrate to a different CSP. Cloud native solutions are hybrid cloud-compatible and can integrate with our data centers. Hybrid deployments are widespread for massive application migrations where the migration from on-premises to the cloud happens over a long period. Typically, the frontend part of the application is moved to the cloud first, starting with components such as the CDN, APIs, and user interface. For cases where low latency and a reduced jitter are required, we can use cloud native connectivity services. These connectivity services require our data center to be in one of the colocations of the CSP and underlying infrastructure changes in our data center, such as new cable connections, are required. Examples are GCP Cloud Interconnect, AWS Direct Connect, and Azure ExpressRoute.

Cloud native architectures offer many benefits. However, we have only scratched the surface of cloud automation, and we have not even discussed the cultural aspect. Let's get onto it now.

DevSecOps culture, IaC, and CI/CD

In the *The evolution of cloud native* section, we discussed Conway's Law, the Agile Manifesto, the rise of Agile software development, and the first DevOps conference in 2009. But what exactly is DevOps?

The culturural aspect

DevOps is a cross-functional combination of development and operations. Key characteristics are shared ownership, workflow automation, and rapid feedback. DevOps uses cultural behavior, practices, and tools to automate development and operations to improve the end-to-end SDLC. Its goal is to improve the software quality and decrease the time from a committed change to production. DevOps is mainly about culture and, as a result, it impacts the software toolchain. The cultural change aspect of DevOps adoption is quite often underestimated. Let's elaborate on the impacts to understand why this is the case.

DevOps adoption means that different disciplines work together, which we call cross-functional teams. The *two-pizza team* topology, created by Amazon's Jeff Bezos in the early 2000s, is a strategy for keeping teams small and efficient by ensuring they are small enough to be fed with just two pizzas. This approach fosters better communication, agility, and productivity within the team. The *you build it, you run it* mentality fosters business agility. It empowers teams to react faster and innovate to deliver customer value. It also results in high-quality outcomes since people are motivated to avoid incidents they get called into. Those things should sound familiar by now. Let's have a look at how this looks when we add security to the mix.

DevSecOps

A mature DevSecOps culture adopts a **shift-left** approach. Functional and non-functional quality controls are performed very early in the SDLC. *Shift left* means testing activities such as requirement definition and design start early, so the testers are involved early. Testing is usually automated to a high degree, including unit tests, integration tests, non-functional tests, regression tests, contract tests, and others. Tools for static code analysis help to analyze code quality.

DevSecOps augments DevOps and suggests embedding security in the software delivery process. This empowers development teams to produce high-quality changes that meet security and regulatory requirements. DevSecOps integrates security tools into the CI/CD toolchain. This integration includes **static application security testing** (**SAST**) tools to analyze the source code for vulnerabilities. **Software composition analysis** (**SCA**) is an analysis of custom-built source code to detect embedded open source software or libraries and validate that they are up to date and contain no security flaws. Other usual security scans include secret scanning to ensure no security keys or passwords are embedded in the code. Vulnerability scans inspect machine images, container images, and source code for common vulnerabilities and exposures. These types of scans have become increasingly important due to a surge in supply chain attacks. A supply chain attack uses third-party tools or services to infiltrate a system or network.

There are many new trends with the word *Ops* in them. One that gets a lot of attention is **AIOps**, which promotes leveraging AI capabilities and embedding those in the DevSecOps approach to identify anomalies and suspicious behavior early. As a result, we want to see improvements in delivery and operation, and we will look into that next.

Measuring the progress

The **DevOps Research and Assessment (DORA)** team published the DORA metrics. Their purpose is to measure and improve the performance and efficiency of the software development process. Providing actionable insights helps identify bottlenecks and improve the process. The four key DORA metrics are as follows:

- **Lead time for changes (LTFC)** is the time from the first code commit to deployment. Shorter lead times mean faster delivery of business value.

  For instance, we can track the time from when a developer commits a change to a production release. On average, this takes 24 hours, which allows the company to respond swiftly to market demands and user feedback.

- **Deployment frequency (DF)** is the number of deployments in a given duration of time. A high frequency indicates the ability to deliver new features and bug fixes and respond to customer needs.

  For example, we release updates to our mobile app twice a week. This frequent deployment helps to quickly deliver new features and bug fixes to users, ensuring the app remains competitive and user-friendly.

- **Change failure rate (CFR)** is the percentage of failed changes over all changes. A lower rate indicates higher quality and stability in releases.

  For instance, out of 50 deployments in a month, 5 resulted in rollback or required hotfixes due to bugs or issues. This gives our organization a CFR of 10%, highlighting areas for improvement in their testing and review processes.

- **Mean time to recovery (MTTR)** measures the average time it takes to recover from a system failure. A shorter MTTR demonstrates the ability to recover quickly from incidents.

Tackling the cultural challenges

Now that we have looked into DevSecOps, we can see that adoption is not trivial. There is a lot to consider. Starting from a waterfall software development approach will be a steep learning curve. A considerable percentage of humans have some degree of resistance to cultural change. If an organization is separated into silos, it will take a while to break those down. DevSecOps requires more collaboration and broader skills. Therefore, it is crucial to provide sufficient training. Training will be required to gain cloud native knowledge including the tools used to build, test, and deploy the code.

As the term *Ops* in DevSecOps suggests, the team also operates the applications. Therefore, the team is motivated to release quality code to ensure they do not need to solve too many incidents. This ownership approach is a crucial differentiator from traditional methods, where development and operations are separated. It also means the team members need the skills to build observability capabilities and react to incidents. Learning all this will require training, which can be a combination of classroom training, online training courses, and pair programming. Providing learning environments for experimenting and creating proof of concepts is also very effective in upskilling our teams. These environments are usually called *sandpits* or *sandboxes*. We use the word *developer* here because they will likely produce application, test, infrastructure, or configuration code. But that term can be used interchangeably with engineer, software engineer, full stack developer, and others.

There are different ways organizations can drive cultural change. Top-down means the change initiative starts at the leadership level, and bottom-up means it begins with the delivery team and eventually reaches the management and leadership levels. For a successful DevSecOps adoption, we will need buy-in from the leadership. Otherwise, the required cultural changes won't happen. The adoption process is mostly successful when it gets adopted first in parts of the organization that already have an agile delivery approach. Those teams will find it easier to experience DevSecOps, and they can start swarming after a while. That means the team members can be augmented and act as mentors in other teams. Getting external help through a DevSecOps consultancy can be good if we are at the beginning of our transformation journey. The external consultants can coach the team, contribute to the code base, and ensure that best practices are applied. For a successful DevSecOps journey, the consultants must transfer the knowledge to the internal development teams.

IaC

The source code is the source of truth for every cloud native solution. Individuals responsible for the infrastructure create the infrastructure or patterns via **infrastructure as code** (**IaC**). IaC defines components such as network constructs, servers, policies, storage, and FaaS in code.

Cloud native versus cloud-agnostic IaC

CSPs offer their own IaC technology and there are also third-party offerings that are platform-agnostic:

- **Cloud native IaC:**

  CSPs have their own IaC service for their platform, including AWS CloudFormation, **Azure Resource Manager** (**ARM**), and Google Cloud Deployment Manager. Those services come with their own IaC language. Compared to higher programming languages such as Golang or Java, the IaC languages are less complex and can be learned quickly. Simplicity benefits individuals with a strong infrastructure background who do not necessarily have much coding experience except for Bash or PowerShell scripts.

- **Platform-agnostic IaC:**

  There are also IaC tools available that use one common language to deploy to several cloud and on-premises platforms. Terraform is a popular IaC tool that can deploy to all major CSPs and thousands of other platforms, including collaboration platforms, firewalls, network tools, and source code management tools. Terraform used to be open source, but when it was shifted to a Business Source License in 2023, the community reacted quickly. The code base was forked, and a new open source project called **OpenTofu** was established.

It sounds as if IaC has the potential to bring significant advantages, which we will discuss next.

Advantages of IaC

What are the advantages of defining our cloud resources via IaC? Whenever we deploy something repeatedly, such as a temporary or new testing environment, the architecture and deployment approach will always be consistent, and the approach is easy to repeat. Typically, we use different parameters for a different environment, for example, a different IP range for a different network segment or a smaller auto-scaling group for non-production environments. The rest of the code stays the same. Hence, IaC is also very efficient in achieving scalability or implementing global deployments. Configuration and code are fully version-controlled in Git. Therefore, it is easy to go back to the previous version.

We can also easily use version pinning if we want our production environment to be further behind than the development environment. IaC also helps to achieve a good DR response time. Instead of manually or semi-manually building a new DR environment, we can fully automate this with IaC and CI/CD technologies, which we will cover in a minute. IaC also helps to meet security and compliance requirements. Security requirements are embedded in the code. For instance, if we only want to allow HTTPS traffic, our code will only open port 443, then we articulate that in the source code. As best practice, the code will be peer-reviewed to ensure we meet our requirements. When we redeploy, we can be sure we don't expose our application since the deployment will deliver a repeatable outcome. All changes are tracked in Git, which helps with auditing and compliance. Some regulatory frameworks require a repeatable approach. That is exactly what IaC establishes. There is also a cost benefit to IaC. Because creating and destroying resources is so easy, it helps avoid over-provisioning. If test environments are not needed, then resources can be easily shut down if they are not required. If we take a complete serverless approach, we will need to worry less about this. We will talk about this later when we get into the strategy.

How do we deploy the cloud resources that we have defined via IaC? How do we build and deploy our application code? How do we execute all the functional and non-functional tests in an automated way? The answer is CI/CD, and we will explore it now.

CI/CD

CI/CD is a combination of continuous integration and continuous delivery, sometimes referred to as continuous deployment. The main difference is that continuous delivery requires a manual approval step, whereas continuous deployment deploys automatically after a code change. CI/CD bridges gaps between development and operations. It enforces automation during the build process, functional and non-functional testing, and deployment.

Defining a structure

There are many ways to structure the CI/CD process and even more combinations of tools. The fine-tuning will depend a lot on organizational and regulatory needs. We will go with a standard structure, where we want to adopt a shift-left approach. The following diagram helps us step through this process:

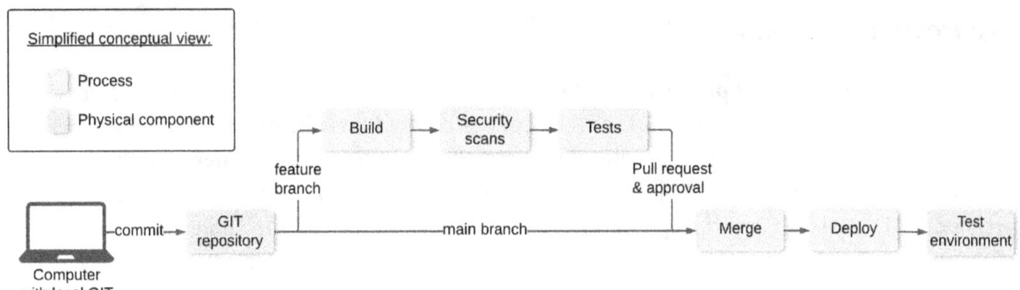

Figure 1.1 - Simplified conceptual CI/CD process

The process starts with the developer using the preferred **integrated development environment** (**IDE**). Sometimes, developers use just a command-line tool. However, IDEs are commonly used because they provide practical built-in features and plugin architecture. This architecture enables the installation of extensions or plugins. Visual Studio Code is a popular open source IDE developed by Microsoft. Even though the software is open source, the available extensions are not necessarily open source. IDEs usually have a built-in Git integration. However, we can install an additional extension that visualizes the Git repository and the Git branches.

Git branching and shift left

A Git branch is a separate version of the code repository created for a new change. There are different branching models, such as trunk-based development or feature branching. We will look into that in more detail in *Chapter 5*, and for our example, we will use the feature branching model. When the developer wants to commit a change to the repository, it is important to work off the latest version in the repo (short for repository). Therefore, a `git pull` command is required to ensure the latest version is in the local copy. After that, the developer creates a new feature branch and updates the code. There are a lot of checks that can now be run automatically to provide early feedback. For example, a security extension could scan the code and identify weaknesses. For instance, if the code is a Terraform template that defines a public Amazon S3 bucket, then the plugin can provide feedback that the bucket should be private. S3 buckets are blob storage constructs in AWS, and misconfigured S3 buckets have been the reason for many data breaches. This early feedback is an example of shift left, and the developer can fix the code before it is validated in the CI/CD pipeline. Code formatting, linting, and syntax validations typically run on the client side. Once the developer is happy with the changes, the code is committed to the Git repo.

Optionally, a commit can trigger a pre-commit hook, executing the steps we just described. It can also auto-generate documentation.

Approval and deployment

The developer then raises a **pull request (PR)**. Someone performs a peer review. The PR gets approved if the code meets the expectations. Then, the code is merged into the main branch. The merge will trigger the pipeline to run. In the beginning, there will be some validation steps similar to the ones the developer had already run. Still, we want to ensure that some validations are mandatory and don't rely on individuals. As a next step, the build process will kick off and run some static code analysis, functional and non-functional tests, and further security scans. Once the pipeline run is successful, an authorized individual can trigger the deployment. These steps are a simple example of a CI/CD pipeline.

We can see the many benefits of automating those steps. Building out the required pipelines for an organization will take a while, but once they are established, the development process becomes much quicker, more reliable, and more secure. But how can we validate that it also runs as expected? Let's find out.

Observability and resilience

We have already covered many aspects of cloud native solutions, including the cultural impact, cross-functional teams, DevSecOps culture, and tooling complexity. We will now examine observability and resilience, two areas that need more consideration during the early design phases of cloud native solutions.

If we do not establish comprehensive observability, we will not know whether we achieve our targets, such as response times. And if we fail, we will not know where the bottleneck is. Therefore we need to have a holistic logging, monitoring, and observability strategy in place. The same applies to withstanding failures. We need insights to validate that our deployment architecture matches the resilience expectations. We will explore both aspects, starting with observability and what it means in a cloud native context. We cannot fix what we cannot see. Observability helps get actionable insight into an application's internal state and measure it by evaluating outputs.

Logging – the observability enabler

Logs are the key enabler for monitoring and observability. The scope of logs is very broad, and they can include operating system logs, access logs, application logs, infrastructure logs, network flow logs, **domain name service (DNS)** logs, and more. Logs enable monitoring, alerting, debugging, incident discovery, and performance optimization. Earlier in this chapter, we clarified that a typical DevSecOps team (aka product squad) writes the code and also manages their application, also referred to as "product." Therefore, the team will be motivated to establish good observability practices and tooling.

A good maturity level can be achieved when the team has a good mix of skills and experience mix across development and operations. Individuals with operational experience know the value of observability. People with a software engineering background also see the value of observability, especially on the application layer.

However, sometimes, the other layers, such as the network or operating system layer, need to be considered more. Getting a holistic picture covering all layers is critical to getting good insights into our systems. It is also essential to be able to correlate data. For instance, if we have a hybrid cloud application, a business transaction might start at the CDN, get to an API layer, and then write to a cloud-hosted queue where the on-premises business logic pulls the data from and writes it to an on-premises-hosted database.

Additionally, there is an on-premises firewall that inspects all incoming traffic. This architecture is complex but also common. If we have performance **service-level agreements** (**SLAs**), we will not only need to measure the end-to-end transaction time. We will need to identify the bottlenecks if we run the risk of failing to meet those SLAs. The problem could be anywhere on the entire traffic path. Good insights will help to pinpoint the bottleneck. Collecting all those logs leads us to another challenge. Because we know we need to collect all relevant logs, it is easy to fall into the trap of over-collecting, leading to alert fatigue. We will examine the typical anti-patterns in *Chapter 10* and discuss how to address those pitfalls.

Log quality

Consistency, standardization, and good quality of log information are foundational for helpful dashboards and meaningful alerts.

A couple of things need to be considered to achieve this. We will need an agreement on the severity levels we want to log. Not all severity levels require logging all the time. The debug level, for instance, should only be logged when we are debugging. If we don't make a sensible decision about when to use what severity level and what levels need to be logged, we will have inconsistent log files. It is also very likely that we will then log too much. This means we need a bigger log file indexer, increasing operational expenses. An increasing size of log volume makes it harder to find relevant information in case of an incident. That is especially the case if we don't have a standardized log structure.

Therefore, we also need to define what information is captured in the log files and the sequence and structure. Structured data formats such as JSON help achieve this, and they help include key-value pairs to provide context. The log entry could include a key of `userID` or `sessionID` and the actual ID as a value. The log entry should contain other helpful contexts during troubleshooting, such as timestamps, transaction IDs, and correlation IDs, to trace and correlate requests between microservices. We should not store sensitive information such as credit card details, customer names, and addresses in log files. Some regulatory frameworks, such as the PCI-DSS, mandate data categories that must not be stored in log files. Centralized logging will also help to find data correlations because logs from APIs, the database, and infrastructure events will be saved in the same storage. Examples of popular open source logging tools are Logback, Graylog, and Log4j. The latter became famous in 2021 due to a vulnerability known as Log4 Shell, which allowed hackers to take control of devices running unpatched versions of Log4j. Therefore, we should always protect ourselves from vulnerabilities, and we will discuss this in more detail in Chapter 6. Some service mesh solutions, such as Istio or Linkerd, provide logs, metrics, and traces out of the box.

What else do we need to consider for logs? We need to ensure that only authorized individuals and systems have access to log files. If they contain sensitive information, they need to be encrypted. However, we will check with our applicable regulatory frameworks and internal security policy to see whether that is allowed. If our source code contains recursions, we should ensure that the same exception or error is not logged multiple times. We must also consider data retention for log files to avoid a bill shock. A sound logging approach will enable a good monitoring and observability capability, which we will discuss next.

Monitoring and observability

A monitoring solution is needed to make sense of the logs, and we need alerts to be notified about any critical events.

OpenTelemetry is an open source observability framework. It is designed to capture and process telemetry data, including metrics, logs, and traces from cloud native applications. It provides a set of APIs, libraries, agents, and instrumentation to help DevSecOps teams monitor application behavior. It fosters standardized data collection and consistent observability across applications and environments. A significant benefit is the interoperability with various backend systems. Because, with OpenTelemetry, we can instrument a standardized code, we can easily swap to different backends and tools. This reduces the vendor lock-in. OpenTelemetry has strong community support and is backed by major CSPs and observability vendors, ensuring ongoing improvements, broad compatibility, and shared knowledge and best practices. When choosing a new observability product, it is worthwhile to make OpenTelemetry support an evaluation criterion.

Popular open source tools that support OpenTelemetry are Prometheus for metrics collection, Grafana for visualization, Fluentd for log collection, and Jaeger for distributed tracing.

When setting up alerts, it is also critical to consider a team roster for on-call times. This defines when a particular DevSecOps team member needs to be available to solve incidents. It should also provide some flexibility and allow temporary roster changes if an individual is unavailable due to personal circumstances. If our team operates across different time zones, the tool must address that. Popular commercial offerings are PagerDuty and Atlassian Opsgenie. Observability helps to gain application insights in real time and to be able to react swiftly to any unexpected behavior. We aim to architect robust, scalable, and elastic solutions. But we also need to address the insights that we gained from an incident to improve resilience, which we will elaborate on in the next section.

Resilience

Addressing resilience in a cloud native architecture is crucial to understanding how the application can withstand failures. Failures can occur on any layer in the architecture and in any of the components involved. AWS released the first version of the *AWS Well-Architected Framework*, Microsoft followed with an Azure version in 2020, and Google released the *Google Cloud Architecture Framework* in 2021. All three frameworks have a *Reliability* pillar or chapter in their framework. Nevertheless, this area is often misunderstood, especially in the early days of a cloud adoption journey. It is the architect's and engineer's responsibility to design and implement the application in a way that addresses possible failures. If we leverage managed services, then the CSP will take a lot of considerations into account, and we can reduce the reliability surface that we need to manage. We will discuss this in detail in *Chapter 7*.

Humans can fail – so can the cloud

Even though the CSP is responsible for the resilience of the cloud services, outages can and will occur. *"Everything fails, all the time"* is a famous quote from Amazon's chief technology officer, Werner Vogels.

There are a variety of infrastructure failure scenarios on the CSP side, such as service outages, AZ outages, region outages, or global services outages, such as a DNS outage. These are just some examples, and, of course, we can also have outages within the actual application. Examples are misconfiguration of load balancing or database connection pools, running out of disk or storage space, not allocating enough compute power such as memory or CPU size, unexpected configuration drift, or software vulnerabilities. We need to consider guiding principles when architecting resilience, and we will step through these now.

Automating recovery

First, an application should automatically recover from failure. This behavior is also known as self-healing. A failure needs to be discovered to initiate an automated recovery process. We put health checks in place. Those health checks can trigger follow-up actions. For example, we can configure health checks on a load balancer, and if a container instance behind the load balancer fails, it will be automatically replaced with a new instance. For this recovery scenario, it is essential to have a quick start-up time. Therefore, lean container images such as Docker Alpine are widely used.

Another guiding principle is that all change must be managed through code and automation. Automation enables a repeatable outcome and allows all changes to be tracked and reviewed. CI/CD becomes one of our best friends when we move into a cloud native world. Write access should be limited to CI/CD pipelines. Developers should be limited to read-only access for all environments except for sandbox environments. If human access is required in an incident, then there should be a break-glass mechanism. That means the elevated permissions are limited to the required timeframe and audit logs capture all manually performed changes.

Resilience and scalability

Recovery procedures must be tested. A working backup routine does not guarantee backup integrity or that the recovery procedure will work as planned. Our business continuity plan needs to address recovery testing. We must validate the documentation during a recovery test and update the documented recovery steps if required. A data criticality framework will help to define the proper **recovery time objectives (RTOs)** and **recovery point objectives (RPOs)**. The RTO defines the maximum time to restore a failed application after an outage. The RPO defines the maximum time we tolerate for a data loss. For instance, if the RPO is 1 minute, we accept the risk that we could lose data for 60 seconds. Therefore, we will need to configure automated backups for every minute. The shorter the RTO is, the more frequently we need to perform backups. We need to consider cost and performance trade-offs to make informed decisions. We must test other recovery scenarios, such as network recovery.

Another resilience guiding principle is that an application should scale horizontally to increase availability. Horizontal scaling means we scale out in the event of a traffic spike. Typically, additional instances are spun up behind a load balancer to distribute the load. If we architect the solution for auto-scaling, capacity guesses become somewhat irrelevant. We still need to consider hard service limits published by the cloud vendors. But with dynamic provisioning and auto-scaling, we rely less on capacity estimates. Auto-scaling also helps reduce the CSP cost since we can right-size based on dynamic demand changes instead of statically provisioning for peak times.

Testing the recovery

Game days are an excellent way to validate resilience and uncover weaknesses that require remediation to improve application reliability or security posture. These are structured events where teams simulate different failure scenarios to test the auto-recovery, the efficiency of human processes, and the accuracy of the recovery documentation. The goals of the game day need to be defined before we can select failure scenarios. We will also need an environment where we can simulate outages. If our applications, including infrastructure, are defined as code and can be deployed via CI/CD pipelines, creating a temporary environment for that purpose will be easy. The game days usually start with a team briefing before the incident simulation commences. Typical scenarios include shutting down servers or containers, throttling network bandwidth, or simulating cloud service outages.

We can simulate outages with fault injection simulators. Netflix developed tools for this purpose and released Chaos Monkey in 2011. It randomly terminates instances. Other tools followed, including Latency Monkey, to simulate network latencies or unreliable network conditions. Nowadays, the major cloud platforms offer cloud native fault simulators: AWS Fault Injection Service, Azure Chaos Studio, and Google Cloud Chaos Engineering.

Once the fault injection has started, the team members need to detect where the problem is by using the observability tools and diagnosing findings. Data recovery needs to be validated. The validation includes data integrity validation and performance testing.

The insights gained will lead to mitigation steps, such as improving data recovery or fixing a misconfigured auto-scaling. The day ends with analyzing what worked well and what did not. These required improvements need to be implemented and tested again at a later stage. Game days are a good way of embedding feedback loops in our DevSecOps culture.

Now that we have explored a holistic picture of cloud native benefits, both cultural and technological aspects, we will finish this chapter by clarifying some common misunderstandings. This knowledge will help us to navigate through the anti-patterns that we will discuss afterward.

Common misunderstandings

By now, we have a good understanding of cloud native. But why are there so many misunderstandings? The concepts are complex and require different ways of working. Technology is changing rapidly, and there is a lack of standardization, which leads to various interpretations. Moving toward cloud native requires a lot of training and a new mindset.

Misunderstandings can lead to the following shortcomings:

- Slow time to market

- Lack of security

- Lack of fault tolerance

- Lack of backup and recovery

- Inefficient DevOps and CI/CD best practices

- Increased operational effort

- Increased **total cost of ownership (TCO)**

We will now examine some common cloud native misunderstandings. Each will result in several of the listed shortcomings.

The shared responsibility model

Not understanding the shared responsibility between the CSP and the customer is a misunderstanding with very severe consequences. The shared responsibility model articulates security and compliance ownership. The CSP is responsible for the "security *of* the cloud." That means they protect the underlying infrastructure that runs the services offered to the customers. Those are the data centers and the infrastructure that delivers cloud services. The customer is responsible for "security *in* the cloud," for example, for their data or ensuring that encryption is enabled.

In an **infrastructure as a service (IaaS)** model, the customer has the highest level of responsibility. The CSP only manages foundational infrastructure, such as networks, data storage, and VMs that can host the guest operating system.

The customer's responsibility is to manage their network constructs, such as a **network address translation (NAT)** gateway. The customer must also manage application-level controls, identity and access management, endpoints, and data.

In a **platform as a service (PaaS)** model, the CSP manages infrastructure and platform components such as the operating system, libraries, and runtime. Customers are responsible for data management and user access for their applications.

The SaaS provider manages most security responsibilities in a SaaS model, including software, infrastructure, networks, and application-level security. The customer is responsible for data protection, account management, and user access.

The following figure shows how responsibilities change when we move from on-premises to IaaS, PaaS, and SaaS. Whether we choose IaaS, PaaS, or SaaS, the following areas will always be our responsibility: data, endpoints, access management, and account or subscription management.

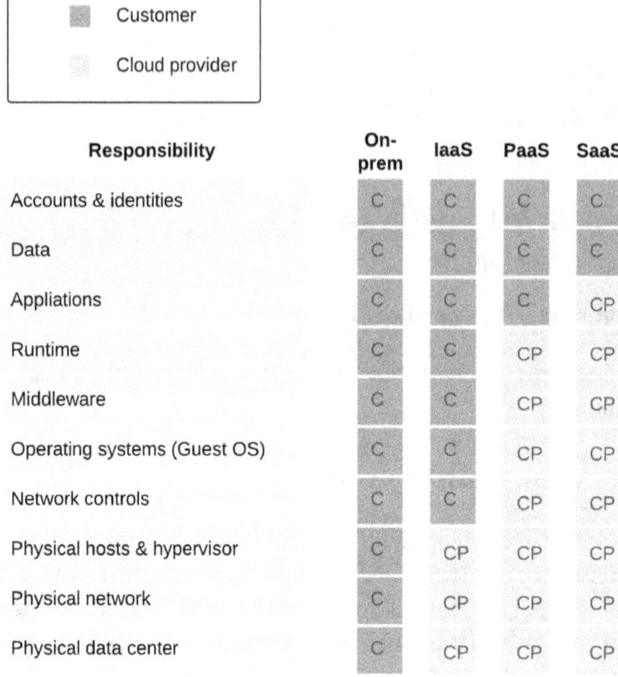

Responsibility	On-prem	IaaS	PaaS	SaaS
Accounts & identities	C	C	C	C
Data	C	C	C	C
Appliations	C	C	C	CP
Runtime	C	C	CP	CP
Middleware	C	C	CP	CP
Operating systems (Guest OS)	C	C	CP	CP
Network controls	C	C	CP	CP
Physical hosts & hypervisor	C	CP	CP	CP
Physical network	C	CP	CP	CP
Physical data center	C	CP	CP	CP

Figure 1.2 - The shared responsibility model

When we look at serverless technologies such as FaaS (AWS Lambda, Azure Functions, and GCP Cloud Functions), the customer's responsibility is between SaaS and PaaS. The customer user is accountable for the serverless service's deployed code and user-defined security or configuration options. Many organizations have a cloud platform team that establishes a platform for the product teams. They will often use a cloud native landing zone offering that provides a preconfigured, secure, and scalable environment designed to streamline cloud adoption, enhance security and compliance, and improve operational efficiency. In large organizations, the cloud platform team typically manages AWS accounts, Azure subscriptions, and Google projects. The cloud platform team will leverage cloud native account vending services such as the AWS account vending service or the Azure subscription vending service to perform this task.

The cloud platform team typically provides a service catalog that contains self-service artifacts, such as containers, network constructs for routing, guardrails, observability tooling, and more. Some artifacts will be provisioned as part of the automated account creation, including networking constructs, logging and monitoring capabilities, and guardrails. The product teams might publish other items to the service catalog or the container registry. In this case, we have a three-tiered shared responsibility model: the CSP, the cloud platform team, and the product teams. This can result in confusion around the operating model, which we will discuss next.

Operating model confusions

The operating model needs to address the responsibility model, and a clearly defined RACI matrix will help everyone understand what to do (**RACI** stands for **responsible, accountable, consulted, and informed**). The RACI matrix should include all phases in the SDLC, from source code to operations. Some example tasks that should be in the RACI matrix are certificate management, DNS management, key management, backup, and recovery.

When I worked for a cloud and DevOps consultancy, I started a new engagement with an educational institution. It was my first morning on site when an administrator accidentally deleted an entire data warehouse environment. Unfortunately, this was the only non-production environment. The data warehouse is a very business-critical application since it manages all the data of university applicants and students. We then tried to recover from backups. Unfortunately, the data recovery had never been tested. The backup data was corrupt and, therefore, useless.

Another administrator then asked whether we could call Amazon and ask them for backups. This question demonstrates that the shared responsibility model is not always understood. The administrator should not have had permission to delete an environment in the first place. Access and identity management, including the principle of least privilege enforcement, is the customer's responsibility. Also, data management, including backups and recovery testing, is the responsibility of the customer. After that incident, we built a self-healing solution for the client and improved the permission model.

Missing out on cultural transformation

Another common misunderstanding is that cloud native is only about technology. We have talked about the DevSecOps culture before. The full potential will only be utilized if we are changing the culture. Otherwise, business innovation will be limited. It is easy to experiment in the cloud, create new proofs of concept, tear them down, or change them, but only with a DevSecOps mindset when mature automation practices are established. We need to put an effort into cultural transformation and leverage training and team augmentation. Otherwise, the resistance to change will continue, and the opportunity for quick change and release cycles can never be unleashed.

The lack of DevSecOps maturity will result in poor governance, limited agility, and slow responsiveness to market needs. A siloed approach where development and operations are separated will be reflected in the application structure as described in Conway's Law. Eventually, the end customer experience will not be as good as possible. Another consideration is that cost management and ownership differ from an on-premises CapEx model. We are shifting toward **operational expenses (OpEx)**, and without cost ownership and cost tagging, we cannot achieve effective showback or chargeback models.

If cloud native is solely seen as a technology enabler, we will not achieve efficient cost management. There will also be security challenges, which brings us to the following fundamental misunderstanding.

Treating cloud like on-premises

Believing that security controls in the cloud are the same as on-premises can also lead to many anti-patterns. This misbelief brings significant security risks and challenges and can dramatically reduce efficiencies and slow down our time to market.

We must manage data encryption, access controls, and backups for an on-premises environment. CSPs offer native security controls for encryption and access control. However, these controls need to be configured by the customer. It is critical to understand the responsibility demarcation, and it shows why understanding the shared responsibility model is so important. In other words, we can establish data security controls much easier in the cloud. Still, we must remember to look into our security and regulatory requirements and assess the attack vector.

Because of the global nature of the cloud, it is also easy to copy data to different regions. Cross-region support is a feature, but it can also be a trap with severe consequences. Since it is straightforward to switch between areas, it is recommended to have a policy-as-code framework in place that prevents that from happening by accident.

To manage network security on-premises, we use firewalls, VPNs, and intrusion detection and prevention systems, which we must manage ourselves. Cloud native offers virtual network segmentation and security features such as NACLs, security firewalls, and managed firewall services. Those controls need to be configured by the customer, but this can be done much easier than on-premises. We can guarantee consistent security controls between environments if those controls are managed via source code and deployed via CI/CD pipelines. This approach has similarities with application security. For on-premises workloads, we need to build all the controls, including vulnerability management and application firewalls. If we utilize a fully managed service, such as a managed database service or FaaS, the CSP is already taking care of the majority. We still need secure coding practices and scan our code, but we don't need to scan the managed runtime environment. The CSP manages that for us; they have comprehensive compliance coverage. The coverage applies at least to the level managed by the CSP and we can download compliance reports for external audits. The customer still needs to take care of the layer above, as described in the shared responsibility model. However, cloud native provides compliance and audit features that can be configured for our needs. Cloud native services include Azure Compliance Manager, AWS Config, and Google Cloud Compliance Resource Center.

Lift & shift will leverage the full cloud potential

Thinking that a lift and shift approach will leverage all cloud benefits is another widely spread misbelief. *Lift and shift* means an application is moved from on-premises to the cloud without rearchitecting and refactoring. Lift and shift does not leverage any cloud native benefits. Instead of leveraging a managed database service, the database will be built using VMs, which requires installing the operating system and database. That means we must patch the database server, scan it for vulnerabilities, and develop and manage the entire security from scratch instead of leveraging built-in features. It would be much simpler if we could migrate our database to a managed database service. That way, we can significantly reduce the operational complexity and simplify the security approach. Cloud native services also have built-in scalability, resilience, and observability features. They simplify the application architecture and make it easier to operate the application. A lift and shift approach is very costly; such an application's operational cost can be higher than on-premises. A driver for lift and shift could be a data center exit strategy. The overall effort will be higher because we need to build all the security controls and building blocks traditionally and then refactor the application toward cloud native. The effort duplication brings many challenges and a high likelihood of a budget blowout.

Containers solve everything

"Moving everything onto containers will make my application cloud native" is another widespread misconception. A containerized application does not necessarily utilize all the cloud native features we have explored. There are several variations of this misunderstanding. Another one is that cloud native requires containers. Even though containers are a fundamental technology in this space, they are not necessarily required. We might be able to use FaaS if that is a good architectural fit for our goal. In that case, we don't need to manage containers or a cluster. A further variation of the container misunderstanding is that Kubernetes is required. Kubernetes is the most popular container orchestration platform, and the CSP offers managed Kubernetes services. There are some excellent use cases for it, such as microservice architectures. However, it comes with a steeper learning curve compared to Faas, and it is often underestimated. It is also worthwhile checking whether the required skills are available in the geographical market where the team needs to be.

Security can be an afterthought

A very concerning misunderstanding is that security can be bolted on afterward. Security must be considered and integrated from the beginning. "*Security is job zero*" is a well-known quote first mentioned by AWS's chief information security officer in 2017. It means that security is everyone's responsibility and should be considered the foundational priority in all cloud and IT operations, even before other jobs or tasks, hence *job zero*. In the DevSecOps section of this chapter, we discussed how security aspects need to be addressed early, ideally starting with security checks in the IDE, having scans embedded in the CI/CD pipeline, and continuing with scans in our environments. A lot of this end-to-end coverage will not be present if security gets retrofitted later on. That means the application has an increased attack surface, and data breaches become more likely because of a lack of guardrails. There might be operational interruptions, maybe because a cloud native firewall that would protect from DDoS attacks or SQL intrusions is not used from the beginning onward. Or certificates expire because the cloud native certificate manager that also renews certificates is not being used. There will also be a risk that compliance requirements cannot be met. These factors can result in reputational damage, negatively impacting our business. Therefore, it is best to address security right from the beginning.

Cloud native versus microservices

Another misunderstanding is that cloud native and microservices have the same meaning. People sometimes use the two terms interchangeably, but they differ in some respects. Cloud native is an overarching approach that includes a variety of practices and tools for developing and running applications in the cloud. It focuses on scalability, resilience, continuous delivery, and leveraging cloud infrastructure. Cloud native includes containerization, orchestration, a DevSecOps culture, and automation through CI/CD pipelines. It addresses the entire SDLC and operations in the cloud. The microservices concept provides architecture guidance specifically on how to break down applications into smaller, independently deployable components. Cloud native applications leverage features and infrastructure. They are designed to run in the cloud. A microservices architecture can be applied to any application, whether hosted on-premises or in the cloud. Microservices hosted in the cloud can be part of a cloud native strategy.

> **Other misunderstandings**
>
> These are the main misunderstandings, and let's just quickly step through a couple more.
>
> Cloud native adoption will automatically save money. This is only true if the solution is architected in the right way. We went through that when we talked about lift and shift and containers. Another one is that cloud native is not as secure as on-premises. This is also totally wrong: the security controls are different from on-premises. If we utilize managed services, then the complexity of the security will decrease.

There are many drivers for adopting a cloud native stack, such as business agility, operational efficiency, time to market, developer productivity, and others. Our key drivers will depend on our business strategy. The cloud strategy needs to align with or be embedded in it to ensure the cloud native adoption delivers the best possible outcome. We will look into the strategy in the next chapter.

Summary

This introductory chapter has already covered a lot of ground. We learned about the evolution and benefits of cloud native. We discussed how culture is part of cloud native and how DevOps evolved to DevSecOps. It is critical to consider security throughout the complete SDLC. We also looked into foundations for CI/CD, observability, and resilience. We also clarified common misunderstandings, which will be helpful for conversations with stakeholders and the remainder of the book. Now that we are equipped with an excellent foundational understanding, we are ready to look into anti-patterns. We will start with objectives and strategy in the next chapter since they will be defined at the beginning of our cloud native adoption.

Get This Book's PDF Version and Exclusive Extras

Scan the QR code (or go to `packtpub.com/unlock`). Search for this book by name, confirm the edition, and then follow the steps on the page.

Note: Keep your invoice handly. Purchase made directly from packt don't require one.

Part 2: Setting Up Your Organization for Success

This second part focuses on strategic areas of our cloud adoption journey. These areas include strategy, governance, FinOps, DevSecOps culture, continuous integration and continuous delivery (CI/CD), and security. Within each area, we will explore common anti-patterns before discussing what good looks like and how to transition into good habits.

This part has the following chapters:

- *Chapter 2, The Cost of Unclear Objectives and Strategy*

- *Chapter 3, Rethinking Governance in a Cloud Native Paradigm*

- *Chapter 4, FinOps – How to Avoid a Bill Shock*

- *Chapter 5, Delivering Rapidly and Continuously Without Compromising Security*

- *Chapter 6, How to Meet Your Security and Compliance Goals*

2

The Cost of Unclear Objectives and Strategy

Every functioning organization has a **business strategy**. We need it from the first day onward. If we run a start-up, we will need it to get funding, and if we run an established business, we will know that it is required to set a vision and objectives that employees can follow. It is common knowledge that a strategy is needed. But why do we have so many **anti-patterns** that revolve around the strategic aspects? In all fairness, it is a fast-moving world: innovation cycles are fast. We need to make sure we refresh our architecture so we can build on top of other technologies to add business value.

This means we need to create an organizational mindset for continuous change and technology adoption. Consumer markets are competitive. Twenty years ago, it was enough to have quarterly or monthly releases of our applications. Now, we need continuous incremental changes. Regulatory frameworks are asking for more rigor, and the number of cyber breaches is increasing. Because of changing external factors, we need to be ready for continuous internal change.

"The only constant in life is change" is a famous quote by the Greek philosopher Heraclitus. To some degree, that is against human nature. But we need to be ready for continuous change and continuous improvement. Therefore, we need guidance regarding the types and magnitude of changes that benefit our organization. That is why we need a strategy. Not only do we need a strategy but we also need one that is up to date and covers all relevant concerns.

In this chapter, we are going to cover strategic challenges and why there are significant consequences if we do not address them. The following are common strategic challenges addressed in this chapter:

- Lack of clear objectives and strategy
- Lack of migration strategy
- Outsourcing of cloud knowledge and governance
- Lack of a partnership strategy
- Gaps in our Cloud Adoption Framework

We now have a clear picture of the learning objectives for this chapter. Let's start with the very first anti-patterns in this book, find out why they put organizations at risk, and then see how those anti-patterns can be turned into best practices.

Lack of clear objectives and strategy

"What we need to do is always lean into the future; when the world changes around you and when it changes against you – what used to be a tailwind is now a headwind – you have to lean into that and figure out what to do because complaining isn't a strategy" is a quote by Jeff Bezos, the Amazon CEO.

Someone who can grow their business from a little bookshop to a global online giant, release Kindle devices, expand the company to a global **cloud service provider (CSP)**, and then shift focus to space flights probably knows a fair bit about strategy and its importance. An incomplete strategy will hold us back during our cloud adoption and we will not be able to leverage the full benefit of the cloud. Therefore, we will now cover the following:

- Common strategic anti-patterns
- Understanding business goals
- Defining technology objectives and principles
- Defining our strategy foundations and leveraging guardrails

We will start with common strategic anti-patterns next.

Common anti-patterns

We will now step through two common anti-patterns and why they are holding back a cloud adoption journey.

The bottom-up strategy trap

The first variation of this anti-pattern starts with a **bottom-up cloud adoption approach** and typically provides some quick wins. Stakeholders of a digital transformation initiative realize that the lead times to release an application should be shorter. Those include waiting times such as onboarding a new vendor because various departments, including Legal, Procurement, and Tax, need approval, or a supplier can only deliver the required hardware in a few weeks. Then, the software products need to be installed, configured, tested, and registered in the asset registry. The sponsor then requests a **value stream map** that lays out the current process and timelines and compares them to what can be done.

It turns out the teams can deliver the product in half the time if they leverage a **cloud native approach**. That sounds great, doesn't it? Especially when we see quick wins and get confidence that the critical go-live deadline can be met. But long-term operational thoughts won't get enough consideration. Standardization across the organization will hardly be considered because the actual viewpoint is the initiative, which might be a project, product, or program of a business domain (group of projects).

The lack of standardization will impact the cultural aspects, such as **DevSecOps** and technology. In this scenario, we will have a business alignment with a project/product or product portfolio but not across the enterprise. This misalignment will result in an inhomogeneous culture and inconsistent technology stack across the organization. It is only sustainable if a business unit does not have synergies with other business units. In other words, the business unit is entirely self-sufficient and cannot leverage the common building blocks of other business units. This scenario is very often not the case, and it illustrates the bottom-up variation of this anti-pattern. Even in this case, **siloing** is still a genuine concern since it can have a negative impact on collaboration, learning, and productivity.

Let's now look into the top-down variation of this anti-pattern, which brings different challenges.

The top-down strategy trap

The technology leadership team has researched and found that words such as *poly-cloud* or *multi-cloud* sound excellent for unlocking all the benefits of cloud native and reducing **vendor lock-in**. What do those two words mean? **Poly-cloud** wants to leverage the strength of a particular CSP. For example, customer-facing APIs might be hosted in **AWS** because of their scalability, **GCP** might be used for ML and AI, and **Azure** might be used for authentication and authorization.

The primary driver for **multi-cloud** is to avoid vendor lock-in, and cloud segmentation is usually driven by capability strength in a broader picture. Poly-cloud and multi-cloud adoptions result in a very steep learning curve. Common scenarios are the following:

- Depending on the usage, it might mean the data team needs to learn how to manage data in multiple clouds

- If the data is managed in one cloud and everything else in other clouds, then the network team needs to be skilled in all the involved clouds to establish redundant links between clouds

We can imagine how complex the operating model becomes when several CSPs are involved. Some foundational constructs, such as **availability zones**, differ between CSPs. Even the term *Private Link*, a service name that AWS and Azure use, works very differently. CSPs also charge **data egress fees**. If we have an application running in Azure and the data resides in AWS, we must pay egress data fees in AWS. Another common side effect of this scenario is that only the **common denominator** is implemented to achieve consistency across cloud platforms, which prevents us from utilizing the CSP features to their fullest extent. The **top-down approach** has good intentions, too, but it does not consider the cultural challenges, the steep learning curve, and the required high degree of collaboration and change management to a full extent.

During a consulting engagement, I helped a university with its multi-cloud governance framework. They wanted to adopt a multi-cloud approach using Azure and AWS. After a couple of days on-site, I discovered this was their third attempt. The first two attempts had already failed over the last three years. And now they have tried the same multi-cloud adoption again. One month later, the engagement was put on hold again. The historic phrase *"There is only one way to eat an elephant: one bit at a time"* showed its relevancy again. In our context, it means that we are more likely to be successful if we take small steps toward a target architecture that can evolve over time. If we start our cloud native adoption journey, it needs to be step by step so we can gain momentum, and a sound cloud strategy needs to address precisely that. For impactful cloud adoption, we need a clear understanding of our business goals and follow on from there. Let's discuss what we need to consider for that.

Understanding the business goals and our current state

How do we move from lacking clear objectives and strategy to a well-architected cloud native strategy? We will start by discussing the strategic aspects.

Strategic aspects

We will need a strong business strategy, and the cloud native strategy needs to be an extension of this. It is crucial to understand that to achieve good business outcomes. We often hear that the technology strategy needs to align with the business strategy. Nearly every business relies on technology. That's why the technology strategy should instead be an extension. This thinking will automatically ensure alignment. This way, we can ensure that our technology decisions provide the best business outcome, whether that requires new features or improving our compliance posture. When we start the strategic improvement initiative, we first need to understand where we are today and where we want to be. As in our top-down scenario, we likely set unrealistic goals when we only know where we want to be. How do we know where we are compared to everything around us? In the real world, we use maps to find out where we are and locate where we want to be, and the map will guide us there. Nowadays, it will likely be a navigation app or system, but the result is the same.

Know where we are

Wardley Mapping, named after Simon Wardley, is a strategic framework that visually represents the components of a business or system, its maturity stages, and its value to the users. They help to understand an organization's environment, identify potential changes, and make informed decisions about where to invest resources. In a Wardley map, we position components of our value chain. A component might be a data repository or something unrelated to cloud.

Wardley maps have two dimensions:

- The vertical dimension describes the **visibility to end users** such as customers or internal users
- The horizontal dimension represents the **evolution of commoditization** ranging from *genesis* through *custom build* to *product* and *commodity*

A Wardley map might help us identify that we rely too much on custom-built components rather than leveraging features that are already a product or a commodity, such as **FaaS**. Now that we know what our business strategy is and what our current standpoint is, we are in a much better position to understand what our technology objectives need to be, and we will discuss that now.

Defining technology objectives and principles

With a good cloud native mindset, we want to support the business in achieving our goal while being highly efficient. Typical drivers for objectives are **business agility**, **time-to-market**, and **global reach**. Let's see how we can address these.

Addressing our objectives

We can achieve these objectives by moving to commodities where they are available and focusing on custom builds where there is a niche need. Increasing resilience is another common objective, meaning we must architect for **fault tolerance** and **recovery**. Enhancing security and compliance would require embedding security and compliance in our **shift left approach**. After defining the objectives, we need to get stakeholder buy-in, which we explore next.

Collaboration and buy-in

Now that we are in a position to articulate objectives, we can collaborate and document them. We will need leadership buy-in to ensure actions will be taken to implement our goals. Building a strong connection to the **chief information officer** (**CIO**) and other members of the leadership team is important. We must establish trust, provide visibility of the new direction, and ensure the leadership team understands our intentions. The strategy must support our development teams but also requires support from the top.

Stakeholder management

The more hierarchy levels an organization has, the longer it takes until everyone receives and digests the information. Even though objectives don't provide clear guidance, it is important to communicate them early. That way, people will not be surprised when they receive directions about the next level of detail. If we get trapped in this anti-pattern, we will probably not have a functioning **community of practice**. In the interim, we must use other communication and collaboration forums such as architecture and engineering stand-up. As a next step, we will define principles to provide early visibility for our stakeholders.

Defining principles

Defining a holistic strategy takes time, but we don't want to leave the stakeholders in the dark during that process. Otherwise, the **technical debt** will continue to build up. An excellent way to provide early visibility is by articulating **cloud native principles**. Those principles enable organizations to establish resilient, scalable, and secure architectures, faster innovation, cost efficiency, and increased agility. Let's go through some principal examples:

- **CSP selection**: This will articulate our only CSP or give unambiguous guidance when we use A over B. An example is "*Use GCP for every product managed under this business domain, otherwise use AWS.*" We will talk about cloud platform selection frameworks later.

- **CI/CD standardization articulation**: Do this to instantiate cloud resources. Use **Terraform** for every infrastructure component created through CSP APIs, such as an API gateway.
- **GitHub Actions usage**: Use these for everything application-related, such as deployments of new serverless functions (FaaS).
- **SaaS usage**: Use SaaS first, then serverless containerized services, and **IaaS** as a last resort if nothing else is viable. This can include content management systems or CI/CD platforms.

Once we have gone through this phase, we will ensure to continue the stakeholder engagement, which we will discuss next.

Continuing the stakeholder engagement

This guidance will help prefer commodities when custom-built is not required, as described in Wardley Mapping earlier. Until we can draft a strategy, it is beneficial to continue socializing the guiding principles and getting the agreement through our existing governance forums. The forum members need to agree to those principles. Acceptance will ensure actions are being taken and make it easier to get a strategy sign-off later. We are now ready to define our strategy foundations.

Defining our strategy foundations

When we move toward defining or reshaping our existing strategy, we need to check that we cover the aspects related to people, processes, and technology. The strategy should start with the vision, and we will explore this next:

- **Vision**: It needs to be clear who the sponsor is, and we will document that in the strategy. The Head of Cloud Platform could sponsor the cloud platform, whereas the Head of Products sponsors product development. Then, we add the guiding principles we have already worked out to the strategy. We need to be very clear about who our CSPs are. If this is not a guiding principle, we need to clarify it. This area can cause confusion if it is not clearly articulated. We want to avoid the need to make case-by-case decisions for individual workloads. Those details are needed to scale and deliver a consistent support model.
- **People**: Once we have a clear picture of the current tooling and the target state, we can identify new skills that the teams will require to get the most out of the tooling. Since DevSecOps is also about a cultural change, we need to identify what training is required. Are individuals already well-versed in **Agile**, or do they need further upskilling? Classroom training can be helpful, but the best hands-on experience will come with an Agile coach embedded in the team. It is the same with the DevSecOps adoption from a cross-functional team point of view. If this is new to the teams, augmenting DevSecOps consultants can achieve a fast learning curve. People need to experience this cultural change to understand how it works best for the team. Job descriptions must be updated, and the Human Resources department needs to be consulted. That is a big change for the organization, and a change manager will be required to help with the organizational transformation.

- **Process**: The criticality of processes is often underestimated. I have seen many cases where organizations implement tooling but the expected outcomes were not achieved because the processes were not mature enough to turn the technology adoption into a success story. For example, if we have a vulnerability tooling in place, it will provide the visibility that we need. However, it does not mean that the vulnerabilities will be remediated. There need to be processes, such as automated ticket generation for critical alerts, and escalation procedures. Otherwise, other things will take priority, and the actual root cause never gets fixed.

- **Technology**: At this stage, we must also articulate the core technology stacks for **container orchestration**, security tools, CI/CD, and observability. The tooling needs to align with the cloud native vision. Legacy on-premises CI/CD tooling can be a burden when moving to a DevSecOps model due to the increased complexity of networking, operations, security, and compliance management. For example, we need to update on-premises firewall rules every time we connect to a new build agent, we need to patch the actual servers and certificates, and we need to provide more compliance evidence compared to a SaaS solution. When exploring new tooling, evaluating whether it also integrates out of the box is important. If we move to a new tooling, such as a new CI/CD toolchain, we also need to think about a **migration strategy**, which we will do in the next section.

To reduce the risk of breaking changes we will need guardrails, which are our next discussion point.

Adding guardrails to our strategy

We need to consider the **quality controls** we want to establish. Since we are focusing on the strategy now, we can discuss it in great detail in *Chapter 5, Delivering Rapidly and Continuously Without Compromising Security*, but holistic coverage is important for now and we will look into some guardrail examples next.

Guardrail examples throughout our SDLC

Quality controls for the early SDLC (software development lifecycle) stage include repository and pipeline creation via updates to a configuration file in a CI/CD platform repository:

- The change requires a pull request approval

- The approval will trigger a **pipeline run** that validates whether the new repository and pipeline names align with the naming standards

- If that is the case, the pipeline creates two new resources: a Git repository and a new CI/CD pipeline

- During the development phase, other **guardrails** will include **code scanning**, **linting**, **documentation generation**, and **least privilege enforcement**

> The value of pre-deployment guardrails
>
> Guardrails can validate **data sovereignty, encryption, reliability**, and various governance, compliance, and cost aspects prior to deployment.

A popular **policy-as-code framework** for this purpose is **Open Policy Agent (OPA)**. As a next step, we can map the required guardrails to our SDLC to get a solid end-to-end picture.

A holistic end-to-end view across the SDLC

Guardrails can be set up throughout our SDCL phases, and the following figure gives us an idea of what a guardrail mapping can look like.

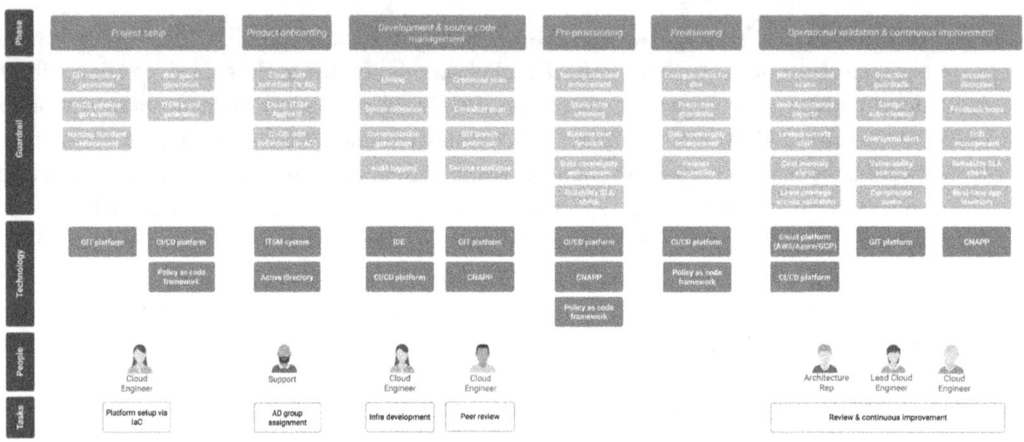

Figure 2.1 – Mapping guardrails to our SDLC

The guardrails can also include **cost optimization controls**, such as budget alerts, underutilization and rightsizing alerts, and **anomaly detection**.

Implementing these guardrails can take years, depending on how much human resources can be allocated. Therefore, it is critical to work out the priorities and technical dependencies. This will help us articulate a roadmap. To visualize the progress of a guardrail area, I like to add a little **Harvey ball** in front of each box. A Harvey ball is a round ideogram that visualizes levels of maturity, or in our case, we can also use them to show progress. If an area is 25 percent complete, it would be color-coded from the top to the right edge of the circle to the right, like a period on a clock from 12 pm to 3 pm. The following diagram illustrates examples of different progress stages:

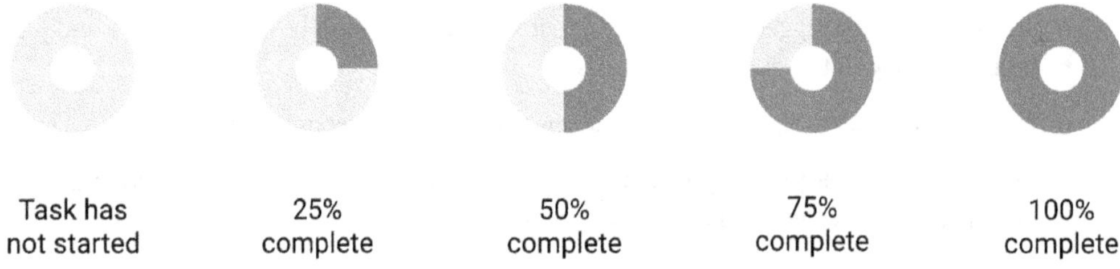

Figure 2.2 – Harvey ball examples

There is still more we need to include in our strategy, which we will explore next.

Enhancing our strategy

"Strategy without tactics is the slowest route to victory. Tactics without strategy is the noise before defeat," said Sun Tzu, the author of *The Art of War*.

The quote illustrates the requirement for a multifaceted approach. Our strategy must include an overarching view of cloud native initiatives covering CI/CD, including security tooling, observability, and all cloud native capabilities. When we define timelines for the roadmap, we need to consider our organization's **maturity level**. If we have gone through the Wardley Mapping process, we will have a good understanding of where we are, but we also need to factor in where we are on our cultural journey:

- **Update frequency**: Because the roadmap is often updated more frequently than the strategy, the roadmap is sometimes maintained in a separate document. However, it can also be part of the strategy document. CSP features and services change all the time, as might our business objectives or regulatory requirements. Therefore, we need to update our strategy regularly.

- **Change management**: When we continue with our strategy, we need to double-check that the previously mentioned change management and training aspects are covered. For the technology aspects, it will be very helpful to cross-check our strategy with the *Well-Architected Framework* of our CSP. We will also cover another framework, called the Cloud Adoption Framework, in a later section.

- **Endorsement**: The sponsor and the governing body must sign off on the strategy. That might be the Head of Cloud and the architecture community. Only if the strategy gets a sign-off can people be held accountable, and only then will people follow the articulated directions. I have seen many organizations that only have draft strategies. People consider drafts more as a recommendation rather than a guideline. We want our cloud native journey to support the business, so we will need the buy-in.

After stepping through strategic mistakes and best practices to define our objectives and strategy, we are ready to look into the next strategy aspect: setting ourselves up for a successful cloud migration journey.

Lack of migration strategy

Some common misunderstandings we discussed in the previous chapter contribute to this anti-pattern and these include the following:

- Confusion regarding cloud benefits

- Underestimating skill gaps

- Underestimating cultural change

- Lack of standardization and service catalog

For example, not having a **well-defined cloud native strategy** will also contribute to this anti-pattern, especially if we think moving to the cloud automatically reduces operational costs. Without clear guidance, we do not know what our target state should look like after the migration. Underestimating the **skill gap** and **cultural change** are also frequent contributors. Another significant contributor to this anti-pattern is the absence of a **service catalog.** After exploring the anti-pattern, we will discuss a migration framework for our applications, how to start on the business case, and how to kick off the implementation and gain momentum. Let's get started with the variations of this anti-pattern.

Common anti-pattern variations

Let's step through three common variations of this anti-pattern, starting with the myth of organic growth of the cloud footprint.

Growing the cloud footprint organically

This anti-pattern starts when an organization wants to organically grow its presence in the cloud. As a consequence, there is no migration initiative, which results in a **slow cloud up-ramp**, typically only for new applications. Some existing on-premises applications might be extended to a hybrid cloud solution because of on-premises scalability issues.

A typical case involves a **content distribution network (CDN)**, a web application firewall, an API gateway, and a queue in the cloud. The cloud native components can handle peak loads, and the on-premises app can pull from the queue. What was initially intended to be temporary can easily become permanent because there is no strong desire to move the rest into the cloud. After all, the team members have never gained sufficient migration experience. The burden here is that **troubleshooting** becomes more complex because errors can occur on both sides. It is the same with evidence collection for **compliance audits**. We have seen organizations that started their cloud adoption 8 years ago but only had 20% of the workloads in the cloud, and the rest was still on-premises. The vast majority of the cloud applications were new applications. The problem is that organic growth is unlikely to gain momentum.

Therefore, we will deal with legacy applications for a long time and won't be able to fully unlock the potential of cloud native stacks.

Lack of migration guidance

Another variation of this anti-pattern is not having a migration decision framework. Without a framework that guides us to which cloud platform to migrate to, we will need to make case-by-case decisions, which will take too long, and the decisions will not be consistent. We also do not know what the actual migration treatment should look like. A **treatment plan** will describe what refactoring steps we take to make an application more cloud-friendly. Organizations that do not have that framework in place make case-by-case decisions. This brings several problems. The decisions will not be consistent because there is a **lack of standardization**, which will increase the operational complexity. The decision process will take longer because it is not standardized. The migration process will take longer because every migration is treated differently. This can be a big burden on the application teams. Because of all the disadvantages, migrations will be perceived as painful and energy-draining. This will then reduce the willingness to migrate more applications. This results in the same outcome as the previous variation of this anti-pattern: we cannot leverage the full cloud native advantages because we are stuck in the legacy on-premises world for too long. It also means that we still need to continue with our data center refresh program. Once the hardware is renewed, we have spent considerable funding that could have been used for migrations.

We can see how this turns into a long-winded story that doesn't seem to end. But how can we fix it? How can we develop a structured migration strategy that helps us standardize migrations, flattens the learning curve, speeds up the migration progress, and delivers robust cloud native solutions that support business agility? We have seen that a slow organic approach does not help us gain momentum. Only once we gain momentum can we accelerate the cloud migration, increase migration efficiency, and improve our applications' operational efficiency and business agility. Now is the time to explore a framework that will help us achieve repeatable outcomes and gain momentum.

Lack of a service catalog

A service catalog contains blueprints that can be deployed in a self-service fashion. The service catalog offers reusable building blocks. Without a service catalog, we will have inconsistent and slow migrations. We need to set priorities for our service catalog items to make sure that high-impact items are implemented first. We also need to make sure that we address our requirements properly, including non-functional requirements. Otherwise, we will run into issues when we ramp up our migration journey.

An example of a service catalog item is a **publish and subscribe pattern**. This service catalog item can be referenced in a CI/CD pipeline. Then, it will create a queue and a notification construct, optionally with **dead letter queues** (**DLQs**). The DLQ can be enabled via an input parameter to the service catalog call. The main CSPs have their native service catalog offerings. SaaS CI/CD solutions, such as Terraform Cloud, also offer that.

The advantages of service catalogs are that they promote standardization and can have reliability and security default configuration. In the context of migration, they speed up migration significantly and help standardize our migration approach, simplifying the operational aspect.

Service catalogs also provide several advantages, including the following:

- They can accelerate on-premises to cloud migrations significantly because building blocks can be reused

- They promote standardization and can have reliability and security default configurations built in

- They can help reduce the operational complexity due to standardization, which brings consistency across environments

To stay away from the migration anti-patterns, we need a framework for our migration journey, which we will explore next.

A framework to navigate our migration journey

We need a robust framework that helps us with decisions and standardized treatments to gain momentum. In 2010, Gartner published the concept of using *R models for cloud migration strategies*. The model provided a framework to classify applications based on their migration suitability. Gartner's framework had 5 Rs. AWS released a framework with 6 Rs, and later on, an updated version with 7 Rs, and the model is called *The 7 Rs for migration*. This is now a de facto framework for cloud migration. Microsoft adopted a very similar framework in their Cloud Adoption Framework shortly after that, and the terminology is also very similar. GCP uses a different grouping. We will stick to the AWS and Azure terminology for the remainder of this book. We will step through the variations in a common order of priorities, with the first one having the highest priority:

- **Refactor**: This means the application is re-architected to leverage its full cloud native potential. This has the biggest potential to improve resilience, scalability, performance, and operational complexity. Refactoring requires more time and effort but can have a long-term return on investment.

- **Replatforming**: This means that an application is slightly modified for the migration. It is also referred to as *lift, shift, and tinker*. Those slight modifications could be an operating system upgrade or moving the database to a cloud native managed database service such as **AWS RDS, Azure SQL**, or **GCP Cloud SQL**. The CSPs offer database migration services for this purpose. This reduces operational complexity and it has the potential to reduce the run cost and improve resilience.

- **Repurchasing**: This is also known as *shop and drop*, meaning an existing on-premises application is replaced with a **commercial off-the-shelf** (**COTS**) solution, typically a SaaS product. It is worthwhile to compare the vendor's website offering with the offerings in the CSP's marketplace. Sometimes, the licensing models differ.

- **Rehosting**: This stands for shifting an application from on-premises cloud native virtual machines, such as **AWS EC2, Azure VMs**, or **Google's GCE**. With this migration path, the CSP's hypervisor is used. This path is often called *lift and shift* and brings us a step closer to a cloud native solution than the *Relocate* strategy. CSPs have migration services that help with this migration type, including **AWS Server Migration Service, Azure Migrate**, and **GCP Migrate for Compute Engine**.

- **Relocate**: This means that an application is moved to the cloud without architectural changes, using the same virtualization hypervisor as on-premises. **VMWare** has partnerships with the major CSPs to simplify this migration type. The *Relocate* strategy is often used when the goal is to move quickly, for instance, because of a data center exit strategy.

- **Retain**: This means that an application is not being moved. This is also called the *do-nothing* decision. This is often done when it is too hard to tackle a migration now or when the application has a set decommissioning date and new features are not required. An example is legacy mortgage systems because the mortgage contracts have such a long runtime. Any new mortgage applications will be managed by a newer application.

- **Retire**: This refers to the decommissioning of systems. This usually happens with small bespoke legacy systems that are performing small jobs. The decommissioning happens often toward the tail end of a migration initiative because the functionality can be absorbed by other applications. This is the desired target state for applications that become obsolete by a cloud migration initiative.

The following diagram provides an overview of the 7 Rs:

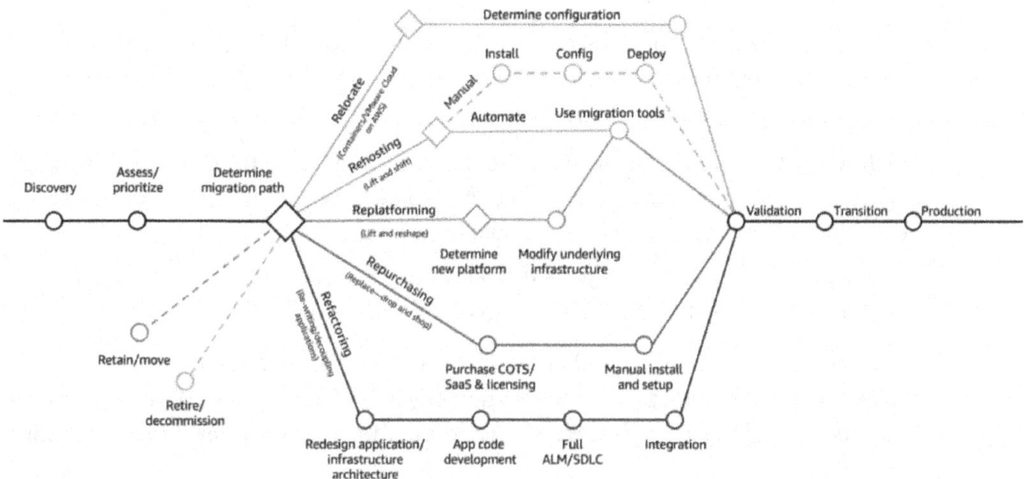

Figure 2.3 – The 7 Rs

(source: https://aws.amazon.com/blogs/enterprise-strategy/new-possibilities-seven-strategies-to-accelerate-your-application-migration-to-aws/)

The diagram summarizes the framework and it provides good guidance to navigate through the migration options. The framework provides repeatable guidance for our target state. Now, we need to categorize our migration candidates to start with a business case, which will be our next step.

Transitioning into the business case

Later, we will investigate how to create a 7R decision tree tailored to our organization's needs, but first, we need to start building out a **migration strawman**. This is an initial, simplified draft of a migration plan. It outlines a list of applications, a timeline of business goals, and the 7 Rs.

Now, we will look into some of the strawman aspects, starting with the creation:

- **Creating the strawman**: The creation of the strawman is often done in a one-day workshop. If it is an on-site workshop, it can be done on a whiteboard that has a drawn timeline representing the business goals and seven sticky notes in different colors. We can then go through the application list and have the application name on a sticky note near the colored sticky, depending on which migration path suits best. Of course, this can also be done on a virtual board with tools such as **Miro** or **Mural**.

- **Purpose**: The purpose of the strawman is to come to a basic structure that can be reviewed and refined later on. It will also help to identify challenges early and build the foundation for a detailed and comprehensive migration plan.

- **Timelines and resources**: At this stage, we can define high-level timelines and the required resources for the migration paths. They won't be accurate, but they will help steer conversations about priorities and which of the 7 Rs should be favored.

- **Cost benefits**: We also need to look up the data center cost savings we can achieve by reducing our on-premises footprint. The numbers are usually known since they are in the budget.

- **Other benefits**: The strawman will be a valuable input to our migration business case. Since we have high-level effort estimates, we can quantify the **migration cost**. We will also quantify the business benefits, such as **increased business agility**, **improved resilience**, and **reduced technical debt**.

- **Business case**: A signed-off business case is critical to gain momentum. This is the sticky point where a lot of organizations fail. Because there is no allocated budget for migrations, they get stuck in the *lack of migration strategy* anti-pattern.

We will fast forward to the next steps because we will step through the migration details in *Chapter 12*. The next goal is to accelerate our migration journey, and we will look into how to do that next.

Kicking off the implementation and gaining momentum

We will kick off a **migration acceleration initiative**, starting with the funding request:

- **Funding**: Our CSP can help us identify a consultancy for that purpose. Our CSP can provide funding or credits for this through their initiatives: AWS **Migration Acceleration Program (MAP)**, **Azure Migration and Modernization Program (AAMP)**, and GCP **Rapid Migration and Modernization Program (RaMP)**.

- **Readiness assessment**: The next step is a **migration readiness assessment**, which analyzes whether our current cloud landscape is ready for the migration initiative and what the gaps are. The assessment considers things such as the operating model, the maturity of the landing zone, and other factors usually defined in the **cloud adoption framework (CAF)**, which we will discuss in a later section.

- **Migration planning**: Before the actual migration starts, there will be migration planning. An approach we have seen working is implementing a proof of concept by picking four to five applications we want to migrate first. They should have different migration paths; for example, one *Rehost*, two *Replatform*, and one *Refactor* candidate. The applications must be complex enough to verify our approach and migration toolset.

- **Proof of concept**: The proof of concept will help in articulating our treatment plan, which is an extension of the 7 Rs. It will also add to our organization's context. We shouldn't start this journey alone. We should have the support of a consultancy that has done that many times before. The consultants must be embedded in our teams to ensure the knowledge transfer works.

- **Treatment plan**: The treatment plan will become a valuable extension of our migration strategy and a feedback loop to validate that the strategy is aligned with the more detailed findings we gained during this process. It will also articulate a **cloud placement decision** if our organization has a poly- or multi-cloud strategy. What else can we see in a treatment plan? Typically, we have guiding questions that step through the required business benefits, such as increased business agility.

- **Simplified treatment plan example**: The following illustration is a very simplified view, but it shows us how **prescriptive guidance** can work. Please note that the order of migration path types does not reflect our priorities, but it works best for eliminating options. We are also not considering the *Relocate* option, since that is mostly relevant for data center exit strategies.

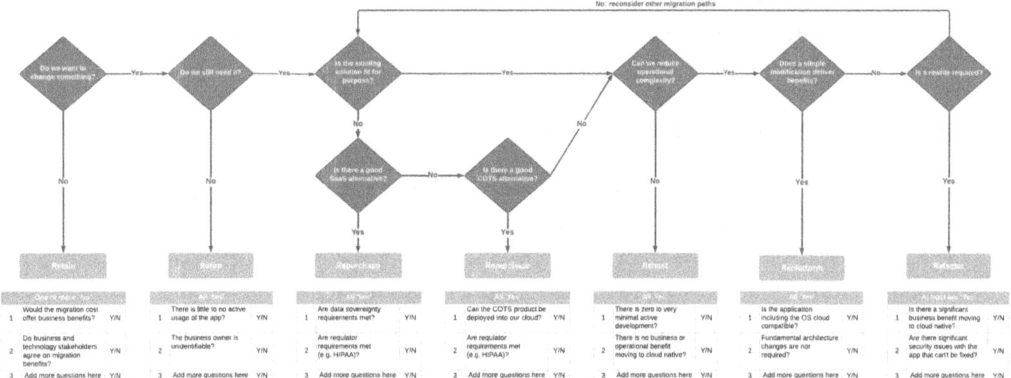

Figure 2.4 – A treatment plan example

The preceding diagram shows a simplified version that can be easily tailored to our organizational needs.

- **Organizational context**: The treatment plan will differ for every organization because it addresses the company's context, business strategy, and cloud native strategy. Once we decide on the migration path, we must identify the required change areas: **data storage and database**, **application refactoring**, and **CI/CD changes**.

- **Quantifying the change**: As a next step, we can quantify the change. We can retest the decision by reviewing the treatment plan with the insight gained. This process will be much smoother if a certified CSP partner helps us because they have done this many times.

Every consultancy will have a different variation of this framework and use different tooling to capture all the findings. That doesn't matter. The critical success factors are having prescriptive guidance and a repeatable approach to the migration path decision. This will help to get a good migration strategy implemented. We will talk about migration factories and tooling in *Chapter 12*. We have enough to start a migration strategy and build a feedback loop using the treatment plan.

If we get external help for our migration acceleration or other cloud native initiatives, we will need sufficient knowledge in our organization to be able to govern those initiatives, and we will explore this in the next section.

Outsourcing of cloud knowledge and governance

It can take years for an organization to realize they are stuck in this anti-pattern because a lot falls under the umbrella of knowledge when we talk about cloud native. Let's elaborate on our understanding of cloud knowledge before we go through how this anti-pattern can start and its impacts.

What does it take to govern cloud native initiatives?

Cloud native initiatives can be complex and critical to the success of a business. Therefore, we need a sound governance approach, which we will explore now.

People and organizational aspects

From a cultural and soft skill viewpoint, we need to understand DevSecOps practices, which we discussed in *Chapter 1*. We need to understand how the change management process works in our organization. We need to know what communication channels to use for **effective communication** and **collaboration** and how to use our collaboration tools for documentation and teamwork.

We need to understand **business drivers** and how we can support them, and articulate our cloud native strategy. This includes aspects such as **business agility** or **resilience** requirements. We have to know our stakeholders, how to engage them, and how to manage relationships and expectations. This includes our business partners, such as SaaS vendors and CSPs. Understanding governance frameworks, how to balance centralized and decentralized governance, the required governance controls, and how to establish a mature level of governance and compliance automation are also critical. In this section, we will step through these aspects in the following order:

- What it takes to govern cloud native initiatives
- Drivers for outsourcing
- Common anti-patterns
- Indicators for these anti-patterns

Technology aspects

From a technology point of view, we need to understand the services our CSP offers and the best practices for combining and orchestrating them. It also includes knowing the well-architected framework and how to apply it strategically and for individual initiatives. It is also critical to know how to define **reusable architecture building blocks** that align with **best practices** and **business goals** and how to turn them into **reusable artifacts** in our service catalog.

We need to stay on top of new cloud native developments to ensure we don't get stuck with old technologies, as we discussed earlier when we looked at Wardley maps. We need to be able to validate whether our **CI/CD toolchain** meets our needs and how to use the toolchain to establish consistent architectures. Understanding networking concepts and how to connect applications to business partners, public internet, on-premises, and, potentially, other CSPs is crucial. We also need to know **deployment best practices**, such as blue-green, to decide what deployment architecture is needed. Of course, we also need to understand **data best practices, microservices, container technology, cost management**, and many more aspects. We must also make sense of business and technology dependencies to build roadmaps.

Operational aspects

We need operational knowledge to understand best practices for **logging, monitoring**, and **alerting**, as well as how to leverage our observability tools and establish **centralized logging** where needed, such as security or audit logs. Operational knowledge includes **managing scalability, optimizing high availability performance, optimizing cloud resource utilization, cloud cost management**, and **FinOps best practices**. Knowledge of security and compliance is also required to implement the right controls. These include data and network traffic segmentation, encryption, network security controls, and others. We need to know how to assess trade-offs such as security versus cost.

This is not an exhaustive list of the knowledge required to deliver our strategy successfully. However, it is a good starting point for understanding what is required and why cloud native knowledge is critical for the organization.

Drivers for outsourcing

The never-ending learning is a big challenge. It is a challenge that some organizations try to avoid. Outsourcing a problem sounds tempting, and this decision can have several drivers. Sometimes, decisions are made without fully understanding the problem space. These are some typical cases:

- Technology is not our core business. Why should we deal with all that complexity? Let's outsource it. Good contract and vendor management practices will do the trick.

- We want lean teams to scale up and down in case we need to react to peak seasons or sudden market reactions. We can do that more easily when we have temporary external resources, such as consultants from a business partner or freelancers. Freelancers are individual contractors.

- Hiring highly skilled technology talent is very time-consuming. If we sign an agreement with a big consultancy, they will give us the best people in the market.

- We want to reduce administrative overheads. We do not need to manage training initiatives, performance reviews, or leave approvals if we have fewer permanent staff and more freelancers or consultants.

Both outsourcing scenarios (freelancers and consultancies) have many similarities. We will now examine how this anti-pattern can unfold in reality.

Common anti-patterns

This section will cover a few common strategy anti-patterns that are holding back organizations.

Knowledge outsourcing to freelancers

I once freelanced for a government organization, and more than 75% of individuals in the information and technology department were freelancers. Every individual contractor brings their own experience, knowledge artifacts, favorite programming languages, coding styles, libraries, tooling, and design patterns. Unknowingly, they might even have their favorite anti-patterns they keep using.

The motivation to be a freelancer is typically independence and a higher remuneration, depending on the job market. The next election had an indirect impact on the government organization. Contracts of freelancers that had been there for more than three years could not be extended. New contractors were brought on board, and they had a smorgasbord of tools, frameworks, and coding practices in front of them. The problem was that they couldn't pick and choose. They had to digest it all. Therefore, the learning curve is steep and there are many unknowns. This increases the time until new team members can be productive, and it also brings additional risk because of the unknowns. The situation can only be fixed by allocating time and budget to remediation initiatives.

Knowledge outsourcing to consultancies

Another time, I was employed by a consulting firm that had a cloud/DevOps engagement with a bank. The customer had a lot of different consultancies in the mix. Business units could decide which consultancy they want to bring in. One third party specializing in software engineering and APIs was attached to one business unit and a different one to another, and there were consultancies specializing in AWS and a different one in Azure. Some consultancies had been there for years, and their technology frameworks had changed during the long-term engagement. Having many consultancies in the vendor mix, combined with changing technology stacks and patterns, made it obvious that there are many moving parts. It became obvious that there was no overarching governance. The CI/CD toolchain and applications became unmanageable. Of course, consultancies also have to rotate their staff, because one of the personal drivers of a consultant is to get new challenges frequently and not get stuck in one place. This needs to be considered in project plans since there is extra time that needs to be allocated for handovers. One of the big global consultancies also brought in many junior consultants to maximize its profit, and the senior consultants did not challenge the quality shortcomings.

If we end up with these types of anti-patterns, not only will the frameworks and technology be inconsistent but so will the quality, levels of automation, observability granularity, log statements, deployment architectures, recovery procedures, and more. As a result, the organization becomes paralyzed and cannot react swiftly to market changes. It is critical to understand that consultants and freelancers need to be treated as accelerators, not as replacements for internal knowledge. So, how can we spot this anti-pattern to make sure we can take the right measures? We will find out now when we investigate the indicators.

Anti-pattern indicators

Cultural indicators

These are examples of cultural observations that indicate problems with knowledge outsourcing:

- **Ramp-up time**: It takes new joiners an unreasonable amount of time to become productive and understand the landscape. This is an especially strong indicator if even senior developers or engineers take longer than three months to get up to speed. They have usually broad experience with tooling. If they take a long time, this is a hint that either the CI/CD landscape is defragmented or out of date, or processes and ways of working are not as agile as they should be. In this scenario, it is a good idea to ask the new joiners what the challenges are and capture structured feedback. We could also engage a third party to assess the current CI/CD and cloud landscape and come up with recommendations and priorities.

- **Resource bottlenecks**: Initiatives are impacted if the most knowledgeable person is away. This strongly indicates that knowledge is not being shared across the organization, which is a major risk for the organization, especially when that individual leaves the organization or requires unplanned leave. Pair programming, shadowing, and reverse-shadowing can close that knowledge gap. We also need a clear definition of ready, which means the requirements are ready to start the design or a design is ready for implementation. This will depend on the definitions within a team.

- **Outsourcing everything**: It becomes obvious that most cloud engagements need to be outsourced. This could be because of internal resource constraints or lacking internal skills and experience. Let's explore this in more detail:

  - **Lack of internal resources**: If we do not have the resources, we must validate that enough time is allocated for our team members to collaborate with the external partner. We must understand and influence decisions to align with our vision, best practices, and operational needs. Otherwise, we will have the technology and framework sprawl, and the team will not know the internals of the application or product produced by the consulting firm. Even if the team has the required training in the cloud platform and CI/CD, they will not know enough about what has been delivered and deployed into production.

- **Lack of skills**: If the internal team cannot implement a new cloud initiative because of a lack of skills and experience, it is obvious that more training is required. We will need a combination of standardized learning for cloud and CI/CD, but we also need contextual learning on how to apply those things in our organization. This can be learned with team augmentation and working alongside an external party. The knowledge transfer must be addressed in the **statement of work (SoW)**, and it needs to be regularly validated during a consulting engagement.

- **DevSecOps culture**: Another giveaway for a knowledge gap is the absence of a DevSecOps culture or manual steps in the CI/CD process. We talked about the DevSecOps culture earlier, and we can improve or establish it through team augmentation. The main reasons for a lack of automation and relying on manual steps in the CI/CD process are insufficient knowledge or cutting quality corners due to rushed deadlines. Both are risks to the organization and need to be addressed by allocating enough time to fix the issue and ensuring the teams have the required knowledge or can gain it through the previously discussed learning methods.

As we can see, the root cause of this problem category is quite often a lack of training and experience to establish an effective governance procedure. But there are also other areas that indicate problems, and we will look into them now.

Indicators in our documents and systems

The following indicators can be found in existing documentation, including contracts, and in systems that we use:

- **Outsourcing contracts are missing fundamental information**: Before the engagement starts, a mutual contract is signed between both parties, commonly known as the SoW. If the SoW does not reference internal CI/CD practices such as code scanning, branching model, CI/CD workflows, coding style guides, and observability standards, this should raise alarm bells. Standards and frameworks must be referenced in a SoW if they are in place. Otherwise, the outcome will not meet our expectations, and we will need to deal with technical debt, governance challenges, maintenance complexity, and avoidable operational complexity. It is time to act immediately if we don't have those standards. If internal team members do not know how to articulate those standards, the next engagement with our trusted cloud consultancy should be establishing or maturing those standards. This engagement will need full support from the technology and business teams. It is a very strong sign that we do not have the knowledge to govern our cloud native initiatives. This means that governance happens outside of the organization. This is a guarantee for failure since this approach will not meet our organization's needs and strategic direction. We need to make this standardization engagement a priority. More importantly, we need someone who can work closely with the consultancy and learn all about the best practices while also doing some theory education such as a classroom or online course.

- **Analyzing the training budget and skill certifications**: Numbers don't lie. Our team members cannot reimburse expenses for training or conferences without a dedicated training budget for ongoing learning unless we use some creative accounting techniques. Some team members might be willing to absorb those expenses. From a corporate point of view, it would be fair to budget for it and pay those expenses. How else could our company expect to remain abreast of the rapid pace of innovation in the technology space without supporting our employees in remaining up to date with our knowledge? In the end, we will achieve a better corporate outcome. We need to work out a training plan that aligns with the experience level of our team structure.

- **Cloud native skills are not reflected in job descriptions**: If the required experience level is not articulated in the job description or is not quantifiable, then we need to work on a skill matrix for each experience level. Then, we can work out a gap analysis to see which areas need improvement. This will help to look up what training we need and what the cost will be. It is important to cover the following areas in the training plan: DevSecOps and Agile, security, CI/CD, governance, and technology, including development, operations, and observability. It is important to get those numbers into the next budget. If any budget during the current financial year can be repurposed, we are already in a better position because we have worked out the training numbers, gaps, and benefits.

- **Over-privileged user permissions**: Another way to indicate we are heading toward this anti-pattern is to validate human permissions in our identity and access management roles. If no one has the skills to validate this, that should ring alarm bells. If we discover that humans have permissions that should not be needed in a mature DevSecOps culture, this is a strong indicator of the immediate need for training. If humans require write permissions to change either database schemes or ingest data into a database, there could be two reasons for this: either the permissions are not required or we are not following least privilege best practices. The likely option is that our teams are not following DevSecOps best practices. In this case, we have to allocate time to establish those capabilities. In our example, we will need data ingestion patterns articulating how tooling can help to import data. If the team doesn't have experience in that area, it will highlight another need for training. By now, we know that learning includes generalized learning provided in a course and pairing up with externals who have done that before.

Similar to the cultural indicator category, we can see that a lack of training and experience is causing problems, and we will later explain how this impacts operations and delivery. We now have a good understanding of how to spot indicators within our documentation and systems and we will move on to operational and delivery indicators.

Operational and delivery indicators

The following indicators become obvious while we operate our applications or when we want to implement changes or new features:

- **Every little change takes an unreasonable amount of time**: This indicates technology and framework sprawl as a result of governance gaps. Those gaps are likely due to a need for more knowledge to govern technology and process decisions. We must upskill our team to govern initiatives, review outcomes, and make recommendations.

- **No long-term fix for outages**: There are outages, and the teams can fix them quickly but do not know how to improve the situation strategically. This indicates a lack of observability and, potentially, a shortcoming in technology refreshes. Both could have happened due to a timeline rush, a lack of observability experience, or tooling. This will require a root cause analysis to determine what actions need to be taken.

- **Significant findings in advisory tools**: An advisory scanning tool, such as a **cloud native application protection platform** (CNAPP) shows many findings. These include unencrypted storage, unattached disk volumes, underutilized instances, missing access logs, reliability gaps, and keys that have not been rotated for over a year. This shows we either operate reactively due to time constraints or have not adopted best practices. The first one could mean that we do not have mature risk management procedures and ownership definitions in place, such as an operating model, and a RACI (responsible, accountable, consulted, informed) matrix that shows responsibilities, accountability, and who needs to be consulted or informed. The second possible reason, a lack of best practice adoption, is another sign that training is required and that the team needs to be given time to implement these best practices. Quite often, a combination of both reasons applies.

We have explored internal indicators, the problems they cause, and how to remediate them. Recovering from these problems can take a long time, depending on the company's size, degree of sprawl, and complexity. It is important to continuously look out for these indicators. But there are also some external indicators for this anti-pattern, and we will go through them next.

External indicators

The following signals are potentially provided by third parties:

- **Significant finding in audits**: Audits reveal many remediation-required findings, including least privilege approach gaps and vulnerabilities in containers and virtual machines. The root causes are the same as those as the findings surfaced by an advisory tool, such as a CNAPP solution.

- **Over-relying on penetration tests**: Penetration tests include findings that could have been avoided with a mature DevSecOps culture, such as out-of-date images, lack of network security controls, or installed malware because we are exposed to supply chain attacks. This indicates we have not addressed practices such as vulnerability scanning in our DevSecOps culture and CI/CD toolchain. This is usually not a technology issue, since most CSPs offer that service. It is very likely a sign that more DevSecOps upskilling is required.

- **Partner feedback**: A CSP or software vendor provides feedback that we are not utilizing the tool enough or correctly. We need a functional relationship with the third party for them to be honest enough with their feedback. The feedback from the CSP could be that our virtual machine uptake needs to be lowered if we have a serverless strategy. This can be a sign that our serverless strategy has not been communicated well or that our teams don't know how to write serverless applications and would rather run apps in the traditional way on virtual machines. A vendor might provide feedback if we have a committed spend and significantly underutilize the tool. One of my previous customers had a committed spend for security and compliance SaaS products but they only utilized 10 % of the license volume. The reason was that only the people who initiated the purchase knew how to leverage the tool but left shortly after the purchase. Luckily, the vendor reached out, and we were able to run some training sessions. This helped with the tool ramp-up and creating visibility of the current maturity level for compliance and security.

Lessons learned

What is the lesson learned from feedback coming from either CSPs or software vendors? They often provide training, and we need to make sure that we utilize that training. Only then can we guarantee that we get good value from our purchase. If the product is our strategic choice, we need to make sure we build good relationships. This will make sure that we get honest feedback, and we can also get answers to questions we might have. We will discuss this in more detail in the next section, where we explore partnership strategies.

Lack of partnership strategy

"Partnership is not a legal contract between two equal individuals. It's an emotional alliance between two people who are committed to each other's success" is a quote by Warren Buffet. We rely on partnerships in our daily lives, for example, with work colleagues, friends, a spouse, and others. On an organizational level, partnerships have the same significance. We want to avoid making partner decisions based on gut feeling and instead rely on logical and strategic thinking and decision-making. No matter what market we operate in, there will be competition, and we want to be ahead of the curve. We won't be able to achieve all our goals alone. Let's look into some anti-patterns that can reduce the value of partnerships, burden our organization, and hold us back.

We will look into two anti-patterns, one for professional services and one for technology partners. We will identify indicators and partner selection considerations and how to improve the partnership with our CSP (cloud service provider). Let's start with the anti-patterns.

Common anti-patterns

Panic-driven partner selection

In a previous role, I worked for an organization that had a tiny cloud platform team, considering the cloud native ambitions they had. Let's refer to them as the customer to distinguish between the consultancy and the customer. The customer relied heavily on a cloud consultancy. The local consultancy has less than 500 employees and operates only in a small part of Asia Pacific. Their consultants are highly skilled, have a wealth of cloud native knowledge, and contribute to the community via meetup talks, conference presentations, and blog posts. They have won several AWS partner awards and have demonstrated true dedication. They could operate with little guidance, were productive, applied best practices, and were always willing to transfer knowledge or work in a team-augmentation approach. The small cloud consultancy was a great cultural fit and understood the customer's business objectives. They also had all the required technology expertise.

Later, the customer had two on-premises outages within a year. Because of service-level agreement breaches, they had to pay penalties for the outages. Additionally, those outages received media attention, which added more pressure.

Only 25% of the applications ran in the cloud, and the majority were hosted on-premises. The leadership team brought in one of the big global consultancies to investigate resilience issues across the organization. The international firm was known for its expertise in process design and management consulting. The international global consultancy started with on-premises analysis and design recommendations. Unfortunately, once the global consultancy commenced the cloud discovery workshops, the budget for the local cloud consultancy was repurposed. The giant consulting firm tried reusing slides that were previously used for businesses 20 to 50 times the size of the customer. The slides were very generic and did not address the customer context. During the first cloud workshops with the new partner, it became apparent that their cloud experience could not match expectations. The experience gaps were significant. The majority of their consultants were very on-premises focused. The people who had some cloud experience were graduates who only had very little time to learn from errors and anti-patterns.

The recommendation slides produced after the discovery phase did not reflect reality. The chosen language was ambiguous. The consultancy did not understand the current automation and compliance gaps, which became obvious during the play-back sessions. When we (the customer) tried to clarify misunderstandings, we realized the consultancy did not understand the fundamental concepts of cloud native. We agreed that the cloud team needed to be pulled into the review process earlier to improve the quality. The consultancy brought in more consultants to capture detailed requirements in the following engagement phase.

We had review sessions where there were 2 members from the cloud team and 12 from the consultancy. The consultancy produced design artifacts that were missing a majority of compliance and security requirements. After a while, some team members of the customer's cloud team spent 50% of their time reviewing and providing feedback. The mentality of the consultancy was very different compared to the previous strategic cloud consultancy. Their behavior was passive, and their main driver was to move stories from "in progress" to "done" on the Jira board. The quality was so low that it did not add value, and the cloud team spent more time hand-holding the consultants to get the quality to an acceptable level. After 6 months, 25% of the intended scope was delivered. It was an exhausting experience and negatively impacted the motivation of team members. This anti-pattern is avoidable if we choose the right vendor for the suitable problem space. Choosing the right partner requires some planning and collection of data points to see how the velocity can improve over time. But those things do not happen if we make reactive decisions.

You snooze, you lose

Another common variation of the *lack of partnership* anti-pattern is being in a passive mode instead of a proactive mode. That typically happens when we do not have a cloud migration strategy and want to grow our cloud presence organically. As a consequence, we don't gain momentum. The migration approach will be slow, as we already covered in the *lack of migration strategy* anti-pattern. Because of that, we will not invest enough time and budget into strategic relationships. When this happens, we might have all required license agreements in place, but we are not necessarily using the tools and platforms correctly. We are probably also not focusing on building enough cloud native knowledge within our organization. We don't have regular collaboration sessions with our partners. We will miss out on the training that our teams could get. We will also not receive valuable feedback or leverage the partner for reviews. All those things will hold us back. Let's summarize the benefits of strategic partnerships to make sure we leverage them.

The value of strategic partnerships

A partnership is a mutual relationship. Partners will want to help us since they want a successful customer story, too. What are we missing out on if we do not build strong strategic partnerships?

- Partners can help us with a training plan, training sessions, and lab environments so that our team members can follow the instructor for more hands-on experience. With a functioning partnership, we can leverage those benefits.

- If we don't have a strong relationship with our partners, they won't provide valuable feedback to improve and be more effective in our working methods. Partners have seen many customer stories and seen first-hand what has gone wrong and what worked. They want to help us because a customer's success also means they have a good customer story.

- We will not receive roadmap insights, which can be helpful to avoid building up technical debt and avoiding bespoke solutions if we know there will be an out-of-the-box feature soon.

- We will also not receive the support we need. The turnaround time for questions we ask will be slower than desirable, or the quality might be lower because stronger relationships get more attention.

- Our innovation will not be as accelerated as it could be if we have a partner who can speed up transformations and ensure we use best practices. The latter might also impact security and reliability.

- Other areas for improvement could be a lack of cost efficiencies that an SME (subject matter expert) from the partner could spot or slower support response times because we are not on a premium partnership contract. AWS, Azure, and GCP have different response times depending on the support level we choose. A higher support level also comes with a higher cost; we must assess the benefits.

What indicators show that we are on our way to this anti-pattern or are already impacted by it? We'll look at these next.

General indicators for this anti-pattern

Undocumented vendor onboarding

A potential sign of a weak relationship is if the vendor onboarding was never documented and has never gone through a formal endorsement process. That is a sign that the partner was never assessed to ensure they met our legal and compliance requirements. We might not know their entire service offering besides the SaaS solution we purchased. In this case, we might miss out on free training that can be provided to our teams. If we have never done the due diligence check, the vendor might not fit our objectives. We must assess whether we want to invest more time and budget into this partnership. If we think the product meets our needs but don't get much support from the vendor, we need to reach out for conversations about what else they can bring to the table. We will only get roadmap insights if we have a **non-disclosure agreement** (**NDA**) with the provider. If there is no NDA in place, then that is a sign that we either don't have meaningful discussions about achieving our business objectives or have a legal issue.

Passive behavior

If we think our business partner is passive, that is another sign of a weak relationship. The symptoms could show in a variety of ways. Their response time could be faster when we ask questions. They might not show up to meetings or be frequently late. We might receive negative feedback from stakeholders within our organization. The partner might never provide feedback about how we use their tool, or they don't offer any roadmap insights. We can see that many aspects can hold back our journey if we don't build strong relationships with our partners.

Lack of cadence

Another indicator that we didn't build a strong relationship is if there is no regular cadence with the vendor. We might not need a strong relationship for a small SaaS solution. Still, it is critical for a partnership with our CSP and vendors of our core CI/CD toolchain or security and observability products. A weak partnership can significantly impact our productivity, reliability, security, and ways of working. What can this cadence look like? Let's start with our CSP.

Let's examine the key areas we want to address when establishing new partnerships or reassessing existing ones and the key benefits of strong partnerships.

Considerations for selecting a partner

Considerations for selecting a CSP

We want to leverage the expertise of our partners, who could be CSPs, consultancies, or technology vendors:

- **Subject matter experts (SMEs)**: They have specialized knowledge and a team of SMEs. First, we need to clearly understand our objectives. CSPs have technical SMEs for security, serverless, network reliability, and others. They also have SMEs for non-technical areas such as compliance, change management, training and education, or particular industries. They might offer classroom training or subscriptions to their online training platform as part of the support agreement. We discussed cadence meetings with account managers and solutions architects from our CSP when we assessed indicators of this anti-pattern. These recurring proactive sessions will help improve our architecture and utilize cloud native features effectively and efficiently.

- **Partner ecosystem**: There is also an ecosystem around CSPs, and professional service organizations are part of that. There is also a significant community aspect. CSPs have community programs such as **Google Cloud Innovators, AWS Heroes and Community Builders**, and **Microsoft Most Valuable Professionals**. Individuals contribute content such as meetup presentations, blog posts, videos, and so on. If our team members are passionate about their cloud platform, they will use those information channels and continue their learning journey. Or, even better, they might contribute. When our employees contribute to the community, our brand name gets known within the cloud community. This will help the organization hire technical talent and be perceived as a technology expert in our industry.

Considerations for selecting a consulting partner

When looking for a new consulting partner, we need to assess their current expertise area and their strategic growth area:

- **Strategic alignment**: If we are looking for a **professional service partner**, we must ensure their strategic goals meet ours. If the consultancy wants to expand its AI and ML practice but we want to focus on IoT, then there is a misalignment. We need to validate the technology aspects where we need guidance, including CSP services, CI/CD, data capabilities, observability, and so on. We will check whether they have sufficient certifications for our CSP and customer success stories. The consultancy needs to sufficiently cover our time zone and potentially be on-site if this is required for workshops. If we want them to help us with a cultural DevSecOps transformation, we must validate and compare their cultural values with ours. We might need help with training, stakeholder engagement, or change management, and we need to validate those capabilities.

- **Current focus areas**: Consultancies are often structured by practices. Individuals in a practice can go deeper in a particular area and help us with in-depth knowledge we don't have in-house. We can also use team augmentation to upskill our team members, increase our maturity level, and help us avoid anti-patterns. Our partners' expertise can help us build momentum, gain speed, and achieve agility. Partners have tools and frameworks to help us accelerate our cloud native adoption. If we get help increasing our efficiencies, we can focus more on innovation and things that differentiate us from the competition.

Considerations for selecting a software vendor

We must also perform a due diligence assessment if we are looking for a **software vendor partnership**. If innovation is at our forefront, we must select a vendor that invests enough in innovation and delivers fast innovation cycles:

- **Public information**: Websites such as **Forrester**, **G2**, and **Gartner** publish market research and indicate vendors' innovation for a particular problem space. We don't want to rely on one opinion; it is good to get several views. Vendors are usually prepared to give existing customer references and establish contact with an existing customer. That way, we can find out how a different organization adopted a product or service, their challenges, and how it helped them.

- **Architecture fit**: We also need to validate the architecture fit. Does the product or product suite meet our integration needs? **Integration** to the source code repository is essential. For instance, if we have a least privilege scanning solution that can identify machine role policies that need to be updated. In this scenario, it would be very helpful to point us to the corresponding code and suggest the code change. That will save a lot of time if we have hundreds or thousands of Git repositories, and it saves us from going on a treasure hunt.

- **Compliance and security**: If compliance and security are vital, we must validate that these requirements can be met. Is everything encrypted at rest and in transit? What data is stored? Is the data stored in my region? Are you **SOC2** or **PCI-compliant**? Do they meet our legal requirements, and can the jurisdiction be in the country we operate in? Do they meet our security requirements? For example, they only use strong cipher suites for encryption. Can they provide training, and do they have integration partners? These are just some examples of things we need to assess.

A technology vendor will know the best practices for their tools and how to use them without building up technical debt. They can also provide insights into their roadmap, which is helpful when we want to make strategic design decisions. For example, if a particular feature is being released soon, we can avoid custom code, or we might be able to join a preview program.

Improving our CSP partnership

There are a few aspects to consider for improving a CSP partnership:

- **Different roles**: Depending on our support plan, there might be more than one contact person, and the concern areas will be split between them. If we are unsure who to contact for what particular area, we need to ask our CSP for clarity. That is important to make sure we get help promptly and can also set up cadence meetings with the right people in the room. For example, an **account manager** might oversee commercial agreements, legal sign-offs, or training plans. That would be our contact person whenever we need help with our support plan, want to ensure we get the best volume discounts, or need help finding a professional service organization.

- **The right contact for the right problem space**: When we set up a cadence with the account manager, we need the right people from our teams in those meetings. They are managers who manage commercials and can contact the legal or procurement teams with any questions or formalities. They can also help to structure bigger initiatives such as a migration program. Sometimes, there is a split between a **business account manager** and a technical or delivery manager. The **technical account manager** will then be the contact for more technical questions and high-level architecture questions. A potential further contact person could be a solution architect with all the experience to help us with architecture or engineering questions. They also have internal connections to SMEs for all cloud native services and industry experts. We can set up various cadence meetings/workshops.

- **Cadence**: If we are rapidly building new architecture patterns or adopting new services, we will need frequent meetings with our **solutions architect** (**SA**), maybe weekly or twice weekly. The meetings with the account manager might only be required every two weeks. It is always good to talk the SA through your thinking because they might have ideas for approaching things differently.

  Example of an architecture cadence: We always found it helpful to talk our SA through new patterns to challenge our thinking and get feedback. Sometimes, the patterns were so problem-space-specific or complex due to regulatory requirements that the SA had to add SMEs to our workshop. We will only get this benefit if we develop a strong partnership. The SA was our first point of contact whenever we had questions regarding the cloud services roadmap. Our organization was typically represented by the lead cloud architect and the lead cloud platform engineer in these meetings. To ensure those meetings and workshops are productive, having the right areas represented and not too many people is essential.

Conclusion

Those are some common aspects and assessment areas for a partnership evaluation. Bigger organizations typically have a third-party assessment framework in place, but not necessarily the small ones. Either way, **holistic due diligence** is required to make an informed decision. A business partner could also identify risks we have yet to spot and help us mitigate them. There are many reasons why our organization can benefit from good strategic partnerships. We know they are crucial for cloud native transformations, and we can now move on to the last anti-pattern in this chapter, which is a lack of CAF.

The cloud adoption runaway train

"It is not the strongest of the species that survive, nor the most intelligent, but the one most responsive to change."

– Charles Darwin

Everything around us changes all the time. Therefore, we need to adapt and adopt. Even though these two words have very different meanings, they quite often go hand in hand. **Adapt** means that we adjust or accommodate. **Adopt** means we take something as our own, such as a methodology that has been proven successful. A CAF helps us along our cloud journey. There is no official definition of a CAF, and every CSP has its own definition. Therefore, we will go with a definition that is precinct and hits the middle ground of the definition the major CSPs use: *A CAF provides best practices, tools, and guidance that help with effective cloud adoption. It addresses the different life cycle phases and ensures organizations achieve their business goals by leveraging cloud native technology.*

The different CAFs of the main CSPs all have the same goal and want to help organizations plan and implement their cloud adoption journey. However, all frameworks have a different structure, approach, terminology, and specific guidance for the CSP services. We will discuss them in this section and also common anti-patterns. Then, we will close off with a summary and the key learnings from this chapter. Let's dive into the CAFs now.

CAFs

AWS CAF

AWS organizes the CAF into six perspectives: business, people, governance, platform, security, and operations. It also outlines the **cloud transformation value chain**, represented by transformation domains. **Technology transformation** enables **process transformation**, which enables **organizational transformation**, which in turn enables **product transformation**. This leads to **business outcomes**, as outlined in the following figure.

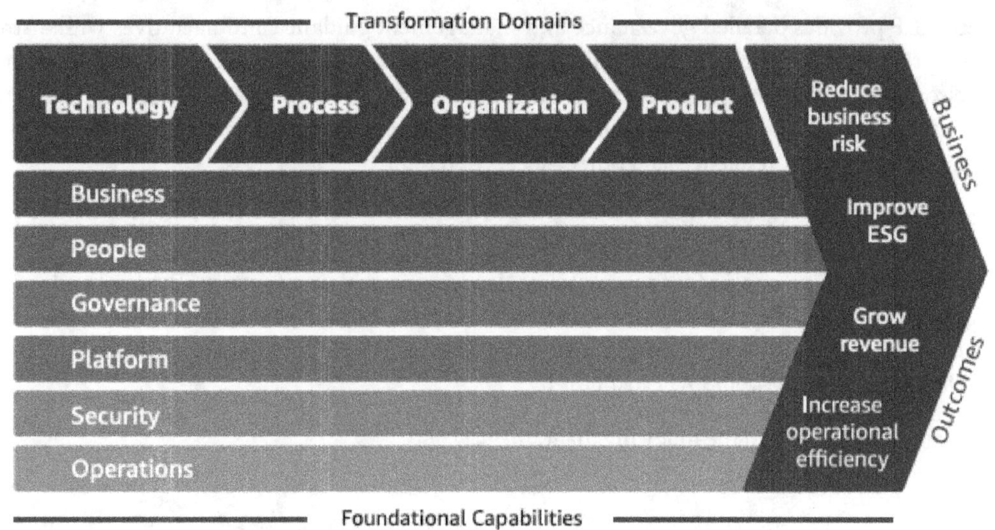

Figure 2.5 – AWS CAF (source: https://d1.awsstatic.com/whitepapers/aws-caf-ebook.pdf)

The previous diagram provides a crisp summary of the AWS CAF, which strongly emphasizes operational excellence and security, and it includes resource references such as the **AWS Well-Architected Framework**, **AIOps**, and **AWS Prescriptive Guidance**.

Azure CAF

The **Azure CAF** is structured by the phases: define, plan, ready, adopt, secure, manage, and govern. The following diagram outlines the phases and how the framework uses methodologies to overcome blockers.

Figure 2.6 – Azure CAF (source: https://learn.microsoft.com/en-us/azure/
cloud-adoption-framework/_images/caf-overview-graphic.png)

The CAF provides detailed governance and management guidance and narratives with a strong enterprise focus. It references **Azure Blueprints** and **Azure Policy** for governance and compliance. It also references the **Well-Architected Framework** and the **Microsoft Learn** training platform. It also references architecture templates, including best practices and considerations for scalability, availability, security, resilience, and other aspects of design.

GCP CAF

The **GCP CAF** is organized into four realms: lead, learn, scale, and secure. The lead realm states we need a top-down sponsor mandate and *bottom-up momentum from our teams' cross-functional collaboration*. The GCP CAF emphasizes continuous learning and innovation and strongly focuses on leveraging data, ML, and AI capabilities.

We can see all realms in the following diagram:

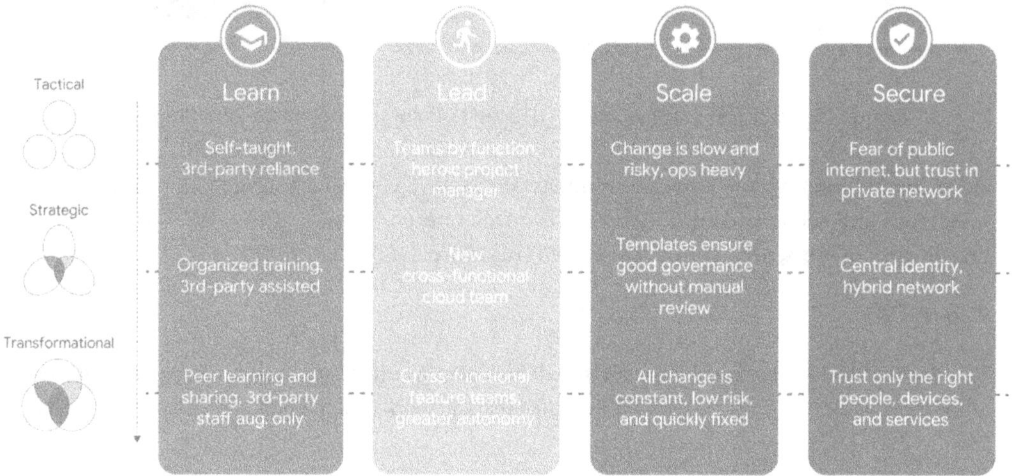

Figure 2.7 – GCP CAF (source: https://services.google.com/fh/files/misc/google_cloud_adoption_framework_whitepaper.pdf)

Communalities between CAFs

All three CAFs have a similar coverage area and address the strengths of the individual CSP.

After comparing the different CAFs, two things become apparent:

- First, cloud adoption is complex, and there is much to consider. That is why some aspects of a CAF are often forgotten, resulting in an incomplete picture of our cloud adoption journey. Therefore, we might forget or insufficiently address aspects such as training, cultural impact, or change management. Those are common reasons why cloud adoption initiatives fail and need to be relaunched. That is not only a costly exercise but also can lead to people leaving the organization because of frustrations that are beyond their control.

- Second, this chapter has already examined areas within the scope of a CAF, including strategy, learning, and the consequences of a lack of cloud knowledge, including governance gaps. In *Chapter 1*, we also examined some cultural aspects. Therefore, we will now focus on two strategic anti-patterns that we have not discussed yet.

Common anti-patterns

Ignoring blueprints and CI/CD best practices

The first variation of this anti-pattern is ignoring blueprints. This is a very common scenario that we have seen multiple times. Let's illustrate this anti-pattern with a scenario and explore the individual steps:

1. The cloud adoption is initiated bottom-up. The leadership team understands it brings great opportunities but does not get involved in governance. However, enough rigor is in place to ensure that common frameworks, CI/CD tools, and programming languages are used.

2. The product team starts developing the first service catalog items to ensure the code can be reused by other teams. CSPs use different terminology for this purpose. Instead of service catalog items, they might use terms such as *products, blueprints, solutions,* or *modules.* For clarity, we will use the terms *product catalog item* and *module.* That way, it is clear that they have been implemented by our organization and not a CSP. Service catalog items can include API gateways, database services, and many more.

3. The team was excited since they were much further ahead in cloud adoption than the rest of the company. After a while, the team encountered a deployment issue. The deployment was successful, but there was something wrong with the deployment artifact, and some of the API functions responded with errors. The Golang code base that was released was a newer version than the one that had been tested in UAT (user acceptance testing) before.

4. A team member fixed the issue by releasing the latest tested version, and the application performed stable again. Luckily this could be fixed within minutes. During a root cause analysis, the team found that a build artifact from the development environment had somehow been released to production.

5. Everyone thought they were practicing good environment promotion, which meant build artifacts could only be deployed to the next higher environment after testing it. We could only deploy a build artifact from development to the test environment, not to UAT or production. It turned out the guardrails were not in place to enforce the use of predefined workflows that validate environment promotion. A new team joiner was unaware of this best practice and set up a custom CI/CD pipeline for the deployment. We cannot blame the new joiner.

We could have protected him and our organization by leveraging guardrails, which was missed in this first incident. CAFs explain CI/CD best practices, including environment promotion.

> **The value of CAFs**
>
> CAFs provide comprehensive guidance on implementing CI/CD pipelines, emphasizing automated testing, integration, and deployment strategies to ensure seamless environment promotion and reliable software delivery.

The AWS CAF describes CI/CD and environment promotion preliminary in the two perspectives platform and operations. The Azure CAF covers environment promotion under the *ready*, *adopt*, and *manage* stages. The GCP CAF describes CI/CD in the *scale* realm. We will now explore what can happen if we do not follow operational best practices.

Ignoring operational best practices

The second variation of this anti-pattern is ignoring operational best practices. We will look into a scenario that I have seen unfolding several times:

- The partner portal team is building a public-facing website for partner integrations. The solution utilizes service catalog items, including one for **Transport Layer Security (TLS)** certificate management.

- We fast-forward and skip the next 13 months. The product owner for partner solutions receives a call. The TLS certificate expired, and a third party wants to know what happened to the website. The product owner is checking with the team.

- They can confirm that the certificate expired but are unsure how it happened. The third-party certificate provider has a default 13-month expiry time for issued certificates. The TLS module did not support automatic third-party certificate rotation.

- Unfortunately, this was not documented in the module documentation. It took a couple of days to get a new certificate issued and imported. For now, this was done manually to get out of this misery. Hopefully, there will be a better mechanism before the next expiry. I have observed this anti-pattern multiple times.

- This scenario happens mainly when the security or network team mandates third-party certificates. This brings additional complexity compared to using cloud native generated certificates, as AWS does with the Amazon Certificate Manager.

- However, even if the CSP does not provide that capability, they will still describe best practices regarding certificate management and renewal in their CAF.

We need to ensure we are across the holistic picture and put the required rigor and automation in place. We also want to ensure we read and understand CAF guidelines in conjunction with the Well-Architected Framework.

Ignoring coding best practices

We are coming to the last anti-pattern variation in this chapter. We will go through an event that was somehow confronting and, at the same time, it made me feel sorry for the person who got more attention than they were hoping for:

- Years ago, I was consulting with a government department. The government department was rushing into the cloud. Some timelines had already been announced by the media, and things had to happen quickly.

- There was hardly any governance. About 80% of the project team were freelancers, including the interim CIO, and the rest were consultants. Of course, there was no training provided, exactly as we described in the knowledge outsourcing anti-pattern. There were no mandated patterns or best practices.

- The expectation was that all team members needed to be on-site for production releases. Communication was poor overall, and planned releases were sometimes not communicated to everyone. Therefore, critical team members missed out and received phone calls on a Sunday questioning why they were not there for the go-live when they didn't even know about it.

- In other words, it was the wild west. No one in charge was interested in understanding the holistic picture, let alone in defining a CAF. Everyone just wanted to survive. When an organization falls into this reactive mode, it becomes very vulnerable.

- It became worse when freelancers were unhappy and resigned within a one-week notice period. New people turned up frequently. One day, the interim CIO came in very stressed. He got emails from the CSP in the middle of the night informing him that cloud credentials had been leaked on a public GitHub repository.

- A phone call from the federal police who were concerned about the government's security woke him up. As a result, every project team member had to sign an agreement that they do not leak confidential information, and they had to complete the paperwork for a police clearance report. He also explained what happened.

- A JavaScript freelancer who had started two months ago wanted to showcase his skills on his personal public GitHub repository. Unfortunately, the developer forgot to remove the access keys from the code. The keys should never have been in the code in the first place. That morning, the federal police raided the developer's home and confiscated all devices. There was no malicious intent.

This happened solely because of a lack of guardrails, training, and best practices for CI/CD and security. All these areas are described in CAFs.

The development security best practices are described in the security pillar and also in the *ready, adopt,* and *manage* stages in the Azure CAF. The AWS CAF describes this from the security perspective and the GCP CAF includes it in the *security* realm.

This was a par excellence showcase of being stuck in the reactive mode, not stepping through the CAF and Well-Architected Framework-provided guidance steps, and just starting the cloud journey without enough consideration. This incident should not discourage us from going cloud native. It should encourage us to look at the bigger picture: the opportunities, the risks, making sensible decisions, but most of all, leverage the prescriptive guidance, including the CAF, and the Well-Architected Frameworks our CSP gives us.

These frameworks are crucial because they provide structured guidance to ensure a smooth and efficient transition to the cloud. They help align our business objectives with our cloud strategy, ensuring that your investments deliver maximum value. A CAF offers best practices for managing security, compliance, and operational excellence, essential for maintaining robust and secure cloud environments.

Summary

In this chapter, we covered strategic aspects of our cloud adoption journey. We started with objectives and strategy. We called out that the cloud native strategy should be seen as an extension of the business strategy. We investigated bottom-up and bottom-down anti-patterns. We discussed how to get started on a migration strategy, including building a strawman, starting a business case, and gaining momentum. We explored the risks of knowledge outsourcing and how a lack of knowledge could result in mediocre quality, bringing reliability, security, compliance, and operational complexity challenges. We discussed the value of partnerships and, finally, we looked into the value of a CAF. By following a CAF, we can avoid common pitfalls, such as architecture gaps due to blueprint ignorance, deployment issues, and leaked secrets. The knowledge gained prepares us to explore the next problem space – rethinking governance, which we will do in the next chapter.

Get This Book's PDF Version and Exclusive Extras

Scan the QR code (or go to `packtpub.com/unlock`). Search for this book by name, confirm the edition, and then follow the steps on the page.

Note: Keep your invoice handly. Purchase made directly from packt don't require one.

3

Rethinking Governance in a Cloud Native Paradigm

In the fast-paced world of cloud native architectures, traditional governance approaches often struggle to keep up with the demands of agility, scalability, and rapid innovation. As organizations embrace cloud native practices, they inadvertently fall into anti-patterns, which are inefficient or misguided behaviors that can slow progress, increase risk, and stifle innovation. These anti-patterns arise from a failure to adapt governance models to the fluid, decentralized nature of cloud environments. This chapter explores how organizations must evolve their governance strategies to avoid these pitfalls and build resilient, adaptable systems. This chapter will cover the following anti-patterns:

- Learning will happen miraculously

- The culture doesn't need to change

- Centralized governance will scale

- Our business is too special for guardrails or standards

- Missing feedback loops

Learning will happen miraculously

In the traditional IT world, governance focuses on a centralized structure of control. This changes with cloud native. Cloud native environments require agility, scalability, and decentralized decision-making. Effective cloud governance ensures compliance, security, and efficient operations, which accelerates innovation. Organizations can leverage automated policies, continuous monitoring, and the adoption of new services without compromising security, aligning cloud strategies with business objectives.

Organizations tend to see *governance* as an all-encompassing word for the technical and non-technical control mechanism for managing infrastructure and defining frameworks on which applications are run. While the all-encompassing aspect tends to lean toward the application of best practices (imagine, if you will, the use of playbooks/runbooks), what tend to be forgotten about are the non-technical aspects of governance, which, in turn, when mismanaged lead to anti-patterns and a breakdown of structure. One of the major factors of this is the pattern covered in this section, dubbed *learning will happen miraculously.*

The cost of ignoring learning

Both upskilling and current stack knowledge in traditional organizations tend to be limited by the mindset of *learn in your own time* or *we do not have time to train you.* Here is where engineers turn to one of two choices. Either engineers will extend their tenure with a company for decades at a time working on one system, or they will look for other roles, thus leading to high talent turnover.

High talent turnover is a major challenge for engineering teams. Each new hire requires onboarding, during which senior engineers must dedicate time to training, impacting overall productivity. At a regular turnover rate of 2-3 years, this is expected, but once it turns into a 6-to-12-month turnover, it becomes a time sink and an overall loss. The 2021 Great Resignation is a good reference to this point. Each new engineer has an initial period where they are onboarded; without the necessary learning material, such as documentation, present, this then becomes a burden.

Time spent handholding, rather than having proper documentation present, leads many engineers to move on to greener pastures, as *death by documentation* is very commonly found among tech-debt-heavy organizations.

This is a position you should avoid ending up in as time and money are lost, as well as losing out on innovation. It has led many organizations' infrastructure and software teams to fold.

Having worked on the product and consulting side of IT, with a stint at a managed services provider, we have come across instances of this. We can see why traditional organizations behave this way. For them, it's **business as usual** (**BAU**) that matters most; looking through a short-term lens, this makes some sense. On a basic level, what an organization focuses on is ensuring that their product is creating value, whether that is monetary or otherwise. When faced with a task such as upskilling or creating documentation, it's easy to just push engineers to "learn in their own time," because, well, the eight hours of the workday should really be spent on the product, in their eyes. I do want to note here that learning outside of hours is critical to career growth; even just an hour a day will pay dividends in the future. However, it should not be the only source of education.

In the long term, it fails; engineering talent ends up being locked into the bounded context of what their product is, and nothing else. How can you innovate or create value outside of your typical knowledge set if you are put in a position where there is nothing to gain from it? For consulting organizations, this is great; this is where they step in and provide value and execute what otherwise could and should have been done by internal engineering talent. For cloud organizations, this is a balance that needs to be addressed. Without the freedom to learn during work hours, barriers are created so that when it comes to service/product improvement, outside help is traditionally required.

Take, for example, the following diagram:

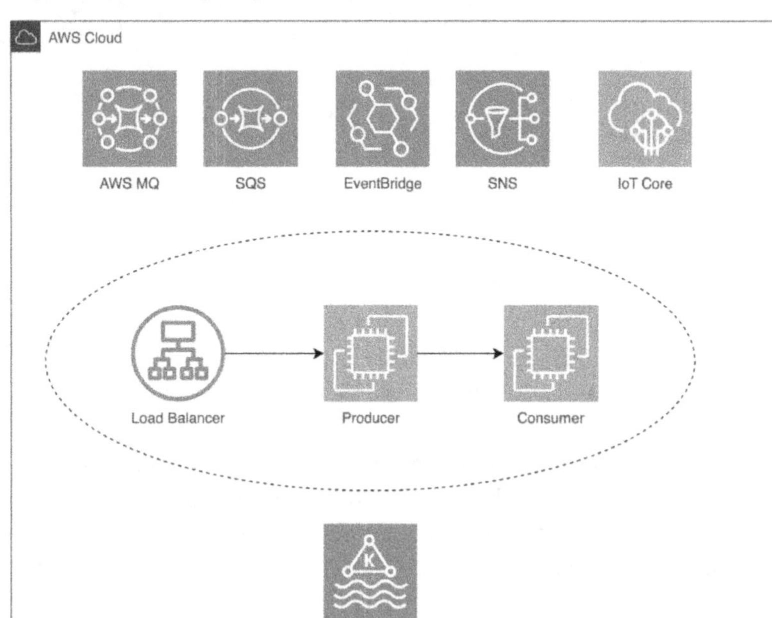

Figure 3.1 - Consumer and producer

Technically, the bound context of the producer-to-consumer setup is a functional model; however, it invites no room for improvement within a BAU or *learn while doing* way of working. The services in this model may be known, but not to the extent where suggestions can be made to improve the design.

Addressing the anti-pattern

When faced with a shared drive full of Word docs or countless Confluence pages, the concept of learning while working on the system, building or supporting seem like the better choice. But organizations tend to take this concept too far. Not long after an engineer starts to understand the product they are working on, their entire time ends up being focused on it, leaving no room for growing their skill sets.

Providing resources and support for ongoing education and professional development is vital. Organizations aim to balance workloads to ensure employees have time to learn and apply new skills without excessive context switching. What we have seen in the decision-making process for learning/ self-education at traditional organizations has been as follows:

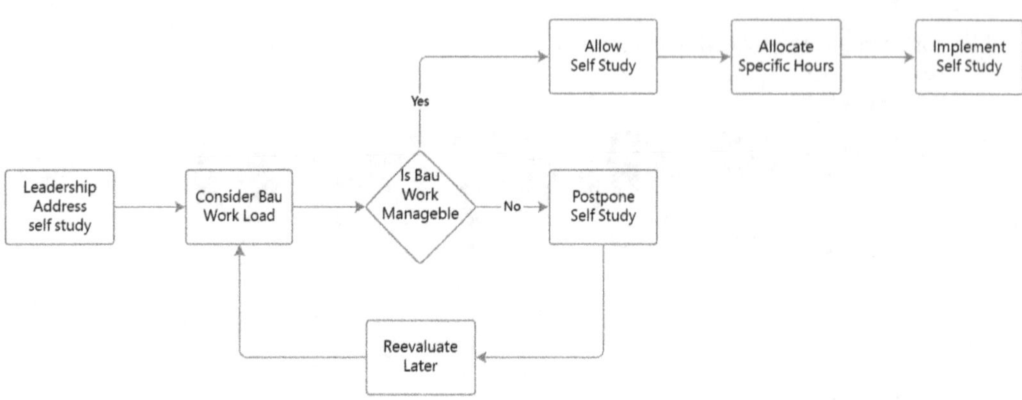

Figure 3.2 - Traditional self-study decision tree

Most fall into a never-ending cycle of postpone self-study -> evaluate later, promising the self-study but never delivering. Going beyond this, cloud native organizations work on addressing the root of the problem. One of the primary reasons the *learning will happen miraculously* mindset persists is the overwhelming burden of unmanageable BAU tasks. This challenge is often rooted in accumulated technical debt, which is not a new phenomenon. By recognizing and actively addressing this issue, organizations can gradually free up time for self-directed learning and professional development. It is essential that this initiative is spearheaded and supported by leadership, who must remain vigilant about the dangers of a growing backlog. Such backlogs should be treated as critical issues requiring immediate and sustained attention.

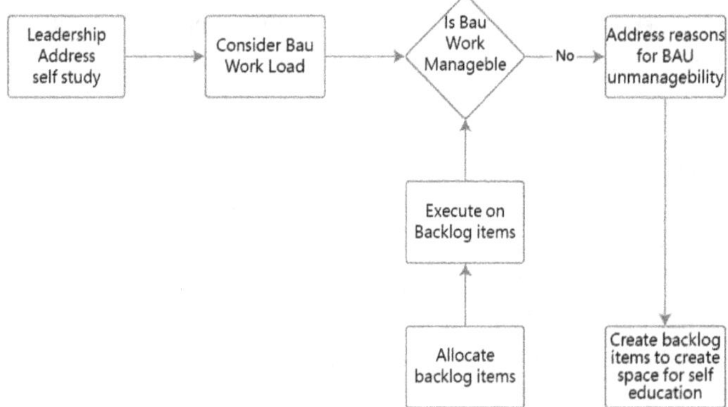

Figure 3.3 - Evaluating the reasons why "REDRAW PLEASE"

This approach is rooted in the belief that knowledge and experience are foundational to creating a lasting impact. When employees are encouraged to learn and grow during work hours, they are better equipped to explore new technologies, implement innovative features, and drive the organization forward. Without this commitment to continuous learning, companies risk stagnation and limit their ability to create distinctive solutions. By integrating education into the daily work environment, organizations not only empower their employees but also ensure their long-term growth and adaptability in an ever-evolving landscape. This support can come in the form of access to training materials, workshops, and dedicated time for learning within the work schedule. This can be easily achieved by blocking out the calendar for training. If that time needs to be repurposed (e.g., for an incident), then that time block gets moved in the calendar. Be strict on rejecting meetings during that allocated time.

The following tables provide a set of holistic options, some internal and others external. *Table 3.1* presents a fair few options, some much harder to achieve than others, but of the lot, certifications and training are the best places to start.

Category	Description	Frequency	Participants	Methods
Onboarding bootcamp	Intensive program for new hires focusing on cloud native tools and practices.	First month of employment	New engineers	Hands-on labs, workshops, mentoring
Continuous learning hours	Designated time during the week for self-paced learning and exploration.	Weekly	All engineers	Online courses, reading, experimentation
Certification and training	Support for achieving industry-recognized certifications (e.g., cloud vendors such as AWS or Kubernetes).	Ongoing	Interested engineers	Online courses, external training providers
Tech talks and brown bags	Informal sessions where engineers share knowledge on specific topics.	Bi-weekly	All engineers	Presentations, live demos, Q&A sessions
Tech debt days	Dedicated time to address technical debt while learning about legacy systems.	Quarterly	All engineers	Pair programming, refactoring sessions, Confluence/ documentation bounties
Mentorship programs	Pairing less experienced engineers with senior engineers for guided learning.	Ongoing	Junior and senior engineers	One-on-one mentoring, code reviews
Technical writing	A centralized repository for documentation, best practices, and lessons learned advertising engineering excellence.	Ongoing	All engineers	Blogs/white papers, internal documentation

Table 3.1 - Internal learning options

Cloud native vendors tend to have their own certification paths. With AWS, we can run through certification training via platforms such as AWS Skill Builder, Tutorial Dojo, or Learn.Cantrill; with Azure, Pluralsight and Microsoft Learn; and the same for GCP but with Google Cloud Training and Whizlabs. The learnings you gain can and should be double-dipped. Say our learnings of how S3 buckets can become a great way to host Static sites via the AWS Developer certificate, a simple blog can be encouraged via that or the outcome of the education leads to internal product recommendations, in particular ones like the S3 Static hosting.

To counteract the development of anti-patterns in cloud native environments, innovative learning events play a critical role. Regularly scheduled activities, such as hackathons, game days, learning communities, and external conferences, ensure continuous educational engagement and operational readiness among engineers. These events foster a proactive culture of innovation, collaboration, and security awareness, essential for navigating the complexities of cloud native technologies. This community approach will also provide external insights that would otherwise not be had. *Table 3.2* details the frequency, participants, and methods of these transformative events:

Category	Description	Frequency	Participants	Methods
Hackathons	Events focused on building prototypes and experimenting with new technologies	Quarterly	Cross-functional teams	Collaborative coding, problem-solving
Game days	Events where critical events, security events, and similar are simulated to gauge reactions	Annually	Engineers	All-day DR tests, security simulations via pen testing or testing
Learning communities	Specialized groups focusing on specific technologies (e.g., DevOps, security)	Monthly meetups	Engineers with shared interests	Discussions, collaborative projects
External conferences	Attendance at industry conferences to stay updated with the latest trends	Annually	Selected engineers	Keynotes, workshops, networking

Table 3.2 - External learning options

In cloud native environments, the myth that "learning will happen miraculously" must be dispelled for organizations to succeed. Governance is about not only technical controls but also fostering a culture of continuous learning. The shift from traditional, centralized control to agile innovation requires addressing the human element, ensuring engineers have the time and resources to develop their skills.

Learning cannot be left to the margins or expected to happen outside work hours. To embed learning into the organization's fabric, companies must offer structured development opportunities and integrate learning into daily workflows. This allows engineers to refine their skills while contributing to business goals, leading to more innovation and a stronger workforce. Sustained success in a cloud native world depends on making learning an integral part of the job. When organizations prioritize learning as a core strategy, they empower teams to drive technological change and ensure long-term success. In the next section, we will explore how this transformation cannot happen without a shift in culture.

The culture doesn't need to change

The driving force for a successful organizational culture over time is change. Marc Benioff, CEO of Salesforce, said it best: "*The only constant in the technology industry is change.*" We may assume that Marc is only referring to the tech we build and work on here. However, what is implied here is that the culture as well as the tech behind the industry changes. Adopting a cloud native approach is more than just implementing new technology; it's about embracing a fundamental shift in organizational culture. Many organizations mistakenly believe they can simply overlay cloud technology onto their existing practices without making significant cultural changes.

This section aims to equip readers with the skills to understand the cultural impact of cloud native adoption. It will also address the dangers of underestimating cultural change, overlooking key stakeholders, and neglecting change management, which can lead to a lack of buy-in and resistance from employees.

The cultural impact of cloud native adoption

When an organization adopts the cloud native paradigm, it must go beyond technology and address impacts on how teams work, communicate, and approach problem-solving. Cloud native adoption encourages practices such as continuous integration, continuous delivery/deployment, and various engineering cultures, such as DevOps/SecOps or platform engineering. These practices necessitate a collaborative, flexible, and proactive culture that can adapt to rapid changes, unlike that of a traditional IT organization.

Spotify – the impact of cultural change

Spotify offers an excellent case study of how embracing a cloud native culture can lead to transformative success. When Spotify decided to move to the cloud, it understood that this shift required more than just technological change; it demanded a fundamental rethinking of their organizational culture. To achieve this, Spotify adopted a unique model centered around autonomy, collaboration, and continuous improvement. The approach to cloud native is best exemplified by their creation of "squads": small, cross-functional teams that operate with a high degree of autonomy.

Each squad is responsible for a specific aspect of Spotify's service and has the freedom to decide how they achieve their goals. This structure allows teams to experiment, iterate, and innovate quickly without being bogged down by bureaucratic processes. The squad model also promotes a culture of accountability, where teams own their work from start to finish, fostering a sense of ownership and pride in the outcomes. In addition to squads, Spotify introduced the concepts of **tribes**, **chapters**, and **guilds** to maintain alignment across the organization while preserving autonomy. The following table goes into detail about each one.

Concept	Description	Impact
Squads	Small, autonomous, cross-functional teams responsible for specific aspects of Spotify's service	Promotes rapid experimentation, innovation, and ownership
Tribes	Groups of related squads working within a broader area of Spotify's service	Ensures alignment and collaboration across squads
Chapters	Discipline-specific groups within tribes that ensure consistency in practices (e.g., frontend developers)	Maintains best practices and technical standards
Guilds	Informal communities of interest that span the organization, fostering knowledge sharing and collaboration	Encourages cross-functional learning and innovation

Table 3.3 - Spotify teams model explained

Take note of the approach; the concepts presented do not create silos, but instead create overlapping groupings where intercommunication is encouraged and endorsed.

Spotify's success story illustrates the power of aligning cultural change with technological change. Their cloud native transformation wasn't just about adopting new technologies; it was about fostering a culture that values autonomy, collaboration, continuous improvement, and learning from failures. This cultural shift has been instrumental in enabling Spotify to innovate at scale, maintain high service reliability, and remain a leader in the competitive music streaming industry.

To truly understand the success of a change in culture, our learning needs to focus on the risks of not changing.

The hidden costs of ignoring cultural change

Organizations tend to focus heavily on the technical aspects, sidelining the human element, which can lead to a cascade of issues. These issues are caused by a combination of leadership decisions, fear of the unknown, and lack of buy-in by leadership. Let's take a closer look at the implications of these issues.

Resistance to change

Employees accustomed to traditional workflows may resist adopting new cloud-based practices, delaying progress and causing inefficiencies. For example, in a multi-cloud consultation with a fintech organization, despite the inefficiencies of legacy processes, such as taking two days to provision a new AWS account and relying on custom scripts, engineering teams were reluctant to adopt cloud native solutions to streamline workflows. The organization also resisted third-party cloud management, so we used native tools from each cloud vendor for the respective cloud teams.

It is clear that engineers' hesitancy often stems from multiple factors, with the learning curve being one of the most significant. With every change comes the inevitable question: "How do we adapt?" This fear is entirely valid.

Consider the example from the *Learning will happen miraculously* section of a long-tenured engineer at a traditional organization. While the business may highly value their deep experience and loyalty, their resistance to change can become a significant roadblock for the broader organizational culture. This resistance is not just about reluctance; it's rooted in years of established practices that have become second nature to them. Their deep expertise, while invaluable, often ties them to legacy systems and processes that are comfortable but outdated. This hesitation stems from a fear of the unknown, a strong preference for familiar routines, and a general reluctance to embrace change. Let's look at how we can overcome this resistance to change.

Overcoming resistance to change

Overcoming this resistance requires persistent and thoughtful efforts:

- **Providing post-project support**: Addressing concerns head-on, reassuring engineers that their expertise is still valued and that the new tools are there to enhance, not replace, their work.

- **Offering comprehensive training and support**: This includes not only surface-level introductions but also deep diving into the new systems, with hands-on workshops, detailed documentation in Confluence, and Markdown files in GitHub, tailored to bridge the gap between old and new ways of working.

- **Fostering an environment that values continuous improvement**: Creating a culture where learning and adaptation are seen as ongoing processes, not one-time events. This helps in gradually easing the engineers into the new methodologies, ensuring they don't feel overwhelmed or sidelined.

For change to be successful, clear actions, not just words, are required to overcome resistance from experienced engineers. It requires building a solid foundation, anchored in clear communication, robust support systems, and a commitment to continuous improvement. This foundation serves as the necessary icebreaker to overcome resistance, allowing the organization to transition smoothly and ensuring that even the most experienced team members feel secure and valued during the transformation.

Let's now address the lack of buy-in.

Lack of buy-in

After overcoming the initial resistance to implementation, the next critical hurdle in driving cultural change is securing buy-in from both employees and key stakeholders. Without a deep understanding of the benefits that cloud native adoption can bring, resistance is almost inevitable. This lack of buy-in often manifests as half-hearted implementation efforts, where the enthusiasm needed to drive the project forward is notably absent, leading to a high risk of failure.

During our engagement with a fintech company, we encountered this exact scenario. Their on-premises infrastructure was plagued by inefficiencies, including the following:

- Lengthy deployment times
- Limited scalability
- Accumulating technical debt
- Lack of resilience

The existing systems, though flawed, were familiar and comfortable, creating a false sense of security that cloud native solutions appeared to threaten. The resistance wasn't just about the technology; it was about challenging the status quo and moving away from long-established routines that, despite their inefficiencies, had become deeply ingrained in the company's operational fabric.

We clearly outlined the numerous advantages of transitioning to cloud services, such as the following:

- Improved agility
- Cost savings to the operating model
- Enhanced security
- Rapid scalability

We explained that the move to cloud native is meticulously designed to streamline operations, reduce risk, and ensure compliance. However, there was still resistance to making the change. This lack of enthusiasm wasn't just a minor obstacle; it was a significant roadblock that resulted in a lukewarm implementation. Teams were hesitant to fully engage with the new tools and processes, treating the transformation as a superficial change rather than a fundamental shift in how the organization operates.

Overcoming lack of buy-in

To overcome this challenge, it was essential to build a compelling case for cloud cultural change by focusing on the following:

Strategy	Description
Connecting technical benefits to broader organizational goals	Ensuring that the advantages of cloud adoption were clearly tied to the company's overall objectives, helping employees see the bigger picture
Extensive training and support	Providing in-depth training sessions to demystify the new tools and processes, aiming to change mindsets and reduce the intimidation factor

Strategy	Description
Creating a culture of continuous improvement	Fostering an environment that values learning and adaptation, encouraging teams to embrace change as an opportunity for growth rather than a threat
Reinforcing long-term benefits	Consistently highlighting the long-term gains of cloud adoption, shifting the organization's perspective from short-term discomfort to future advantages

Table 3.4 - Strategies of change

In the end, overcoming the lack of buy-in required more than technical solutions; it demanded a holistic approach addressing the cultural and psychological aspects of change. By aligning the cloud native strategy with the organization's core values and ensuring that every team member felt included and valued, we could turn skepticism into support and transform what initially seemed like insurmountable resistance into a collective drive toward successful cloud native adoption.

The next section addresses poor communication and features a case study from Grammarly.

Poor communication – a case study

A failure to clearly communicate the reasons for change and its benefits can lead to confusion and anxiety among engineers. This was evident during an engagement that we led to set up cloud foundations on AWS and deliver a **minimum viable product** (**MVP**) in a short timeframe. The project sponsor, the head of architecture, was delighted with the outcome. Although leadership was ecstatic, during an all-hands meeting, it became evident that the broader team was unclear on the project's purpose and rationale.

The questions raised by the audience revealed a glaring communication gap. The project sponsors had failed to adequately inform the wider organization about the cloud native transformation, resulting in unnecessary anxiety and concerns. This experience underscores the vital importance of clear and consistent communication throughout the cloud native adoption journey. Leaders must ensure that everyone within the organization understands not only the reasons for the change but also the benefits it brings and how it will impact their roles. This alignment is critical to the success of any transformation initiative and helps to mitigate resistance by fostering a sense of shared purpose and commitment to the new direction. Take, for example, Grammarly, who have publicly posted their findings on just this.

Grammarly, over a two-week period in October 2022, found the following:

- 15% of workers say poor communication made them consider changing teams

- 25% of workers say poor communication strains their relationships with their current team

- 22% of workers say poor communication has made them consider finding a new job

These factors all lead back to being blockers for cloud native cultural change.

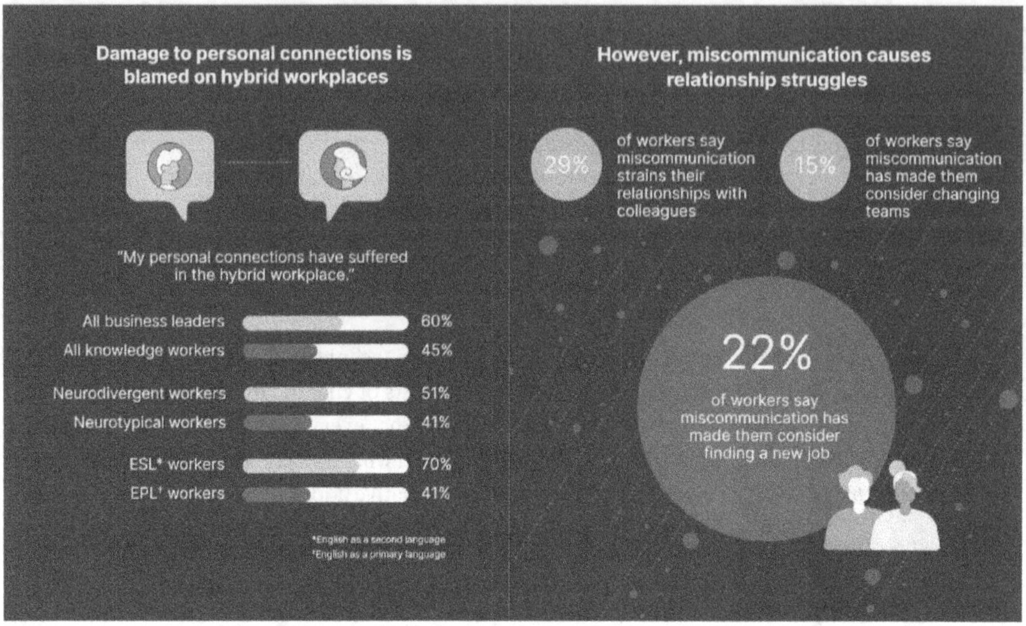

Figure 3.4 - Snippet from Grammarly case study
(https://www.grammarly.com/blog/poor-communication-work-stress/)

Overcoming poor communication

Leadership plays a pivotal role in fostering buy-in for cloud native adoption. It's not just about mandating change; it's about communicating a vision that resonates across the organization.

Leaders must clearly and persuasively articulate the benefits of cloud native adoption, linking these advantages to both the organization's broader goals and the personal aspirations of team members. By doing so, they can transform skepticism into enthusiasm, turning obstacles into opportunities for growth. An inspirational leader leads by example, embracing the change themselves and demonstrating its value in tangible ways.

Patience and persistence are also key, as buy-in is not achieved overnight; it requires continuous engagement, ongoing education, and celebrating small wins that collectively build momentum for the broader transformation. To address all that we have read so far, the next section will give us strategies and frameworks that can be adopted.

Effective strategies for cultural change in cloud native adoption

To successfully adopt a cloud native approach, effective strategies include the following:

- **Promote cross-functional collaboration**: Break down silos by encouraging cross-functional teams to work together. Adopt an agile and DevOps/DevSecOps/modern engineering culture to foster innovation and ensure diverse perspectives are considered in decision-making.

- **Encourage experimentation and learning**: Create a safe environment for employees to experiment and learn from failures. Promote a growth mindset and provide opportunities for continuous learning and development.

- **Empower teams with autonomy**: Give teams the autonomy to make decisions and take ownership of their projects. This empowerment can lead to increased innovation, faster problem-solving, and greater job satisfaction.

- **Foster open communication**: Maintain open, transparent, and consistent communication. Regularly update employees on the progress of cloud initiatives and provide forums for feedback and discussion.

- **Change management frameworks**: Utilize structured approaches such as Prosci's ADKAR Model and Kotter's 8-Step Change Model to manage change effectively.

The journey toward cloud native adoption emphasizes the need for cultural evolution alongside technological advancements. As demonstrated by companies such as Spotify, successful cloud native adoption extends beyond technology to foster a culture of autonomy, collaboration, and continuous improvement.

Overcoming resistance, rooted in fear, entrenched practices, or misunderstanding, is crucial. Through educational initiatives, leadership endorsement, and cultural reengineering, organizations can align new tools with their core objectives, helping every stakeholder embrace the transition.

The next section will discuss the *centralized governance will scale* anti-pattern. The lessons from these cultural shifts highlight the importance of scalable governance structures in supporting complex cloud environments.

Centralized governance will scale

Reflecting on the history of the IT industry reveals that centralized governance has long been the norm. Traditionally, every component within an organization was deemed critical, leading to a governance structure where all decisions, improvements, and oversight originated from a single point of authority. Initially, this model functioned effectively, managed by a small team led by a senior engineer or program manager.

However, as organizations grew, this centralized approach often became cumbersome and slow-moving. As organizations embrace cloud native more broadly, the importance of robust governance frameworks becomes increasingly apparent. Effective governance is essential for maintaining security, ensuring compliance, and optimizing operational efficiency. A common assertion within the field is that centralized governance can be effectively scaled across diverse organizational structures.

This section delves into the nuances of this approach, the dangers of insufficient decentralized governance guidelines, and the challenges posed by entrenched bureaucracy and the lack of a dedicated **cloud center of excellence (CCoE)** or **community of practice (COP)**.

In this section, we will gain insights into the best practices for establishing a CCoE in the cloud and the critical anti-patterns that organizations should strive to avoid. This section will explore how organizations can successfully transition from rigid, centralized systems to more dynamic, decentralized governance frameworks that better support their evolving needs.

Centralized governance – navigating challenges and crafting solutions

While governance implementation is indispensable, an absence of decentralized governance guidelines can turn an anchor into a shackle, removing agility and any potential for innovation in the long and short term. It's paramount to embrace standardization, be it in technologies or practices, empowering engineering teams to navigate these established frameworks. A benefit of decentralized governance is its ability to hasten decision-making, amplify autonomy, and swiftly pivot in response to the ever-dynamic market landscape. The following subsection provides some insights into the absence of decentralized governance.

Challenges posed by the absence of decentralized governance

The lack of decentralized governance can lead to several challenges:

- **Inhibited innovation**: Excessive centralized oversight, lacking flexibility, can deter teams from proactively improving existing processes. This rigid control stifles the exploratory mindset essential for technological advancement.

- **Operational bottlenecks**: Centralized decision-making often introduces delays, impeding agility when rapid responses are crucial, especially in dynamic fields such as serverless computing and AI development.

- **Declining team engagement**: Without the autonomy to drive meaningful change, teams may experience diminished motivation and engagement, leading to reduced productivity and innovation.

The following figure illustrates the contrast between centralized and decentralized governance:

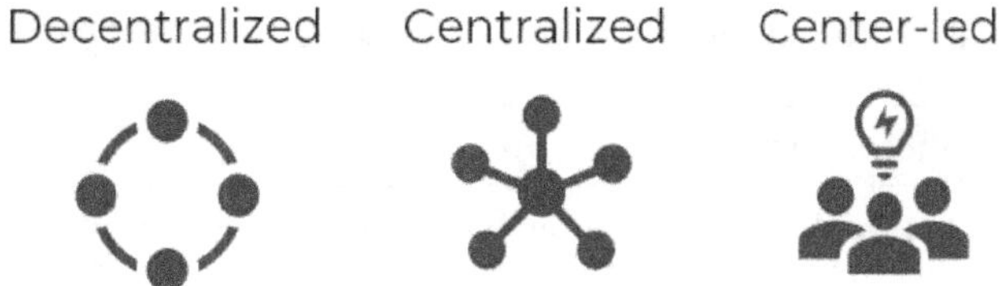

Figure 3.5 - Centralized versus decentralized (Redraw please)

Centralized models, reminiscent of traditional IT frameworks, typically concentrate authority and decision-making at the core of the organization. This central dependency creates a bottleneck, where every decision, no matter how trivial, must be escalated up the hierarchy, often leading to delays and reduced responsiveness. In contrast, a decentralized cloud native model distributes authority closer to the sources of information and action. This proximity empowers teams to make decisions quickly based on their direct understanding of the issues, fostering a more agile and responsive environment.

When decision-making is removed from those involved in the day-to-day operations, it can lead to a sense of disempowerment among team members, who may feel their expertise and insights are undervalued. This can reduce job satisfaction and increase turnover, further destabilizing the organization. Centralized models struggle to scale effectively in dynamic environments. As organizations grow and operations become more complex, the central bodies become overwhelmed with decision requests, leading to slower response times and potential missed opportunities in fast-moving sectors. For example, we have worked with large critical infrastructure organizations such as large telecom companies, where engineers on the ground might discover innovative ways to optimize network traffic, but their inability to implement changes without lengthy approval processes can lead to frustration and a sense that their technical expertise is undervalued. This detachment not only hampers innovation but can also lead to decreased job satisfaction and increased turnover, further destabilizing the organization.

At scale, decentralized governance has seen much success. Take the AWS example that follows.

Two-pizza team – decentralized governance

Decentralized governance is well illustrated by AWS's *two-pizza team* framework. This model champions small, nimble teams that wield the autonomy to make swift decisions, thus creating a culture of innovation and agility while ensuring alignment with broader organizational goals.

Take, for instance, the team behind Lambda, the serverless computing service from AWS. Their capacity to swiftly integrate customer feedback into new feature additions exemplifies the competitive edge fostered by decentralized governance, bolstering AWS's stature as a frontrunner in the serverless computing arena.

Each two-pizza team, dedicated to specific services or features, thrives on the autonomy to innovate and drive their agenda forward, making rapid adjustments to better meet customer demands and stay ahead in the market. The advantages of the two-pizza team are highlighted in the following table:

Advantage	Success Metric
Increased agility	Smaller teams move faster and adapt quickly without cumbersome processes.
Enhanced autonomy	Having fewer team members reduces misunderstandings and enhances alignment on fast-moving projects.
Improved communication	Having fewer team members reduces misunderstandings and enhances alignment on fast-moving projects.
Greater accountability	Clear responsibilities within small teams improve accountability for actions and results.
Faster decision-making	Streamlined decision processes due to fewer bureaucratic layers and necessary approvals.
Increased focus	Smaller teams focus more intensely on specific objectives without broader organizational distractions.

Table 3.5 - Detailed advantages of the two-pizza model

Centralized governance solutions

Following a detailed exploration of the challenges posed by centralized governance, it becomes imperative to address one of its most debilitating factors: **calcified bureaucracy**. This phenomenon represents processes that become so rigid and outdated that they severely hamper an organization's ability to innovate and adapt, qualities that are crucial in the rapidly evolving landscape of cloud technology.

Symptoms of calcified bureaucracy

One of the most glaring signs of this calcified bureaucracy is slow decision-making. In many traditional organizations, decision-making processes become bogged down by an accumulation of management layers and procedural steps that no longer contribute value. These layers are remnants of past structures, held in place by sheer inertia rather than necessity, leading to delays that are not only frustrating but also costly in terms of lost opportunities. This symptom is mostly felt by larger and older organizations; we have heard this multiple times from those who work within or have contracted with government bodies where by sheer bureaucracy, change is stifled.

Another symptom is resistance to change. Although we looked into this component in depth in an earlier section, it also relates to centralized governance. Traditional organizations often exhibit a profound reluctance to adopt new technologies or methodologies, rooted in a fear of disruption. This fear is not unfounded, as new technologies can unsettle established roles and processes. But the resistance also stems from comfort with the status quo and an avoidance of the unknown. Such resistance can prevent organizations from staying competitive in industries where technological adaptability is key to survival.

Strategies for disrupting calcified bureaucracy

To combat the inertia of calcified bureaucracy, especially in settings that require the high agility provided by cloud technologies, organizations can adopt several effective strategies:

- **Streamline processes**: It is crucial to conduct regular reviews of all processes with the aim of streamlining them. This involves cutting out redundant steps and simplifying procedures to enhance operational efficiency and responsiveness.

- **Empower teams**: Delegating decision-making authority directly to the teams on the frontlines can dramatically increase agility. This empowerment allows those who are most intimately familiar with the issues at hand to implement solutions swiftly and effectively, without the delay of climbing up and down the hierarchical ladder.

- **Promote a culture of continuous improvement**: Cultivating an organizational mindset that values the continuous evaluation and refinement of processes ensures that they remain relevant and effective. This culture encourages innovation and the willingness to experiment, which are vital for leveraging cloud technologies to their fullest potential.

By addressing the symptoms and root causes of calcified bureaucracy, organizations can not only enhance their adaptability and efficiency but also foster an environment that is conducive to innovation and rapid technological adoption.

The transition from a calcified to a dynamic and responsive bureaucracy is not just a shift in processes but a transformation in organizational culture, aligning it with the demands of the cloud era.

In the following section, we will delve into the critical role of a CCoE in navigating the complexities of cloud governance and ensuring that organizations maintain agility while avoiding the pitfalls of bureaucratic stagnation. These frameworks are essential for clarifying roles, streamlining decision-making, and fostering a culture of continuous improvement in cloud native environments.

Lack of a CCoE

The purpose of a CCoE is to establish a centralized team or function that plays a critical role in driving cloud adoption, governance, and best practices across an organization. We might ask ourselves here: *"Why do we need a centralized team if we move to a cloud native organizational structure?"* Simply put, by establishing a CCoE, organizations can effectively manage their cloud environments, optimize business operations, and deliver enhanced value to their customers and communities.

By tightly linking cloud initiatives with the organization's broader business objectives, the CCoE ensures that cloud adoption is not just a technological shift but a strategic move aligned with long-term goals. A key function of the CCoE is the development and enforcement of best practices and standards for cloud usage. These standards are essential for maintaining consistency and efficiency across the organization.

The CCoE establishes guidelines for resource provisioning, cost optimization, and security controls, ensuring that all cloud activities align with the organization's operational and strategic needs. AWS offers an insightful whitepaper on the topic of structuring a CcoE. Let's dive deeper into its key recommendations.

CCoE structure

AWS has released a whitepaper for setting up a CCoE to transform organizations. Based on this whitepaper, the CCoE is typically divided into two teams:

- **Cloud business office (CBO)**: The CBO aligns the products and services offered by the CCoE with the needs of enterprise customers and leadership. It acts as a bridge between technical teams and business stakeholders, ensuring that cloud initiatives are aligned with organizational goals and priorities.

- **Cloud engineering**: This team codifies the differences between standard cloud service configurations and the organization's enterprise standards. They package and continuously improve these codified patterns as self-service deployable products for customers.

Let's explore the strategies for building an effective CCoE.

Recommended strategies for creating a CCoE

The following are some of the recommended strategies for creating a CCoE:

- **Define clear goals and a long-term vision**: The CCoE should have clearly defined, measurable goals that align with the organization's overall business objectives. Establishing a long-term roadmap with ambitious projects will drive cloud adoption and innovation.

- **Develop deep cloud expertise**: The CCoE needs detailed knowledge of the target cloud platform, including its services, performance, monitoring, cost optimization, and security best practices. This expertise is essential for guiding the organization through successful cloud adoption.

- **Establish cloud governance and policies**: The CCoE is responsible for developing and enforcing cloud governance policies to ensure cost-effectiveness, security, and compliance. This includes defining cloud architecture principles, deployment standards, and automation practices.

- **Measure success and iterate**: The CCoE should collect metrics and KPIs related to cloud projects and compare them to established goals. This data helps determine whether the CCoE is providing the intended value and identifies areas for improvement. The CCoE strategy should be adapted as conditions develop.

In summary, a well-established CCoE is vital for managing cloud environments effectively. It ensures that organizations can optimize their operations, innovate rapidly, and deliver significant value to their customers while maintaining compliance and security. Without such a centralized function, organizations risk falling into fragmented efforts, missed opportunities, and increased friction and inefficiencies, especially in global projects.

As we conclude our examination of centralized governance and the importance of establishing clear roles and responsibilities, it's critical to recognize that not all organizations are alike. While a well-structured governance framework is essential for maintaining security, compliance, and operational efficiency in cloud environments, some organizations may resist standardization, believing that their unique business needs are too specialized for such practices.

In the next section, we will explore this mindset in detail, discussing the risks and challenges associated with rejecting standardized governance frameworks and how it can lead to inefficiencies, increased risk, and missed opportunities in cloud operations.

Our business is too special for guardrails or standards

This is a common misconception. In our experience, nearly every organization believes its IT environment is too unique or complex for the implementation of standardized guardrails or governance practices. However, when audit time approaches, these same organizations often find themselves scrambling to establish the very controls they initially resisted. The perceived complexity masked a deeper hesitation to implement the necessary controls. Regardless of how specialized a business may seem, when it comes to compliance with government, financial, or industry-specific standards, these requirements must be met.

The true challenge lies not in the uniqueness of the business but in its willingness to overcome this reluctance and establish the essential governance structures.

In this section, we'll explore the importance of data insights, the critical role of **governance, risk, and compliance (GRC)** policies, and the necessity of a clear **responsible, accountable, consulted, and informed (RACI)** model.

Understanding the concept and benefits of guardrails

Guardrails in cloud governance are critical tools and predefined policies and practices that direct teams toward the compliant and secure usage of cloud resources, fostering an environment where innovation flourishes without compromising on safety.

As the foundational elements of centralized governance, these guardrails offer a well-balanced approach, allowing for flexibility in operations while ensuring that essential controls are firmly in place. They function as both guidelines and boundaries, empowering teams to effectively utilize cloud resources within a framework that enforces crucial safeguards to comply with regulations, standards, and organizational policies.

By promoting consistency, scalability, and accountability across the organization, guardrails ensure a uniform approach to managing cloud resources. The strengths of guardrails and details on why to use them are outlined next.

Key strengths of guardrails

The following are a range of benefits offered by guardrails:

- **Enhanced security**: Guardrails enforce security protocols across an organization, ensuring practices are followed that protect sensitive information and critical systems. These protocols might include mandatory encryption for data in transit and at rest, restricted access based on the principle of least privilege, and automated security updates. By standardizing security measures, guardrails reduce risks and strengthen the cloud environment's security.

- **Compliance assurance**: Automate compliance with regulatory requirements, lowering the risk of breaches and fines. Guardrails enforce data sovereignty laws by restricting data storage to specific regions or ensuring adherence to regulations such as HIPAA or PCI-DSS. This automation minimizes manual oversight, helping organizations maintain compliance with ease.

- **Consistency and standardization**: Enforce standardized policies and procedures across all teams, ensuring the consistent deployment and management of cloud resources. This reduces configuration errors, improves interoperability between cloud services, and simplifies onboarding and training for new team members.

- **Audit and reporting**: Guardrails improve governance by offering audit trails and detailed reports on cloud usage and compliance. These features help organizations identify inefficiencies, manage risks, and provide accountability for internal audits or external reviews, supporting the continuous improvement of cloud strategies.

Guardrails streamline the path to production in a cloud native environment by integrating compliance directly into the deployment process. Tools such as AWS Config conformity rules, AWS SCP, and Azure Policy regulatory rules allow developers and engineers to focus more narrowly when releasing updates or new features. This focus does not create silos but instead establishes clear boundaries on permissible actions. Consider the following diagram, which illustrates a group of AWS accounts within an AWS organization.

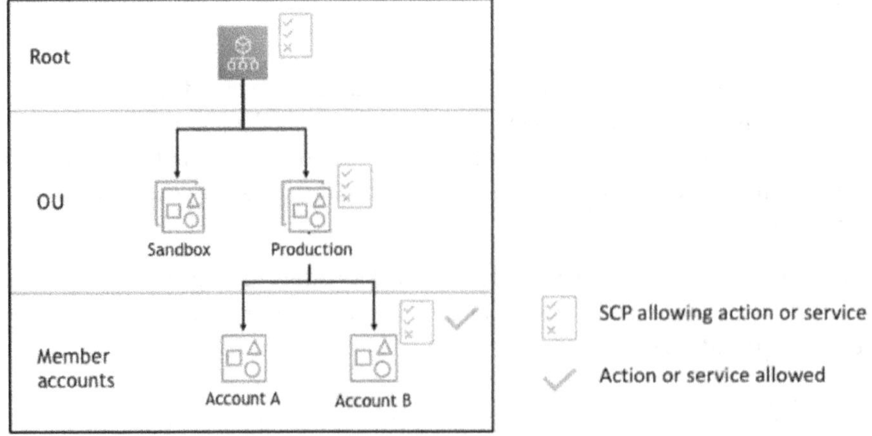

Figure 3.6 - AWS organization OU with member accounts (Redraw Please)

In this example, apply account-level rules specifying that only explicit resources can be deployed, such as Lambda functions or Fargate tasks. This setup forms a consistent guardrail, ensuring that deviations only occur with explicit approval, thus maintaining compliance and control during deployment. To optimize the use of guardrails, it is essential to distinguish between the different types of guardrails to consider. The next section will provide a detailed overview.

Understanding which guardrails to use

As our understanding of guardrails grows, to better utilize them, we should look at segmenting them into two sections: proactive and detective.

Proactive guardrails are essential in cloud governance because they prevent issues before they occur, while detective guardrails identify and address issues after they have happened. Proactive guardrails play a crucial role in securing the cloud environment and ensuring compliance, minimizing the reliance on reactive measures. Essentially, both preventative and proactive guardrails are designed to stop the creation of non-compliant resources in the environment. For simplicity, we'll refer to them collectively as proactive guardrails.

The benefits of proactive guardrails include the following:

- **Minimize security breaches**: Implementing proactive measures and best practices from the start significantly reduces security incidents. For example, enforcing IAM policies that grant only necessary permissions can prevent excessive privileges.

- **Ensure continuous compliance**: Automated checks during deployment verify adherence to regulations, maintaining continuous compliance. For instance, guardrails can enforce GDPR compliance by tagging personal data and restricting deployment to approved regions.

- **Reduce operational overhead**: Proactive guardrails prevent issues before they occur, reducing the need for manual intervention and saving resources. For example, enforcing resource tagging ensures accurate cost allocation from the start, streamlining cost analysis.

- **Standardize deployments**: Guardrails ensure consistent configurations across the cloud, reducing complexity and improving manageability. For example, IaC templates with guardrails standardize security groups, patching schedules, and monitoring for all web servers.

- **Accelerate secure development**: Embedding security and compliance checks in the deployment process speeds up secure application delivery. For example, guardrails in CI/CD pipelines automatically scan code for vulnerabilities and compliance before deployment.

Detective guardrails work by detecting resources that violate security policies after they've been provisioned. When combined with automated remediation, they are known as **remediation controls**.

The benefits of detective guardrails include the following:

- **Identify issues**: These guardrails continuously monitor the cloud environment to detect and flag non-compliant resources or actions after they've occurred, providing insights into potential security breaches, misconfigurations, or policy violations that may have slipped through preventative measures.

- **Address after the fact**: Detective guardrails allow for the identification and remediation of issues post-deployment. While they are not ideal for serious security issues, they are useful for identifying and resolving minor compliance deviations or overlooked settings.

- **Monitor and report violations**: Detective guardrails provide ongoing monitoring and detailed reports on violations, helping organizations maintain visibility into their cloud environment. For example, AWS Config rules can monitor and report on resource configurations that violate organizational policies, while AWS CloudTrail can log unauthorized API calls or changes to critical resources.

By understanding and implementing both detective and proactive guardrails, organizations can build a secure, compliant, and efficient cloud environment that not only protects against potential threats but also optimizes operations and costs.

The next section will detail the RACI model, further explaining how roles and responsibilities can be delineated to enhance organizational efficiency and clarity in cloud governance.

RACI model

It is essential to clearly delineate roles and responsibilities within the organization. This clarity is crucial to avoid the pitfalls of ambiguous accountability and inefficiency that can derail cloud initiatives. The **RACI model** is a responsibility assignment matrix that serves as an effective tool to define these roles and responsibilities, ensuring that every task within the cloud operating model is executed with precision and accountability.

In this section, we will explore the RACI model for cloud governance, illustrating its components and detailing how a poorly implemented RACI model can lead to further cloud native anti-patterns.

The RACI model helps in clarifying who is responsible, accountable, consulted, and informed for various tasks within a cloud governance framework. The following is a table outlining how the RACI model can be applied to key tasks in cloud governance:

Task	Responsible (R)	Accountable (A)	Consulted (C)	Informed (I)
Define cloud governance framework	Platform engineering team	CIO/CTO	Security team, compliance team	All stakeholders
Establish governance policies	Platform engineering team	CIO/CTO	Legal team, security team	All employees

Task	Responsible (R)	Accountable (A)	Consulted (C)	Informed (I)
Implement security controls	Security team	CISO	Platform engineering team	All stakeholders
Monitor compliance	Security and compliance team	Compliance officer	Security and platform engineering team	All stakeholders
Cloud resource provisioning	Platform engineering team, operations team	Platform engineering manager	Application owners, security team	All stakeholders

Table 3.6 - RACI breakdown example

Understanding and addressing the following anti-patterns in cloud governance RACI models is crucial, as these pitfalls can significantly undermine the effectiveness of cloud operations, leading to operational inefficiencies, unclear accountability, and increased risk. By recognizing these common mistakes, organizations can better align their governance structures with their strategic objectives, ensuring smoother execution, enhanced collaboration, and more reliable compliance across cloud environments. The following table highlights the typical challenges with the RACI model and the solutions that should be applied:

Challenge	Solution
Overloading and ambiguous roles	Clarify and limit roles by ensuring each has a well-defined scope. Avoid assigning too many tasks to one role and review roles regularly to prevent bottlenecks.
Using RACI as a catch-all	Use RACI selectively by focusing on key governance areas. Avoid excessive granularity and ensure it remains practical for addressing specific issues.
Lack of collaboration	Foster cross-team collaboration by involving all relevant teams, including the CCoE, in RACI development. Encourage open dialogue to cover all responsibilities.
Not keeping RACI updated	Regularly review and update RACI to align with evolving governance practices. Ensure it reflects changes in cloud strategy and responsibilities.

Table 3.7 - Resolving challenges with the RACI model

This leads us to the importance of a robust cloud GRC framework. While the RACI model helps clarify roles and responsibilities, cloud native GRC policies provide the necessary structure to address the complexities of modern cloud operations, particularly for organizations that consider themselves too unique for standardized guardrails and practices.

In the next section, we will delve into how cloud native GRC frameworks can fix these issues, offering a comprehensive approach to governance that balances the need for flexibility with the demands of compliance and security.

The necessity of endorsed GRC policies

No business is too special or unique to bypass the need for robust GRC policies. These frameworks are essential for effectively managing risks, ensuring compliance, and establishing a solid governance structure within any organization. Without endorsed and consistently enforced GRC policies, businesses are likely to encounter inconsistent implementations, increased operational overhead, and vulnerabilities that could have been easily mitigated.

Key elements of GRC policies

The following are the key elements of GRC policies, with a description of each:

Key Element	Description
Governance	Establishes the framework for decision-making, accountability, and oversight within the organization. This includes defining roles and responsibilities, setting strategic objectives, and creating processes for monitoring and reporting. Effective governance ensures that cloud initiatives align with overall business goals and that there is clear accountability for cloud-related decisions.
Risk management	Involves identifying, assessing, and mitigating risks that could impact the organization. In cloud native governance, risk management covers concerns such as data security, vendor lock-in, and compliance risks associated with cloud adoption.
Compliance	Ensures adherence to regulatory requirements, industry standards, and internal policies. In cloud environments, compliance may involve ensuring data residency requirements are met, maintaining proper access controls, and implementing necessary encryption standards.

Table 3.8 - Elements of GRC policies

The critical importance of enforcing GRC policies

Even the most meticulously crafted GRC policies are rendered ineffective without proper enforcement. When these policies are not consistently applied or accountability is unclear, they devolve into mere guidelines, lacking the power to drive real governance or mitigate risks effectively. This lack of enforcement can create significant governance gaps, leading to increased operational overhead, vulnerabilities, and diminished trust in the organization's ability to handle incidents and maintain compliance.

Note the following challenges of enforcing GRRC policies.

Challenges in enforcing GRC policies

Following are the challenges in enforcing GRC policies:

- **Inconsistent application:** When GRC policies are applied inconsistently across different teams, departments, or projects, it creates discrepancies in how governance is executed. These inconsistencies can result in gaps where certain areas of the organization are inadequately governed, leading to vulnerabilities that can be exploited. The inconsistency also makes it difficult to measure the effectiveness of policies, as different teams may interpret and implement them in varying ways.

- **Lack of accountability**: Without clearly defined roles and responsibilities, enforcing GRC policies becomes a challenge. When accountability is not established, there is no clear ownership of compliance, making it easy for non-compliance issues to go unnoticed or unresolved. This lack of accountability can lead to a culture where policies are seen as optional, further undermining the governance framework.

- **Increased operational overhead**: Inconsistent enforcement of GRC policies necessitates additional resources to manage and correct deviations from established standards. This reactive approach is not only resource-intensive but also inefficient, as it often involves addressing issues after they have already caused disruptions. The need for continuous corrections increases operational costs and diverts resources from more strategic initiatives.

- **Complexity across layers**: Enforcing GRC policies across various layers of the organization, such as network, infrastructure, operating systems, applications, data, edge computing, and **web application firewalls (WAFs)**, adds a significant level of complexity. Each layer may have its own unique requirements and challenges, making it difficult to ensure cohesive policy enforcement. Additionally, managing cross-layer controls, such as credential scanning and ensuring consistent policy application, requires sophisticated coordination and monitoring. The complexity is compounded in environments where different layers are managed by separate teams, potentially leading to gaps in enforcement and increased risk.

Without rigorous enforcement, even the best-intentioned GRC policies fail to provide the security, compliance, and risk mitigation that organizations need to operate safely and efficiently in the cloud. Consistent enforcement ensures that GRC policies are more than just theoretical guidelines; they become integral parts of the organization's operational fabric, driving compliance, reducing risks, and fostering confidence in the organization's ability to navigate the complexities of modern cloud environments. With this in mind, we proceed to our final section, on missing feedback loops.

Missing feedback loops

In the dynamic realm of cloud computing, feedback loops are essential due to the rapidly evolving nature of the field. **Feedback loops** facilitate continuous improvement, allowing organizations to adapt and refine their cloud governance practices over time.

In this section, we delve into the critical consequences of missing feedback loops, emphasizing the importance of a robust change management process and the necessity of shifting left to foster a proactive culture. We'll explore how these concepts can be seamlessly integrated into an operating model, supported by real-world examples and discussions on cloud anti-patterns to illustrate these key points.

What are feedback loops?

Think of feedback loops as the radar system of cloud governance. Just as a radar scans the environment to detect changes and potential threats, feedback loops monitor the effectiveness of our cloud strategies in real time. They provide us with continuous insights into how well our governance frameworks are performing, highlighting both successes and areas for improvement.

In the fast-paced world of cloud computing, where new technologies and threats emerge regularly, these loops are vital to ensuring our policies and practices remain relevant, effective, and aligned with our overall business objectives. Feedback loops operate by collecting data from every layer of our cloud infrastructure, from network configurations to application performance, and security incidents to compliance checks. This data is then analyzed to identify patterns, trends, and anomalies, providing us with actionable insights. By integrating these insights back into our governance strategies, we can make informed adjustments that enhance our cloud environment's security, compliance, and efficiency.

Why we can't ignore feedback loops

Whether you are a Dev/DevOps/DevSecOps/platform engineer, feedback loops are essential throughout the entire cloud native organization for not only efficiency but also responsiveness. In the case of alarms, they are immediate feedback providers when, say, CPU/memory or storage has hit a critical point, potentially bringing down our entire app.

Now, feedback loops are nothing new to a traditional IT organization; they have been around for some time via monitoring tools such as Nagios and Zabbix. However, they only address a portion of the entire feedback system. With cloud native, we want that to be from end to end – deployment tooling, operating systems, containers, serverless function invocations, all of it. The question to ask is how much of it makes sense and will impact our organization if left ignored. To better understand this, let us look at why we can't ignore feedback loops:

- **Continuous improvement**: Feedback loops are critical for identifying weaknesses in our governance framework before they escalate into larger issues. Whether it is tightening security controls, optimizing resource allocation, or refining compliance practices, feedback loops give us the ability to make continuous, data-driven improvements that keep our cloud environment secure, compliant, and efficient.

- **Improved responsiveness**: Feedback loops enable us to pivot quickly in response to new challenges, whether it is a sudden change in compliance requirements, a new security threat, or a shift in business strategy. With regular feedback reviews, we can adapt our governance practices on the fly, ensuring that our cloud operations remain agile and aligned with our organizational goals. Here, we want a proactive setup with a reactive response mechanism.

- **Enhanced decision-making**: Gone are the days when decisions were made based on intuition or incomplete information. Feedback loops equip us with the hard data needed to make informed decisions. By monitoring key metrics, such as compliance rates, security incidents, and cost trends, we can gain a clear understanding of what's working and what needs adjustment. This data-driven approach empowers us to make decisions that are not only effective but also aligned with our long-term strategic objectives.

As we implement these feedback loops, we're not just creating a reactive cloud governance framework; we are building a proactive organization that is equipped to handle it.

Cost of time and effort

In the fast-paced world of cloud native development, missing feedback loops can severely hinder the efficiency and effectiveness of the development process. A lack of timely feedback not only slows down the development cycle but also increases the pressure on developers, leading to frustration, errors, and missed deadlines.

Consider a scenario where a development team uses GitHub Actions to automate the deployment of their applications to AWS. While GitHub Actions offers a streamlined way to build, test, and deploy code, the absence of robust feedback loops in this process can lead to significant challenges.

Without immediate feedback, the team might push changes to the main branch and initiate the deployment process, only to discover much later that the deployment failed due to a misconfiguration in the infrastructure or a bug in the code. This delay in discovering the issue means that developers are left in the dark for longer periods, unaware that their changes have introduced a problem. Consequently, they continue to work under the false assumption that everything is functioning correctly, which compounds the issue.

Slowed development cycle and increased pressure

The absence of feedback loops in this deployment process slows down the entire development cycle. Instead of receiving immediate notifications about deployment failures or performance issues, developers only learn about these problems after they have had a chance to manifest and potentially affect the production environment. This delayed feedback forces the team into a reactive mode, where they must scramble to diagnose and fix issues long after they have been introduced. The lack of proactive alerts means that problems are often discovered at the worst possible time, during critical production hours or just before a major release.

This reactive approach not only slows down the development process but also places increased pressure on developers. With no early warning system, developers are forced to take on the additional burden of troubleshooting and resolving issues that could have been prevented or caught earlier in the pipeline. The stress of constantly firefighting can lead to burnout, reduced productivity, and a decline in code quality as developers rush to meet deadlines. To avoid these pitfalls, it is essential to implement robust feedback loops throughout the development and deployment process.

This exact scenario happened to a client of ours. We had built their pipeline from end to end, as an MVP, to show how well GitHub Actions and Kubernetes work together. To ensure consistency, we provided tests post-container build to ensure that the app could run. Given that it was a Docker container, portability was critical, so rather than testing on another cluster, we tested in the pipeline. Post-MVP, more pipelines were built but did not include the testing we had created patterns for prior, and containers were shipped to Kubernetes clusters. Without proper testing, chaos ensued.

We would assume that non-production environments and test environments are not entirely business critical, yet in this case, the new containers brought down the clusters as they had caused other dependent APIs to fail, thus impacting other teams. In the case of GitHub Actions, integrating feedback mechanisms such as automated testing, infrastructure checks, and real-time monitoring can provide developers with the information they need to make informed decisions quickly. For instance, if a deployment fails due to a configuration error, an immediate notification should be sent to the development team, detailing the cause of the failure and suggesting possible fixes.

By incorporating these feedback loops, the development process becomes more agile and responsive. Developers can address issues as they arise, reducing the risk of problems escalating into major incidents. This proactive approach not only accelerates the development cycle but also relieves the pressure on developers, allowing them to focus on writing high-quality code and innovating without the constant fear of unforeseen issues derailing their progress. The following diagram provides insights into where to apply feedback in the development pipeline:

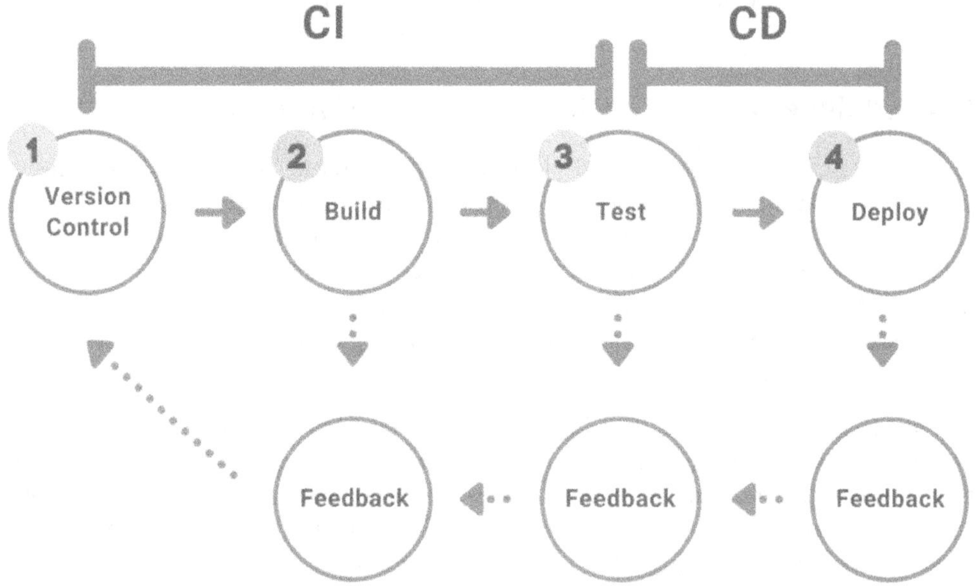

Figure 3.7 - CI/CD pipeline with feedback loop (Redraw please)

Feedback loops give us the ability to adapt to change, for better or worse. This leads us nicely on to our next section, on change management. Building on our discussion of feedback loops in cloud governance, it's essential to understand how adopting the shift-left approach further enhances these practices by proactively addressing potential issues early in the development process.

The role of change management in cloud governance

Just as in traditional IT organizations, in cloud native organizations, change management is still critical; it is how they are invoked and run that is different. With a proper feedback loop system, we can rely on when we make changes, the impact of success and failures are known, prior to getting there change management will need to run its course.

In traditional IT organizations, for most environments, from development to production, changes would require some form of change request via an **IT service management system** (**ITSM**). The change request would then need to be brought in front of a **change advisory board** (**CAB**), where then, and only then, can the change proceed.

Cloud native organizations cannot get rid of change management altogether as no change management leads to the following:

- **Inconsistent implementations**: We've seen time and again that changes are implemented inconsistently across teams and environments, leading to significant gaps in governance and security. It is like building a house without a blueprint: it may look stable on the surface, but it is only a matter of time before it collapses under the weight of these inconsistencies.

- **Resistance to change**: Engineers push back against new processes because they feel uninformed or uninvolved. It is like trying to force a square peg into a round hole: it just doesn't fit. The result is lower adoption rates and the potential for conflict, which can derail even the best-laid plans.

- **Operations disruptions**: It can cause interruptions that lead to downtime, inefficiencies, and a heightened risk of errors. It is like navigating a stormy sea without a compass: without clear direction, we're likely to get lost and struggle to stay on course.

By understanding these difficulties, we can develop a well-organized change management procedure that confronts these concerns directly.

The GitOps model is one that cloud native organizations are adopting or have adopted to adhere to a modern management process. In a GitOps model, change management is deeply integrated into the version control system, leveraging Git as the single source of truth for all infrastructure and application configurations. This approach to change management ensures that every modification to the system, whether it is a code update, configuration adjustment, or infrastructure change, is tracked, auditable, and reversible. The process is inherently collaborative, with changes proposed, reviewed, and approved through **pull requests** (**PRs**), ensuring that all stakeholders have visibility and input before any changes are implemented.

When a change is proposed via a PR, it triggers a series of automated processes, including testing, validation, and deployment. This not only speeds up the change process but also reduces the risk of errors, as every change is thoroughly reviewed and tested before being merged into the main branch and applied to the live environment.

The following table details this further:

Stage	Description
Pull request	A developer or engineer proposes a change by creating a PR in the Git repository. The PR includes the specific changes to code, configurations, or infrastructure as code (IaC) files.
Automated testing	The PR triggers automated testing pipelines that run unit tests, integration tests, and security scans to ensure the change doesn't introduce any issues.
Code review	Team members review the PR, providing feedback and suggesting improvements. The review process ensures that multiple stakeholders agree on the change before it is merged.
Approval process	Once the reviews are complete and any requested changes are made, the PR is approved by authorized personnel, such as senior developers or team leads.
Automated deployment	After approval, the change is automatically merged into the main branch. This merge triggers a deployment pipeline that applies the change to the relevant environments (e.g., staging, production).
Monitoring and rollback/ forward	Post-deployment monitoring ensures that the change behaves as expected. If issues arise, the change can be quickly rolled back by reverting the PR, restoring the system to its previous state.

Table 3.9 - Details of a GitOps change request

Integrating change management into the operating model

To effectively integrate change management into a cloud governance operating model, organizations will adopt the following practices:

- **Define clear objectives**: The first step in any successful change initiative is to define clear objectives. What do we want to achieve with this change? Articulating our objectives will simplify the remaining steps.

- **Engage stakeholders**: This includes executives, IT teams, and end users – anyone who will be affected by the change. By involving them from the beginning and consistently, we will ensure their support and comprehensive preparation.

- **Provide training and support**: Now that we have our team in place, it's time to provide them with the training and resources they need to succeed. This could involve workshops, webinars, or even personal coaching sessions. By investing in our team's development, we will reduce resistance to change and improve implementation success.

- **Monitor and review**: Finally, it's crucial to continuously monitor the impact of changes and gather feedback from stakeholders. This will help us identify areas for further improvement and make data-driven decisions.

The shift-left principle

This approach is about integrating quality and security practices early in the development life cycle, rather than waiting until the end to address these critical aspects. By shifting these processes to the left, closer to the beginning of the development cycle, we gain the foresight to prevent problems before they even arise.

The benefits of shifting left

The benefits of shifting left include the following:

- **Early detection of issues**: Imagine discovering a bug during the design phase rather than after deployment to production. The shift-left approach enables us to identify and resolve issues early, saving considerable time, effort, and headaches down the line.

- **Improved quality and security**: By embedding quality and security practices from the outset, we ensure these elements are integral to the development process. It's like having a superhero team of quality and security experts working tirelessly to keep our applications safe and secure, from day one.

- **Faster time to market**: Late-stage defects have a notorious way of delaying releases. With shift left, we can bid farewell to those last-minute problems. By addressing issues early, we can deliver our applications to market faster than ever before.

In a previous consulting engagement, we enhanced the development process for a multinational finance group preparing to launch operations in Australia. This approach ensured full compliance with Australian cybersecurity controls and PCI-DSS requirements while safeguarding against the storage of **personally identifiable information** (**PII**) on public cloud infrastructure. To achieve this, we integrated security and compliance checks directly into our CI/CD pipeline.

Bitbucket pipelines were employed to automate build and deployment processes, and AWS Config with Security Hub was incorporated to continuously monitor resources for any deviations from established policies.

For those unfamiliar with AWS Config, it is a service that provides a detailed view of the configuration of AWS resources within your account. Similar services exist across other cloud platforms:

- In Microsoft Azure, the equivalent service is Azure Policy, which allows you to create, assign, and manage policies to enforce rules across your resource configurations

- In Google Cloud Platform, Cloud Asset Inventory offers a way to view, monitor, and analyze all Google Cloud and Anthos assets across projects and services

These services are crucial to ensuring compliance with organizational guidelines and regulatory standards. AWS Config, for example, leverages **function as a service** (**FaaS**) to correct any detected issues. The same can be run in Azure and Google, via Azure Functions and Cloud Run.

By shifting left and implementing automated governance checks, we could detect and address security vulnerabilities and compliance violations early in the development process.

Excellence in cloud governance goes beyond implementing best practices; it necessitates fostering a culture of proactive engagement and innovation, where teams are equipped and empowered to anticipate challenges and drive continuous improvement.

Creating a proactive culture

Cultivating a proactive culture in cloud governance begins with leadership. As leaders, we must model the behaviors we want to see in our teams by engaging in the technical details, emphasizing the importance of quality and security, and actively supporting our teams. This sets a clear standard for proactive behavior, which is essential for maintaining robust cloud governance.

However, leading by example is only the first step. To empower our teams, we must provide them with the necessary knowledge and tools to implement best practices from the outset. This includes investing in comprehensive training programs, offering access to the latest cloud governance technologies, and curating a library of technical resources. Importantly, recognizing and rewarding proactive behavior, such as identifying security vulnerabilities early or suggesting improvements, reinforces the value of these actions and helps embed a proactive mindset across the organization.

The strategies are discussed here in more detail:

- **Lead by example**: Effective cloud governance starts with leadership. As leaders, it's essential to model the proactive behaviors we expect from our teams. This involves engaging directly with technical details, demonstrating the importance of quality and security, and actively supporting our teams. By doing so, we set a standard that encourages others to follow suit.

- **Provide training and resources**: Leadership alone isn't enough; we must also empower our teams with the knowledge and tools they need to succeed. This includes investing in comprehensive training programs, curating a library of up-to-date technical resources, and ensuring access to the latest cloud governance tools and technologies. Properly equipped, teams are better positioned to implement best practices from the outset.

- **Recognize and reward proactive behavior**: Finally, it's crucial to acknowledge and reward those who demonstrate proactive behavior. Whether it's identifying potential security vulnerabilities early or suggesting enhancements to the cloud governance framework, celebrating these contributions reinforces their value and encourages a culture of continuous improvement across the organization.

A proactive culture requires an environment that you can play/build on. The sandbox environment here becomes critical to achieving a proactive culture and helps avoid one of the earlier anti-patterns, *learning will happen miraculously*.

Empower and uplift

By integrating sandbox environments into our development process and fostering a proactive culture, we significantly reduce the likelihood of unexpected issues in production. This approach ensures that changes are thoroughly tested and validated, leading to more reliable and confident production releases. We achieve this by doing the following:

- **Automated testing**: Implementing automated testing within sandbox environments ensures that changes meet our quality and security standards. This early detection of potential issues reduces the risk of surprises when changes are moved to production.

- **Continuous integration and continuous delivery (CI/CD)**: Utilizing CI/CD pipelines to automate the deployment of changes from sandbox to production ensures consistency and reliability. This streamlined process minimizes the risk of human error and enhances the efficiency of our development cycle.

- **Regular feedback and review**: Continuously gathering feedback from sandbox testing allows us to refine and improve our development process. By using this data to make informed, data-driven decisions, we can optimize our cloud governance framework and ensure ongoing improvement.

In cloud computing, the lack of feedback loops and effective change management hampers efficiency, causing inconsistent implementations, resistance to change, and operational issues. A GitOps-driven approach, where every change is tracked and reviewed through PRs, ensures transparency, accountability, and alignment with business goals.

Feedback loops are crucial for continuous improvement and faster decision-making, while the "shift-left" principle catches issues early in development. Strong leadership, proper training, and sandbox environments for testing build a resilient governance framework that reduces risk, speeds up innovation, and improves production confidence.

Summary

In cloud native environments, governance must evolve to keep pace with the agility and innovation that these architectures demand. Traditional governance models, often centralized and rigid, are ill suited for the decentralized, fast-moving nature of cloud technologies. As outlined in this chapter, organizations must shift from outdated, control-heavy methods to more adaptable and flexible governance strategies.

This includes addressing critical anti-patterns, such as the assumption that learning happens on its own or the belief that a centralized approach will scale effectively. By fostering a culture of continuous learning, encouraging feedback loops, and establishing clear, decentralized governance practices, organizations can avoid these pitfalls. Ultimately, cloud native governance is about empowering teams with the autonomy to innovate while maintaining security, compliance, and operational efficiency.

Get This Book's PDF Version and Exclusive Extras

Scan the QR code (or go to `packtpub.com/unlock`). Search for this book by name, confirm the edition, and then follow the steps on the page.

Note: Keep your invoice handly. Purchase made directly from packt don't require one.

4

FinOps – How to Avoid a Bill Shock

"FinOps is the practice of bringing financial accountability to the variable spend model of cloud, enabling distributed teams to make business trade-offs between speed, cost, and quality."

– J.R. Storment, Executive Director of the FinOps Foundation

How do we know what the return value should be for the money we put into something? To explore this quote further, we can compare similarities with when we build a house and need to set a budget. We know how many rooms we need, how much garage space we need, and what insulation level, air conditioning, or heating capacity, depending on the climate zone. Those are immediate build expenses. However, there are also long-term considerations that we need to consider. Do we want better insulation and a solar system to reduce the ongoing electricity cost? This means there is more upfront cost, but there is a long-term benefit of ongoing cost reduction.

In the same way, we need to consider the short- and long-term benefits of FinOps. It becomes more complex because our cloud landscape is more dynamic than a static building construction. FinOps needs to be an ongoing discipline. But how do we strike the right balance between paying the right price, implementing the right solution, meeting timelines, and getting the right value?

"Price is what you pay; value is what you get" – this is a famous quote by Warren Buffett. In other words, we need to focus on the value we receive from an investment rather than just looking at the price. In our case, the investment is all the effort we put into building an enterprise cloud platform and the applications we run on top of it. We need to assess the value gained, such as business agility and increased resilience, instead of solely focusing on cost reduction.

This chapter's goal is to understand how we can get good value out of our cloud native landscape. We will focus on the following areas:

- Missing out on the power of good tagging practices
- Not leveraging cloud native tooling
- Ignoring non-obvious **cloud service provider (CSP)** costs
- Focusing on cost savings over driving value

There is a lot to unpack, and we will go through it step by step. Before we can measure the value, improve our cost governance, and deal with cost ownership, we will look into enabling cost allocation in the cloud. It all starts with metadata, also called tagging or labeling within the scope of cloud resource management. Let's dive into it.

Missing out on the power of good tagging practices

Tags are key-value pairs that act as metadata for cloud resources. **Tagging** is the practice of assigning tags to cloud resources to describe them. Tags help organize, manage, and track resources efficiently.

Tags are helpful not only in providing a cost breakdown but also in managing, identifying, organizing, searching for, and filtering resources. The benefits of tagging are as follows:

- **Resource management**: Tags help organize resources by categories, based on products or projects, environments, cost centers, business units, and others. This makes it easier to search for particular resources.
- **Security and compliance**: Tags can be used to enforce identity and access policies and control access to resources. For example, if a resource tag describes a database holding credit card information, we can implement a policy ensuring that humans cannot read the data.
- **Automation**: Tags can be used to drive deployment and auto-scaling behavior or automated shutdown of resources.
- **Operational efficiencies**: Tags can be useful for troubleshooting during an incident since they provide additional context. They can also be useful for fine-grained monitoring and to drive alerting behavior.
- **Cost management**: Tags help allocate and track costs. We can use them to break down costs and organize our resources. For the remainder of this section, we will focus on this aspect.

Even if tagging is as simple as describing key-value pairs, many things can still go wrong, and we will discuss two anti-patterns.

Common anti-patterns

Tagging-related anti-patterns often start with shortcomings in our tagging standards or tagging enforcement, and we will look into these areas next.

Lack of tagging standards

The first one is the lack of tagging standards, which I have seen many times. There are several reasons why this anti-pattern can occur. It could be that cloud native adoption did not get enough focus because an organization is trying to increase its cloud footprint organically and is never gaining momentum for cloud migrations. It could be because a company is trapped in a reactive mode and cannot operate strategically or because of competing priorities.

This is how things usually unfold. An organization is adopting the cloud. However, the cloud adoption model has gaps, especially in governance, automation, standardization, and service catalog offerings. As a result, decentralized product teams are provisioning cloud resources and managing them differently. Applying tags is optional. Even though teams will eventually decide to apply tags, the tags between teams will not be consistent.

That means we will have resources that are not tagged at all or only have some tags, and there is a high chance that the tags themselves are inconsistent, whether it is the key, the value, or both. Therefore, we will miss out on many FinOps guardrails, which we will analyze after the second variation of this anti-pattern.

Lack of tagging enforcement

The second variation is that there are mandated tagging standards but they are not enforced. As a result, we will probably have better tagging coverage than the previous variation. However, we still rely on human perfection.

Every engineer must ensure they have all tags assigned to each cloud resource. That means the key and the value need to be a perfect match.

During a consulting engagement, I analyzed the tags in place across different cloud environments. Over time, the tag for the cost center had changed multiple times. The customer used the following combinations for the key: "cost-centre" (UK spelling), "cost-center" (US spelling), "costcentre" (all lower case), "CostCentre" (Pascal case syntax), "costcentre," and "costcenter."

Because tags are case-sensitive in AWS, this resulted in six different tag categories. Therefore, the billing report also visualized them in six different variations, requiring manual rectification to achieve a cost breakdown. Another common mistake is to use names for the product owner tag value. The individual then leaves the organization and their account gets deactivated. We then have an invalid tag and do not even know in which department the previous application owner was. This makes it hard to track down the new application owner, assuming there is no ownership vacuum.

As we can imagine, this is not an exciting activity that must be performed every month and adds the risk of human error.

Consequences of poor tagging practices

There are several impacts if consequences" we do not have sufficient tagging in place:

- **Cost allocation becomes challenging**: We cannot allocate cost to cost centers, profit centers, or departments. This makes it difficult to track and manage budgets. A common result of unclear cost allocation is the lack of ownership and accountability.

- **Cost optimization becomes challenging**: Without sufficient tagging, we will have difficulties identifying the owner of underutilized or unused resources. Therefore, no one will act to right-size resources or turn off unnecessary ones.

- **Inaccurate financial reporting**: Financial reports rely on accurate tagging. This means we need to manually allocate costs or accept inaccuracy. In the latter case, that means we cannot fairly distribute the cost.

- **Incomplete tagging also results in imprecise budgeting**: This can lead to budget overruns and insufficient forecasting. Without a correct reflection of our current spending, we will struggle to predict future expenses.

- **Insufficient showback or chargeback processes**: "Chargeback consequences" models, where costs are billed back to the departments or product teams that incurred them, rely heavily on accurate tagging. Without accurate tagging, implementing a fair and transparent chargeback system is challenging and requires a lot of human data wrangling. With showback models, departments are shown their cloud spending without actual billing. Insufficient tagging can reduce transparency, leading to disputes, confusion, and potentially mistrust.

- **Lack of ownership**: Without a functioning chargeback process, there cannot be clear ownership, which is critical for good value realization. Therefore, we will miss out on good FinOps practices, including overspending, because we have underutilized cloud resources.

- **Lack of policy enforcement**: Cloud governance policies often depend on tags to enforce rules and best practices. Insufficient tagging can weaken governance, leading to uncontrolled costs. Tags provide visibility into how resources are being used across the organization. Without them, it is difficult to ensure resources are consequences" used efficiently and according to policies.

Spotting untagged resources

Common root causes of inadequate tagging are inconsistent deployment methods, a lack of leveraging a policy-as-code framework, a lack of tagging standards, and a lack of automation that misses out on tagging enforcement. Validating the tag keys and values will bring us certainty. There are different ways how to do that depending on the CSP We will look into it now by starting with AWS.

Untagged resources in AWS

If we have access to the console or cloud shell, we can do the validation ourselves. If we want to find untagged resources in our AWS account, we can use the resource search feature in the AWS Resource

Explorer with a filter query that uses the `tag:none` value. As we can see, this is fairly straightforward, and we will now explore how to solve this problem in Azure.

Untagged resources in Azure

In Azure, we can use PowerShell commands for this as in the following:

```
$resources = Get-AzResource

$untaggedResources = $resources | Where-Object { -not $_.Tags }

$untaggedResources | Format-Table Name, ResourceType,
ResourceGroupName, Location
```

In the preceding snippet, the following occurs:

- The first command gets all resources

- The second command filters all resources that are not tagged

- The third command displays all untagged resources in a table format showing the resource name, resource type, resource group name, and location (Region)

We will now look into the required steps in GCP.

Untagged resources in GCP

In GCP, we can also use the cloud shell to search for unlabeled resources, as shown here:

```
gcloud asset search-all-resources \
--scope='projects/<project_name>' \
--asset-types='container.googleapis.com/NodePool' \
--filter=-labels:*
```

If we have not enabled the cloud asset API yet, we can do this with the first command. The second command lists all Google Kubernetes Engine node pools that do not have a tag. In the scope, we need to replace `project_name` with our project name. The `labels:*` filter reduces the search result to unlabeled resources.

If we don't have access to the console or cloud shell, we can ask someone with permission to run the preceding commands and validate the tagging coverage and accuracy. Otherwise, we can also contact the person managing the CSP's bill and validate with them how accurate the current cost breakdown is. It is a good idea to validate both options since there might be different opinions within our organization. In that case, it will be helpful to set up a workshop and go through the evidence, including the last bill, and the cost dashboards from our CSP, and run some commands to validate the tags.

Once we understand our current status and shortcomings, we must identify our target state. For this chapter, we will solely focus on FinOps-related tags and not tags that might be helpful for security, compliance, observability, or other operational aspects. *What does good look like, and where do we start?*

Adopting a tagging taxonomy

We will start by defining a tagging taxonomy and establishing standards for tag keys, values, and syntax.

Tag keys

We need to know what information we want to extract from our tags and specify the valid and required tag values and keys. Typically, information includes the following:

- **Cost center and/or business domain/unit or portfolio name**: If there is no 1:1 mapping between cost centers and business units and both are relevant for a showback or chargeback approach, we will need both.

- **Level of detail**: The need to add a second hierarchical view to the previous tag value (cost center and portfolio) depends on the organizational structure and size. Therefore, adding another tag value for products, projects, or team names is optional. A portfolio could include several products, and we might want cost segregation. Some organizations use project codes until applications transition into **business as usual** (**BAU**) mode. In that case, we must have at least one mandatory tag from the project code or cost center. Product codes are more fine-grained than cost centers. Environments such as `dev`, `test`, `uat`, `preprod`, and `prod`. should also be addressed in our tagging strategy. This gives us good insight to validate how much cost we spend per environment.

- **Business owner**: This should be the job title or role, not the name of an individual. It helps us identify the business owner if we have a showback model and need to deliver a cost breakdown. If we have a chargeback model, we know who to send the billing information to and provide cost recommendations and forecast insights.

- **Technical owner**: This needs to be a job title or owner as well, and the information is useful for the same reasons as the business owner. Sometimes this could be the same job function across the organization, in which case, we can consolidate those two tag values.

- **Application and/or service identifier**: This information is useful for linking information to our application inventory. In that case, we can answer cost-related questions about our application inventory. Adding an application function tag is helpful.

  The term *application function* is sometimes called *application role*, and it describes whether a component represents a database, presentation layer, business logic, or data tier. It is not necessary for an accurate showback or chargeback model, but it gives us good insight into where we spend our money. It will tell us whether the CSP cost occurred on the presentation layer, the business logic layer, the integration layer, or the data layer. This provides us with additional data points when we are considering refactoring our application.

Tag values

We also need to standardize our tagging values. We must agree on whether we want single values or can have lists in the key. The values need to be clearly defined. Examples are the correct format for a cost center, which is a combination of two digits and four characters, or valid application functions, like db for the database, `api` for the API layer, `int` for the integration layer, and so on. Ideally, those tags are assigned as part of the CI/CD pipeline. In that case, we can validate both the key and the value with our policy-as-code framework.

Syntax

The tagging syntax is also important for keys and values. Syntax examples are everything in lowercase (`costcenter`), camel case (`costCenter`), pascal case (`CostCenter`), snake case (`cost_center`), and kebab case (`cost-center`). No matter what syntax we use, it needs to be consistent, and we need to check that the syntax is supported by our CSP. This applies to both the tag key and value.

Continuous improvement

Once we have established our taxonomy, we need to continue establishing other tagging best practices to achieve a good cost-control governance model.

Tagging automation and enforcement

We want to make sure every resource that supports tagging has a valid tag. We can use tools such as AWS Tag Policies and AWS Config, Azure Policy, or Google Cloud Resource Manager. This will ensure compliance and prevent untagged resources. If we have a service catalog, the tags should be a mandatory input parameter.

For the application function, we can include default tags in the service catalog item, for example, the database or API gateway. There are different ways we can ensure a good tagging implementation:

- We can implement policies with **OPA** or the policy frameworks of our CSP to make sure untagged resources can never be deployed except to a sandpit environment.

- When we use the development frameworks of our CSP, we can also validate tags and labels in a similar approach to unit tests. The AWS **cloud development kit** (**CDK**) supports assertions, which we can use to validate tags. The **Azure Resource Manager** (**ARM**) template test toolkit can be used to validate the structure and properties of Bicep or ARM templates. In GCP, we can write unit tests with the Google Cloud SDK to validate labels.

- Some **infrastructure as code** (**IaC**) tools, such as Terraform, support tag declaration on a deployment level. This way, we can define common tags like *cost center* on a deployment level and only need to define fine-grained tags not defined on a deployment or service catalog level.

If we have a policy-as-code framework, we can enforce tagging and deny the creation of untagged or insufficiently tagged cloud resources. That policy could be skipped for sandpit environments where we automatically tear down resources regularly. If we have a mature DevSecOps culture in place, we want to warrant that tags can only be modified by our CI/CD pipelines. In that case, we can use guardrails to make sure tags cannot be modified by human access.

Regular audits using cloud native tools

We should conduct regular audits of tags to ensure they are correctly applied and up to date. CSPs offer tools such as AWS Tag Editor, Azure Cost Management, and Google Cloud's Resource Manager. Once we generate compliance reports, we can identify missing or incorrect tags and take corrective actions.

Continuous improvement

Any findings in our tooling or audits need to be addressed to ensure they are permanently remediated and do not become a permanent burden. Once we have our tagging established, we can get valuable insight. The following Azure diagram illustrates how the tag inheritance feature can be used. When enabled, tag inheritance applies billing, resource group, and subscription tags to child resource usage records. In that case, we do not have to tag every resource. This is a very powerful feature.

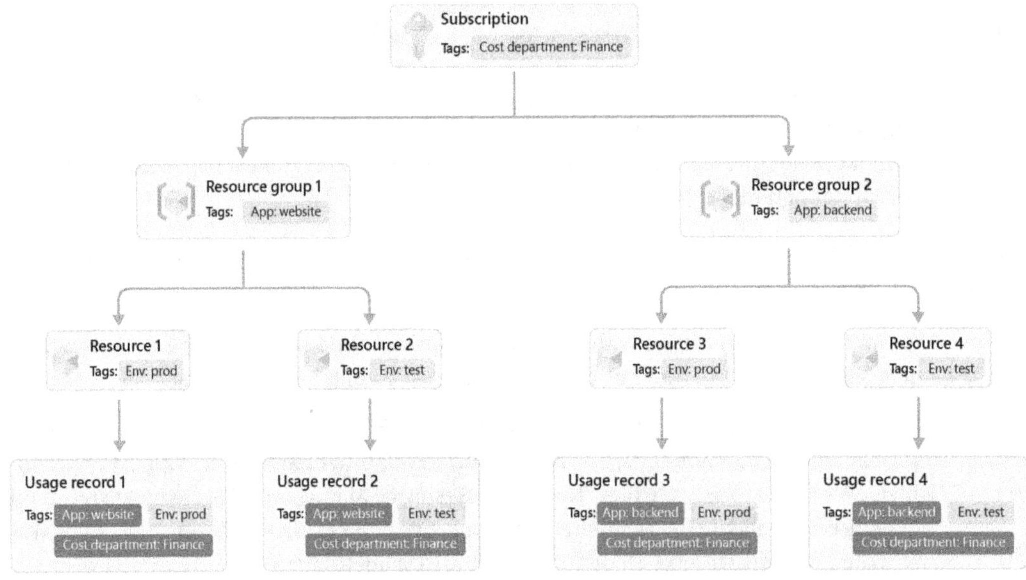

Figure 4.1 – Azure example showing tag inheritance (source: https://learn.microsoft.com/en-us/azure/cost-management-billing/costs/enable-tag-inheritance)

Now, we know how to set our organization up for a solid tagging implementation. Once we have established a robust tagging framework and procedure, many other FinOps-related services can leverage it and provide good visibility. This includes cost anomaly detections, budgets and cost alerts, rightsizing recommendations, and planning for a committed spend discount plan.

We have stepped through tagging anti-patterns and how to remediate them and turn them into best practices utilizing cloud native services. We have not discussed third-party tools, so we will now explore whether there is a space for them.

Not leveraging CSP FinOps services

The major CSPs offer various FinOps services, including cost analysis tools, cost reports, budget management, rightsizing recommendations, savings plans, cost trend analysis, forecasting, and alerting. The offerings are mature but not always used. That is especially the case if cost savings do not become a high priority because other challenges like security, resilience, and compliance must be tackled first. Before we explore the anti-pattern, we want to make it clear that commercial third-party cost management tools can have their place.

Two main drivers can trigger us to consider third-party tools for cost management and FinOps practices. The first one is if we have a multi-cloud or poly-cloud strategy. In that case, we might want a unified view across multiple clouds. This will depend on our operating model. If we are prepared to use different FinOps services per cloud (for example, GCP and Azure), then we don't need to go down that track. This will add cost management complexity if a team is using several cloud platforms. This could be a centralized cloud platform team that is responsible for creating cost dashboards.

The second driver is whether we want to include more than our CSP platform in our FinOps approach – for example, to include CI/CD tooling or SaaS monitoring solutions. In that case, we must define our requirements and assess the benefit of third-party tools. Some CI/CD tools have native cost control features, such as GitHub with a Plans and Usage feature. If we are OK with looking into several dashboards, we probably do not need to invest in another FinOps third-party tool. We need to consider the cost trade-off. How much additional time do we spend on our processes compared to license fees for a commercial offering? Now, it is time to explore how we can find ourselves in the anti-pattern of not leveraging cloud native FinOps services.

Common anti-patterns

The power and scope of FinOps services that are provided by our CSP are often overlooked, and we will explore two related anti-patterns next.

Billing will sort itself out

Not using any cost control services is common at the beginning of cloud adoption or when an organization tries to grow its cloud presence organically without implementing a chargeback model.

My very first cloud experience on a production scale was at a government organization. My manager knew that I had AWS experience. He gave me his credit card so I could create an AWS account for a project team. That happened again several times. A few months later, in December, we had the end-of-year celebration, which was paid for with the same credit card. Consequently, the credit limit was reached and the monthly AWS payment bounced in January.

In February, AWS tried to charge for February and January, which resulted in another bounced payment, and the same happened in March. By that time, we had already received several automated warning emails that AWS accounts would be closed if we were not paying.

If we had given cost management a higher priority, we could have had alerts and reacted proactively. Instead, we were reacting to emails we got from AWS and involved procurement. They were not prepared to react swiftly since the government organization had strict processes in place. Eventually, the payment method was moved from credit card payments to an ongoing purchase order. However, cost controls were only implemented a year later using the cloud native capabilities.

After a couple of months, a project manager asked me to change the billing currency from **US dollars** (**USD**) to Australian dollars, which I did. Unfortunately, the procurement department was not prepared to pay the next invoice since the currency did not match the currency in the purchase order. This is another hiccup we can avoid if we are familiar with our internal cost management practices. Collaboration between departments helps to cross those organizational boundaries. An approach we have seen working well is having a cross-functional team that has regular cadence meetings with extended team delegates. Those delegates include procurement, finance, and recruitment. This helps to catch any surprises early and address them swiftly. This story should make one thing very clear: *tooling is only a part of a successful FinOps adoption*. It is critical to have clear processes and responsibilities defined as part of our operating model. Now is the time to investigate another variation of this anti-pattern.

Rushing into a third-party product

We already explored the reasons why a commercial third-party offering might make sense. We will now examine a scenario where one is not required. Both scenarios have one thing in common: a low cloud adoption maturity level. In this variation, we want to achieve quick wins.

That could be the case because value realization has never become a high priority due to other burning issues, like security, compliance, and reliability (especially after outages). Another driver could be that we are changing our financial approach from a cost center to a profit center approach. Because we need to rush, we are not considering the long-term cost impact enough.

In a previous company, I was in a situation where we had already implemented the foundational cost management capabilities in a development organization, including cost breakdown, forecast, budget alerts, anomaly detection, and committed savings plan. Unfortunately, the cloud platform team was totally swamped with helping other teams and did not have enough time to fine-tune to rigorously test those features to release them into the production organization for all business units.

In the meantime, a new financial year commenced, and the company changed from a cost center to a profit center approach. That meant the costs needed to be distributed accurately. However, there were gaps in the tagging implementation for legacy applications. Therefore, a team manager had to spend more than a day per month getting the cloud bill splitting right. The **leadership team** (**LT**) became aware of that but they only knew half the story. They underestimated the business benefit of the existing cost management service catalog items that were already deployed in the production organization.

One of the LT members attended a conference and saw a presentation of a FinOps tool with a nice user interface. He was curious and asked some questions after the presentation. That was enough for the sales team to flag the company as a hot opportunity. The vendor followed up with a lunch invite. Judging by how much the product appreciation increased, it must have been a very good lunch. As a next step, there was a very strong desire to implement a proof of value. Because the company was operating in a very regulated environment, this resulted in a comprehensive vendor selection process.

This pattern results in locking ourselves into an ongoing expense. Third-party FinOps license fees are typically based on our cloud spending. The higher the cloud spending, the more we pay for our commercial tool.

Impacts

By going through the anti-pattern, we have already seen some of its consequences, and we want to briefly summarize them now:

- **Lack of value optimization**: If we are not using a FinOps tool, we cannot optimize the value of our cloud native stack. We will not be able to optimize our resources and make the right financial trade-off decisions, for instance, about whether to opt for a savings plan.

- **Lack of cost visibility**: We will not be able to provide an efficient and correct charge-back approach. Therefore, we cannot direct ownership toward the business stakeholder, which means there is no motivation to optimize the value realization.

- **Increased vendor management effort**: If we use a third-party product, we will have an additional vendor that needs to be managed. We have talked about partnerships before. Is this a strategic partnership?

- **Increased ongoing cost**: If we use third-party tools, we will be charged a license fee, which is typically based on our cloud spending. The more we spend, the more we pay for the license. The provider has no incentive to reduce our cloud costs because that would also reduce their revenue.

- **Manual overhead and delays in financial reporting**: We will have an increased manual effort to manage our financial reporting, which will also take longer. Hence, it will be difficult to understand real-time expenses or adjust budgets and forecasts accordingly.

Even if we have the right tooling in place, we still need to establish mature processes and responsibilities that align with our operating model. Otherwise, we will not unlock the potential of our tooling. We will explore the process and cloud native services next.

Cost management seen through the SDLC lens

We are now stepping through FinOps capabilities, and we will align them with a simplified overview of a **software development life cycle (SDLC)**. The following table provides an overview of the SDLC phases and a logical name of the FinOps service for this phase. We will go through each of the phases and discuss what we need to consider for establishing a good business value for our application stack.

We have already looked into tagging, which needs to be established during the *implement and test* phase, which makes up the majority of this phase. Therefore, we will merge this phase with the *deploy* phase when we go through the SDLC. We can see that the *maintain and improve* phase has the longest list of considerations. We need to take those insights on board to plan and design for improvements in our iterative delivery.

Plan & design	Implement & test	Deploy	Maintain & improve
Design principles	Tag policies	Preventive guardrails	Detective guardrails
Cost calculator	Tagging	Organization setup	Cost explorer
Budget and alerts	Tagging enforcement	Automated cost estimate	Advisory tools
Architecting for cost efficiencies	Data life cycles		Cost anomaly detection
			Rightsizing recommendations
			Committed spend

Table 4.1 – SDLC phases and supporting FinOps services

We will now look into FinOps services that support the first phase: *plan and design*.

Plan and design

FinOps considerations and tooling for the *plan and design* phase are as follows:

- **Design principles**: Internal guiding principles and SLAs, such as RTO and RPO, will drive our cost model. The individual Well-Architected Frameworks from the CSPs will also provide guidance. If a solution needs to be resilient, it will have a fail-over database, which adds to the cost. Once familiar with our requirements, we can start designing a solution with a drawing tool. There are many options available. Diagrams.net is a free drawing solution, and Lucid Chart is a popular commercial offering with enterprise collaboration features. The diagram will help us fully visualize the services we want to use.

- **Cost calculator:** We can then use our CSP's pricing calculator. AWS Pricing Calculator, Azure Pricing Calculator, and Google Cloud Pricing Calculator provide a user-friendly user interface and support most of their cloud services. They all support committed spending savings plans, provide a shareable URL for the calculation, and reports can be exported. With all cost calculators, we need to be careful to select the correct region, since prices differ. We will also need volume estimates. For API services, we typically need to estimate how many API calls we have; for data services, we need to know the data volume and growth and whether we need a fail-over database or an additional read-only database. For any egress data, for example, from one cloud to another, we also need to know the volume numbers. If we implement a new solution, then some of these numbers will be covered in the business case and design. For other metrics, we do have to make rough estimates, and we can fine-tune them either during the *design* phase or build feedback loops once the solution is deployed and used.

- **Budgets and alerts:** All major CSPs have budget and alert services. There are different ways in which budgets can be defined – either in a static manner, where we define a monthly budget, or a monthly percentage increase. There are also ways to create dynamic budgets. The ML-empowered service can learn from previous spending and estimate cost trends for the next months. This is a good method to reduce human effort and still be in a position to leverage cost guardrails. The following AWS screenshot shows a budget definition for 12 months. The **Auto-fill budget amounts** feature prepopulates the last 11 months based on the initial budget figure and the monthly percentage increase.

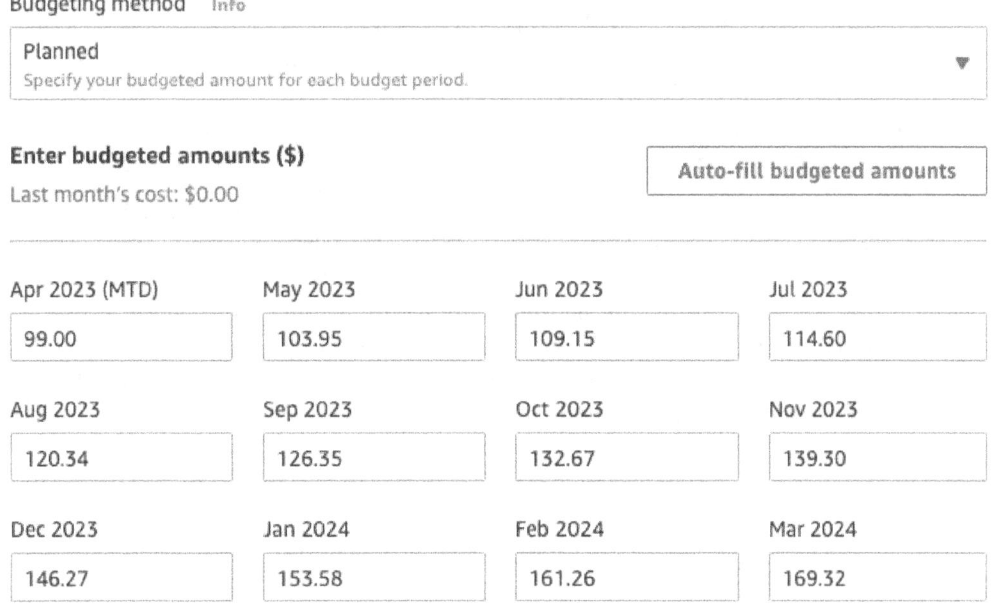

Figure 4.2 – AWS example – budget definition (source: AWS console)

The budget can then be used to configure triggered alerts if we are either hitting a certain threshold or if the trend indicates that we will be above the expected amount at the end of a defined period. These alerts help uncover unexpected costs before we receive the next bill.

- **Architecting for cost efficiency**: When we use cost management and forecast tools, we can establish cost transparency. This enables us to include financial aspects in our architecture decisions. For example, we might shift toward a serverless architecture and move to smaller instances for our containers because horizontal scaling has more cost savings potential. Being able to make informed decisions will also help us plan for the right guardrails that we can utilize during later stages in the SDLC.

Implement, test, and deploy

These are measurements we can take that help us during the *deploy* phase. The first one is part of the *implement and test* phase, and the others are part of the deployment:

- **Data life cycles**: We can establish data life cycles in our application code. Examples are different storage tiers that the data will reside in during its lifetime. For operational data, we can define that the data needs to be in the hot storage tier for 3 months, then it gets moved to an infrequent access tier, and then it goes to an archive for another 6 months. For regulated workloads, such as PCI-relevant applications, we can make sure that the data is only deleted after 7 months. By establishing predefined life cycles, we can reduce the cost and also establish standardization across the organization.

- **Preventive guardrails**: The first deployment-related measurement in this group is preventive or proactive guardrails. We can limit the size of instances we allow in development environments. Guardrails will ensure that instances above a certain size cannot be deployed. It is important to communicate those restrictions so that they are understood and do not cause frustrations amongst the development teams.

  Another use case for cost-related deployment guardrails is denying the creation of high-cost services in workload accounts because they are already established in shared accounts and can be consumed from there. Preventive guardrails can be established via AWS Service Control Policies, Azure Policy, GCP Organization Policy Service, or **Open Policy Agent** (**OPA**) policies. We also need to review access controls to ensure that only authorized individuals are able to deploy to production. This will help accidental or unauthorized spending. We also looked into the benefits of guardrails and non-cost-related guardrails in *Chapter 3*.

- **Organization setup**: Setting up an organizational structure for your cloud environments can also help with cost control and breakdown. This feature is offered in different ways depending on the CSP. In AWS, it is called AWS Organizations, Microsoft calls it Azure Management Groups, and within GCP, it is called Google Cloud Resource Manager.

  We can apply preventive guardrails at an **organizational unit** (**OU**) level. In that case, none of the accounts under our "development" OU can deploy super large instances. We can also use the OU structure for a cost breakdown, for instance, if we have all shared services, such as application logging or a data lake, under a shared services OU.

- **Automated cost estimate**: Some deployment tools provide cost estimates for the stack that will be deployed. HCP Terraform provides this feature, and there are also some open source tools that we can embed in our CI/CD pipelines. The developer can review the estimated cost before proceeding with the deployment. This helps to catch little errors such as picking the wrong instance type, but those errors can have a big cost impact.

Maintain and improve

We will now explore the measures we need to take during the *maintain and improve* phase. Most importantly, we need to establish the right processes, ownership, and accountability to utilize the tooling. There is no point in having nice dashboards and automated recommendations if no one is looking at them, or not taking any action. With the insights and learnings we gain during this phase, we can establish a feedback loop that will help us improve our FinOps practices going forward:

- **Detective guardrails**: Detective guardrails allow the deployment, but a non-compliant rule will be flagged on a dashboard and can trigger a notification. We could do this for very large instances in our development OU. That way, we are not blocking the team from deployment but can still provide visibility of this finding. It is also a common practice to test guardrails first in detective mode before turning them into preventive guardrails.

- **Cost explorer and usage reports**: AWS Cost Explorer, Azure Cost Management, and GCP Cost Management have many features in common that will help us gain cost insight. All three offerings provide a cost breakdown by service, cloud resource, project, account, or resource group. Customizable cost reports and dashboards help visualize spending patterns and identify cost drivers. The following screenshot from the AWS console shows a cost and usage report. We can see a breakdown based on services, and we can modify the timeframe granularity.

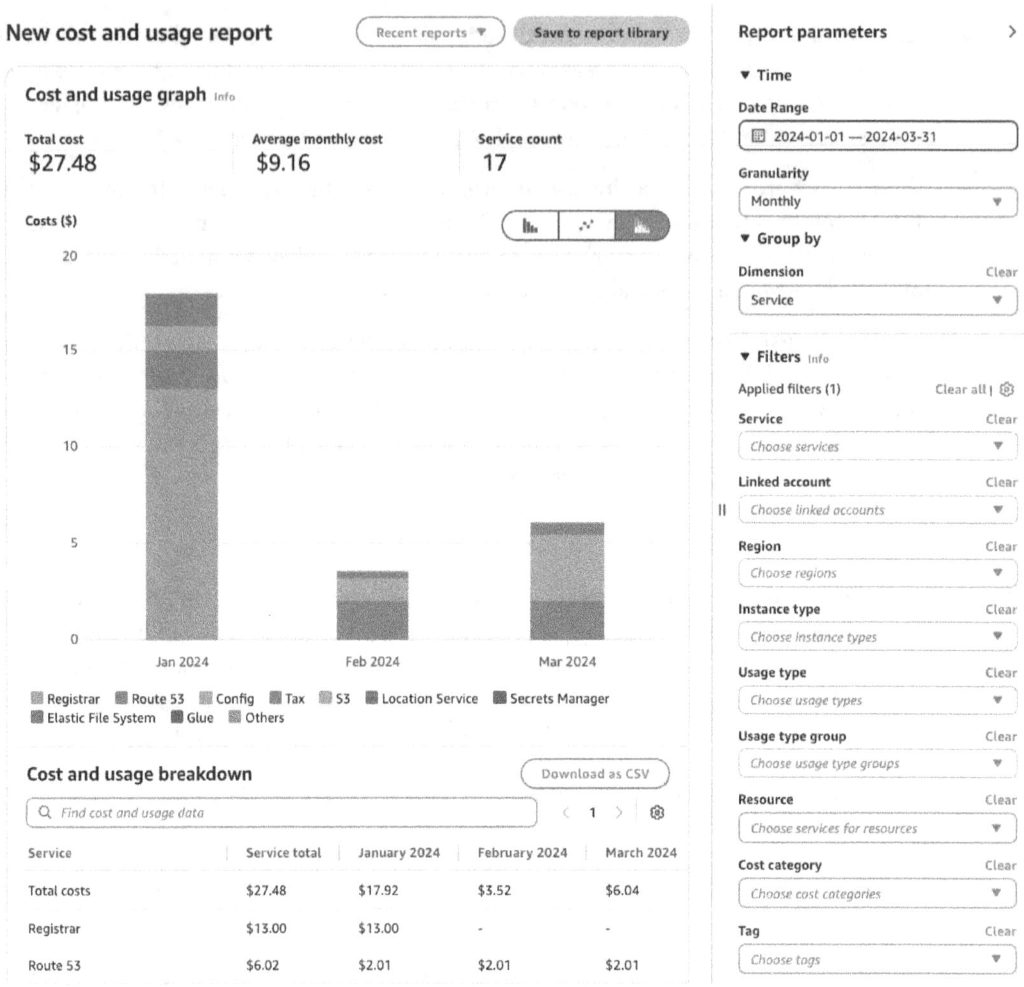

Figure 4.3 – AWS example – cost and usage report (source: AWS console)

- **Advisory tools**: These tools provide insight into where we can reduce our spending. AWS Trusted Advisor gives insights into various improvement areas, for example, underutilized instances. Azure Advisor takes a similar approach and also provides cost recommendations, for instance, purchasing Azure Reservations. GCP has a similar offering with the Google Cloud Recommender, and cost-related recommendations include deleting unused disks. Those insights will help to get an initial overview of where we have areas for improvement.

- **Rightsizing recommendations**: Rightsizing recommendations help us to adjust the sizing of our workloads. This will help to reduce the costs and use the funds gained otherwise. AWS has rightsizing recommendations and the Compute Optimizer service to help with that. This feature is partly included in GCP Cloud Recommender and Azure Advisor, which we already discussed. GCP and Azure also have Rightsizing Recommendations as part of the Azure Cost Management and Billing Services and Google Cloud Active Assist. It is critical to test the rightsizing first in the lower environments before rushing into a production change to avoid sizing issues.

- **Cost anomaly detection**: These services help us identify unusual traffic spikes and unusual spending patterns. We can trigger alerts to get notified immediately and investigate. The reason for an unusual pattern could be an error in a deployment. The AWS offering is called AWS Cost Anomaly Detection, Azure and GCP have this feature as part of the Azure Cost Management and Billing and Google Cloud Cost Management service, respectively.

- **Committed spend**: Committed spending plans are another way to reduce our cloud bill. Committed spending can be applied to various resource types, such as instances (virtual machines), containers, or FaaS. Plans can have a one-, two-, or three-year time span. It is recommended to go with a one-year plan since computing technology always evolves. In a year, we can then get a plan for a newer instance generation that is more powerful and can handle more load. There are several strategies we might want to apply to our savings plan:

  - First of all, if we have a decentralized governance model, then the business units or product portfolios will be responsible for setting up their plans. They are the ones who know their applications the best, but also the business target and expected growth.

  - The second strategic aspect is that we might want to have more than one savings plan. That way, we can stagger them and adjust them more frequently. One savings plan could start in January and the other one in July. This gives us the flexibility to update twice every year.

The following GCP screenshot shows the **committed use discounts** (**CUDs**). It shows us the potential cost savings when we opt for a general-purpose memory instance and a Cloud SQL Database VM.

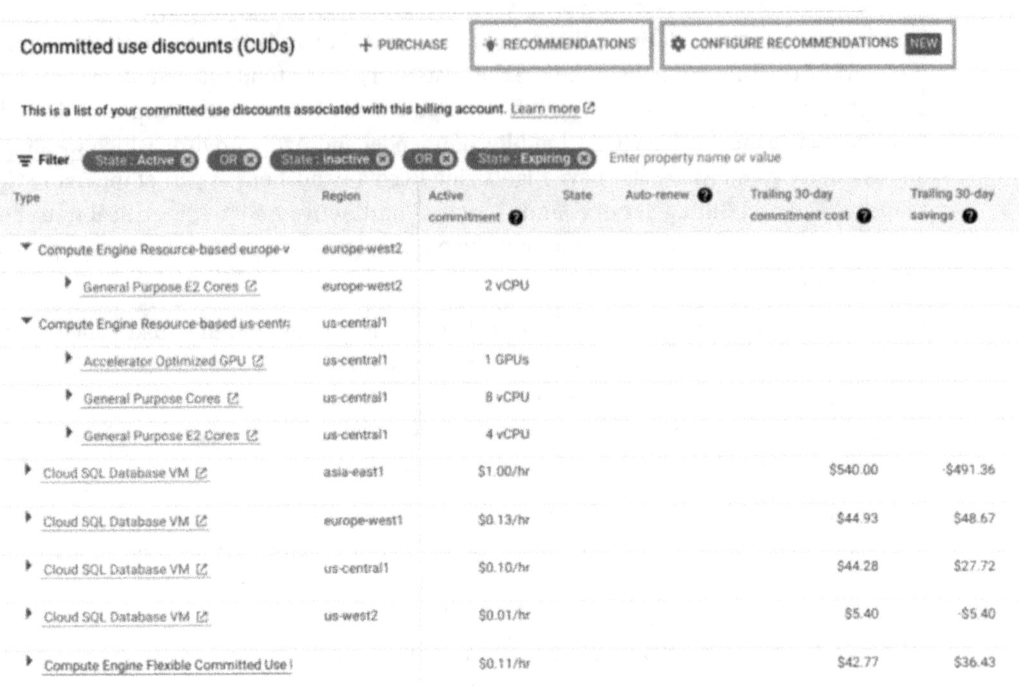

Type	Region	Active commitment	State	Auto-renew	Trailing 30-day commitment cost	Trailing 30-day savings
▼ Compute Engine Resource-based europe-v	europe-west2					
▶ General Purpose E2 Cores	europe-west2	2 vCPU				
▼ Compute Engine Resource-based us-centr:	us-central1					
▶ Accelerator Optimized GPU	us-central1	1 GPUs				
▶ General Purpose Cores	us-central1	8 vCPU				
▶ General Purpose E2 Cores	us-central1	4 vCPU				
▶ Cloud SQL Database VM	asia-east1	$1.00/hr			$540.00	-$491.36
▶ Cloud SQL Database VM	europe-west1	$0.13/hr			$44.93	$48.67
▶ Cloud SQL Database VM	us-central1	$0.10/hr			$44.28	$27.72
▶ Cloud SQL Database VM	us-west2	$0.01/hr			$5.40	-$5.40
▶ Compute Engine Flexible Committed Use		$0.11/hr			$42.77	$36.43

Figure 4.4 – GCP example – Committed use discounts (source: https://cloud.google.com/static/billing/docs/images/cud-dashboard.png?dcb_=0.5258774275081315)

As we can see, there is a lot to digest if we want to leverage all the tooling our CSPs give us. Before moving on to the next section, we want to reiterate a couple of callouts:

- We always test sizing-related changes in lower environments before a production change
- Tools are great, but we need ownership and accountability to ensure actions are being taken
- We need to understand what our applications are doing to make informed trade-off decisions.

Now, we move on to cloud cost, which is not obvious and might be overlooked when we define our cloud strategy or design.

Ignoring non-obvious CSP cost

"The real cost of a four-dollar-a-day coffee habit over 20 years is $51,833.79. That's the power of the Compound Effect," says Darren Hardy, author of *The Compound Effect*.

Those four dollars might not include a service tax and then the compound effect is even higher. Where are we going with this? Cost models in the cloud are far more complex than a cup of coffee. There is a fair chance that we have had coffee cost surprises in the past, but there is a nearly 100% chance that we have had some sort of cost eye-openers in the cloud, either because we left an instance running after a demo or because there were some cost aspects we didn't consider.

Different abstraction levels, such as IaaS, PaaS, or fully managed services, have different price components. So do database and storage solutions, API offerings, or logging and monitoring solutions. The more cloud resource types we use, the more complex the cost landscape becomes. That is even more so the case when we have a hybrid cloud landscape, especially if we use several CSPs for a poly-cloud or multi-cloud strategy. These complex scenarios increase the likeliness of unexpected costs, especially if we do not create cost estimates during the design and do not validate the real cost against the planned cost. The problem is that the longer we wait to uncover unexpected costs, the more we will evolve our architecture, but potentially toward a direction we might regret when we see the cost impacts. The longer we wait, the harder it will be to remediate. Therefore, we want to uncover some common mistakes that lead to this anti-pattern. Let's start with the first one.

Common anti-patterns

Some of the ongoing CSP costs are not obvious and so can unnecessarily increase our bill if we do not address that in our architecture. We will talk about two common anti-patterns next.

Ignoring data transfer cost

Ingesting data into our cloud typically does not result in data transfer fees because CSPs want to attract customers to bring more applications into their cloud. However, this is different for other transfer cost types, and some have the potential to be underestimated or even overlooked. We will go through common categories that can cause surprises. The prices themselves keep changing, so we will look into areas that need to be considered rather than particular prices:

- **Egress transfer fees**: These are fees that occur when we export data from our CSP to either the internet, another cloud platform, or our data center. In a previous engagement, a cloud consultancy was helping with a large-scale data lake solution. The solution required ongoing data exports to a data analytics platform that had not been migrated to the cloud yet and was still running on-premises. The consultancy provided a cost forecast. The CSP called out that they could not see the egress data transfer cost in the cost estimate. Somehow, that fact got missed. Design decisions were based on the fact that egress data fees were not factored into the ongoing cost. It turned out that the egress fees would have been several hundred thousand USD per year. This resulted in a big dispute. The consultancy had to rectify things at their own expense and risk, and they had to compensate parts of the already occurred egress data fees.

  This scenario also highlights that a multi-cloud DR (disaster recovery) strategy is a very expensive exercise. When we want to recover in a different cloud platform, we need to make sure that the data is continuously replicated. This gets often forgotten when risk and business continuity teams want to minimize the risk of a CSP going into receivership. A possible outcome is a multi-cloud cost disaster, which is hard to recover from. It is also worthwhile noting that different regions have different prices. For example, exporting data from the US region to the public internet might be cheaper compared to exporting data from an Asian or South American region to the internet.

- **Transfer fees between regions and cross-region architecture impacts**: Data transfer between regions involves transfer fees. Similar to the preceding example, the price depends on the origin and destination regions. Cross-region replications are common when we have ambitious DR goals. A complete region outage can happen, but it is very unlikely. A cross-region DR strategy can protect us from that risk. Data transfer fees within the same continent are usually lower compared to cross-continent data replications.

- **Data transfer fees within the same region (across AZs)**: Several cloud native services also charge data transfer fees within a region. These fees are lower compared to cross-region and egress transfer fees. AWS charges an intra-region data transfer fee if several EC2 instances (virtual machines) are deployed across several AZs and need to transfer data between each other. This was at least the case when this book was written, and it could change at any time. Azure has dropped the intra-region transfer fee for virtual machines and GCP does generally not charge this fee. We have already pointed out that these things can change quickly. Therefore, it is important to use our CSP's cost calculator and try several combinations of data transfer volumes.

Not considering long-term storage costs

When we rush deadlines or do not have predefined service catalog items we can use, it is just too easy to forget about the cost aspects of a solution. We focus on technical details to solve the immediate problem that is required for a launch or a proof of value outcome. We will now look into common pitfalls that will drive up the CSP bill:

- **Data life cycle**: A common error is forgetting to configure a data life cycle for blob storage or shared drives. In that scenario, the accumulated data increases continuously. Because blob storage is fairly cheap, it can take a while until we realize the continuously increasing cost. The price for data hosted in databases, fully managed logging services, or disk volumes is higher, and the bill shock might be more obvious. The following diagram illustrates the possible transitions for AWS S3, which is a blob storage service. We can see how the *Standard* tier can transition into cheaper tiers. The cheapest one is called *S3 Glacier Deep Archive* and requires data retrieval time.

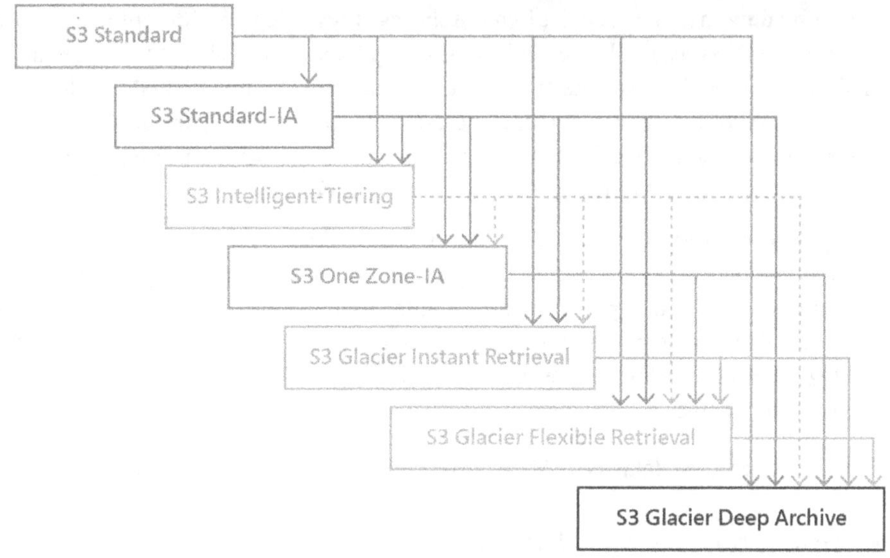

Figure 4.5 – AWS example – data life cycle transitions for blob storage
(source: https://docs.aws.amazon.com/AmazonS3/latest/userguide/
lifecycle-transition-general-considerations.html)

- **Disk back-ups and unattached volumes**: During a previous project, we were tasked with establishing a self-healing mechanism for a **data warehouse** (**DWH**) solution. Parts of the DWH landscape were hosted on virtual instances.

That itself is already an anti-pattern, but it was an old third-party product that had never been architected for the cloud by the vendor. We were addressing the self-healing scenario of addressing instance failures and also disk volume failures. For that purpose, we automated a combination of hourly snapshots (i.e., incremental backups) and full backups for all three volumes for an instance in a test environment. All of a sudden, priorities changed, and we had to help out for a couple of days in a different problem space. Because we were trying to achieve quick DR results, we did not implement a backup data life cycle during our testing. By the time we got back to focus on the auto-healing solution, there were already hundreds of backups that had been taken.

The next CSP bill was significantly higher. The first reaction of the product owner was that virtual high-volume disks were much too expensive. They are pricier than slower ones. But the real problem was that there was no data life cycle in place. This gap can bite very quickly, and in that case, it did.

- **Standby databases or read replica databases**: These are two different use cases. Standby **databases (DBs)**, also called secondary DBs, help improve availability. If the primary database fails, the standby DB can take over the data load after an automated DNS fail-over from the primary DB to the secondary DB. If the data volume of the primary database increases, the secondary or read replica database size will increase, too. This means we pay more for storage for several databases, which we need to factor into our costs.

- **Logging**: It is rare to see a clear logging strategy that has been rigorously implemented. Sometimes, we see production environments that even log the "info" log level. This produces a lot of log volume, and we need to pay the price for it. If this anti-pattern is paired with a missing data life cycle, then it becomes even worse. We need to have a clear understanding of what needs to be logged, where the log files need to be shipped to, and how long we need the log files in hot versus infrequent or cold storage.

Now that we have covered data-related cost issues, we will look into a couple of other cost factors.

Other non-obvious cost factors

Data transfer cost and long-term storage cost are very common gotchas, but there are also others, and we will analyze them now.

Idle or overprovisioned resources

Idle resources can occur when we create a proof of concept and forget to clean up afterward. They can also be the consequence of a manual scale-up event, for example, for a product launch, a stress test, or a sales event like that on Black Friday. Then, the team forgets to scale down once the event has passed, and the next monthly bill will be a harsh reminder to scale back again. The main CSPs offer rightsizing recommendations. These are visible in the console, as we can see in the next GCP screenshot. They also provide API support, and we can implement automated alerts if a rightsizing recommendation is detected. We could also automate the actual rightsizing, but this would require upfront testing prior to a workload adjustment in production.

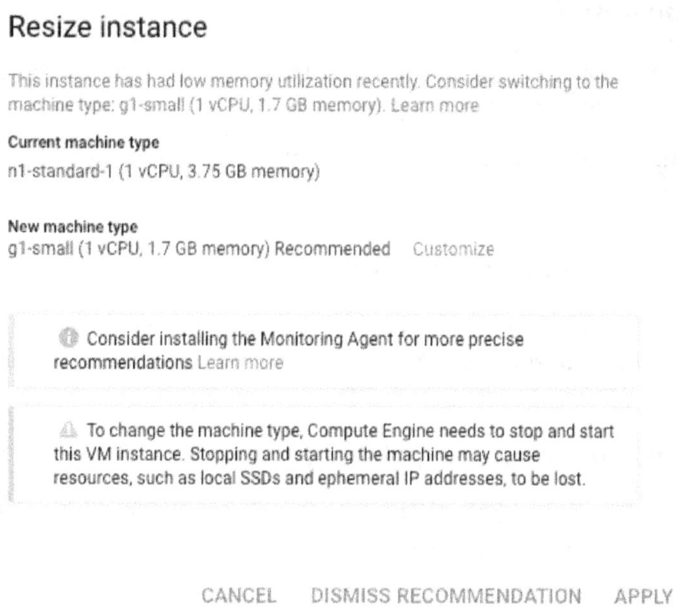

Resize instance

This instance has had low memory utilization recently. Consider switching to the machine type: g1-small (1 vCPU, 1.7 GB memory). Learn more

Current machine type

n1-standard-1 (1 vCPU, 3.75 GB memory)

New machine type

g1-small (1 vCPU, 1.7 GB memory) Recommended   Customize

> Consider installing the Monitoring Agent for more precise recommendations Learn more

> To change the machine type, Compute Engine needs to stop and start this VM instance. Stopping and starting the machine may cause resources, such as local SSDs and ephemeral IP addresses, to be lost.

CANCEL   DISMISS RECOMMENDATION   APPLY

Figure 4.6 – GCP example – rightsizing recommendation (source: https://cloud.google.com/compute/docs/instances/apply-machine-type-recommendations-for-instances)

Compliance tools

Compliance is required for regulated industries, and it is not trivial. Any services that support compliance automation come with a price. If not all our workloads are regulated, then it makes sense to differentiate where and when to use compliance tools.

If we use compliance tools from a vendor and also from our CSP, we need to make sure that we are not doubling up too much. Often, we cannot avoid some degree of overlap, because we must avoid gaps.

Machine learning services

Machine learning (ML) services require a lot of CPU power to train models. Rightsizing and continuous utilization verification are important here. For example, we need to find the right balance between the amount of training data we require versus the benefit of a higher accuracy level in our learning model. Otherwise, a cost surprise is nearly guaranteed.

Public IPv4 addresses

IPv4 addresses are limited, so the main CSPs started charging for public IPv4 addresses assigned to virtual machines. The charge is minimal, but we need to consider it for large-scale deployments.

After stepping through the most commonly overlooked cost aspects, we will now explore what the consequences are.

Impacts of missing non-obvious cost

Now that we have a good understanding of the cost factors we need to consider, we will explore the consequences of not addressing them. Here is a spoiler alert: The impacts go beyond an increased CSP bill.

The cross-region inconsistency price tag

An aspect that is often overlooked is that there is not necessarily a feature parity between regions. A service might not exist in the secondary region, or the service does exist but only has a subset of features.

I encountered that during a previous consultant engagement when the serverless DB offering existed in both regions, but one region was lacking several features, including an out-of-the-box point-in-time recovery. Therefore, the second region required a different design, different IaC, and different DR testing scenarios. This additional design, build, and operational effort is not visible on the cloud bill. However, our teams will need to dedicate more time and pay great attention to detail, and the operations risk increases.

Architectural multi-region DR strategy impacts

If we have not considered multi-region data transfer fees, we will realize that the cost of our multi-region DR strategy significantly exceeds the budget. This will depend on the risk/cost trade-off decision we need to make. If we decide to rectify the solution and move to a single-region DR solution, then we need to adjust our architecture and implementation and migrate the existing backups to the primary region.

Architectural multi-cloud strategy impacts

If we have a multi-cloud strategy where we need to continuously transfer data between CSPs, the data transfer fees will be shocking. If we haven't considered this in our CSP selection process, then we have made an architecture decision that is difficult to revert, especially if we have progressed in our cloud adoption for a significant amount of time.

In this case, we need to make a trade-off decision between long-term cost savings, reducing operational complexity, and increased migration and testing efforts. Another critical point to consider is the architectural benefits we could gain.

A common consequence of multi-cloud adoptions is that only the common denominator is used across clouds to make sure we have a consistent approach. For example, everything needs to be on a virtual machine or a container. Therefore, we cannot utilize the full cloud native potential, such as managed API gateways or DBs. This increases the operational complexity. By unwinding a multi-cloud strategy, we can leverage those benefits.

Increased cloud runtime cost

This is the most obvious impact. The cost will be higher than we budgeted for. If we don't adjust our architecture, this will have a long-term impact that will only get worse when we move more applications to the cloud or when the applications become more popular and create more traffic.

Other impacts

If we have many idle resources, such as disk volumes that are not attached to a virtual machine, it will be difficult to identify the right resources during an incident. The idle resources will still be relevant for an external audit and will trigger additional administrative effort. If we have idle virtual machines running, this will also unnecessarily increase the carbon footprint impacting potential sustainability goals.

Those are the key impacts, and we definitely want to avoid them if the business benefits do not match or exceed the additional cost. Some signs should trigger us to investigate further, and we will look into them next.

Indicators

There are several indicators for this anti-pattern. We will go through them now and start with the most obvious one:

- **Bill shock**: We received our CSP bill, and we can see that the cost trend is steeper than expected or that there is a big spike that does not match the cost trend of the previous months.

- **Lack of insight**: Earlier in this chapter, we discussed FinOps tooling. If we are missing out on mechanisms like budgets, alerts, and rightsizing recommendations, then there is probably some hidden cost that we are not aware of. Enabling those features will help us gain clarity.

- **Lack of ownership and accountability**: If product teams are not motivated to optimize value generation, they will not be motivated to identify unexpected costs and consider them in architecture decisions.

- **No committed spending plan or spot instances**: If we do not have a committed spending plan such as the AWS Savings Plan, Azure Reservations, or GCP committed use contracts, we pay the full price for compute power, fpr example, instances, containers, and FaaS. If we have workloads that can have outages, such as batch job operations, or instances in a lower environment, then we need to consider leveraging AWS spot instances, Azure Spot Virtual Machines, or GCP Preemptible VMs. Both those measures should be combined and if neither of them exists, we are overspending, even though it is not visible in our cloud bill.

- **Lack of strategy assessment**: If we have a multi-cloud or multi-region strategy and the business value never got reassessed, then there is a chance that we lack current insights.

- **Untracked trial services**: CSPs and SaaS providers offer free trials. If we do not track the time or free-tier usage, we will have to pay extra after the limits are reached.

- **No deployment cost forecast**: Some deployment tools provide a cost forecast before the deployment is performed. Those estimates might not be 100% accurate because the data transfers and volumes will vary, but they give valuable insight if we get something fundamentally wrong. If we accidentally deploy a too-large instance, we can see the unexpected additional cost.

Remediations

Let's have a look now at how we can get to a target state that gets us into good shape:

- **Upfront cost calculations**: When we need to architect a new solution, we create a solution diagram that shows all the components that trigger cost. This overview will show what cloud services we need to consider. We will need non-functional requirements such as volume metrics, number of requests, data growth, RTOs, and RPOs to come up with solid estimates.

  A data flow diagram can also help to identify the data transfer fees. The same applies when we want to enhance existing architecture. If the current state is already deployed and launched, then we can work out the actual cost from the CSP bill. We can then compare it with the target state to identify how our costs will change.

- **Establish FinOps tooling**: We discussed this in the previous section, *Not leveraging CSP FinOps services*, so we will keep it short here. FinOps tooling helps us establish good cost insight and uncover non-obvious costs. Now that we understand data transfer, storage, and other cost gotchas, we know what to look out for.

- **Well-architected reviews**: Once a solution's design has matured, we can perform a well-architected review. The well-architected framework from our CSP will guide us to ask the right questions and validate our design. We could also involve a consultancy to get an independent opinion. We can do the same for workloads that are already deployed. In that case, we can also use previously discussed advisory tooling to help us validate the current state.

- **Service catalog**: A service catalog will help us achieve a good self-service experience with a repeatable outcome. This can also help us with our cost approach. Storage service catalog items can have a built-in data life cycle. The user only needs to select which standardized life cycle they need. That way, we can ensure that a life cycle is always in place.

- **Lack of guardrails**: Preventive guardrails can prevent certain cost impacts, including the deployment of really large instances to a development environment. Another preventive guardrail could be that users can only deploy product catalog items or endorsed cloud services. Detective guardrails can notify us if a guardrail is not compliant.

- **Encryption keys**: Customer-managed keys come with an additional cost for the actual key storage or versioning and also for each operation, including key creation, encryption, and decryption. Some regulatory frameworks require customer-managed keys, and some mandate even a dedicated key store solution. This means the physical storage is dedicated to one cloud customer. Dedicated services come with an additional price tag and that includes AWS CloudHSM (**HSM** stands for **hardware security module**), Azure Dedicated HSM, and Google Cloud HSM.

- **Other architecture considerations**: If we use a **content distribution network** (**CDN**), we need to pay an additional fee. However, it will provide additional protection at the edge. Because data is cached at the edge, not every request needs to fetch data from our backend systems. Therefore, depending on our architecture, it can reduce the data transfer fees for our backend components, but the overall cost will still be higher compared to not using a CDN.

After gaining a solid understanding of unexpected costs and how to spot and remediate them, we will explore how to focus on driving business value.

Focusing on cost savings over driving value

"It's not whether you're right or wrong that's important, but how much money you make when you're right and how much you lose when you're wrong," is a quote by George Soros, one of the most successful global investors.

Making strategic cloud decisions is different from trading. However, we must make the right decisions to optimize our cloud value. Instead of buying and selling, we need to put the right capabilities in place and move on from them when the time comes. This will help us increase our ROI. To prepare for that, we must evolve our architecture, ways of working, and cultural approach while ensuring our teams have access to training during this continuous transformation journey. These are the critical internal and external factors we need to consider when driving value for our cloud native stack:

- **Changing business requirements and competitive advantage**: Requirements can change because our business evolves, the market we operate advances, or we try to branch out into new market segments. Either way, we want to release new features quickly. Therefore, we must innovate faster, experiment, and maximize the output.

- **Technology advances**: We previously discussed Wardley Mapping. Cloud services, such as FaaS, have become commodities. To support business agility, we must avoid undifferentiated heavy lifting and refresh our technology stack. If we can use fully managed services like FaaS instead of containers or instances, then we do not manage patching, auto-scaling, and the security of the operating system and applications.

- **Compliance and security requirements are changing**: We must protect our customer data, implement more controls, and ensure customer data can be deleted when requested. Therefore, we can rely on low-budget manual solutions because they do not scale. We need to drive automation.

- **Vendor and partner ecosystem**: Reducing software vendor or consultancy fees can result in higher long-term costs. We need to understand how well the third-party roadmap aligns with our organization for SaaS solutions. For consultancies, we need to understand how their strategic approach aligns with our vision. We discussed that in detail in *Chapter 2*.

- **Talent and skill availability**: When we determine what technology or framework we use, we must consider whether we already have the skills in-house or sufficient skilled resources in our job market. Saving five percent on licensing or operational cloud costs can be outweighed by not finding resources or paying a higher consultant rate or salary. The availability of skilled professionals who understand cloud native technologies can influence how effectively we can build and maintain our architecture.

- **Training and collaboration**: We must ensure our teams are well trained in architecting and implementing the cloud native stack in the best possible way for our business. Saving money on training and collaboration will result in technical debt and a considerable price tag.

Optimizing business value is a prominent driver. However, during the early stages of cloud adoption, businesses often focus too much on cost reduction. In this section, we will explore how a cost focus can hold us back in our cloud adoption. Let's look into the common anti-patterns now.

Common anti-patterns

We will now explore two common anti-patterns and the consequences that come with them. We will start with the impacts of focusing solely on cost reduction instead of looking at the holistic picture.

Penny pinching

Going for a bargain can sometimes be tempting; everyone has done it before. The comparison is easy when we get the same product and quality for a reduced price. It becomes more complex when dealing with cloud native solutions and the long-term operational aspects we must consider.

A couple of years ago, I worked with an engineer who ran a cloud hosting business on the side. His target group was small businesses that needed managed applications. The engineer was managing parts of the top half of the shared responsibility model, which is security in the cloud. The customer offering included a standard three-tier web architecture with public and private subnets. The private subnets needed outbound connectivity to the internet for some reason. This was also a security anti-pattern, but we now focus on leveraging business value.

To establish the connectivity from the private subnet to the internet, a **NAT gateway** (**NAT-GW**) solution was required. The engineer compared the prices of the CSPs' fully managed NAT-GW services and the cost of hand-crafting a NAT-GW solution from scratch. A fully managed service comes with additional costs that cover ongoing patching, high availability, security controls, out-of-the-box logging and monitoring integration, and much more. Nevertheless, he decided to go ahead with the hand-crafted solution. That meant he had to manage the ongoing image updates for the virtual machine, the ongoing patching process, the security controls, the logging and monitoring, and so on.

That solution would also result in a lot of additional compliance effort for a regulated solution since they needed proof of things such as least privilege enforcement, log integrity, logging of elevated user access, and much more, even though this was only a small-scale hosting business with only 100 customers.

This approach does not scale if we want to grow our customer base and business value. The lesson learned might take a while until we realize the consequences of building up technical debt. This is also a common consequence of poorly planned cloud migrations where a *lift and shift* migration plan is prioritized over strategic value gain by refactoring an application to leverage all cloud native benefits.

Not investing in continuous improvement

In a previous engagement, I worked for a customer that had to meet several regulatory requirements because they were a financial services organization. Collecting the required evidence manually for an external audit took 3.5 months in one year. This was a full-time effort for one cloud team member assigned to the audit. This time span covered the cloud stack. Other teams were involved in the on-premises workloads.

Screenshots, log file examples, and process descriptions were to be provided for all environments handling credit card information. The cloud team relied mainly on external resources from consultancies. Therefore, the internal staff was reduced to a bare minimum.

We already knew we had to improve our approach for the next year and shift toward automation. We evaluated several SaaS tools that could help improve the security and compliance posture and reduce the audit effort to the bare minimum. If our organization is in good shape, we can provide the external auditor with read-only access to the compliance automation tool. They can then validate that the required controls are in place. This means the overall effort on both sides is reduced, but we can also get ongoing assurance insights that help us continuously improve.

Unfortunately, the company decided not to invest in continuous improvement and allocated the budget to other initiatives. The following external audit was even more challenging. Instead of the previous version of the compliance framework, we had to adhere to a new version, which was more thorough. It increased the overall effort, and we had to hire a contractor for 3.5 months to meet the audit timeline and ensure the under-staffed cloud team was still functioning and could continue maturing the cloud platform.

The key takeaway is that the overall spending for an additional temporary resource to add a couple of band-aids could have been invested into a strategic improvement that would have resulted in a sustainable solution and reduced the long-term effort. Getting things wrong is not unusual, but we need to use what we have learned to improve. Making the same error twice in a row is painful to watch. In hindsight, it felt like watching a car crash in slow motion. Thankfully, no physical harm occurred, but the pain was not forgotten. Let's move on and summarize and quantify the impacts of focusing on cost savings rather than driving value.

Impacts

Focusing on cost saving over driving value has some significant negative long-term impacts, and we will explore them now:

- **Missed business opportunities**: If we do not drive the improvement of our value chain, we will miss out on customer experience improvements that can differentiate us from the competition. If we do not continuously improve our cloud native stack, we will increase our tech debt, and the time to market for current features will decrease. This will be a disadvantage if we want to innovate, react to market changes, or comply with regulatory requirements.

- **Increased operational complexity**: Without continuous improvement, we will miss out on fully leveraging the cloud potential. Managed services are being innovated and improved at a much quicker pace compared to what we could achieve ourselves. If we do not refresh our architecture, it will be out of date soon. These operational benefits of managed services include built-in observability and resilience. The avoidable increased operational complexity will burden our teams since the operational effort will be unnecessarily high.

- **Decreased productivity**: Penny-pinching can negatively impact a team's morale. The result will be less engagement, motivation, and collaboration. Therefore, productivity will be lower than it could be when we aim for value creation.

- **Compromised security and compliance**: Solely focusing on cost reduction can lead to underinvestment in security tools, monitoring, and compliance services. This increases the risk of security breaches, data loss, and non-compliance with regulations, which can have significant impacts. Not enabling services such as network firewalls, intrusion detection systems, or vulnerability scanning will expose our applications to vulnerabilities and result in non-compliance with regulatory frameworks like PCI-DSS.

- **Reduced user experience**: Cost-cutting measures can negatively impact service reliability and availability, leading to dissatisfied customers and potential churn. Reducing redundancy or backup frequencies to save costs might result in service outages or data loss, impacting reliability and customer experience.

- **Loss of revenue and growth potential**: Minimizing cloud spending can impact our architecture and restrict our ability to scale quickly for demand peaks. This can limit our ability to leverage ad hoc market opportunities, such as trading spikes due to business news or temporary retail peaks like on Black Friday.

Focusing on cost optimization has significant impacts and can damage our business and reputation in the long term. But how can we realize we are on the wrong path and must react? We will look into this next.

Problem indicators

It is not always easy to realize whether we are already en route for this anti-pattern, and therefore, we will explore some of the early signs:

- **Service downgrades and performance issues**: Growing complaints about slow application performance, higher latency, or frequent service outages can indicate a focus on cost reduction. Performance degradation due to under-provisioned resources, such as a lack of auto-scaling or edge computing, indicates that cost is prioritized over business outcomes.

- **Reducing security controls**: Reducing investment in cloud security tools, services, or personnel or a noticeable decline in security monitoring and compliance activities are signs of cost reaction. These measures can increase the risk of data breaches and compliance failures, demonstrating a dangerous trade-off between cost savings and essential security controls.

- **Lack of standardization**: Immature standardizations include a lack of coding standards, standardized CI/CD pipelines, container-based images, service catalog offerings, and others. The consequence is increased operational complexity and a slower time to market, which will decrease value creation.

- **Lack of chargeback and accountability**: Without a chargeback model, we do not have clear responsibilities. Therefore, the product teams will not drive the ROI. In that case, we will likely have a centralized cost-focused governance approach. An immature operating model also falls under this category.

What does good look like, and how do we get there?

We need to tackle the following problem spaces to achieve a valuable outcome. If we tackle these challenges in time and sufficiently, they become enabling areas:

- **Ownership and accountability**: Clear demarcation of responsibilities is required. The cloud platform team might be responsible for establishing all network infrastructure and managing the service catalog. The product team will be responsible for the application, data, and ongoing optimizations. This includes right-sizing compute instances and deciding which backup and data life cycle plans must be used to meet all requirements and avoid underutilization. Establishing a chargeback model will help drive economic behavior. This brings us to the next point.

- **Committed spend and spot virtual machines**: Ownership and accountability will also trigger cost-saving thinking within product teams because cloud costs saved can be spent on innovation. If the teams understand their responsibility, they will be interested in leveraging cost-commit plans to leverage discounts. It will also trigger spot instances for test environments or batch jobs that can afford interruptions. Spot virtual machines are cheaper to run compared to on-demand instances.

- **Taking a long-term delivery view**: Projects have a short-term view because they only plan for the project's time span. Afterward, the project will be moved to BAU status, and an operations team will operate it. However, the solution might not necessarily improve over time. This results in insufficient legacy architectures that do not leverage the latest cloud native features. Moving to a product team approach brings operational responsibility closer to the product team. The product team will be very interested in reducing the operational complexity and continuously improving the application.

- **Technical debt register**: It will help us keep track of any tactical decisions we make. This could be an old Java runtime that we are using or a DB engine that is not our strategic choice. If we later create a new application container image with a newer runtime, we can remediate the technical debt because we will have clear visibility.

- **Data insights**: Rather than just focusing on the total cloud cost, we get a better picture when we have data points and can build correlations. That way, we can find out how much the online sales number increases because we can release more frequently, as we invested more into our CI/CD pipeline maturity.

- **Partner ecosystem**: Having a partner strategy in place is a good starting point, but we also need to make sure we build a good relationship. Partners such as CSPs, SaaS vendors, or consultancies are experts in the field, and they can provide valuable advice on what we can improve or where we can co-innovate to create new business opportunities.

- **Investing in long-term gains**: A short-sighted view of expenses will result in missed strategic opportunities. If we assess the value of mature CI/CD pipelines that provide repeatable, secure, and reliable outcomes, we can reduce our time to market. Examples include automated performance, reliability, or regression tests.

- **Temporary environments and auto-destroy**: Establishing sandpits where developers can experiment with new cloud services or the CI/CD toolchain will contribute to education. Sandpits bring the risk of a cost surprise because, typically, not all resources get destroyed after they are no longer needed. We can implement an auto-destroy mechanism to make sure resources can be removed at certain time intervals, for example, every weekend. We can do this with cloud native CI/CD tooling, SaaS solutions, or open source solutions such as AWS Nuke. The implementation is an upfront investment, but it will eventually pay off. The same applies to temporary environments that can be shut down outside business hours.

We explored a lot in this chapter and will now summarize what we learned so that we can digest the information quickly.

Summary

We started with tagging, our daily bread and butter, to achieve an accurate cost breakdown. We need clear tagging standards and enforcement to establish a functioning chargeback model. We explored cloud native FinOps services such as cost explorers, budgets, alerts, and cost anomaly detections. Those are valuable features for gaining early insight and cost alerts rather than passively waiting for the next cloud bill shock. We explored data transfer fees and how they can occur within our cloud platform and for hybrid or multi-cloud traffic. We then closed by exploring business value creation instead of taking a short-term cost minimization stance. Only a long-term perspective can help us maximize the business value we can achieve with our cloud native stack.

Now, we are ready to tackle the next challenge, which is security and compliance goals.

Get This Book's PDF Version and Exclusive Extras

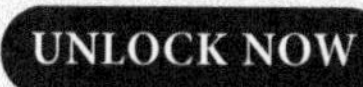

Scan the QR code (or go to `packtpub.com/unlock`). Search for this book by name, confirm the edition, and then follow the steps on the page.

Note: Keep your invoice handly. Purchase made directly from packt don't require one.

5

Delivering Rapidly and Continuously Without Compromising Security

So far, we have looked at the organizational changes required for cloud native development. In this chapter, we will start to look at the cultural and development practices that are required for a shift to cloud native. When shifting to cloud native software development, we're sold the dream of rapid delivery and secure systems. However, this can only be achieved in practice with corresponding organizational and cultural change. Let's explore how common anti-patterns in our software delivery life cycle can interrupt our journey to becoming a high-performing cloud native organization.

In this chapter, we're going to cover the following main topics:

- Underestimating the cultural impact
- Frequent change to meet business needs
- Guardrails
- Shifting left
- Self-sufficient teams

Underestimating the cultural impact

Delivering cloud native projects rapidly and securely is primarily a cultural change. The technical and business process changes required to excel at cloud native delivery support cultural changes. We need to align the mentality of the team working on the project toward shared ownership of outcomes, breaking down the silos that may be present in the existing delivery process. The team that produces a change or feature should be responsible for its delivery into the production environment. This shift is the most fundamental aspect of delivering rapidly. In this section, we will start by reviewing a typical deployment process that we see often in clients who are just beginning their cloud native journey.

The siloed model – a long road to production

Let's examine a well-intentioned yet siloed delivery process that is usually the artifact of taking an on-premises approach to releases and applying it to cloud native delivery.

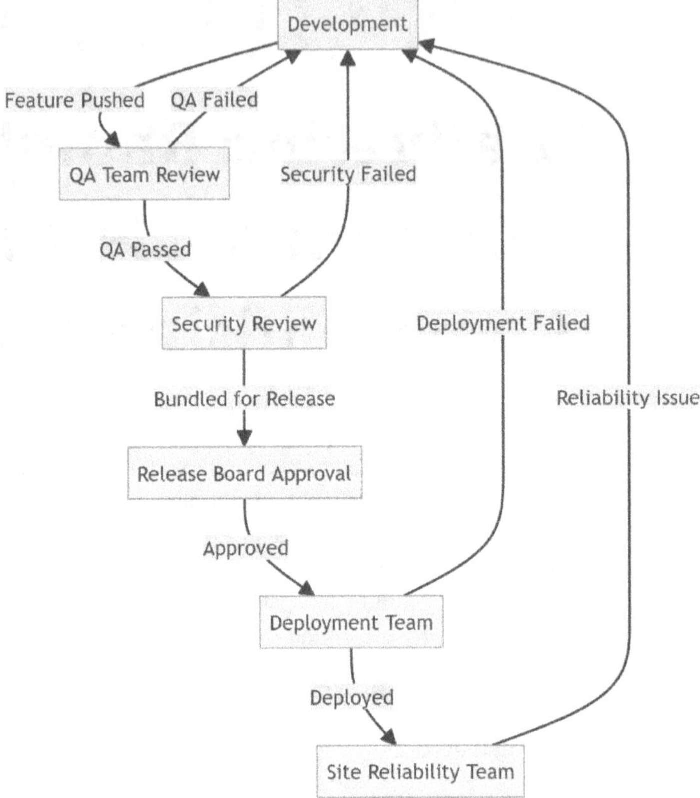

Figure 5.1 – A typical siloed release process – many touchpoints with little end-to-end ownership

This model works when releases are large, cumbersome processes that take significant effort to deploy, and the consequences of pushing a bad change are complex to recover from. We might use this model when deploying to a fleet of on-premises customer servers of varying capacity and capability. In the cloud, these constraints do not exist. We can make rapid changes with quick remediation if something goes wrong; a single, unified, homogenous production environment simplifies deployment and remediation.

Under this model, we heavily scrutinize all code before it reaches our production environment. However, its rigidity is also its downfall. When something inevitably goes wrong in one of these stages, the process, more commonly, is that the developer, who has already begun working on the next feature, must drop what they're doing to create a fix applied at the level of review reached. It's unlikely that this last-minute change will go through the review process as the process cannot afford to start over.

DORA – measuring the road

"If you can't measure it, you cannot improve it." We understand that the siloed model is limiting when applied to cloud native software, but as we change our delivery process, how do we know that our changes are shifting our business in the right direction?

Earlier, in *Chapter 1*, we introduced the DORA metrics to measure how well teams perform. If you are interested in the science behind these metrics, we recommend reading the DORA report or *Accelerate: The Science of Lean Software and DevOps: Building and Scaling High Performing Technology Organizations*. To recap, these metrics are as follows:

- Deployment frequency
- Lead time for changes
- Change failure rate
- Time to restore service

If these are the metrics that most accurately predict team performance, we can see that ownership of delivery is not optional.

Deployment frequency is suboptimal in the siloed configuration as we are tied to such an arduous release process. This release process also dictates our lead time for changes, as any changes must be aligned with the estimated schedule. We are also deploying much larger bundles of code at a time so that the chances of one of the features in the deployed bundle causing a change failure is now much higher, as the likelihood is now the sum of the likelihoods of each of the sub-components. Finally, the time to restore service is also much greater due to either rolling back a large change or sifting through a large release to find the culprit and apply a hotfix (which is also unlikely to go through the release process).

Leaving aside the metrics for high-performing teams, we also run into another issue around ownership. Who owns this change and is responsible for its success? The developer who wrote it? The change approval board that approved it? If it's a security issue, does ownership lie with the security team? Siloing the release process also means siloing the ownership; without end-to-end ownership of the process, problems are much harder to fix.

Empowered teams – increasing your speed

This brings us back to the concept of empowered teams. If your team wrote it, you are responsible for its entire journey into production. Or, more succinctly, *"You build it, you run it."* We can't just throw all of our teams in the deep end and expect them to swim; they need to be supported. This is where those siloed teams from before come into play. They shift from being the gatekeepers of the journey toward the production environment to enablers of the dev team to undertake that journey themselves.

> **Note**
>
> Empowering and supporting teams to own their output is the core of rapid and secure delivery.

Hence, to deliver rapidly without compromising security, the cultural shift is one of the most essential aspects, while also being an aspect that companies fail to target. For a team to own its output, each must have the skills and capabilities required to deliver a piece of work end to end, either internally through forming cross-functional teams or externally through an enabling team. Later in this chapter, we will explore ways to approach this from a shift-left and push-down approach. The key here is not to hand all control over to delivery teams but to ensure they are empowered and supported by those traditionally siloed functions to own their output.

The easiest way to do this is to provide both the carrot and the stick to the development team. Enabling teams must produce platforms and artifacts the development team can consume to do their jobs in line with company standards. This might be in the form of authentication libraries, infrastructure as code patterns, common UI component libraries, and so on. Then, the enabling team should seek to automate guardrails to enable the developers to ensure that the code they are producing meets the same standards that had been manually enforced. This could be through the use of QA testing suites, **static application security testing** (**SAST**), and automated ticket creation systems for site reliability alarms in the observability platform. By enabling developers in this way, we empower them to own their output and shift left the responsibility of the deployment process.

DevSecOps – the super-highway to production

Let's now revisit our deployment model:

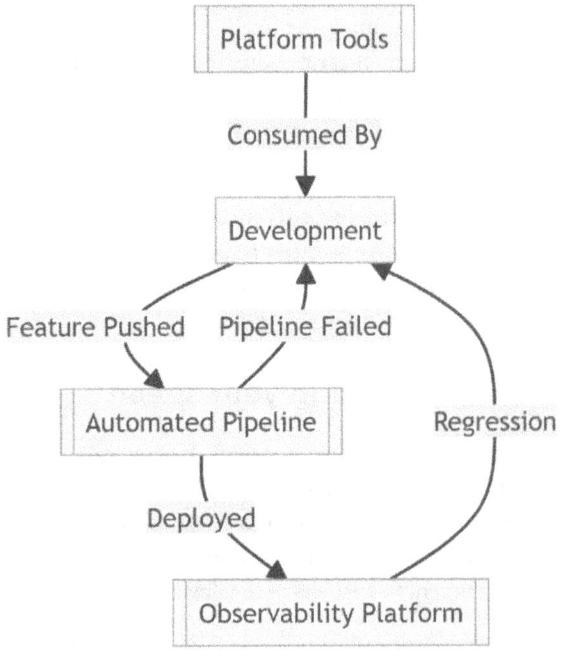

Figure 5.2 – Target state for ownership of deployable artifacts

Our other teams have remained in the organization. Instead, they are maintaining three sets of artifacts:

- **Platform tools**: The systems and artifacts that developers consume to produce software artifacts that align with the responsible team's requirements, such as shared auth libraries, structured logging libraries, or cloud infrastructure modules.

- **Automated pipeline**: This pipeline codifies each team's expectations instead of relying on a manual review. As mentioned earlier, this may include QA automated tests, SAST, or container scanning tools.

- **Observability platform**: This platform codifies the expectations around the application's performance and alerts developers for situations outside of normal operating parameters while storing information about these events.

The key difference here is that instead of the development team interfacing with five different teams to push features out to production, the development team is empowered to own the code they produce and deploy artifacts that meet a baseline standard to production. They can also see how the artifacts they produce perform through the observability platform. Hence, we've shifted the culture away from gatekeeping to enablement. This is the crux of DevSecOps, enabling software teams to develop, secure, and operate the code they write.

The magnitude of this change is typically underestimated in organizations undergoing a cloud native transformation. People can take offense to being taken off the critical path, considering that they relinquish some power they previously had. The mindset to install in these teams is that they are no longer at odds with the development team by stopping them from deploying to production but instead are stewards of their specialty for the development teams, producing artifacts and providing insights that help guide the development teams toward their own secure, high-quality, observable artifacts.

As a result, development teams become more cross-functional, and team members need to upskill in security, quality assurance, and site reliability engineering under the guidance of these enabling teams.

We can now see a few distinct advantages of reducing these friction points:

- Deployment frequency increases as we no longer bundle on a schedule but instead deploy as soon as possible. This also results in a much shorter change lead time, as once a change is ready and passes our pipeline checks, it can easily be deployed to production.

- We are now deploying much smaller units of code that often contain only a few features, which decreases the likelihood of the change failing and reduces our change failure rate.

- We have a platform to observe our application, which means that a change that results in an outage can quickly be identified, and a fix can be pushed through the automated pipeline. This is a key difference as, typically, hotfixes needed to be applied out of band, and we could not afford to run the fix through the whole pipeline. Instead, the automated pipeline can still be used as the developers do not need to interface with other teams to deploy the rectification. Hence, we have shifted toward a process of **continuous improvement and continuous delivery (CI/CD)**.

Staying on the road

Another fallacy that companies can quickly fall into is the belief that delivering features using DevSecOps and CI/CD principles will result in a large increase in development velocity, which means tighter deadlines. While it is true that the underlying improvements in the process will translate to the faster delivery of features, focusing solely on delivery timelines will ultimately undermine efficiency gains by the cultural shift.

If you are migrating from a fixed release schedule with tight deadlines and rigid business processes, it can be tempting to translate that directly into delivery schedules in the new paradigm. Instead, by decoupling feature work from the release process, we allow our development teams to obsess over output quality and only release features when ready from a multifaceted perspective. This ensures that we retain our increase in development velocity without compromising on code quality, and this leads us to a sustainable, rather than temporary, increase in development velocity.

Conway's law states, "*Organizations which design systems are constrained to produce designs which are copies of the communication structures of these organizations.*" When we allow our teams to be siloed, we inevitably constrain their output to a particular part of the development/deployment process and their responsibilities and produce a deployment process replicating those teams' communication pathways. Therefore, the logical conclusion is that to maintain all of the cultural changes we have prescribed in this chapter, we must encourage our teams to become self-sufficient. This enables the automated, independent production of change that we desire.

Drawing a new map

Finally, as we shift to fully cloud native, one of the hardest anti-patterns to break can be the coupling between services and the compute they run on. New services are cheap to create, maintain, and run. Hence, we can form bounded service contexts that encapsulate a business domain.

Domain Driven Design is a great read in this space; it goes into this topic in great detail. This allows us to evolve our architecture to meet our business domain needs rather than apply our business needs to our architecture because we installed a particular number of servers. Later in this book, we will dive into translating your business problems into application code and introduce the concepts of coupling and cohesion. The key for this chapter is to break the mentality that your architecture must fit into a predefined configuration. Conway's law also applies to your architecture, and just as we break down silos in the deployment process, we must also break down silos between development teams to enable us to build the right solution in the right place.

As we can see, the cultural shift required to create genuinely cloud native solutions can take some organizations by surprise, so it is crucial to consider its magnitude. The key shift in thinking is about empowering and enabling teams to be self-sufficient and own their delivery from feature inception to running it in production through a cultural change from a siloed ownership and delivery model to a lean ownership model where developers are responsible for the changes they make, supported through DevSecOps enablement. Empowered development will allow us to deliver change faster, so let's dive into how to enable frequent atomic changes to meet our business goals.

Frequent changes to meet business goals

In the previous chapter, we introduced the concept of the empowered development team. We worked on reducing the silos in the release process to allow ownership of the end-to-end release process. With this process, we can release much more frequently. Let's explore the development changes that are enabling us to work under this new paradigm.

Pruning Git branches

Most deployment strategies will be multi-stage. For example, you may have environments called *development, integration testing*, and *production*. The understanding is that earlier environments have changes deployed first, so we can test our changes before being released to the production environment. Having multi-stage deployments is a pattern we recommend as it allows for the testing of features, either by the development team or through automated tests against a live environment, before we deploy the changes to production. With this strategy, adopting a pattern such as Gitflow may be tempting, where each environment is a self-contained branch. Let's look at a typical Gitflow implementation.

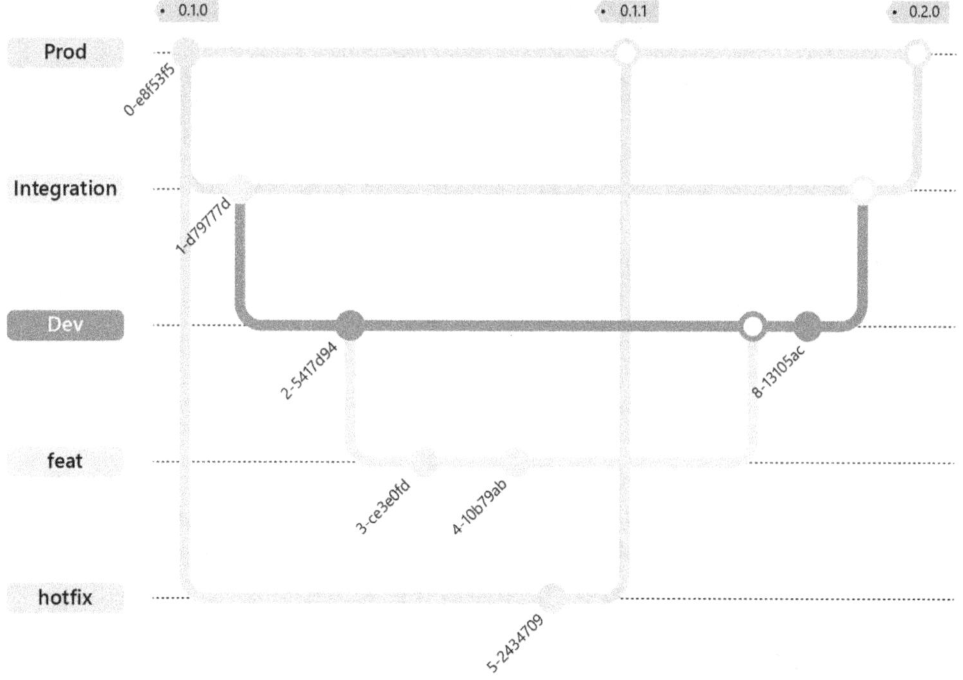

Figure 5.3 – Typical Gitflow branching model

This anti-pattern produces a false sense of security as we assume the changes are thoroughly tested in the lower environments before we push them to higher environments. However, with more people working on the code base and teams applying hotfixes, each branch's contents will tend to drift over time. In the preceding diagram, we can see that we applied a hotfix to production, and the first time we tested our deployed feature alongside the hotfix, it was actually in the production environment. This uncertainty is the risk we run when maintaining environment-specific code bases. It also leans toward a backslide in cultural attitudes, as the temptation to introduce manual checks between environment promotions can be detrimental. Instead, the principle of a single code base deployed multiple times limits our environmental drift. An excellent online resource, *The 12 Factor App*, (12factor.net) adopts this as the first factor.

So, how do we operate a single code base effectively? Selecting a revision-based branching strategy, such as trunk-based development, is the easiest way to ensure that we operate from a single code base. Instead of an environment running the latest configuration in an environment branch, we have rules for running the last known correct configuration in a single branch, which we will promote to higher environments on an as-needed basis. Let's take a look at the typical trunk-based development model.

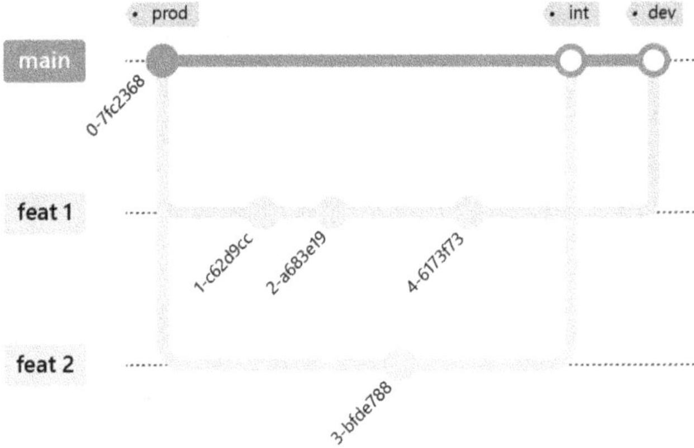

Figure 5.4 – Trunk-based development branching model

In this example, each environment is deployed off the main branch, with lower environments having the most recent changes for testing and higher environments trailing behind on the main branch. By continuously integrating and deploying, we reduce our change lead time and increase our deployment frequency.

Decoupling integration and release

Now the complexity of promoting each environment is taken care of, we run into a problem not apparent in the branch or code base per environment system. How do we test or change features in one environment but stop them from blocking other features from deploying in higher environments? In the previous system, we could cherry-pick commits to promote specific features. The answer to this is twofold: we want an easy way for developers to test their features before merging them and an easy way to manage merged features in different environments.

The simplest solution to manage merged features is to decouple the expression of a feature in the end product from its inclusion in the code base. For example, a feature can be complete and merged but not present in the deployed system. To achieve this, we use a concept known as **feature flags**.

Feature flags allow us to guard specific clauses in our application. A simple example would be a **Download to CSV** button on a table; we might add the button on the frontend, but we still need to implement the download logic. Hence, we would surround the rendering of the button with an `if` statement, and if the feature flag is off, then we wouldn't show the button. When the development team works on this feature locally, they can turn the feature flag on for testing. The deployed environments don't have the feature flag turned on, so we can merge the feature into the main code base without impacting the deployed application. Once the feature is complete, we can turn the feature on in lower environments to test the feature in an actual environment. By decoupling the development of a feature from its expression in the end app, we also decouple the release decision for a feature from being technically driven (i.e., the feature is present in the code base and, therefore, it will be present in the deployed application) to a business decision; we can add features on demand.

To truly decouple the feature release decision from the technical implementation, it's crucial to store feature configuration within the application environment. In this case, an anti-pattern would be to have files checked into version control called `features.prod.yml` and `features.dev.yml`, as, once again, we are creating checked-in concretions in our code base.

The best methodology for feature flagging is to check in a file to version control that defines the feature flags available and their state. In this file, we prefer to use something other than Booleans for feature flags as they become hard to extend later. Typically, we rely on enums. An example enum might consist of values called `Baseline`, `Configurable`, and `Off`. In this scenario, `Baseline` ensures a feature is on in all environments and is turned on by default when we deploy new environments. These flags represent mature features that are stable enough to be always on and are safe to use as the basis for new features. `Configurable` flags are features that we want to be able to change the expression of in various environments. These might indicate yet-to-be-released features, features that are undergoing testing, or features that are incomplete but in a usable state. These features need a way to be either on or off in deployed environments. We can achieve this through application configuration if the system is small or backed by a database table if the feature list is extensive. Finally, we have features configured as `Off`; these are feature flags that should not be available on any environments but are for features that are a work in progress and need to be able to be expressed locally.

To address the problem of developers needing to test locally, this is where the advantages of building cloud native software shine. A common anti-pattern we see is attempting to replicate the cloud in a local environment, and many services do this. However, there is no substitute for actively running your code in the cloud. With cloud native software, using principles such as **infrastructure as code (IaC)** and serverless/managed services, there is no reason why developers cannot spin up an isolated development cloud environment. This practice allows your developers to truly develop in the cloud. It also ensures your IaC avoids its anti-patterns, such as hardcoded references, as we regularly create and destroy new environments. The development team can now also test infrastructure changes independent of deployed environments. This decoupling feeds into the concept of empowered teams; developers can now control the code that runs, the infrastructure it runs on, and the services it interacts with.

They also gain familiarity with the deployment process and get closer to the ideal of "*You build it, you run it.*" By allowing our developers to test in the cloud with a blast radius limited to the ephemeral environment they are testing in, we enable much more destructive types of testing. My load test on my ephemeral environment will not impact your testing on your ephemeral environment. By allowing this type of comprehensive testing in the pipeline, we reduce our change failure rate.

Reversing the inevitable

No system is perfect, and as we increase the rate at which we deploy, the likelihood of one of those changes going wrong is eventually a certainty. According to the DORA report, the change failure rate is one of the metrics we should track for organizational performance. Although we strive to keep this metric as low as possible if a failure occurs, another DORA metric, **mean time to restore (MTTR)**, comes into play. Three key anti-patterns prevent you from optimizing your MTTR when the cause is a change failure:

- Mutable artifacts

- Destructive changes

- No reverse definition for a change

The first anti-pattern is using **mutable artifacts**, and all artifacts produced must be immutable. When your automated build pipeline produces an artifact as a deployment candidate, we must preserve the artifact throughout subsequent build pipeline runs. This immutability can be as simple as container versioning in a container registry or having all previous versions of an internal library available for installation at any point. By having immutable artifacts, it is simple to roll back the system to a known correct configuration. We can simply deploy an earlier artifact, and then we can triage the fixes in lower environments until we are ready to deploy to production again.

The second anti-pattern is **destructive changes**. Deployment of a new version of the system should allow us to roll back to previous instances of the application. For example, a destructive change would be dropping a database table or dropping a data store. When we deploy these changes, we can never roll the system back to the last known correct configuration because we have lost the system's state in the destructive change. If a destructive change is required, it should go through a deprecation schedule before the final destructive change is applied to ensure that removing the functionality will not impact other application areas.

The final anti-pattern is **no reverse definition for a change**. This anti-pattern primarily applies to stores of application state, such as databases or infrastructure changes. It is closely related to the second point: a change fundamentally cannot be reversible if it is destructive. The extension this rule applies is that any change to the system state, architecture, or data must be recoverable. This functionality exists for some tooling, such as Terraform comparing deployed infrastructure to a state file or a SQL Server project deployed via DACPAC. In other scenarios, the migration must explicitly define forward and reverse operations, such as through database SQL migrations using a tool such as Flyway or Entity Framework migrations. The common anti-pattern we see here is that the draft changes contain a detailed upward migration, and no one builds or tests the downward migration.

This strategy means that significant work is often required when we need to roll back a change, as the reverse migration may need time to be created or may be non-functional if testing is not performed. This results in high-pressure, high-risk situations where we must craft changes while production is impacted, resulting in corners being cut to "just get it running again."

To summarize this section, complex release processes allow bad practices due to the high barriers between development and production. We can optimize delivery and increase service uptime by removing those barriers and supporting good practices. The key is frequent, flagged, well-tested changes that are immutable, non-destructive, and easily reversible when required. This allows us to develop faster, but we still need to ensure that our developers are doing the right thing, to do so we typically employ guardrails.

Guardrails

We've talked about empowering developers to do more and fully own the changes they produce. However, developers are not the experts; we see this fundamental anti-pattern in adopting the shift-left mentality. We should not expect developers to become experts in security, **site reliability engineering (SRE)**, DevSecOps, and so on. Developers will need a passing knowledge of these topics but should be able to deploy with certainty without being experts.

Keeping your developers on track

A common anti-pattern that we see in this space is that because we are shifting responsibility left toward the development team, the development team needs more permissions in the cloud environment to do their job. The exact opposite is true. Developers should have a constrained set of permissions to diagnose, inspect, and support the cloud environment. Instead, the escalation of privilege should occur in the CI/CD pipelines, and this is how we enable our developers by providing tooling with elevated permissions. By doing this, we ensure that our developers can deploy independently but not outside the confines of the CI/CD environment. This process limits the chance of environmental drift through manual configuration, which preserves disaster recovery functions.

The primary method of enabling developers to deploy with confidence is to provide guardrails in the deployment process. These guardrails define an acceptable set of actions a developer can take to achieve their objectives. For example, an infrastructure guardrail might prevent a **content delivery network (CDN)** from being deployed without a **web application firewall (WAF)** in front of it. A code-level guardrail might avoid the use of insecure hash functions. In both instances, we prevent changes from meeting a minimum standard when deploying them to production.

We might deploy guardrails to meet regulatory compliance requirements. For example, a cloud-wide policy that prevents any resources from being deployed in particular regions to support data sovereignty requirements might be employed. This example would be perfect for a **service control policy (SCP)** from **Amazon Web Services (AWS)**. These allow us to enforce boundaries of acceptable use at different levels of granularity, from organization-wide to individual accounts. For example, we lock various accounts to a specific region, and globally, we prevent all accounts from deploying resources in export-controlled areas.

An anti-pattern in the security space is mistaking pentesting as a guardrail in the critical deployment path. Pentesting is a vital security step but should be outside the deployment path. Instead, it should run alongside the deployment process. We should automate all steps in the path to deployment. If you want to test the application security dynamically, consider using a **dynamic application security testing (DAST)** framework on one of the pre-prod environments as a pre-promotion check. The essential factor for guardrails is that developers should be able to access guardrail evaluations on demand.

Types of guardrail

We commonly see two main types of guardrails: preventative and detective.

Preventative guardrails are proactive guardrails that specify the outer bounds of what developers can do; these are punitive, preventing the pipeline from deploying if the guardrails are activated. This methodology is suitable for applying easily defined heuristics (i.e., our hashing should not be using the MD5 hash algorithm). The common mistake we see with preventative guardrails is that they typically get implemented, and then the developers are left to fend for themselves. If the guardrail fails, they have to go back and fix it. A better workflow is to have observability into guardrail activation. These metrics will tell you where developers have the most trouble and allow you to make developers' lives easier by providing training, libraries of correct implementations, or, even better, an enabling artifact.

Next, we have **detective guardrails**. These reactive guardrails scan your environment for non-compliance, then either raise the issue or take corrective action. For example, we could enable our developers to deploy storage with public access through a CDN. However, if we tag particular storage containing PII (personally identifiable information), this tagging process might be out of band with the deployment of the storage itself. In this case, we could add a detective guardrail that checks for storage with public access, checks whether that storage account has the tag indicating that it contains PII, and then activates the guardrail. This type of control is typically the least favorable, as it requires an insecure configuration to be present in the environment to detect it instead of evaluating it proactively.

A typical driver of guardrails is security. Several tools exist to perform SAST to pick up common errors and allow the security team to define custom rules they want to look for. This space has excellent open source tooling (such as Semgrep) and many proprietary solutions. There is some upfront work to codify the anti-patterns you want to catch, but each codified heuristic is something that the security team no longer needs to review manually. Many available tools are not limited purely to security heuristics but can also check for anti-patterns such as deeply nested loops or cognitive complexity.

The case for guardrail observability

Building guardrails is essential, but it is also important to monitor them. Developers use observability platforms to understand user behavior better and make changes to the applications they build to support it. We should do the same for our development team, who are effectively our users. By monitoring our guardrails, we can see the common friction points for our developers and proactively fix common issues. Let's imagine our preventative guardrail from before requiring developers to deploy a WAF in front of a CDN. We might notice that our developers are hitting this guardrail very often, and hence, using the metrics we collect around guardrail activations, we build an enabling artifact. This artifact allows developers to avoid activating the guardrail and produce more secure artifacts without additional rework.

The key to enabling artifacts is to abstract away standard configurations using sensible defaults. Continuing with our WAF and CDN example, as a security team, we may introduce a default WAF that gets added to every CDN deployment if a developer forgets to specify one explicitly. If we already have a detective and preventative guardrail for this scenario, the enabling artifact minimizes the number of activations we encounter. When tracking metrics for these units, we recommend monitoring everything. Metrics about the enabling artifact tell you how often we activate the default WAF. These metrics can be helpful to track as they are a great way to measure enabling artifacts' impact on the development team.

If enabling artifacts are the counterpart of preventative guardrails, the equivalent of detective guardrails is automated remediation. For our PII tagging solution, we could listen for the guardrail activation event and kick off a process that revokes public access to the bucket. This enables our system to be secure without outside intervention for simple use cases.

So, for a vulnerability or misconfiguration in our application, the preference is to have a sensible default added through an enabling artifact, such as a library or automated pipeline tool, then for cases outside of this to have them caught by preventative guardrails, and finally, if a misconfiguration makes it to production, then automated remediation or a manual process is initiated to rectify it.

These tools can exist in the pipeline and environment at all times. The final layer of security in this system should be pentesting, but it's important to note that this needs to occur asynchronously with the deployment and development of the application. Ideally, the findings from penetration testing will feed back into our system of guardrails to help us develop new enabling artifacts and preventative/detective controls to stop the issue from resurfacing.

Example guardrails

In cloud environments, there are unusual ways in which systems interact, as not only are you able to give deployed infrastructure and services the ability to interact with each other but also to interact with the underlying definitions of those resources. Now, we will go through some common guardrails that are easily applicable. By no means will this be exhaustive, but it will give you a head start. For our example, we will use AWS.

The guardrail examples we will use are as follows:

- Overprivileged IAM accounts
- Public S3 buckets
- Data sovereignty requirements
- Publicly accessible remote administration tools

A simple place to start would be IAM permissions policies. I won't go into detail about the principle of least privilege here, we'll save that for a later chapter, but it's common to see overprivileged accounts or roles defined. Typically, this arises because the user can't find the correct permissions to perform the actions they require, so they end up assigning a long list of permissions, or wildcard permissions, while trying to make it work. This is actually a great candidate for all three methods of control discussed earlier; we can build common permissions policies that contain pre-approved policies for completing common tasks, for example, connecting our Lambda functions to a specific DynamoDB table. We can then also add a preventative control, such as an SCP in our account or organization to forbid access to particular APIs that are not in use. Finally, we can add a detective control that monitors all our active roles for policies that contain wildcard permissions, and revoke all associated grants and trust policies when one is discovered.

Another common misconfiguration that is a good candidate for guardrails is public access to S3 buckets. Any scenario using public access to an S3 bucket is typically better served through the use of a CloudFront distribution and an origin access identity. We can build an enabling artifact here in the form of a Terraform module that sets up a default configuration for a bucket and disables public access. We can build a preventative guardrail that checks our infrastructure plan to prevent this configuration. Finally, we can build a detective guardrail that scans our deployed infrastructure to ensure that no public buckets exist, and if they do, revoke public access.

Many businesses also have the constraint of data sovereignty requirements; data for entities in a region must be stored in that region. Through the deployment of resources into regions that meet our data sovereignty requirements, we can be compliant. However, we are not provably compliant, as this approach requires the constant enforcement of a process. Instead, we can use a preventative control: we can build SCPs that lock resources in an account from being deployed in any region apart from the ones we specify. This approach must be proactive, as it only applies to new calls to the AWS API.

The last common misconfiguration we see is directly opening remote administration tools to the internet. For example, your EC2 instances might expose port 22 to allow SSH for your developers, but now the attack surface for those instances just increased by every version of SSH those instances are running. This should be enforced at the network level, and typically, it's good practice to have a detective guardrail (alongside preventative guard rails) in this instance. The temptation for a developer to open the SSH port in a **network access control list** (**NACL**) and forget to close it is surprisingly high. As such, we could create an AWS Config rule to check for open port 22 with unrestricted access and automatically close it.

Hopefully, through reading this section, you have come to understand the types of guardrails that can be configured and how to enable your developers to best work within the boundaries you set, without impacting their development velocity. The importance of monitoring your organization's guardrails has also been discussed, with these metrics providing us with a clear insight into both our security posture and developer experience. Finally, we have also looked at some common misconfigurations and explored how guardrails and enabling artifacts could mitigate the risk to the business. So, now we have the tools to enable our developers to securely and safely own their output, let's look at how we can shift left the responsibility of producing secure artifacts onto our development teams.

Shifting left

We have touched on the requirement to shift left the responsibility of producing functional, secure changes to the development team. The focus so far has been on the externalities of the development team. This section will be about the effect of shifting left on the development team and the techniques we can use to meet the new expectations imposed upon them. We recommend reading this chapter if you are a developer, as you will learn some valuable tools, or as part of an external function, as it will allow you to support the development team better.

Development as an iterative process

A common anti-pattern involves invoking **quality assurance** (**QA**) once a feature is complete in the eyes of the developer rather than a process that takes place iteratively over the software development life cycle. We spoke earlier about ephemeral environments, which are helpful for a developer to develop their feature in isolation and provide an environment where somebody can test the feature in its incomplete state. Different companies have different QA functions, which may come from a dedicated QA role or exist as part of the product team. The key here is that ephemeral environments allow you to involve the QA function much earlier in the process.

Another anti-pattern here is using long-lived feature branches with ephemeral environments. We develop the feature on multiple small branches, each containing a portion of the work required for the entire feature to operate. The ephemeral environment allows us an alternative deployment with enabled incomplete features. We establish a fast feedback cycle between developers and the QA process by getting QA involved from the first commit. Shifting left the QA to be parallel or integrated with the development allows us to mitigate the risk that a significant feature may fail QA once we have completed the feature, requiring significant rework to fix. It also brings us closer to a no-silo model by fostering collaboration between QA and development functions.

Test first, code later

One of the anti-patterns that teams typically seem to acknowledge but fail to implement correctly is **test-driven development** (**TDD**) and, by extension, **behavior-driven development** (**BDD**). When asking development teams whether they use TDD or BDD, they usually answer in the affirmative, but when asked when they write their tests, they respond that they write the tests after the code. Cognitive dissonance aside, true BDD involves defining the behavior of your system and writing a test that can check for compliance with that behavior before actually implementing the system. Another fallacy that comes into play when implementing BDD is a waterfall-style approach to coding tests, specifying all the edge cases you foresee and writing too many tests upfront. A lot of system behavior and requirements only emerge through the actual implementation of the system, and writing too many tests up front just hampers this discovery process. Instead, an excellent approach to use in BDD is the red, green, refactor system. You define your desired behavior and write simple tests to ensure the system fulfills the desired behavior. These tests will fail (red), and we will then implement a system that passes these tests (green). Through the design of this system, we then refactor the implementation and the test suite to exhibit the desired behavior accurately and test the emergent behavior of the system. We must create the initial desired behavior with the product owner to ensure that the desired behavior test accurately reflects the behavior required in the end product. This process will shift left the desired behavior's description to a point before we write any code.

Once we create tests, they should enter the deployment pipeline's critical path. This practice ensures that future changes to the system do not prevent it from exhibiting the desired behavior required. A common anti-pattern that teams can fall into in this stage is failing to trust their tests' output fully. In an extreme case, this might look like accepting a certain percentage of failed tests as "par for the course." This lack of confidence in the tests undermines the value of the entire test suite, as developers no longer have confidence that their changes do not cause regressions on existing behaviors.

The second and more common pattern is the existence of intermittent test failures. Intermittent failure commonly occurs when tests are not properly isolated, and the side effects of one test may influence the result of another test. Typically, in this scenario, the developers rerun the pipeline until the intermittent test passes. This behavior is counterproductive for two reasons: firstly, we're increasing the time developers are waiting for pipeline executions to finish, and secondly, we have a failing test that we are ignoring. In this scenario, rather than putting up with the inconvenience of multiple pipeline runs, we should be adequately reestablishing the boundaries of our tests and creating a new test that checks for regression of the intermittent behavior. By vigorously enforcing these test suites, we shift left the responsibilities of detecting and rectifying regressions to the developer responsible for the regression as part of their development process rather than waiting for the regression to become apparent in the end product.

Shared ownership of output

Consider Fred Brooks's famous quote: *"What one programmer can do in one month, two programmers can do in two months."* While tongue-in-cheek, the sentiment holds when we program in isolation. The increased communication channels and distribution of knowledge can make the development process more demanding, which leads us to our third common anti-pattern, **isolated development**. We have seen software teams where they only interact with each other in the daily standup. This system falls back into our old patterns of slow feedback cycles. If I have a daily standup and need the output from one other developer on my team to progress my feature, it may be complete 5 minutes after the standup, and I would need to wait until the next day to hear about it. I've seen high-performing development teams on a virtual call all day, splitting off the primary call to pair and mob program as required. The key differentiator here is that the high-performing team sees their delivery as a shared output rather than an individual output. This differentiator also needs to be reflected in how we track productivity metrics, which should reflect a team's productivity, not the individual's. Management of the individual is informed by feedback from other team members, as the team is the value we want to optimize.

Small and regular changes, merged back to the code base, are also crucial from a code review perspective. Show a developer a 12-line pull request, and they will have plenty of comments. Show them a 1,200-line pull request, and you'll likely get zero comments. Maybe you will get a response of *"Looks good to me."* The main enemy of this approach is long-running feature branches. If you're not regularly merging code with the main branch, then the reviewer does not stand a chance of understanding the scope of the change. Development processes that support small, atomic changes are essential here, such as trunk-based development and feature flagging, as discussed earlier in this chapter. When working toward deadlines, there is typically a tendency to approve pull requests with more relaxed standards to integrate changes in time. This approach, however, is a false economy. By approving lax changes, such as code that does not conform to coding standards or code with high cognitive complexity, we are simply robbing ourselves of future velocity and building up technical debt. The other side of this coin is that when we rigorously enforce coding standards at the pull request stage, we slowly start to see an uplift in the team, and future pull requests from the same team member are less likely to have the same mistakes. The failure to enforce coding standards is the key to our false economy. Enforcement versus non-enforcement of the coding standards eventually brings you to an equivalent or increased development velocity.

Experimenting and getting feedback early

We have examined the feedback loops in a typical software development business function. However, you should also look at feedback loops that may be more specific to your business. An example might be that an order-matching engine from a financial system might require the last six months of data to be fed into the system to ensure it reaches the same target state as the existing engine. To shift this left, we might use a smaller time range with dummy data that developers can run locally to get instant feedback. The key to shifting left is identifying these feedback loops and either putting them into the hands of developers directly or enabling developers to interact with the business unit responsible in the early stages of development. This business process optimization ensures that we are breaking down the chance of a late part of the process coming back with significant changes. To facilitate this, we recommend mapping out all the parts of the deployment process that occur once a change leaves the hands of a developer and finding the areas where this process experiences the most failures (i.e., requires rework by the developer). These parts of the process are your best candidates for shifting left. It's important to note that, once again, you need metrics on the process to identify these stages, so observability in your deployment process is a significant factor in its efficacy.

Shifting left also requires the development team to be the source of truth in tackling a feature. The development team must be allowed to experiment before committing to a solution. A great way to approach this is through timeboxed technical spikes, possibly multiple in parallel if different approaches need testing for their efficacy. The crucial factor here is allowing developers to experiment, with the culmination of their work validating an idea or assumption rather than introducing a change or a new feature. This process is another area where ephemeral environments shine. Having a consequence-free sandbox to test a proof-of-concept idea allows the development team to, in the words of

Mark Zuckerberg, "*move fast and break things.*" Even though this approach does not aim to produce a tangible outcome, typically, these technical spikes, if successful, will form the basis of a new change or feature. So, even though the goal was not to create a change, the technical spike often does not result in lost productivity.

Building in security from the start

The final requirement of the shift-left methodology is ensuring that security is part of the cloud native solution from the inception of the changes. Developers must all be conscious of the effects of their decisions on the overall solution security posture. Developers do not need to be security experts. Instead, they must shift their thinking from "*Does it achieve the required objective?*" to consider the new attack surface their changes could provide. An excellent way to guide a development team that is newly adopting shift-left methodologies into their way of working is to undertake threat modeling of a change as part of the development process. By shifting into the mindset of an attacker, we can quickly identify threats and put mitigations into place to defend against them. This exercise is even more effective if the security team is involved in the first few attempts. While the team's goal is to become self-sufficient (a topic we will touch on soon), using enabling teams is essential to set a consistent quality across teams.

By shifting left, we have enabled our developers to produce secure, complete, and production-ready changes. Using appropriate tooling and business processes has increased the development velocity and given our developers the control and proper safeguards to apply themselves to finding the best solution. Now we have teams that are expected to own their output, we will next look at how to make these teams truly self-sufficient.

Self-sufficient teams

With all the changes we have made in culture, process, tooling, and delivery, we expect our teams to become self-sufficient change factories. But how can we adjust our team's internal structures to ensure that the team can organize and support these new ways of working?

Trifecta leadership

Spotify popularized a model known as the *Squad Model*. While, typically, it also ascribes much larger structures beyond the independent squads, we will focus on the structure of the squad itself. There is valid criticism of the larger model. However, this does not take away from the validity of the atomic team structure. The crux of the team is that it is a unit that works on a specific product. It contains a trio of leaders who orient the squad's development efforts. These leaders are the engineering manager, responsible for the team's technical direction; the product owner, who represents the customer; and the scrum master, who organizes the team's efforts. By encapsulating the responsibilities of a team within the team itself and allowing the team the ability to work across the entire product, we can now scale these squads horizontally without linearly increasing management overhead. We are now venturing into scalable, agile delivery, which matches well with the requirements for cloud native development.

The key to successfully implementing this format is understanding that while the leadership is a trifecta, there is minimal overlap in actual responsibility. A common anti-pattern in this space is all developers reporting to the engineering manager. Developers are the implementers of change, and there is much more nuance to producing change in a system than technical direction. Instead, developers become stewards of the changes that they are making, understanding the product thinking behind it and the technical direction required to implement it. A great way to communicate this is through a concept called *commander's intent*. This refers to the abstraction of leadership direction to encompass the goal, allowing for flexibility in our method. In its original form, the order might require us to move to a particular position on the battlefield, but the intent is to take a specific hill in concert with other units. If we focus on the *how* (moving to the positions), we might miss opportunities to accomplish the *what* (taking the hill).

Similarly, if we dictate the steps a developer must take to implement a feature, emergent opportunities that are only visible to the implementer might be overlooked. This situation is where the trifecta leadership and collaborative model of squads is potent. Not only can we communicate the commander's intent of a particular change but developers also have local sources of authority to present these new opportunities for strategic direction.

Previously, I worked in an organization that used a particular framework to attempt to safely scale agile development while retaining complete control over the product teams. This framework implementation resulted in a misalignment of strategic direction. In other words, the process did not empower the teams to be self-sufficient and capitalize on opportunities, as the requirement was to surface such opportunities at multiple layers before we could take action. The self-sufficient team is the antithesis of this paradigm. Rather than asserting control, we seek to empower and provide strategic direction while enabling strategic opportunity.

The topology of your teams

In their seminal work, *Team Topologies*, Matthew Skelton and Manuel Pais identify four types of teams in a DevSecOps-focused organization, as follows:

- Stream-aligned teams
- Enabling teams
- Complicated subsystem team
- Platform team

The stream-aligned team is an expert in a business domain, aligning its output with the strategic direction of that business area. This team is your organization's primary type, directly focused on changes that will solve your business's or its customers' problems. Note that the organization of these teams is by business domain, while Conway's law assumes that these domains will naturally be bounded contexts within our architecture. We should not constrain the team to own and operate only a particular part of the code base.

The enabling team supports the other team types in achieving their goals by providing technical guidance and enabling artifacts to the development team. For example, a dedicated security team might assist teams with unique security problems in their development process. It's important to note that the existence of these teams does not absolve other teams of their responsibilities. These teams are enhancers, not replacements for self-sufficiency.

The complicated subsystem team deals with a subsystem that takes deep technical or engineering capability. This type of team is generally the only time we assign a team to a particular part of your organization's architecture, and typically, the role of this team is to abstract the complicated subsystem so that other parts of the business can interact with it. A typical example might be a bank that still has a mainframe; we manage the mainframe with a complicated subsystem team that provides interfaces for other teams to interact with.

The platform team is the development team for your developers; they build internal products for which your other teams are the consumers. The platform might consist of standardized build pipelines and guardrails, enabling artifacts and tooling such as Git, ticket management software, and so on. As we discussed before, your metrics and customer development teams should guide this team's strategic direction. These teams have three main modes of operation:

- **Collaboration**: This involves teams working together for some time. These might be teams with closely related changes in progress, a stream team working with the platform team to develop new tooling, or a team working with a complicated subsystem team to evolve the service.
- **X as a service**: This model typically refers to complicated subsystem teams abstracting away technically complex functionality behind a service that other teams can consume.
- **Facilitating**: This involves teams working together to achieve a particular team's goals. For example, the security enabling team might facilitate changes to the authorization logic required by a stream-aligned team. This mode typically also involves empowering the team to be self-sufficient moving forward.

When identifying these modes of operation, a few anti-patterns arise. The most common one is assuming that too many parts of your organization are complicated subsystems. The critical distinction is that complicated subsystem teams focus on something technically complex. A complex business domain is not a complicated subsystem. This method of thinking returns us to the trap of aligning our teams with our existing architecture rather than our business domains and allowing the architecture to grow out of the natural bounded contexts of those emergent domains.

When enabling teams need to facilitate the goals of stream-aligned teams, a common mistake they make is to assume that, as the experts in that area, they should just make the required changes. Fundamentally, to foster team self-sufficiency, the enabling team needs to mentor the stream-aligned team to improve the team's capabilities.

Finally, it can be tempting to use the X-as-a-service pattern liberally for things that are the entire organization's responsibility. A key example is security. Security is not a system we can develop in isolation and provide to developers as a service. It is the responsibility of every member of every team. We can build our platform tooling and enabling teams to incentivize and foster good security practices. The purpose of the X-as-a-service mode of interaction is to remove technical responsibility from the service consumers, which is counterproductive in the case of security.

Champions and the T-shaped engineer

As we shift from a traditional delivery model to a cloud native delivery model, we also broaden the horizon of services we can consume. Rather than solving business problems in the same ways over and over again, we have the opportunity to leverage cloud native services. However, as we broaden our horizons, inevitably, we must educate our teams on the best practices for these new types of services. In the traditional model, every developer could understand the architecture and code patterns required. It is unreasonable to expect all of our team to become experts overnight; however, each of our developers will need to acquire a broad knowledge of cloud native services to identify when certain patterns should be used. This broad knowledge forms the top bar of the T-shaped engineer, a wide but shallow knowledge that is typically acquired through self-learning. When they use certain patterns repeatedly, they develop a deep understanding of specific implementation idiosyncrasies of the services involved, developing a deep knowledge. This forms the column of our T-shaped engineer, a deep but tightly scoped expertise. The idea is that with a few T-shaped engineers on the team, we have a diversity of technical opinions available to guide the technical direction of the team.

For business-wide, job-zero initiatives, such as security, accessibility, or code quality, we recommend electing champions within the teams to provide self-sufficient teams with the internal capability to meet their goals. It is then the responsibility of the governing group behind this initiative, which may be an enabling team, to support these champions in developing their field. This may include supporting self-learning through certification pathways, funding them to attend conferences, and providing internal knowledge-sharing opportunities. The key here is that the company must invest in its people for the initiative to succeed and yield results. It is simply not enough to continue business as usual. In the cloud space, technology and practices evolve rapidly; as a company, to maximize your return on cloud investment, you must invest in people.

Building cloud native capability within teams takes time; it is important to recognize the need to provide teams with all the tools and opportunities to become self-sufficient. To achieve this, we explored using a trifecta leadership of the product owner, engineering manager, and scrum master. We also looked at ways for teams to organize their interactions with each other. Finally, we looked at how we can grow initiatives in the organization and provide diverse opinions by encouraging T-shaped engineers and champion programs.

Summary

Through ownership of output and team empowerment, we have transformed our development teams into genuinely self-sufficient powerhouses. We have tempered their output with automated processes and guardrails to ensure that they are working within the constraints required by our business. We have also looked at mitigating the impact any one negative change can have on the overall system. These atomic changes will form the basis of our new development model going forward. Next up, we will be looking deeper into maintaining security and compliance in cloud native environments.

Get This Book's PDF Version and Exclusive Extras

Scan the QR code (or go to `packtpub.com/unlock`). Search for this book by name, confirm the edition, and then follow the steps on the page.

Note: Keep your invoice handly. Purchase made directly from packt don't require one.

6

How to Meet Your Security and Compliance Goals

In today's digital world, keeping your organization secure is an ongoing process—it's never just a one-and-done deal. With the rise of cloud environments, the stakes have never been higher. This chapter will dive into some of the biggest challenges we face, from the risks of over-privileged access to the misconception that one penetration test before launch is enough. We'll also break down supply chain security and clear up any confusion about the shared responsibility model. Whether you are deep into IT or just getting started with cloud security, you'll find practical tips to help protect your organization.

This chapter will describe common security and compliance anti-patterns. These anti-patterns expose your organization and make it challenging to pass an external compliance audit.

The following topics will be covered in this chapter:

- How to Manage Permissions Without Over-Privilege
- Importance of Continuous Compliance in Security
- Proactive Monitoring
- The Shared responsibility model
- Supply chain insecurity

How to Manage Permissions Without Over-Privilege

In this section, we are going to explore the permissions that we need within our cloud architectures, as human beings to do our everyday jobs, whether that be as a Solution Architect, DevOps Engineer, or even in a finance role in account. Each person needs different permissions for their role in business. We'll then look at the permissions you need to apply to services and devices to access the resources needed by an individual in a role. And at the same time we're going to ensure that we're approaching these permissions with the bare minimum access that's needed to be effective at the role involved, the principle of least privilege.

These are the sort of actions that will stop us, as human beings, from making large-scale mistakes that could cost you your business reputation.

Securing High-Privilege Accounts

From the first moment we register ourselves a Cloud provider account, we create a set of credentials to set up our Cloud architectures as we desire. Each cloud provider may define this differently, however the big three cloud providers define them as such:

- **Amazon Web Services (AWS)**: The email address that is used when you register with AWS is considered the high-privilege account (aka the root account)

- **Microsoft Azure (Azure)**: Here it is called the "Global Administrator"

- **Google Cloud Platform (GCP)**: This is referred to as the "Owner" role.

This level of access is both convenient and very high risk due to:

- **Unrestricted access to all resources and actions**: Giving someone unrestricted access to your cloud environment might make things easier, but it's a major risk. With full control, users could accidentally delete key resources, misconfigure security settings, or access sensitive data they shouldn't see. And if their credentials get compromised, attackers could do serious damage—everything from wiping out infrastructure to leaking confidential information. This is why the principle of least privilege is critical—it keeps access limited to what's necessary, reducing the chance of accidental mishaps and minimizing the fallout if something goes wrong.

- **Potential for irreversible damage**: Too much access means opening the door to mistakes you can't undo. Someone with full control could accidentally wipe out databases, corrupt backups, or even shut down production. Once that damage is done, there's no guarantee of getting it back—data could be lost permanently, and downtime could cost you. That's why it's crucial to limit access and put safeguards in place so no one can make changes that can't be reversed. It's all about avoiding a single point of failure that could bring everything down.

- **High-value target for attackers**: Accounts with unrestricted access are like gold to attackers. If they get hold of one, they can steal sensitive data, disable services, or take over your entire system. The damage would be immediate and far-reaching, hitting your security, reputation, and bottom line all at once. That's why these accounts need to be locked down with strong controls like multi-factor authentication, and permissions need to stay limited. It's all about making sure you don't become an easy target.

Some fundamental best practices can be followed to ensure your highly privileged accounts are as secure as possible.

- Set yourself a strong password and store it in a secure password vault.

- Enable Multi-Factor Authentication. This ensures that you have to physically prove you are the owner of the account to log in with either a 6-digit code or biometric information. More on this later in the section "*Implement Multi-Factor Authentication (MFA)*".

> **Important Note**
>
> For a root account or similar, if it's a unique account and not a role, try to use a hardware token instead and store this somewhere safe.

- Create User accounts or implement a single sign-on provider and assign relevant permissions to the users.

- Do not allow high-privileged accounts to have programmatic access

- Monitoring account activity. If usage at this account level is detected, ensure that an alert is sent to relevant leadership or management

- Limit the use of this account level. Sometimes we need to log into this account level but it should be by exception, not rule.

Consider the high-privilege accounts to be of similar importance to your building lease or trading license. This is proof of who you are as a Business in the Cloud world, and if someone compromises this account, it's going to be difficult to prove you are who you say you are.

Even if you are not using the root-like access accounts, the account should be secured as above.

Over Privileged Users and Services

How many times have you heard the following phrases or similar?

> *"Give me access to everything, it's just easier!"*

> *"just give them a temporary admin role to save time".*

Over privileged access in a Cloud environment means that the user may not need all the permissions that have been assigned to them.

Imagine a bustling office where everyone, from the intern to the CEO, has a master key to every door. While this might seem convenient, it poses a significant security risk. Anyone could access sensitive areas, confidential files, or even the CEO's office, whether they need to be there or not. This scenario mirrors the issue of over-privileged users in cloud environments.

The first type of over-privileged user is the default account your cloud provider sets up for you and by now you should have secured that access control.

Now whether you're a single developer, just getting started or a multi-million-dollar valued corporation, you're going to need to ensure that you're only using permissions that you require. Similarly, if you allow resources to perform actions on services, you'll want to ensure that the service accounts deployed for this are only given access to the specific resource/object/file/service.

Permissions for Humans

In the cloud world, an over-privileged user is like an employee with a master key. They have more access rights and permissions than necessary to perform their job. This situation often arises because it seems easier to grant broad permissions rather than tailoring access to fit specific roles. However, this convenience comes at a high cost to security and in some cases, compliance, for example:

- Increased Risk of Breaches

- Human Error

- Accountability Issues

In essence, managing user access in cloud environments is about striking the right balance between convenience and security. By addressing over-privileged users and adopting best practices like least privilege and RBAC, organizations can protect their cloud resources and maintain a secure, efficient environment. Remember, in security, less is often more—especially when it comes to permissions.

As far as compliance is concerned, you'll need to look at your specific standards and what the implications of over-privileged users might be. For example, PCI DSS will require the principle of least privilege otherwise you'll fail an audit and further impact commercial priorities.

Permissions for Services

In cloud computing, a service account is like a machine in a factory. These accounts are used by applications and automated processes to interact with cloud services. An over-privileged service account has more permissions than necessary to perform its function, much like a machine with access to every part of the factory.

So why is this a problem?

- **Security vulnerabilities**: Service accounts can be an easy target for attackers. If compromised, they can be used to access sensitive data, disrupt services, or escalate privileges within the cloud environment.

- **Unintended access**: With all the extra permissions that an over privileged service account may hold, it could lead to unintended actions such as deleting data or modifying configurations.

Let us now learn how to manage over privileged access for both human users and service accounts.

Applying the principle of least privilege

Managing over privileged access for both human users and service accounts is crucial to maintaining security and operational efficiency. Follow the steps below to achieve the principle of least privilege:

Understand access requirements

When setting up access requirements try to:

- Begin by identifying the specific access requirements for each user and service.

- Determine the minimum set of permissions necessary to perform their job functions.

- Define roles based on these requirements and ensure that roles are tailored to specific tasks or responsibilities within your organization.

Role-Based Access Control (RBAC)

Role-based access controls can be more secure, so it's always worth investigating if this is possible. When creating roles consider the following:

- Develop roles with specific permissions that align with job functions and assign users to these roles. This approach limits access to only what is needed for their role.

- Separate roles by function and responsibility to prevent overlap and ensure clarity in permission allocation.

Leverage Identity and Access Management Tools

There are many varying toolsets that can help you manage your Cloud's Identity and Access controls. Consider the below best practices whilst making use of these tools:

- Use IAM tools provided by your cloud vendor to create and manage roles and policies that enforce the principle of least privilege.

- Assign roles to users and services instead of granting direct permissions to ensure that access is controlled and auditable.

- Implement control policies to set permission boundaries and prevent users from exceeding their intended access. Use access policies to define what actions users and services can perform, and apply these policies consistently across resources.

- Develop custom roles tailored to your organization's specific needs, ensuring that roles contain only the necessary permissions for users to perform their tasks. Custom roles help prevent the use of overly broad permissions that come with predefined roles.

- Utilize centralized IAM solutions to manage user identities and access across all cloud services. This approach allows for consistent policy enforcement and streamlined access management, reducing the complexity of handling permissions.

Implement Multi-Factor Authentication (MFA)

When it comes to securing cloud environments, **Multi-Factor Authentication** (MFA) is an essential step, but it's not without its own challenges.

- Within your Cloud's Identity and Access Management dashboards or control panels, ensure you mandate the usage of MFA for accessing sensitive resources to add an extra layer of security, reducing the risk of unauthorized access even if credentials are compromised.

- Ensure you use an MFA mechanism which also does not present as a single point of failure. For example, you log into your work email account, your social media, or even your cloud account and you set up a virtual MFA device using an app on your phone (e.g. Google Authenticator). You then lose your phone and now you can't log in to any of your accounts until you've gone through a sometimes lengthy process to prove your identity and reset MFA.

- Some people prefer a hardware MFA solution such as an RSA key, which will provide you the 6-digit code we're most familiar with, or a more popular Yubikey-style device, which provides a single-touch method of secondary authentication. This way they don't have to rely upon a technology that is considered almost disposable or easily replaceable. However, these methods still can get misplaced just like our keys or phones. And as they are small, they're easy to conceal too in the event of someone wanting to steal them in order to access resources they shouldn't.

There are at least 2 compromises available to us here.

- Virtualized MFA software platforms that provide backup and multiple access across different devices (e.g. 1Password, Authy, LastPass, etc).

- Applying multiple MFA methods to an account, if it's supported. This way you can apply your phone's Authenticator and a hardware device. This way you always have access to one or the other.

> **Top tip:**
> If you can use biometric (fingerprint, facial recognition, etc) authentication, do so! Biometric authentication adds an extra layer of security by tying access to something unique to the individual, making it much harder for attackers to fake or steal.

Regularly Review and Audit Permissions

Conduct regular audits of permissions to ensure they remain aligned with current job functions and responsibilities. Remove or adjust permissions that are no longer needed.

Use automated tools and scripts to identify and report on over privileged accounts and unnecessary permissions. Tools of note across the big 3 Cloud providers are:

- **AWS**

    - **AWS Identity and Access Management (IAM) Access Analyzer**: Spots externally shared resources and flags overprivileged permissions, keeping your IAM policies secure and in check.

    - **AWS Config**: Tracks changes to resources, ensuring your IAM roles and permissions stay compliant and free of misconfigurations.

    - **AWS CloudTrail**: Logs API activity, giving you visibility into who's doing what and flagging any unusual behavior.

- **Azure**

    - **Azure AD Privileged Identity Management (PIM)**: Monitors and controls access to critical resources, helping you identify and correct overprivileged accounts.

    - **Azure Policy**: Enforces compliance and audits resources to make sure your permissions and access controls meet security standards.

    - **Azure Security Center**: Provides a full view of your security posture, automating the detection and correction of risky permissions.

- **GCP**

    - **Google Cloud IAM Policy Analyzer**: Analyzes access across your GCP setup to spot overprivileged accounts and assess associated risks.

    - **Google Cloud Asset Inventory**: Offers a clear audit trail of resources and permissions, highlighting potential security gaps.

    - **Google Cloud Security Command Center**: Centralizes your security view, whilst keeping track of permissions, roles, and risky configurations.

Use Temporary and Fine-Grained Access

Other considerations to make with identity access could be:

- Utilize temporary access credentials, such as AWS **Security Token Service (STS)**, Azure Managed Identities, or GCP Service Account keys with time-limited access, to reduce the risk of long-term credential exposure.

- Apply fine-grained permissions to restrict actions users and services can perform, such as specific API calls or access to particular data sets.

Implement Logging and Monitoring

As you may read later in *Chapter 10*, understanding what is happening in your architecture is important. The same goes for your Identity Management and this can be done with Logging and Monitoring:

- Enable logging and monitoring to track access and actions performed by users and services. Use cloud native tools like AWS CloudTrail, Azure Monitor, and GCP Cloud Logging.

- Set up alerts for suspicious activities or attempts to access resources beyond granted permissions.

Educate and Train Users

And lastly, to round of the principle of least privilege, we need to ensure that our users are well educated in our security goals:

- Provide regular training to users on the importance of the principle of least privilege and best practices for maintaining a secure environment. Educate them about the potential risks and consequences of over privileged access.

- Conduct threat modeling workshops to help users understand potential security threats and how to mitigate them. By analyzing threats, users can better comprehend the importance of appropriate access controls and the role they play in protecting the organization.

- Keep users informed about updates to access policies and procedures. Ensure they understand the rationale behind these changes and how they align with overall security strategies.

Not all logging is the same

As mentioned in the previous section, logging is important. However, it's important to note the difference between application logging and security logging.

Application logging is all about tracking the performance and behavior of your software. It's the bread and butter of debugging and performance tuning. When something goes wrong, these logs tell you what happened, where, and why. They're focused on the internal workings of your application—like tracking user activities, errors, and system events that help you improve the user experience.

On the other hand, **security logging** is your line of defense against threats. These logs are designed to catch anything suspicious, from unauthorized access attempts to unusual patterns of behavior. They're not just about what's happening inside your application, but also what's happening around it—like who's trying to get in and what they're doing once they're there. Security logs give you the insights needed to detect and respond to potential breaches before they escalate.

In short, while application logs help you keep things running smoothly, security logs are there to keep things safe. Both are essential, but they serve different masters. Make sure you're paying attention to both because missing the mark on either one can leave you exposed.

Reliance on long-term static credentials

A common anti-pattern within cloud management and security is that once we've configured a user, we often forget to manage that user. We make errors sometimes and we also occasionally copy and paste the wrong thing at the wrong time.

Static credentials are the type of credentials that we set in the management console, on our laptop, or in our own emails. Occasionally, they're long-lived beyond 90 days (about 3 months), sometimes beyond 120 days (about 4 months). As time passes since the password is set, the more chance that it has been compromised. Common breaches can be:

- Loyalty card systems having their databases copied to a public source.

- Service providers leaving development API's open and public by accident

- Copy and pasting the credentials into a source code repo

- Leaving a backup of the data on the bus or train on a USB stick

This is not a limited list of potential breaches either, be creative, if you can think it, it's probably happened.

Once a bad actor has access to your data, it's already being sold on the dark web or used in malicious ways. This data could include your name, email address, usernames, and passwords.

> **Top tip:**
> Keeping passwords for a long time is bad, reusing passwords across different systems is just as bad!

As human beings, we like to reuse patterns in life as this helps make things feel familiar. So that password that's been resold on the dark web has probably been used at work and in our cloud environment, which then means it is prone to attack through guessing mechanisms. Once a bad actor has a list of email addresses and passwords, they'll start applying those to many other services, purely as a guess, to try and compromise and get access to resources that they wouldn't have had access to before.

By way of example, if I've just received a user table dump from the dark web that came from a coffee shop loyalty program that shows the below:

Username: "`user1@bigcorp.com`"

Password: "Thi!Sh0uldHaveB33nMySuperStrongPassword"

From this, we're already identifying the company the person works for, their potential username for corporate ID, and their password. This person used best practices when it came to setting their password. However, having the password breached like this doesn't help no matter how strong your password is.

Now that this password is out in the open, there's a very good chance this is also the password for their corporate email, VPN, single sign, etc. As time goes on, this gets around the internet and eventually gets into the wrong hands and then potentially used.

One cloud provider, AWS, suggests rotating passwords every 90 to 120 days as a password is deemed leaked and compromised after this point. This can be done using IAM user controls within the console or similar features within other cloud providers.

When rotating passwords, we also need to remember that sometimes we have other static credentials, such as a Developer using the AWS CLI, AWS CDK, or SDK, and have provided an access key and secret key to their application. These also need to be rotated, either using native cloud features or custom rotation policies using Lambda or other functions.

Static credentials can also exist for databases and APIs, which can often last for years or even a decade in some cases. Cloud providers offer dedicated secret vaults that allow you to store credentials securely and rotate them, so the passwords are not used in plain text or environment variables and are rotated sufficiently.

API keys are a lot harder to change, as they may be used by customers, not just your application. In this case, you need to reduce the blast radius by ensuring that an access key, IAM identity, or API key can't be used to access anyone's data but that customer's data, and ensure you have fine-grained controls to isolate customer data in a multi-tenancy system. You can read more about this in the last section of this chapter, "*Supply chain insecurity*".

Threat modeling

Prior to any planned permissions being given out to people or systems, it's important to understand the threat level presented to you at the time of making these decisions.

Ask yourself the following 4 questions:

- What are we working on?
- What can go wrong?
- What are we going to do about it?
- Did we do a good enough job?

Once you've answered these 4 questions, you should have a much better picture of the threat level presented at the time. This is basic threat modeling.

Threat modeling is all about getting ahead of the game when it comes to security. It's a process where you break down your system to spot potential vulnerabilities and figure out how they could be exploited. By thinking like an attacker, you can identify where the weak spots are and take steps to shore them up before they become a problem. It's about being proactive, not reactive, giving you a way to prioritize and address risks so you're not caught off guard. In short, threat modeling helps you stay one step ahead of any potential threats.

Threat modeling as a practice could be a whole book of its own and is a lot to go into but the one major anti-pattern seen here is the ignorance or naivety of it as a practice.

Make sure all your staff who work with code or infrastructure are trained in threat modeling. Don't just make it one-off training either, this should be revisited yearly, and part included as part of standard onboarding processes for human resources.

Importance of Continuous Compliance in Security

When it comes to launching a new application or system, there's often a rush to check off that final penetration test before the big go-live moment. But here's the catch: relying on just one test is like giving your car a once-over before a road trip and hoping for the best. Security and compliance require ongoing attention and effort. In this chapter, we'll unravel the true meaning of compliance and why it's essential to integrate it into your security strategy beyond that one-time test.

Myth busting the One-Time Test

You must have heard this myth *"One penetration test is all I need"*.

Let's bust this myth right now. One penetration test before launch is not going to be enough to guarantee the security of your application. It'll give you a great picture of where things are right now, that snapshot in time, and may be enough to give you a red light/green light, "go/no-go" situation.

But what about next week? Next month?

Security threats evolve over time, sometimes even overnight. Security needs to be an ongoing process, something you're always working on and always have visibility of. Not just at the last minute. Bake it into your application, architecture, and infrastructure. Make it part of your workplace culture.

Overnight changes

Back in November 2021 on the 23rd, many millions of software developers, CTO's, CIO and engineering managers went to bed blissfully unaware that anything could be wrong with their application stack. Like something from a movie scene, these people were all rudely awakened the next morning to what is known as one of the most serious security exploits ever.

"Log4Shell" (CVE-2021-44228) was a vulnerability found in the popular Java logging framework, Log4J. It was rated as a 10 on the CVE index, the highest rating that can ever be given, and allowed bad actors to execute arbitrary code on servers using Log4J. The vulnerability lay dormant since 2013 and was only found 8 years later and took almost another month to patch.

But once this became a known vulnerability, this was Day 0. The moment of panic. The moment when you are most vulnerable because the exploit is known to the world, arming hackers with a weapon to be used at will by anyone wanting to cause malicious damage. At the same time, the authorities, "the good guys" in our movie scene, are looking for ways to work around and patch protect from the effects of this vulnerability.

If you were a Java software developer or a CTO with a Java stack, would you want to be blissfully unaware of this situation? Or would you rather be woken up to an alert or an email, arming yourself with the right information at the right time to mitigate this circumstance?

The Importance of Continuous Security and Compliance

The story of Log4Shell is a stark reminder that security is never a one-and-done task. Even if your system passes a penetration test today, new vulnerabilities could be discovered tomorrow. The only way to stay ahead of these threats is through continuous security monitoring and compliance validation.

Compliance Is More Than Just a Checklist

Compliance is not just about a bunch of checkboxes or avoiding harsh fines. It's about protecting your intellectual property, your organization, and your reputation and building a level of trust with your customers. When you integrate compliance into your security strategy, you are not just adhering to a bunch of loose guidelines, you're also safeguarding yourself and your systems against massive threats.

Imagine compliance as the framework that holds your security strategy together. Without it, even the most advanced security measures can fall apart under the weight of a new vulnerability or regulatory requirement. That's why it's critical to make compliance an ongoing process, not just a once-a-year audit.

Compliance Frameworks

There are many compliance frameworks and blueprints that you can look toward using. It's worth noting that once you adhere to a certain compliance framework, it's like a badge of honor, a seal of trust, that customers and vendors alike can see and know you adhere to certain standards. Some of the popular frameworks to date are:

- **ISO/IEC 27001:2022 - Information security, cybersecurity and privacy protection**: Focused primarily on information security management systems (ISMS) it provides a blueprint for continuously protecting sensitive information and controls related to implementing and maintaining the integrity of data protection. ISO27001 requires regular audits to ensure standards are maintained and is a globally recognized standard.

- **PCI-DSS - Payment Card Industry Data Security Standard**: PCI-DSS is focused on securing payment card data for any organization that processes, stores, or transmits it. The standard lays out strict requirements, from encryption to access controls, ensuring that cardholder information is protected against breaches. Compliance isn't optional—if you handle payment cards, following PCI-DSS is a must to operate legally and securely.

- **SOC-2 - Systems and Organization Controls 2**: SOC 2 is all about making sure your organization's security, availability, and privacy controls are up to par, especially if you're a tech or cloud service provider. It's split into two types:

- Type I checks your controls at a specific point in time, while

- Type II looks at how well they perform over time.

This standard is key for proving you can handle customer data securely and reliably.

Each one of these standards requires a yearly audit to show compliance.

There are many other frameworks globally, but these are potentially the most popular that we see in the wild.

As has now been mentioned repeatedly through this section, it's important to maintain these standards long term, and as such, each framework has its yearly re-audit and re-compliance.

The ongoing success of compliance and passing the audits does not come from yearly auditing which may incur a couple of months of preparation, whilst pulling engineers or operational staff out of billable roles for a massive chunk of time. Instead, success comes from making these frameworks part of your culture. Everyone should have these frameworks as part of their daily routine, this way passing the audit will be second nature. Not something to be prepared for.

This is what we call *"Continuous Compliance"*.

The Role of Automation in Security and Compliance

Given the pace at which threats evolve, manual security checks simply aren't enough. Automation plays a crucial role in ensuring that your security posture remains robust and that compliance is maintained continuously.

Automated tools can help you monitor your systems in real time, detect potential threats, and ensure that your security controls are always aligned with the latest compliance standards. By automating these processes, you're not only improving efficiency but also reducing the risk of human error.

Each of the big 3 cloud providers offers continuous compliance tooling to help ensure standards are maintained:

- **AWS**: AWS Security Hub gives you a central place to see what's going on with your security across AWS. It pulls in data from various AWS services and third-party tools, continuously checks your environment against best practices, and helps you prioritize issues that need fixing.

- **Azure**: Azure Security Center (now Microsoft Defender for Cloud) does something similar for Azure. It keeps an eye on your resources, offering security assessments, threat protection, and a dashboard to track your compliance. It's not just for Azure, though—it also covers hybrid and multi-cloud setups, so you're protected no matter where your data lives.

- **GCP**: Google Cloud **Security Command Center** (SCC) is GCP's answer to centralized security management. It gives you a clear view of your Google Cloud environment, keeping tabs on misconfigurations, vulnerabilities, and threats. SCC also helps you stay compliant with industry standards, all while integrating with Google's security services to spot and respond to issues quickly.

There are also third-party solutions available to achieve this externally of your Cloud environment. You'll generally provision it access to view your cloud account using a role or access credentials and let it scan regularly. Consider this, a fresh pair of eyes looking at your architecture, offering capabilities that might go beyond what the native tooling may do. These tool sets come with their own costings, so it could be a security vs cost-optimization trade-off.

Building a Proactive Security Culture

To reference *Chapter 5, Underestimating the cultural impact*, to truly protect your organization, security and compliance need to be ingrained in your company's culture. This means everyone—from developers to top executives—should understand the importance of security and be committed to maintaining it.

Regular training sessions, security drills, and awareness programs can help build this culture, ensuring that every team member knows their role in keeping the organization secure. When security is everyone's responsibility, you're far less likely to be caught off guard by a new threat.

> **Top Tip:**
>
> Don't do your own penetration test—bring in an independent reviewer. You're too close to your own setup, which means blind spots are easy to miss. An external expert will bring fresh eyes, spot weaknesses you didn't see, and give you a truly unbiased assessment that stands up for compliance.

Wrapping compliance up

So, you've passed the penetration test and launched your application. What's next? This is where the real work begins. Ongoing security assessments, regular compliance checks, and a commitment to continuous improvement are what will keep your application secure in the long run.

Remember, security isn't just a destination; it's a journey. And on this journey, there's no room for complacency. The moment you let your guard down, you open the door to potential threats. But by making security and compliance a continuous process, you can protect your organization against whatever challenges lie ahead.

The story of Log4Shell isn't just a cautionary tale—it's a call to action. It's a reminder that in the world of security, there's no such thing as *"enough."* One penetration test before going live might give you a temporary sense of security, but it's the ongoing work—continuous monitoring, compliance validation, and a proactive security culture—that will truly protect your organization.

In the end, security is about more than just protecting your systems; it's about building trust, safeguarding your reputation, and ensuring the long-term success of your organization. So don't stop at the go-live moment. Keep pushing forward, keep improving, and keep your security and compliance efforts at the forefront of everything you do.

Proactive Monitoring: Don't Wait for the External Audit to Spot Issues

Launching a new application or system is an exciting milestone, but it's also a critical moment for ensuring your security measures are up to scratch. Relying on a single vulnerability scan or penetration test before go-live is like giving your car a once-over before a cross-country road trip and hoping for the best. Security is not a one-time event; it's an ongoing process that requires constant vigilance. By integrating regular security assessments and leveraging automation, organizations can maintain continuous compliance and tackle vulnerabilities before they turn into big problems.

Importance of Ongoing Security Assessments

One-off security assessments give you a snapshot of your current state, but they don't account for future changes or emerging threats. To stay ahead of the game, you need a mindset focused on continuous improvement and proactive defense. Consider the following best practices:

Vulnerability Scans and Penetration Tests

Regular vulnerability scans and penetration tests are essential for spotting and fixing security weaknesses. These assessments shine a light on vulnerabilities that attackers could exploit, allowing you to take action before it's too late.

Continuous Monitoring

Set up a schedule for regular scans and tests to ensure your security posture is always up to date. This approach helps you catch new vulnerabilities and address them promptly, keeping your systems secure. By way of example, many organizations will organize quarterly perimeter scans of their architecture and then a yearly external, more in depth, penetration test. This way they can get insight into any network or application vulnerabilities.

Proactive Defense & Continuous Compliance

By running regular assessments, you can anticipate threats and bolster your defenses against evolving attack vectors. Staying ahead of potential attacks is key to maintaining a strong security posture. These assessments don't have to be orchestrated activities but can be automated systems that then send alerts to relevant stakeholders.

Comprehensive Coverage

Make sure your vulnerability scans and penetration tests cover all bases, from networks to applications and infrastructure. A holistic view of your security posture ensures that no stone is left unturned. Key points here may be:

- **External network port scanning**: What network ports and protocols are exposed?

- **Application penetration tests**: Can we exploit anything that is exposed?

- **Source code scanning**: You can scan source code in pipelines or at rest in its repository.

- **Internal configuration checks**: Check resources are configured appropriately and won't cause any issues if exposed by accident (or on purpose).

Don't forget, some things will be exposed on purpose, like HTTPS or SMTP ports. So make sure the versions are secured and up to date.

Automating Security Processes

Making continuous compliance and security assessments feasible requires automation. By automating routine security checks, organizations can streamline efforts and ensure consistent protection while freeing up resources for more strategic activities. Consider the below whilst implementing:

- Automation takes care of repetitive tasks, freeing up your team for more critical work. From running regular vulnerability scans to deploying patches, automated processes ensure security measures are applied consistently and efficiently.

- Use automated tools to perform scans, analyze results, and generate reports. Automation allows you to scale security efforts without overwhelming your team, keeping you covered across large environments.

- Automated tools can detect anomalies and potential threats faster than manual processes, enabling quicker responses and minimizing potential damage.

- Automation supports an agile approach to compliance, allowing for more frequent checkpoints and adjustments based on real-time insights. This agility ensures your security measures stay in line with best practices and regulations.

Continuous Compliance Validation

Annual compliance checks are a thing of the past. With today's dynamic threat landscape, continuous compliance validation is the way forward. This involves regularly evaluating and updating security controls to stay aligned with current standards. Consider the example of Agile Compliance. **Agile compliance** means integrating compliance checks into your regular development and operational processes, ensuring that compliance is an ongoing focus rather than a last-minute scramble.

- Establish several compliance checkpoints throughout the year to continuously validate your security measures and ensure they meet evolving requirements.

- Use insights from ongoing assessments to make real-time adjustments to your security posture, keeping your organization resilient and ready for whatever comes next.

- Encourage collaboration between security, compliance, and development teams to ensure security and compliance are woven into every stage of the development lifecycle.

The Role of External Audits

While internal assessments and automation play vital roles in maintaining security, external audits provide a fresh perspective and additional assurance. These audits, conducted by independent third parties, can identify blind spots and offer insights that internal teams might overlook.

- External audits provide an objective assessment of your security posture, highlighting areas for improvement that might be missed by those too close to daily operations.

- Auditors assess your security practices against industry standards and regulatory requirements, ensuring that your organization meets or exceeds compliance benchmarks.

- Successfully completing an external audit can enhance trust with customers, partners, and stakeholders by demonstrating your commitment to maintaining a robust security posture.

- External auditors can offer practical, actionable recommendations to enhance your security strategy and close identified gaps.

Building a Proactive Security Culture

To support continuous compliance and security assessments, fostering a proactive security culture is crucial. This means valuing security as an integral part of operations, supported by leadership and embraced by everyone. Educate your team by:

- Regularly educating employees about the importance of security and compliance. Empower them with the knowledge to identify and respond to potential threats.

- Securing buy-in from leadership to prioritize security initiatives and allocate necessary resources. Leadership support drives cultural change and keeps security a top priority.

- Capture lessons learned from security incidents and assessments. Use this feedback to refine security policies and practices, promoting continuous improvement.

To summarize, security and compliance aren't just boxes to tick off before going live—they're ongoing commitments that demand constant attention and adaptation. By embracing continuous security assessments, leveraging automation, and adopting agile compliance practices, you can maintain a robust security posture and stay ahead of potential threats. This proactive approach not only protects your assets but also builds trust with stakeholders and ensures long-term success in an ever-evolving digital landscape. By integrating security into your organization's fabric and utilizing external audits for additional insight, you can confidently navigate today's complex threat environment.

Misunderstanding the shared responsibility model

In the world of cloud computing, the shared responsibility model is a fundamental concept that dictates how security and compliance duties are divided between cloud service providers and their customers. Despite its importance, this model is often misunderstood, leading to gaps in security and increased risk. This chapter explores common misconceptions about the shared responsibility model and offers guidance on how to navigate and leverage it effectively to enhance your organization's security posture.

Ultimately, we explore the difference between *"Security of the Cloud"* and *"Security in the Cloud"*

Understanding and Addressing Misconceptions in the Shared Responsibility Model

The **shared responsibility model** is a framework that defines the division of labor between cloud providers and their customers when it comes to security and compliance. While the provider is responsible for securing the infrastructure that runs all services, the customer is responsible for securing their data, applications, and configurations.

Responsibilities of Cloud Providers

Cloud providers, such as AWS, Azure, and Google Cloud, are responsible for the security of the cloud. This includes the physical security of data centers, the underlying hardware, network infrastructure, and foundational services.

Providers ensure that the physical infrastructure and network components are secure, protecting against unauthorized access and tampering. They also maintain compliance with various industry standards and certifications, offering customers a secure platform to build upon.

Responsibilities of Customers

Customers are responsible for security in the cloud. This means they must secure their applications, data, and configurations within the cloud environment.

Customers must protect their data through encryption, access controls, and regular backups whilst ensuring that applications running in the cloud are secure from vulnerabilities and potential exploits is the customer's responsibility. Customers must also implement robust identity and access policies to control access to cloud resources and data.

Shared Responsibility Model Across "The Big 3"

Whilst the shared responsibility model is a common framework across all providers, each of the big three cloud vendors (AWS, Azure, and GCP), implements it with slight variations that customers need to be across.

AWS (Amazon Web Services)

AWS addresses its shared responsibility model by using 2 different terms or phrases. *"Security of the Cloud"* and *"Security in the cloud"*

- In the former, *"Security of the Cloud"*, AWS is responsible for protecting all of the infrastructure that runs the services offered in the AWS Cloud. This includes hardware, software, networking and facilities.

- In the latter, *"Security in the Cloud"*, the Customer is responsible for ensuring that their data, operating systems and applications they run on AWS are secure. This also includes configuration and access controls.

The below diagram details the demarcation areas of the AWS Shared Responsibility Model.

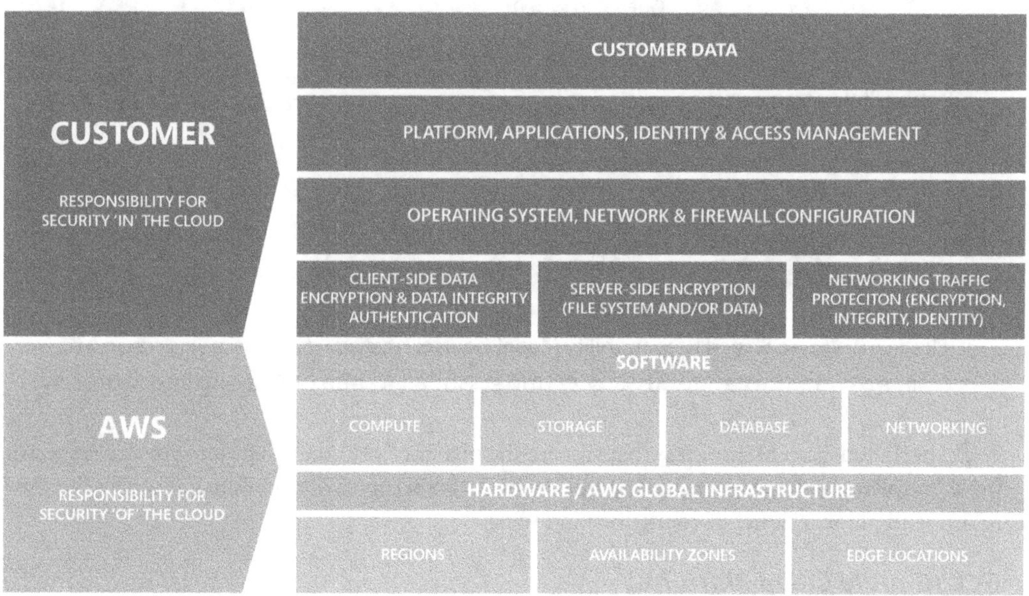

Figure 6.1 – AWS Share Responsibility Model
(source: https://aws.amazon.com/compliance/shared-responsibility-model/)

Microsoft Azure

Azure follows a similar shared responsibility model, where Microsoft is responsible for the security of the underlying cloud infrastructure, including data centers, physical hosts, and networking. Customers are responsible for securing their workloads, applications, data, and configurations within the Azure environment. Azure also emphasizes the importance of using their built-in security tools to manage and monitor the customer's responsibilities effectively.

This image shows us the divide of responsibility:

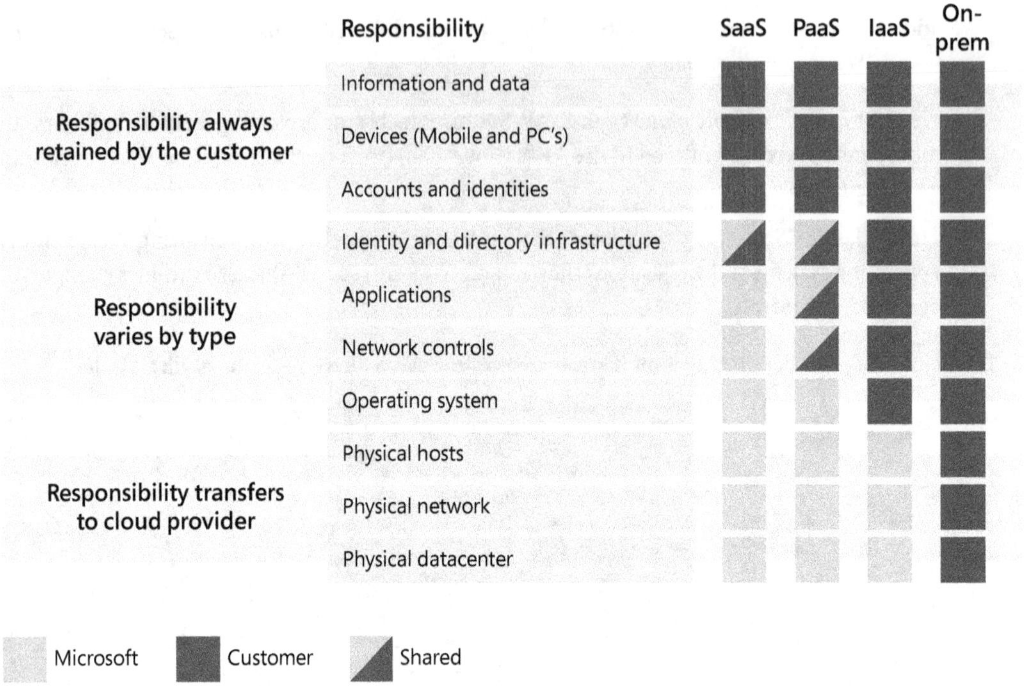

	Responsibility	SaaS	PaaS	IaaS	On-prem
Responsibility always retained by the customer	Information and data	Customer	Customer	Customer	Customer
	Devices (Mobile and PC's)	Customer	Customer	Customer	Customer
	Accounts and identities	Customer	Customer	Customer	Customer
Responsibility varies by type	Identity and directory infrastructure	Shared	Shared	Customer	Customer
	Applications	Microsoft	Shared	Customer	Customer
	Network controls	Microsoft	Shared	Customer	Customer
	Operating system	Microsoft	Microsoft	Customer	Customer
Responsibility transfers to cloud provider	Physical hosts	Microsoft	Microsoft	Microsoft	Customer
	Physical network	Microsoft	Microsoft	Microsoft	Customer
	Physical datacenter	Microsoft	Microsoft	Microsoft	Customer

Legend: Microsoft | Customer | Shared

Figure 6.2 – Azure Shared Responsibility Model (source: `https://learn.microsoft.com/en-us/azure/security/fundamentals/shared-responsibility`)

The expectation from Microsoft is that you are the owner of your data therefore you are responsible for it. You also maintain ownership and responsibility for accounts and identities as well as any device or user end points you might configure and utilize.

GCP (Google Cloud Platform)

Google also adheres to a very familiar model to the other providers where Google is the owner of the global infrastructure, network, and foundational services and therefore responsible. Similarly, Customers are expected to manage their data, applications, and access controls.

Unlike other providers, note today, Google operates a slightly augmented Shared responsibility model called "Shared responsibility and Shared fate". This adds geographical location and Industry also into the considerations.

Geographical location awareness starts with looking at your responsibilities depending on where you deploy your workload and where your customer data resides. E.g. If you deploy in the EU, you may find yourself having to abide by the requirements of GDPR (General Data Protection Regulation) and you will then have to ensure your data doesn't leave the EU.

Various Industries may have different regulatory compliance frameworks, which then may stipulate how you handle data. For example, the Payment Card Industry Data Security Standard stipulates how payment processors look after their data and isolate certain data types.

In both situations, Google has a separate Responsibility Matrix to ensure services and architectures are secure by design.

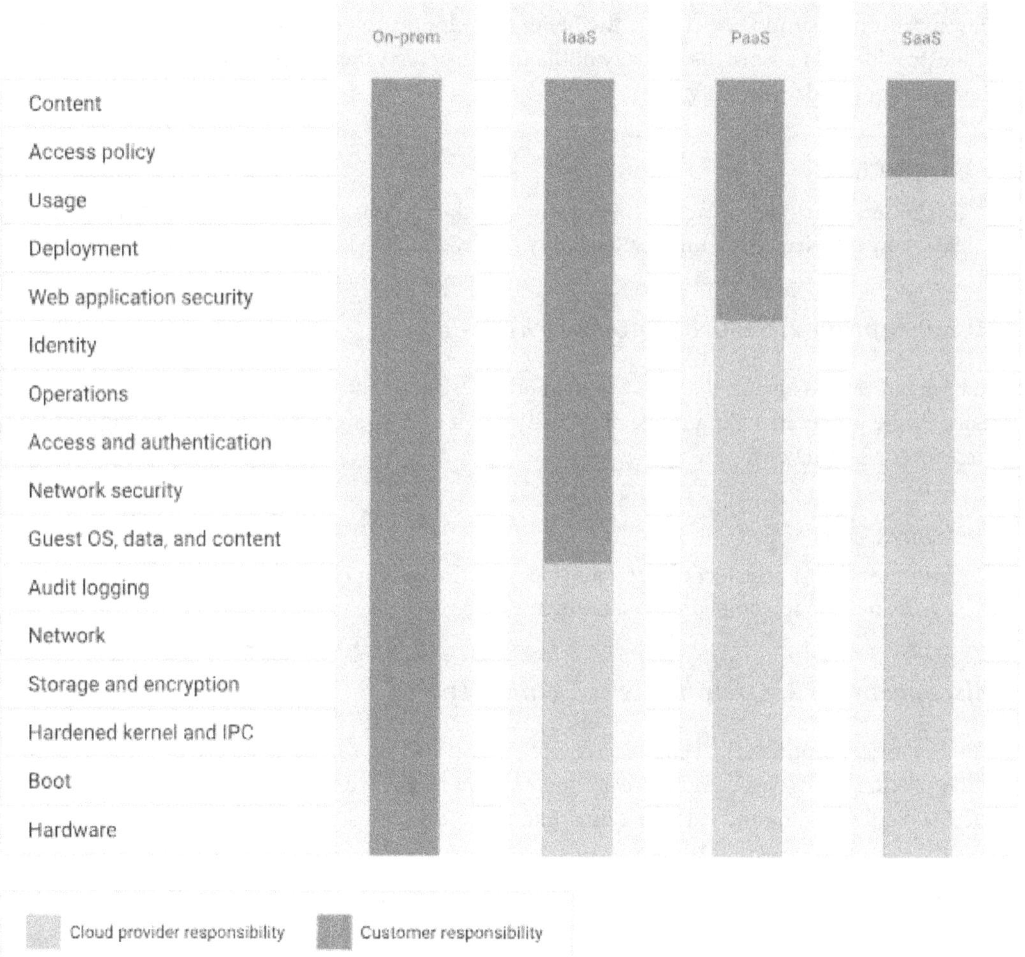

Figure 6.3 – GCP shared responsibility shared fate (source: https://cloud.google. com/architecture/framework/security/shared-responsibility-shared-fate)

Common Misunderstandings

Despite the clarity of the shared responsibility model, several misconceptions persist that can lead to security oversights and vulnerabilities.

Misconception 1: The Provider Handles Everything

One common misunderstanding is the belief that cloud providers handle all aspects of security. While providers do ensure the security of the infrastructure, they do not manage customer-specific configurations or data security.

> **Reality Check**
>
> Customers must take an active role in securing their applications and data within the cloud environment. Neglecting this responsibility can lead to data breaches and compliance failures.

Misconception 2: Security Tools are Built-In

Some organizations assume that using a cloud provider automatically includes comprehensive security tools. While providers offer a range of security services, it is up to customers to configure and use these tools effectively.

> **Reality Check**
>
> Customers must select, configure, and manage the appropriate security tools to meet their specific needs and compliance requirements.

Misconception 3: Compliance is Guaranteed

Another misconception is that compliance with industry standards is guaranteed by using a compliant cloud provider. However, compliance is a shared responsibility, and customers must ensure that their specific configurations and data-handling practices meet regulatory requirements.

> **Reality Check**
>
> Customers should conduct regular compliance assessments and audits to ensure their operations within the cloud meet all relevant standards.

Cloud Provider Proof of Compliance

With the latter misconception, it's worth noting that each of the cloud providers will provide you attestations of their compliance to their part of the shared responsibility. An example of this is that a Cloud Service may become FedRAMP or HIPPA compliant. But how do we prove this?

- **AWS**: AWS Artifact is your quick-access portal for grabbing all the compliance documentation you need when using AWS. Whether it's SOC reports, ISO certifications, or PCI-DSS attestations, Artifact has it all in one place, saving you the hassle of hunting down the paperwork when you need to prove your environment meets industry standards.

- **Azure**: Azure Compliance Manager not only gives you access to the necessary compliance reports but also helps you manage your compliance posture with a clear dashboard and built-in workflows. It's all about making compliance easier, giving you the insights and tools to stay on top of regulatory requirements without getting bogged down.

- **GCP**: Google Cloud Compliance Reports Manager keeps things straightforward, providing a centralized spot to download the compliance documentation relevant to your Google Cloud services. It's all there, from SOC reports to ISO certifications, so you're never left scrambling when it's time to show your compliance credentials.

Common Misconfigurations

To put these common misunderstandings into more practical terms, the most common misconfigurations seen in the wild, due to misunderstanding or ignoring the shared responsibility model, are listed here:

- Inappropriate access controls leading to unauthorized access to sensitive data and systems, further leading to data breaches, compromised accounts and insider threats.

- Not encrypting sensitive data stored in the cloud or during transmission between systems leading to data exposure, especially in the event of a data breach or interception during transit, resulting in loss of confidentiality and regulatory non-compliance.

- Not patching Operating Systems or applying updates to applications and software, leading to vulnerability to known exploits and attacks, leading to potential system compromise, data breach and exploitation to malicious actors.

- Using overly broad or permissive security group settings or firewall rules that allow unrestricted inbound or outbound traffic. This can lead to increased risk of unauthorized network access, exposing systems to potential attacks such as Distributed Denial of Service (DDoS), port scanning, or unauthorized data exfiltration.

- Incorrectly configuring cloud storage services such as Amazon S3, Azure Blob Storage or Google Cloud Storage, allowing access to sensitive data, leading to accident data exposure and then leading to significant reputational damage.

This is not an exhaustive list however the scope for loss of data, reputation and then significant damage to reputation will eventually lead to commercial failure.

In summary, understanding the shared responsibility model is crucial for effectively securing your cloud environment. By recognizing the distinct roles of cloud providers and customers, organizations can ensure that their security measures are comprehensive and robust. Educating your team, implementing strong security controls, and leveraging provider tools are essential steps in navigating this model successfully. By embracing your responsibilities, you can protect your organization's data and applications, ensuring compliance and building trust with stakeholders in today's dynamic digital landscape.

Supply chain insecurity

One of the key areas that gets neglected in security is the Supply Chain. Think of your business as a series of interconnected parts and you are the middle link. You have vendors, suppliers, and partners all linked into each other like a bicycle chain. All of a sudden one of those links is compromised and you have a weak point in your chain. You're all potentially at risk

In a cloud-based environment, your data and systems are often intertwined with those of third parties. This interdependence can expose your organization to vulnerabilities if your partners don't have robust security measures in place. A breach in one part of the supply chain can have cascading effects, leading to data leaks, service disruptions, and reputational damage.

However, we cannot go through our day-to-day business without the chain of relationships between vendors and customers. These relationships are essential to us doing business. Therefore we have to look at how we trade information and data, safely and securely.

Challenges in Supply Chain Security

Common challenges in supply chain security can arise from:

- **Lack of visibility**: Often, organizations of all sizes can have limited insight into the security practices of their vendors. This lack of visibility makes it challenging to assess and manage risks effectively.

- **Varying security standards**: Different vendors may have different levels of security maturity, from zero trust to not having an enforced standard and ad hoc controls. While some may have rigorous security measures, others might not meet the same standards, creating gaps in your security posture.

- **Complex relationships**: Managing relationships with multiple vendors can be complex. Ensuring consistent security practices across all partners requires effort and coordination.

- **Third-party access**: Vendors often need access to your systems and data to provide services. Without proper access controls, this can lead to over privileged access, increasing the risk of unauthorized actions.

Avoiding Supply Chain Risks

To try and mitigate the risk of an insecure supply chain, try and adopt the following best practices:

- **Vendor-based risk management**: Have your new vendors complete a security audit or a risk evaluation prior to onboarding. Check they are following security best practices. It's crucial at this point to set up a foundation for your risk tolerance, maybe categorize your different levels of risk based on the level of access to your environment they may need. It's also important to respect regulatory requirements in these audits such as GDPR, CCPA, and HIPAA. You could also consider geographical location to be a factor in your prioritization.

- **Scheduled review of risk**: Having completed the risk assessment shouldn't be a one-off activity. A vendor is generally out of your purview and things can change rapidly. If our vendor acquires a new CTO or CEO and they announce cost-cutting measures or improved efficiencies they may deem a certain security standard or practice to be changed or even removed if they believe it to be of excessive overhead. This may change your vendor's risk profile, but you will not be aware of it.

  This is where a regular review of the risk or a yearly security assessment may help identify any changed risk.

- **Scheduled review of requirements**: Just as much as things may change at your vendor, things will change within your own organization as well. You may deprecate systems, add in new systems, or change data locations. In this case, the access requirements of your vendor relationship will change too. It's easy to grant new access to extra services but we often forget to remove the old access. This review should identify excessive permissions where possible

- **Incident response across the chain**: What happens when there is a security incident somewhere in your supply chain? "Great question" I hear you exclaim. Because of the potential for tight dependencies on each other in the relationship and shared risk at this point, you will want to develop an Incident response plan. This needs to be concise actions and clear communication. Who reports what to whom? Why? Which members of who's team need to enact what? At this point, honesty is the best policy, as they say. Ensure the policy removes any element of blame to ensure a swift outcome of the incident response plan.

It's worth noting that each cloud vendor also offers a series of playbooks/runbooks to help in the event of a security breach.

AWS	AWS Incident Response Playbook Samples	`https://github.com/aws-samples/aws-incident-response-playbooks`
Azure	Incident response playbooks	`https://learn.microsoft.com/en-us/security/operations/incident-response-playbooks`
GCP	Data incident response process	`https://cloud.google.com/docs/security/incident-response`

Table 6.1 - Cloud Provider Incident Response Playbooks

These playbooks, in most cases, are designed to augment your own processes and not be depended on as a sole resource.

Examples of Supply Chain Insecurity

Quite often, you'll not realize you have a supply chain security issue until it's too late. These examples of real-world supply chain insecurities can help you learn by mistakes others have made in the wild:

Example 1

A common example of this is providing vendors, suppliers or customers with third party API keys or access keys to your systems. These often don't get rotated because of complexity in systems at the third-party side and/or lack of policy. The third party may also not store the credential in a secure way, leaving the keys exposed. This means that your system can be breached due to their lack of robust security.

Example 2

In 2016, a small npm package called left-pad caused a huge disruption across the JavaScript world. Left-pad's job was simple—add padding to the left side of a string—but it was a dependency for thousands of projects, including major ones like React. Out of nowhere, the developer, frustrated with a separate dispute, decided to pull left-pad from npm. Instantly, projects around the globe broke down, leaving developers scrambling to fix the sudden mess.

This incident was a harsh lesson in supply chain insecurity. It showed how fragile our software ecosystems can be when we rely on external dependencies without safeguards in place. If something as small as left-pad could bring down so many projects, it's clear we need to be more vigilant. This means verifying the integrity of packages, having backup plans, and thinking carefully about every dependency we include in our projects. Even the smallest component can cause a major headache when it's gone.

Summary

In today's digital landscape, supply chain security is not just a nice-to-have, it's a necessity. By proactively managing the security of your supply chain, you can protect your organization from the risks associated with third-party relationships and maintain the trust of your customers and stakeholders.

From this, you've got a solid handle on how to lock down your cloud environment by putting the principle of least privilege into practice. This gives you the tools to cut down the risks tied to over-privileged users and ensures you've got tighter control over who can access your critical resources.

Throughout this chapter we have reviewed and understood the following:

- Application of the prinicpal of least priviledge

- Continuous compliance in security

- Provactive monitoring of security

- The shared responsiblity model

- The importance of supply chain security

In the next chapter, we continue on to discuss the business logic that makes your application and common anti-pattern in some software development practices.

Get This Book's PDF Version and Exclusive Extras

Scan the QR code (or go to `packtpub.com/unlock`). Search for this book by name, confirm the edition, and then follow the steps on the page.

Note: Keep your invoice handly. Purchase made directly from packt don't require one.

Part 3:
Turning It into Actions

This final part will follow on from the previous part and describe common anti-patterns, how to avoid them, and how to transition to good habits. The areas we will explore include applications, data, networking, observability, operations, migrations, and testing. This final part will summarize how to prepare ourselves and our organization for a successful cloud adoption journey, how to spot anti-patterns, and how to define the best outcome. We will close by discussing achieving good stakeholder alignment, enhancing our roadmap, and setting our organization up for continuous improvement.

This part has the following chapters:

- *Chapter 7, Expressing Your Business Goals in Application Code*

- *Chapter 8, Don't Get Lost in the Data Jungle*

- *Chapter 9, Connecting It All*

- *Chapter 10, Observing Our Architecture*

- *Chapter 11, Running It Without Breaking It*

- *Chapter 12, Migrating from Legacy Systems to Cloud Native Solutions*

- *Chapter 13, How Do You Know It All Works?*

- *Chapter 14, How to Get Started with Your Cloud Native Improvement Journey*

- *Chapter 15, Transitioning to Cloud Native Good Habits*

7

Expressing Your Business Goals in Application Code

The **business logic** that makes our company technology unique and provides a competitive advantage is usually the business logic that we employ. Expressing our business rules as **application code** can drive forward automation, reduce cycle times, and increase productive output. However, when we move that logic to the cloud, we can be trapped by some **anti-patterns** that we would normally get away with in the old monolithic, on-premises architectures we are evolving.

In this chapter, we're going to cover the following main topics:

- Lift and shift
- Stateful applications
- Tight coupling, low cohesion
- The comprehensive definition of done
- Other pitfalls

Lift and shift

When we move applications to the cloud, we need to shift our thinking from deploying an application as an independent unit to the application being the emergent behavior of the interaction of various services. In this section, we will explore the typical process of shifting an application to the cloud, the strategies we can use, and how to increase the maturity of our cloud native solution.

Building in the cloud versus building for the cloud

When we migrate applications to the cloud, the simplest method is to package up the existing deployment in a VM, deploy it to the cloud, and call it cloud native. This thinking limits the actual usage of the cloud to simply reflect the existing topologies we had in our on-premises environment. But what have we achieved? We still have the same limitations of the system we just migrated from but without any of the advantages of the cloud. We've just moved our code from our server to someone else's server. We may gain some efficiencies in maintainability, organizational complexity, and onboarding time. However, this is not unique to cloud hyperscalers, and we could achieve the same results with most other VM hosts. This **lift-and-shift** mindset gets us into the cloud but falls short of fully utilizing it. This mindset is the difference between building *in* the cloud versus building *for* the cloud. Once the application is in the cloud via this lift-and-shift methodology, we can make improvements and optimizations not only to the application itself but also to its surrounding infrastructure and architecture.

I previously worked for a company that had an existing on-premises solution. This on-premises solution was distributed to customers via remote deployment. The client provided a machine, and a specific onboarding team logged in to that machine and ran a playbook to set up the application. This lift-and-shift mindset persisted into the *cloud native* hosted offerings they provided. The onboarding team provisioned a new instance and database in the cloud, and then somebody installed the application, and the client accessed the cloud instance. This process was the company's first iteration of providing services in the cloud. However, the manual processes have been persistent and difficult to shake. These processes are a classic example of building in the cloud versus building for the cloud. It can be challenging to relinquish control of these business procedures to automation. However, unless we utilize the advantages that the cloud provides, we fail to recognize the actual efficiencies of this shift. A good approach that would have allowed for much faster cycle times and reduced new customer entry barriers is shifting to self-serve, on-demand onboarding, using a cloud factory approach, as we will see in more detail later in the chapter. Similar techniques were adopted in their future cloud native applications, built from the ground up. However, this brings us to a new anti-pattern, having the attitude that "we'll build it right this time."

The myth of "We'll build it right this time"

One of the anti-patterns we often see is software teams wanting to burn everything to the ground and start again to become cloud native. This all-or-nothing approach not only fragments your business into **legacy** (your original application) and **greenfield** (your brand-new application) development but also means that you neglect a product that customers are using to work on a product that will likely not have users until at least parity with your on-premises solution. The timelines of these projects are often wildly underestimated and require reskilling and re-resourcing to get the cloud native skills you need. The all-or-nothing approach frequently means that critical decisions around your application and its architecture are made upfront at the point in time when your organization likely has the least cloud experience on hand!

When shifting to the cloud, AWS has the 7Rs of migration strategies to use, which we went through in *Chapter 2*. To refresh your memory, these are refactor, replatform, repurchase, rehost, relocate, retain, and retire.

You'll notice that *rebuild* is not one of the options. To take full advantage of cloud native services in an existing application, we must choose an option that will eventually lead us down the refactor path. The easiest way to start is to build a cloud factory for our existing application.

Cloud factories

The lift-and-shift part of a cloud migration is unavoidable. Running the existing application in the cloud is the first step to migrating it to become cloud native. When deploying an on-premises application, there is a significant lead time, as it involves hardware provided by the customer, with customer-controlled access and rollouts with manual steps. As discussed in our earlier example, a common anti-pattern in this space reflects that process in the cloud environment. Customers use different **firewalls**, **hypervisors**, **hardware**, and **security** in an on-premises environment. The rollout process typically requires manual intervention to deal with the idiosyncrasies of the particular client.

When deploying in a cloud environment, we get to specify these options ourselves. We say how big our VM is, how we configure our firewall and networking, or what operating system we use. Instead of multiple unique customer environments, we're deploying the same cloud environment multiple times, meaning all the quirks are identical for each implementation case. We can now automate the provisioning workflow with certainty, reducing onboarding from a process that might take weeks with multiple client contacts to a process that can run in a pipeline and might take 30 minutes. Creating a cloud factory for your application is a crucial first step for migrating on-premises applications to the cloud without rearchitecting to a multitenant model. We will delve deeper into this in *Chapter 12*. As we start to transition our application to the cloud, the question still remains: how will we refactor this while retaining the end functionality? The answer is through the use of the strangler fig pattern.

Cloud native through the strangler fig pattern

A strangler fig is a plant that grows on a host tree. Sometimes, the host tree dies, leaving only the strangler fig. The **strangler fig pattern**, coined by Martin Fowler, is similar. It lets us take our existing applications and make them cloud native by slow degrees, eventually replacing our legacy solution altogether. Through this mechanism of action, we also allow for the deferral of system-wide architectural decisions until later in the process, once the cloud maturity of our organization has improved. The first stage of cloud migration is to take our existing application to the cloud – that is, rehost. You can also technically take this approach without the rehost phase and instead redirect traffic to our on-premises instance, although this requires additional networking and solid authorization strategies to be in place. This simple transition is depicted in *Figure 7.1*. We start with an on-premises instance and replace it with a cloud instance. The switch is transparent to the end user.

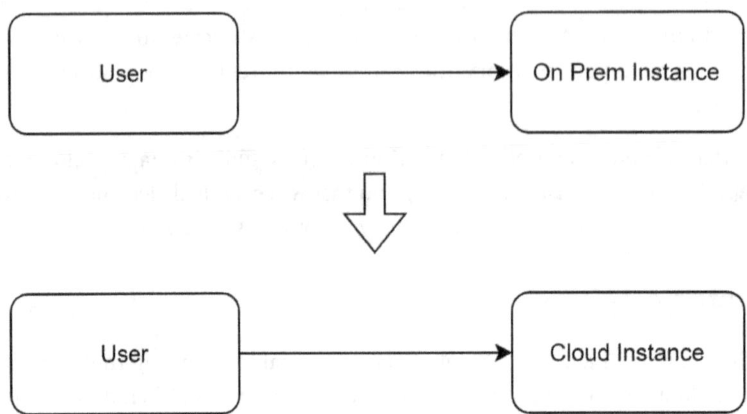

Figure 7.1 – Initial migration of an application from on-premises to the cloud

By completing this stage, we have already achieved some efficiencies; provisioning is faster by removing the dependency on physical hardware and utilizing cloud factories, colocation costs have disappeared, and we mitigate the operational overhead of disparate systems. However, we're not cloud native; the overheads around OS patching and database maintenance still exist, and we're still operating in a manner that matches our infrastructure topology to our customer base.

The next stage of our migration is a simple but critical phase that supports the future iterations of our application. We need to add an **API proxy layer**. All hyperscalers have a managed service that performs this function; in AWS, it is **API Gateway**, Azure has **API Management**, and GCP has **Apigee** and **API Gateway**. Some open source projects provide similar functionality for specific environments, such as **Kubernetes**. The key here is that we are introducing a layer between our end user and our application that can perform **Layer 7 routing** as defined in the OSI model. This model will allow us to inspect incoming traffic and decide actions based on HTTP request properties. In contrast to the architecture in *Figure 7.1*, we now have an additional architectural element, the API proxy, which is once again transparent to the end user.

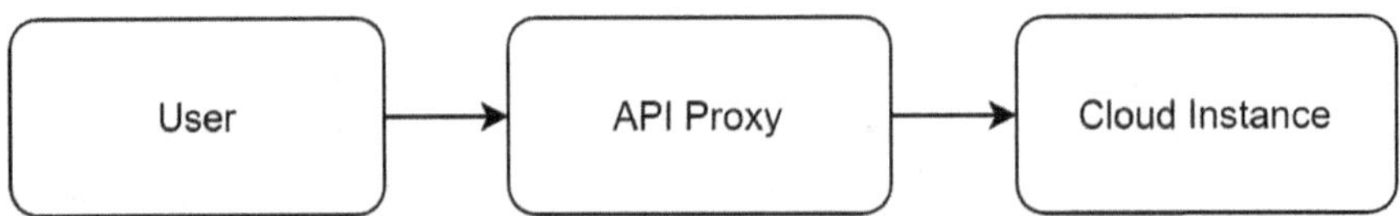

Figure 7.2 – Addition of an API proxy to the cloud instance

Functionally, we have yet to start using the API layer's capabilities to their full extent, but we have achieved some operational efficiencies as part of this change. If we were using **Transport Layer Security (TLS)**, we would likely have a provisioned TLS certificate. Switching to a fully managed proxy allows the TLS termination to occur at the proxy layer, freeing us from the operational overhead of managing this with a manual or semi-automated process. The key is that our application is no longer bound to our deployed instance. Typically, we build on-premises applications using a monolithic architecture, as the deployment of these applications is tightly coupled to the topology of the hardware we deploy them on. In the cloud, these limitations no longer constrain us. It is detrimental to the ability of development teams to operate in this environment. Using the monolith architecture usually results in high internal coupling between components, making it difficult to predict the blast radius of a particular change without knowing the full scope of its use throughout the application.

The solution is to use the Layer 7 routing capabilities of the API proxy to decompose our application into new cloud native implementations. For example, many applications have a user management system so users can log in to the application. Traditionally, someone might achieve this by storing passwords in a database, ideally, hashed and salted. This approach is a definite source of risk for most companies. **Insecure hash algorithms, timing leaks**, and **password database security** are all things your company is directly responsible for under this model. By migrating this to a managed service, we significantly de-risk our operations. We can also make changes at this stage to make our solution more cloud native through replatforming some of the easier migrations, such as databases, to a compatible managed database service. Continuing our architectural evolution, we break down the monolithic application into components in the following figure:

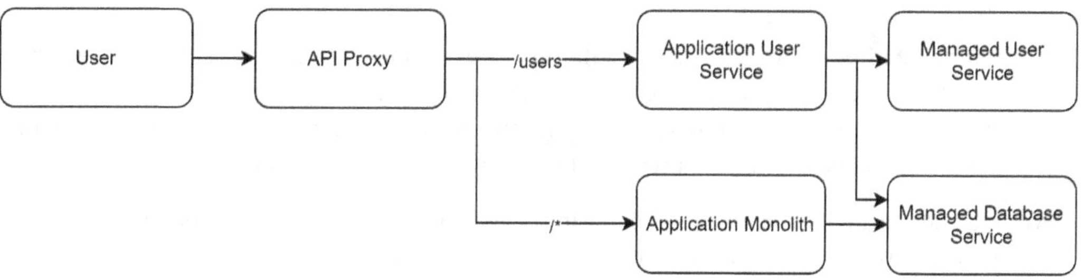

Figure 7.3 – Beginning to decompose the monolith into domain-driven microservices

Under this new architecture, we have separated concerns for our user management and our newly replatformed application monolith. Our user service provides an abstraction behind our API proxy for performing actions such as resetting passwords, updating email addresses, and other user-centric functions. At the same time, our original monolithic application still contains all the functionality external to users. We've managed to refactor one part of our application to be truly cloud native and use managed services. Most importantly, we don't need to know how the entire application will be architected to achieve this. We need to understand this particular domain and the services available to accelerate it. We've also broken any coupling that may have existed between the user service and unrelated parts of the application. Under this new model, changes to the user service have a blast radius limited to the service itself without unforeseen side effects on the rest of the application.

In some simple cases, we may only have two targets for the API proxy: the new cloud native service and the old legacy service. However, as you perform this method of replacing or migrating functionality, it is also worth reevaluating your architecture and seeing whether you can reduce coupling within your application or increase cohesion within a specific domain by breaking out disparate services. Rarely, the perfect solution to a problem requiring refactoring to become cloud native is to build a cloud native monolith.

Slowly, we can continue to break down the service into its emergent domains. We establish bounded contexts within our application, representing highly cohesive parts of our business context. For more information on bounded contexts and domain-driven design, I recommend reading *Domain Driven Design* by Eric Evans. We then decompose our architecture into these domains and look to utilize cloud native services wherever possible. As a part of this shift, if our application supports multiple customers, we can also build multitenancy into these services. Eventually, we will reach a point where we have integrated the entire application into a series of cloud native services backed by managed services that provide equivalent or improved functionality. As the final step in our architectural evolution, we have removed the monolith and left only the new application services. This is reflected in *Figure 7.4*.

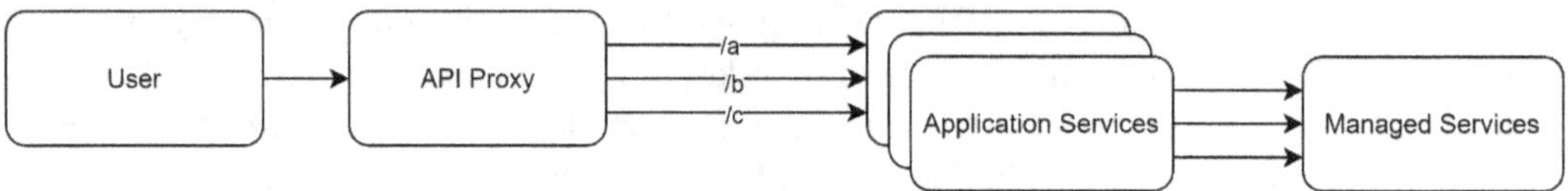

Figure 7.4 – The original monolith is deprecated and is truly cloud native

By using the API proxy to slowly and methodically decompose the monolith, we have effectively accomplished the desired result: removing the legacy monolith and adopting cloud native services. At this point, it is possible to remove the API proxy; however, in most cases, the application proxy still provides benefits by acting as a central entry point to your application.

We have examined typical anti-patterns in the initial cloud migration, including unproductive migration strategies such as one-and-done migration or retirement and rebuilding. We have also explored how the strangler fig pattern allows us to keep servicing our current clients while modernizing our application. Now, we have a path to becoming cloud native that does not require broad sweeping solutions all at once but can be part of a longer-term digital transformation focusing on client outcomes rather than technological puritanism.

Now that we have dived into the migrations of existing applications, we can start to look at how the applications themselves are constructed to be cloud native. The first stop on this journey is addressing where we store the state for our applications.

Stateful applications

Most applications are driven by a series of **stateful processes** at their core. These states might be **ephemeral** – that is, they might not be data with long-term context, such as a user session that is only active while the user is on a website. In other scenarios, we might persist these states for longer-term storage. For example, an online store might require maintaining the state of a shopping cart, collecting payment, and shipping the items. These are all states that need to be persisted in our architecture somewhere. In a single server model, conflating the system's local and external state is trivial. In this section, we will look into the scalability and robustness of these patterns to examine how we can manage the state cloud natively.

The stateless server

A common anti-pattern when building cloud native applications is to store state locally to a server. Most cloud services have options, like **session affinity**, to enable you to migrate applications to the cloud with a locally stored state. However, we should refrain from using these patterns in new or refactored cloud native applications. Two main patterns allow us to achieve this in the cloud.

In the **state assertion pattern**, the client presents a **verifiable state representation** to the backend server. We typically use this pattern for transient state, the quintessential example of which is replacing user session tokens, which we can match to the ephemeral state stored on the machine, with a user session assertion like a **JSON Web Token (JWT)** or **Security Assertion Markup Language (SAML)** response. In both cases, the client stores their state, and we can verify that the client's state has not been altered through cryptographically secure signatures. This pattern comes with some caveats, for instance, the fact that these tokens (unless encrypted) are transparent to the end user, so we should never include secret information that we don't want the user to see in the assertion. They are also prime targets for token theft, so good practices around **token lifetimes**, TLS, and **storage of the tokens** on the client's device are all paramount with this pattern.

The second pattern is using **external state storage**. If the data we are handling is not transient and requires use by multiple parties, then we must persist the state to storage external to the server. The type of data being stored decides how we store it on the backend, too. The key here is to move the state out of our application, which provides numerous benefits in the world of the cloud.

We typically encounter three kinds of state data. Of course, there are always exceptions and edge cases, but as a general rule, we can choose external state storage suitable for our use case.

Transient state data is data that represents a substate of a system at a point in time, but it is inconsequential if the data gets deleted. This might be because the data itself is a cache of other data sources that can be reconstructed or because the nature of the data is transient anyway, for example, **short-lived session tokens**. Typically, we store this data because we require it at short notice. Think of it like your short-term memory. It holds values that you are currently actively working with but might be replaced at any point. Cloud services have solutions tailored toward high-performance workloads and can be leveraged for more cost-effective solutions. For high-performance workloads, we can use services like **ElastiCache** in AWS, **Memorystore** in GCP, or **Azure Cache** in Azure; these all mirror the concept of traditional deployed cache services. Other emerging solutions in the space, like **Momento**, allow for cache as a service. If latency is not mission-critical, other proprietary solutions might be more cost-effective and scalable with only minimal impact on latency, for example, TTLs on DynamoDB (a NoSQL service from AWS) tables or even fully SaaS solutions such as Momento. The critical difference from the self-managed paradigm is that these services are managed, and all have options to be automatically scalable, allowing us to focus on those parts of our application that deliver value, our domain logic.

Persistent state data is data the system needs a persistent reference to with context in a semantic model. These might be items such as orders we want to keep a log of or bank accounts for which we want to maintain a balance. The way in which we store this data can have different modalities, such as **relational** versus **non-relational**, **normalized** versus **denormalized**, or **structured** versus **unstructured**. Typically, these representations of state can be thought of as records that might be akin to our long-term memory. At the time of writing, this is an exciting space, as there are leaps and bounds of progress being made in the serverless offerings for relational databases like **Aurora Serverless** on AWS or **Cloud Spanner** on GCP. For non-relational databases, most cloud providers have well-established, truly serverless offerings (truly serverless in the way that they scale to zero). AWS has **DynamoDB**, Azure has **Cosmos DB**, and GCP has **Cloud Firestore**.

Supporting data is typically data that has little meaning without the context of persistent data. This might be data like photos, PDF documents, or other types of files that we want to store because it provides additional information. The difference between persistent and supporting data is that supporting data can be thought of as an object rather than a record. This distinction is also reflected in the way the services are named, usually referred to as blob or application stores. AWS has **S3**, GCP has **Cloud Storage**, and Azure has **Azure Blob Storage**. Once again, all of these are managed services, and their throughput and capacity will scale with our requirements.

The question is, when do we commit state to an external service? The general rule of thumb is that any state that requires persistence beyond one transaction should be committed to external state management. The local state is fine within the context of the transaction for processing purposes, but the external state is necessary for anything breaking this boundary. A parallel we can draw, which we have all likely suffered with in the past, is a multi-page web form, where every time you submit a value that is incorrect, it forgets the previous pages and takes you back to page one. That is the risk we run with local state that crosses translation boundaries.

These data types are the most common when serving Online Transaction Processing (OLTP) workloads. The storage and consumption patterns are different when serving analytical (OLAP) workloads. When analytical functionality is required, persisting data to an analytical store purpose-built for your use case is usually recommended, such as a data warehouse. Each of the hyperscalers has slightly different approaches in this space: GCP has the fully managed serverless solution **BigQuery**, AWS has **Redshift**, and Azure has **Azure Synapse**. This area also has significant contenders outside of the hyperscalers, like **Snowflake** and **Databricks**.

Now that we've discussed removing the state from the local server, let's explore the new possibilities for resiliency and scalability this opens for us in a cloud native environment.

Resiliency and scalability in a stateless server paradigm

Werner Vogels, the CTO of AWS, once mentioned that *"Everything fails, all the time."* If we persist state locally to our server, then that state is only as durable as that single server. Large companies, such as hyperscalers, employ legions of engineers to ensure their applications are durable, available, and bug-free. Most people embarking on a cloud native transformation won't have access to the same level of resourcing that these large companies do. This is where the **stateless cloud paradigm** allows us to trade on margin by using managed services to store our state. These managed services do have legions of engineers behind them. If we persist state external to our application, suddenly, the fault tolerance of our application becomes less consequential.

Server died? Start another one and investigate the cause. Our state was off the server, so it doesn't matter whether the server went down. Our new server will pick right up where the old one left off. Even better, run multiple stateless instances of your server in a self-healing group. Cloud services also allow us to automate this part of our system. AWS uses **Auto Scaling groups** and **Elastic Load Balancing**. GCP has managed instance groups for VMs or **Cloud Run/Google Kubernetes Engine** for containers, as well as **load balancers** to distribute traffic. Azure uses **Virtual Machine Scale Sets** and **Azure App Service** to a similar effect. All these services allow us to mitigate the risk of single-point failures in our system for the parts of the cloud that are our responsibility and typically contain the most bugs. It's important to note that managing the state does not even need to be a process we entrust to our own code; we can go even further and use a fully managed state as a service.

State as a service

Typically, we build state machines to replicate business processes. For example, we might onboard a new tenant in a distributed microservice architecture system. In the past, I have seen people build complex code in poorly documented and typically fragile ways. For example, a central tenant service called out to each of the microservices to orchestrate them, but this tenant service was touched by every team that needed onboarding actions to be performed. The result was unbound states and error-prone onboarding that resulted in a wide array of edge cases, with no one easily able to grasp the full complexity of the system.

We want a state machine that tells us if the requested action has been completed. Here is where managed services can also be of benefit. Solutions such as **AWS Step Functions**, **Google Workflows**, or **Azure Logic Apps** allow us to outsource the maintenance of the state to the cloud itself. This is an excellent solution for when centralized orchestration is required. In our previous example, we want to onboard a tenant, so we make a state machine that creates a new tenant in the tenant service, provisions a new user as the admin in the user service, and sends an email to that user to log in. Once the user has accepted the invitation, there may be more stages, such as provisioning new data for the tenant, prompting the admin to add other users, or setting up retention policies on user files.

We could do this in a distributed way with eventing and service-specific state, but typically, that results in unbound and undocumented behavior without appropriate oversight. The state machine as a service approach also allows us a single pane of glass to view our state machine structure and how various instances of state are progressing through it. When the tenant onboarding system breaks, we can immediately see where the error is by viewing our well-defined state machine.

The anti-pattern we typically see in this system is people using state machines for systems that do not cross bounded contexts (i.e., they don't require orchestration). In these scenarios, we should instead rely on state representation internal to the bounded context, such as updating an order item from "ordered" to "packed" and then to "shipped." The state transitions in this scenario are simple, linear, and within a bounded context. Hence, external state orchestration is not required. The final piece of the state puzzle is configuring our applications.

Application configuration as state

Fundamentally, our application behavior is an emergent property of our application state filtered through our business logic. The anti-pattern here is defining application configuration in the same code we use to define our business logic. Application configuration is just another form of state, one that typically differs between deployed environments. Our code should be agnostic of the environment it is deployed in, instead, configuration should be managed through deployment itself. There are two places we typically store application configuration:

- Externally in a key-value store or secret manager. We touched on this approach in *Chapter 5* for feature flags.

- Internally in the template used to create new instances of our application, like through environment variables. This is typically for bootstrapping values, such as service discovery endpoints or database connection strings.

The difference between the local state in the configuration domain and the local state in the transaction domain is that the state in the configuration domain must satisfy two criteria to be effective:

- It must be immutable; the configuration must not change due to external factors except for the service's redeployment

- It must be universal; all copies of the application must be provisioned with identical copies of local state

These two paradigms ensure that our transactions are agnostic of the actual backend service completing the request. In the external case, we have a little more flexibility but need to be careful of the effects of rotation and cache invalidation.

State allows our application to provide meaning through the lens of our business logic. However, improperly handled state can cause issues with resilience and scalability. Luckily, in the cloud landscape, there are many battle-tested tools that provide ways for us to store our application state. We can even shift our state machines entirely to the cloud with cloud native offerings while also reducing operational complexity to a minimum. While state is the lifeblood of our application, the health and malleability of our code are normally measured through two other properties; coupling and cohesion.

Tight coupling, low cohesion

In software design, two measures of interrelatedness are often used as a litmus test for sound system design. These are **coupling** and **cohesion**. Coupling refers to disparate services calling each other to accomplish a task. High coupling implies that the services are heavily interdependent and are challenging to operate in isolation without worrying about dependencies or side effects. Cohesion is the opposite. Coupling measures the relationships between services, and cohesion focuses on the relationships inside the service. If a service has low cohesion, it tries to do many disparate things simultaneously. We commonly see low cohesion and high coupling as an anti-pattern in cloud native software development. In this section, we will explore how these anti-patterns tend to be reflected in cloud environments and how to avoid them.

The Lambdalith versus single-purpose functions

A common anti-pattern we see is low cohesion in deployed infrastructure. Typically, this anti-pattern gets introduced through siloed infrastructure teams; for information on why this might be a lousy idea, see *Chapter 5*. Let's assume we have a serverless function on AWS, a **Lambda function**, and every time we want a new one, we need a sign-off from the infrastructure team to create a new function for us rather than being empowered to create a new Lambda function ourselves. Then, we get a feature that should only take a day to implement but should really be a serverless function. Rather than wait for the infrastructure team to deal with their backlog of tickets and provide us with our function, we see a tantalizing preexisting Lambda function that, if we just added some extra routing, could also handle this other functionality. Compound this effect over many features, and suddenly, we end up with a significant monolithic serverless function. Hence the moniker, the **Lambdalith**. The problem is that these serverless functions have low cohesion. This means that by modifying our function, we have a large blast radius that could impact utterly unrelated functionality simply due to process inefficiencies and siloed ownership.

I previously worked with an organization that had an architecture team separate from the infrastructure and development teams. Creating a service required the interaction of three teams and was aligned to a monthly cadence. This particular organization had teams aligned to business domains; each business domain typically had a few services they managed. While feature development was rapid, the event of a new service being added to support those features was exceedingly rare. These containers grew to significant complexity with low cohesion between application parts. **Conway's law** was alive and well, and the architecture closely followed the team topologies to a fault.

In any process, be it online sales or provisioning new infrastructure, the more difficult this process is, the less likely it will be completed. Typically, people ask how much friction is suitable to ensure we still produce secure, deployable artifacts. The answer almost always is as little as humanly possible. We should enable teams to take ownership of their own output by providing them with a safe and secure platform in which they can achieve their goals. Infrastructure and architectural resources should be available to support them at all points. However, if the development team cannot drive the process, you will find that the process will be woefully underutilized.

The truly cloud native antithesis of the Lambdalith is the single-purpose serverless function. In this pattern, each function does exactly one thing and does it well. For example, a **single-purpose function** might handle the HTTP POST method on a specific API endpoint. This does not mean it cannot share code with other single-purpose functions. Typically, grouping these functions into pseudoservices with high internal cohesion makes sense. However, each deployed function should be completely agnostic of its peers in the pseudoservice group. This grouping might be performed by having several single-purpose functions deployed from the same repo (or parent folder if using a monorepo). This pattern provides us with high cohesion in our deployed units. Each unit is only concerned with satisfying the requirements for a single type of request. There is a limit to the level of atomicity to which we should break these units down. Namely, they should never be so atomic that we must chain multiple together.

Chaining serverless functions

Another anti-pattern we commonly see is the chaining of serverless functions in the call stack. This form of coupling can have an extremely negative effect on your solution's performance and cost-effectiveness. For example, consider a serverless function that uses a typical synchronous **backend for frontend** (BFF) approach to call some business logic in another serverless function that queries a database. This situation is illustrated in the following figure.

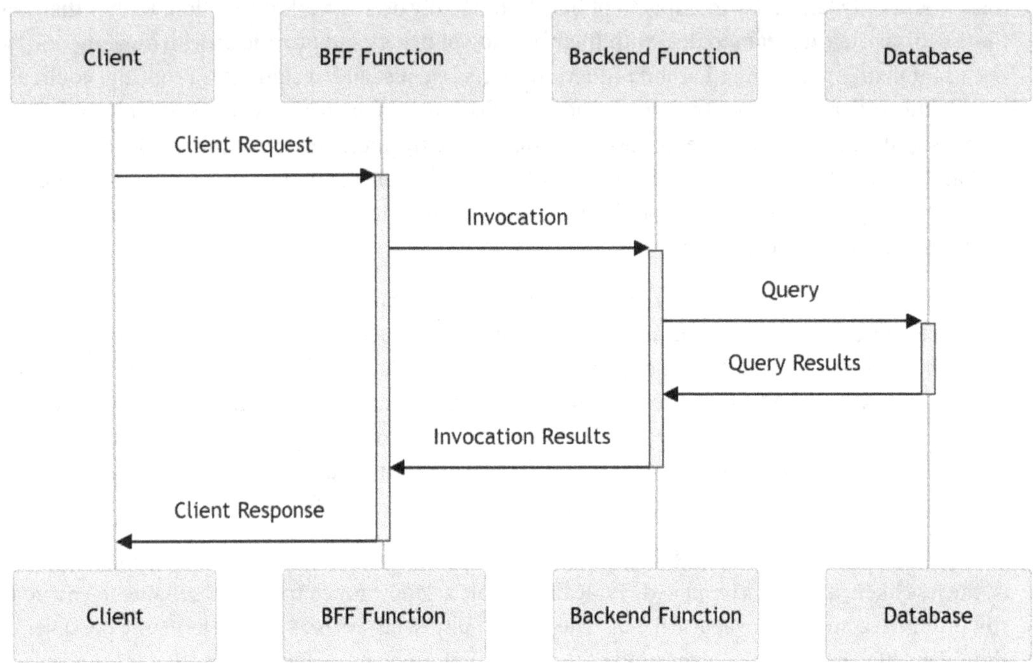

Figure 7.5 – Chained invocations of serverless functions

As we can see in the figure, each preceding call runs whilst waiting for the subsequent call to complete. With this invocation pattern, we are doubling our running compute. In a containerized or VM-level environment, this is not an issue, as our compute resource can serve other requests while we wait for the chained call to finish. However, in a serverless function environment, our function can only serve one invocation at a time. This means that while we wait for the second serverless function in the chain to complete, our first lambda function cannot serve any other requests. Therefore, we are doubling our computing costs and resource consumption without any tangible benefit. Some cloud providers, such as GCP, are building platforms that allow this unused computing power to be better utilized. However, most default implementations are limited to completing a single request at a time. Chained functions are a prime example of coupling that can be converted to high cohesion internally in a single function. We more often need to perform the reverse operation and decouple coupled services.

Decoupling coupled services

When we call services as dependencies from another service, we increase the blast radius of changes to the service being depended on to include our dependent service. This is a form of tight coupling that can be very detrimental to the performance of our application. The more services we chain together, the less reliable our service becomes, as we are now dealing with the product of the reliabilities of each service in the chain. Let's say each service has a 95% reliability rate. If we combine 4 services in a single call, our reliability decreases to 81.4% (0.95^4). Typically, this problem arises as it fits our mental model of services very well. As programmers, when we need to perform some work internal to our application, we call a function and await the results. Extending this model to a multiservice architecture, we call another service and await the results.

Luckily, cloud providers have a cloud native way to solve this tight coupling problem. It requires two changes in thinking to implement correctly:

- We need to break the idea of synchronous feedback. Sending an HTTP 202 return code and performing work asynchronously is just as, if not more, valid than a synchronous response with an HTTP 200 response all in one call.

- We need to stop thinking of each of the services that need to work as dependents and start thinking of them as isolated units of work that need to be completed.

The key to implementing these solutions in a cloud native environment is to decouple these services by putting a managed service in the middle. AWS has **Simple Queue Service** and **EventBridge**, GCP has **Google Pub/Sub**, and Azure has **Azure Event Grid** and **Azure Service Bus**.

These managed services all provide similar functionality. They act as a message broker between our services so that our services do not need to talk to one another synchronously to pass information between them. They differ slightly in how they operate. Some are **simple message queues**, and others are **complete event bus implementations** with publish and subscribe functionality.

The result of using any of these services is similar. Instead of our reliability now being the result of a series product, we have decoupled the services to concern themselves with the reliability of the managed service. Let's take our four unreliable services and attach them to our managed service, allowing for asynchronous execution. Assuming our managed service has four 9s of uptime (99.99% uptime), our result is four services, each with 95.98% reliability. If any of our services goes down, the other services will still operate.

Implementing **dead letter queues (DLQs)** can further improve the reliability of these services. If one of our services cannot process messages, we can send the backlog of messages to be processed to the DLQ. Once we have fixed our service and everything is operational, we can automatically replay the events from our DLQ and complete the outstanding work. This means that instead of a single service failure impacting all systems, the blast radius of a single system is limited to the system itself. The system will eventually be consistent once all unprocessed messages have been replayed. When we need to eventually trace these events through our system, perhaps to troubleshoot why they ended up in our DLQ, we need to correlate their path, which brings us to an essential part of distributed systems: telemetry and event correlation.

Telemetry and event correlation

You can't improve what you cannot measure. Understanding precisely the degree of coupling within a deployed application can be challenging. Typically, we come across an anti-pattern using traditional logging systems with distributed systems. Traditional logging systems do not provide the granularity (level of detail) and traceability (correlation with other messages) required to debug and improve distributed systems. Typically, when we debug a distributed system, we are trying to piece together the result of an action across multiple deployed units. This is where robust **telemetry** comes into play. We can tag all of our requests, messages, and invocations with a **correlation ID** on entry into our distributed system, and then use this correlation ID to trace the effect of that action across all of our deployed units and managed services. We will go into more detail on telemetry systems in *Chapter 10*. However, we can utilize the correlation aspect of modern telemetry systems to assist us in decoupling applications. By following our traces, we can reveal dependencies between systems that previously would have required us to look into the source code or environmental configuration to find. Once we identify the dependencies within our application, we can slowly move from tightly coupled dependencies (one service calling another) to loosely coupled dependencies (two or more services joined by a shared, managed message bus or queue).

Tight coupling and **low cohesion** are anti-patterns we are typically shielded from in an on-premises environment. In the cloud, these patterns become dysfunctional, leading to poorly performing applications and unexpected side effects. The key to rectifying these anti-patterns is, firstly, to be able to measure the coupling and cohesion, and, secondly, to work to decouple tightly coupled services while increasing internal cohesion. Typically, modeling cohesion and coupling should be part of the architectural planning for a feature and form part of the definition of done. Let's explore some common pitfalls and address the comprehensive definition of done.

The comprehensive definition of done

When creating software in **siloed release models**, as discussed in *Chapter 5*, we looked at empowering teams to own the delivery of their outputs from conception to deployment and beyond into operations. However, this requires the development team to also take ownership (with support from other teams) of the functionality and responsibilities that the siloed release pipeline previously hid from the team on the path to production. Hence, we need to revisit the definition of *done* (and, in some cases, the definition of *ready*) for our software teams. Previously we have visited the cultural and business shift required to make this happen, but in this section, we will discuss building these requirements intrinsically into your definition of done.

Ignoring security

Security is a critical factor in the delivery pipeline. Neglecting sound security practices can lead to a gradual accumulation of risk for the company, often unnoticed until a breach occurs. This omission can result in a blame game and severe consequences. To develop secure applications, it's crucial to integrate several security practices into the **software delivery life cycle** (**SDLC**). These practices should be part of the definition of done for any work, and their review should be as rigorous as code review before deployment.

Ignoring **open source** or **external dependencies** is an anti-pattern. In the software world, many open source packages provide base functionality on which we build our business logic. However, each package we pull from an external source represents a possible vector for malicious code to be added to our application. Maintaining and alerting on a **software bill of materials** (**SBoM**) gives you an indication of the health of your project. Many tools exist to help you manage the versions of software packages used. A typical pattern for managing dependencies at a language level is to use a read-through private artifact repository for your language, populating this artifact registry with internal packages to be used and allowing it to pull and cache upstream packages. This repository will enable you to have a single pane of glass containing all dependencies and versions of your application, GCP, AWS, Azure, and many niche players, all of which can export and monitor SBoMs from their respective artifact repository services. Pull requests should be instrumented to ensure that the packages they add do not add any new vulnerabilities, and maintenance should be done regularly, informed by the SBoM, to address any new vulnerabilities that have been found.

Not having a **threat model** for your application or building one and ignoring it is an anti-pattern. Typically, when we see the shift from a dedicated security team to a supported and empowered development team, the development team uses the security team to produce a threat model but fails to address it throughout the SDLC. The preliminary threat model should form part of the definition of ready for the team. The threat model should be fundamental in deciding how to tackle a problem and must be verified to ensure the built solution correctly mitigates the identified risks. Thus, the threat model should be a living document as a change is implemented, providing details on how risks are mitigated so that the changes can be merged confidently. Once in production, the application should be monitored through a **cloud native application protection platform** (**CNAPP**) to catch any risks or misconfigurations that might not be addressed by the threat model. The key to effective threat modeling is to choose the correct level of granularity. If you are a stock market making changes to the settlement engine, then the proper level of granularity might be every merge. Other lower-risk environments might only require threat modeling on a less granular level. The idea is to find the correct amount of friction that mitigates the risk to the proper level without compromising on the necessary level of security for your application.

The final *ignoring* security anti-pattern to address is born out of the increased flexibility the cloud gives us, and that is the failure to address defense in depth. In an on-premises environment, the delineation between what is inside the network and what is outside the network is evident. You have a physical cable going to a firewall that serves as the ingress point for all your traffic. Your solution might have some software-defined networking downstream, but there is a clear separation. In the cloud environment, all of a sudden, different services run in **virtual private clouds** (**VPCs**) and outside VPCs. Endpoints can be addressable over the internet or through endpoint projections into your network. Some services exist in **cloud provider-managed networks** and require additional networking. All of this means that it is less clear where traffic is flowing. There is tooling to help with this but, fundamentally, the highly configurable nature of cloud environments means that misconfigurations can present a larger risk surface. Managed cloud services already have strong **identity and access management** (**IAM**) tooling. This should be complemented with robust, **zero-trust authentication and authorization** tooling in your code that is validated at every application level. Many organizations are still early in their journey of implementing zero-trust architecture. Hence, it should be considered a North Star principle rather than an absolute requirement. The key is asking yourself, *"What happens if we accidentally expose this service to the internet directly?"* This limits the blast radius of cloud misconfigurations and ensures that if an internal service is accidentally exposed to the public, it still authorizes incoming traffic. This blast radius consideration also needs to be considered from a CI/CD perspective. One client I worked with had a single repository and project for all infrastructure. This resulted in highly privileged CI/CD accounts with enormous blast radii spanning multiple disparate systems. Having a robust defense-in-depth strategy means that as application architecture shifts to more of a self-serve model, the platform that our developers are building on top of is secure enough to tolerate failures at each level. Just as we must ensure our developers are building secure platforms, we must also ensure we are building observable ones.

Ignoring observability

In the monolith, logging stages to the console was enough to debug our application. This worked because the application was a simple arrangement (infrastructure) of complex objects (our code). In the cloud native world, we shift much of that complexity into the infrastructure, giving us a complex arrangement (infrastructure) of simple objects (our code). This requires much more robust **logging** and **telemetry practices** than logging into a console. We will dive into this topic in significantly more detail in *Chapter 10*. However, we will go through some aspects in this section that should form the basis of the definition of done.

The first anti-pattern is ignoring spans and only using logging. Logging provides us with point-in-time information about the state of our application. Spans are different. They provide us with context for a period of execution in our application. As part of our definition of done, we should include the addition of spans that provide meaningful information about executing subsections of our code. Throughout the execution of the span, we should also ensure that we are adding enough enriching data to make the diagnosis of issues easier through our observability platform. For any deployment that exceeds the scope of a single instance, we must also consider correlation to allow us to group spans together and trace their path through our distributed application. Trying to piece together the execution context of a request from a series of log entries across multiple services is significantly more difficult than reading a correlated span flame graph.

The second anti-pattern is collecting metrics with no functional output. We quite often see a company collecting many metrics but no alerting or deviation monitoring. We have the data to check whether our application is performing as intended. However, we are missing that crucial step that actually tells us when it isn't. With comprehensive monitoring, alerting, and rectification procedures, we can ensure that our system's non-functional requirements, such as latency and error percentage, do not fall outside of acceptable margins. Therefore, as part of our definition of done, we should ensure two things:

- Firstly, we must ensure that the changes being made have monitoring set up. This might be through synthetic traffic, **application performance monitoring** (**APM**), observability tooling, and traditional logging.

- Secondly, we must ensure that the right people are notified when this tooling detects a problem. This might be done by automatically creating a ticket in your ticketing system, notifying users on a messaging channel, or other means. The important thing is that regressions are identified, and people know rectification must occur.

By including these two items in our definition of done, we can provide certainty that as we add new functionality or modify existing functionality, we don't breach the non-functional requirements of the system. This level of observability also gives us insight into which parts of our applications are candidates for optimization as part of our continuous improvement process. Previously, for clients where users complained about the slowness of the application, we filtered our metrics to rank requests by two factors: how often they were called and how long the typical transaction took. We found that three endpoints were consistently called and consistently slow. With some query optimization, we reduced the response time by two orders of magnitude. The change took about three days in total, and the end users were significantly happier. Without collecting these metrics and utilizing their outputs, we would have needed significant testing in a production environment to get the same level of insight. Observability is great for finding the cause of an incident (i.e. when something goes wrong) but what about stopping incidents from occurring in the first place?

Ignoring reliability

The final part of this section discusses ignoring **reliability**. This is an anti-pattern that we see all too often in cloud migrations. Teams care about having their features work without considering their continued operation. This is where the mentality of *You build it, you run it* can be beneficial. Development teams that also own the operation of their output are more likely to consider reliability because they are invested and want to avoid call-outs at nighttime or during weekends. Cloud native services provide significant tooling to ensure reliability and continuity of service. However, utilizing these services can mean the difference between an outage of seconds and an outage of days. Any company that wishes to conform to internal or external **service-level objectives (SLOs)** or has a contractual **service-level agreement (SLA)** must ensure that they treat reliability as a critical aspect of their definition of done.

The first anti-pattern we will address is an aspect of the deployment process. As we discussed in *Chapter 5*, development teams should own the deployment and operation of their changes. The anti-pattern we often see in this space utilizes the same deployment strategy across our environments. In a development or test environment, it is typical for us to use **all-or-nothing** deployment strategies. This strategy is sound when we want to guarantee that the version of the code we are calling is the latest version and maintain fast feedback loops between the deployment and testing cycles. Applying this same methodology to a production environment means that if our change breaks functionality, the change either breaks everything or nothing. We might even have avoidable downtime on a successful deployment as the new services might take time to come online. For production systems, we care about two things: **early feedback** on a problem and **quick rectification** of a problem. Many cloud native deployment approaches will allow us to make incremental or quickly revertable changes to preserve our system's operation, especially when using highly managed services such as API gateways or functions as a service. These strategies usually come at the cost of additional time to deploy or additional resources provision. They also normally require external state management, as any internal state will be lost on deployment. Some of the methods we can use are the following:

- **Rolling deployments**: These deployments take a set of resources running the same application (say, a set of three containers that might all be running our user service) and then incrementally update each one in series until all services are running the new version, waiting for each service to become healthy before starting to deploy the next. This allows us to mitigate the avoidable downtime that comes with waiting for services to become ready-to-serve traffic in an all-or-nothing approach but does not provide us robust options for returning the application to a good state in the event of a failure that is only present at runtime.

- **Blue-green deployment**: In this strategy, you have two separate groups of resources. One set of resources serves your production traffic using the latest known production stable version of the application (blue) while the other is deployed (green). After you have ensured that the newly deployed system is working, you cut across to the new system, which might be through **aliases** or **internal DNS**. You can then decommission the old blue target resources. In the event of a failure, it is trivial to point the references, DNS or otherwise, back to the old deployment of the application.

- **Canary deployment**: In this strategy, you follow the same deployment methodology as the blue-green deployment strategy. The critical difference is cutting over from the blue to green resources. Instead of an instantaneous cutover, we slowly redirect some traffic to our new instances. This becomes our canary in the coal mine; we can test the services with a subset of production data, and if something goes wrong, we will only impact a small subset of requests instead of all requests. Otherwise, if all is well, we progress to all traffic heading to the new resources, and the old resources can be decommissioned.

These methodologies do not need to be applied only to your application code; this pattern can be used anywhere you have an expensive rollout process. One client I worked with had a database that had to be updated once a month. Each month, the data used to build the database was either modified or appended. Ingestion of the new data and verifying that it was correct took 15 minutes, and the client could not tolerate 15 minutes of downtime. Hence, we created two tables: one for the most recent data and one for last month's data. Each time new data needed to be ingested, we would populate whichever table contained the oldest data with the latest data. We would then check this table against the current table in use. If all was well, we would update the view consumed by the end users to point to the table containing the new data. This allowed a seamless transition between datasets without taking the system offline and allowed quick fallbacks to the last known good configuration if there was an issue. Understanding which deployment strategy suits your purposes is essential, and selecting an appropriate deployment strategy needs to form part of the definition of done.

The second reliability anti-pattern we will examine is the failure to address **disaster recovery** correctly. Cloud services have sensible defaults to prevent data loss events, such as storing objects in multiple regions or automating database backup processes. This process is usually tunable to meet your **recovery point objective (RPO)** – that is, how much data we can tolerate the loss of. Despite how protective cloud services are against data loss events, protection against service loss events is usually heavily dependent on your architecture. The critical metric data loss prevention does not address is the **recovery time objective (RTO)**. Restoring a database from a backup may take a significant amount of time. Likewise, standing up a new instance of your infrastructure may not be a short process. If your application catastrophically fails, then having a plan in place to restore service to your end users is extremely valuable. The first mistake teams generally make in this space is creating one copy of their infrastructure, calling it a day, and then moving on with new features. In this scenario, disaster recovery has been completely ignored. In the event of a catastrophic failure, not only will the team be scrambling to recreate their service but there's no defined process to do so. The second scenario we commonly see is people having a theoretical disaster recovery strategy. They have a list of steps to take in case of a failure, but if the strategy is theoretical, so are the chances of it actually working. An untested strategy is a waste of keystrokes. Any disaster recovery strategy needs to be simulated regularly. The time to test it for the first time (and likely the first time much of the team sees the strategy) should not be when there is a critical outage. Typically, disaster recovery has a few options; the key is that all options must be tested. The possibilities we typically look at for recovery are as follows:

- **Cold recovery**: This strategy is for non-critical services. A cold recovery assumes you are starting from nothing, provisioning a new instance of your application, and restoring from backups to restore service. It is important to note that not having a disaster recovery plan is not the same as having a cold recovery plan. Like all plans, cold recovery must be documented and tested regularly to ensure the process meets your RPOs and RTOs.

- **Warm recovery**: This strategy involves having a second (or more) minimal copy of your application running in a different location that can be quickly scaled up to take over from the service if it fails. Ideally, this **failover** and **scale-up** would be automated, but while automation is being built, it is perfectly acceptable to manually fail-over. An alternative architecture to warm standby that uses the same principles involves keeping the supporting structures of your application running, however, only starting your application when failover is required. This variation on the strategy is commonly referred to as the **pilot light strategy**.

- **Hot recovery**: This strategy involves running your application in a multi-active architecture. Much like we can run multiple servers to ensure that we can tolerate the failure of any single server, this pattern takes the same approach but with your entire architecture. The failure of any active deployment means that traffic can be redirected to the healthy region.

The concept of **chaos engineering** is important to illustrate here. Remember the quote by Werner Vogels, *"Everything fails, all the time."* Chaos engineering reinforces this by purposely introducing failures into your system, ensuring that your system is fault-tolerant. Another good strategy to use is the concept of game days, especially for manual processes. These simulated events run through the disaster recovery strategy with the responsible team to ensure that everyone is familiar with the process. Therefore, as each feature or service is completed, the disaster recovery strategy must be updated to include the requirements of the new changes and needs to form part of the definition of done.

Security, observability, and reliability are intrinsic parts of changes to our system that are often ignored. By addressing these intrinsics as part of our definition of done, we ensure that our development teams are not just building applications that are built to exhibit the features they are creating but also providing a platform that our end users can trust. These parts of our system form a fundamental baseline of cloud native operability, but there are many other pitfalls we can fall victim to.

Other pitfalls

There are several anti-patterns that commonly manifest in cloud native application development. This section will dissect some of these anti-patterns, their lineage from traditional software development, how to identify them, and the proactive mindset shifts required to evade them. In our scenario, cloud native applications have the capability to scale to any size we choose, sparking fascinating interactions between our software and the potential solutions to our problems. By understanding these anti-patterns and adopting a proactive mindset, we can empower ourselves to make informed decisions and avoid potential pitfalls.

Solving cloud native problems without cloud native experience

I was working with a customer trying to migrate their existing data structures into an **OpenSearch** cluster. We had well-defined schemas into which the data had to be marshaled. The problem, however, was that the client attempted to copy their relational data structures directly across to OpenSearch with no denormalization in between. This meant that to marshal the data, we needed to perform multiple lookups to fetch related data structures. These lookups created a situation in which a single request for a model could balloon out to thousands of downstream requests for all of its associated data. Despite our continued protests that the data structures needed to be denormalized or migrated to a high-performance, read-only copy of the relational database, the client wanted to preserve the system's *flexibility* by retaining the original relational shape in a non-relational datastore. We implemented many improvements to push the model as far as possible, including batching requests and local caching for repeated values. However, some requests were simply too deeply nested to optimize. The solution initially proposed by the client was to scale the cluster, so the client scaled the cluster until more performance bottlenecks were hit, and then the client scaled the cluster again. We had an interesting call with the cloud provider. They informed the client that they were provisioning more infrastructure than the cloud provider had provisioned for some subsidiary services. This is the first anti-pattern we would like to address. The easy access to virtually unlimited cloud resources comes with the temptation to solve performance problems by throwing more resources at it, and the resulting cloud bill will scale equally as quickly. We should often look inward at our application instead of outwardly at the infrastructure it is running on to solve problems around application performance. Scaling our infrastructure vertically to solve performance issues will only take us so far. This indicates that an alternative specialized solution may be required, your service has low cohesion, or your application is poorly optimized.

This brings us to the second anti-pattern, which can also result in the first anti-pattern. This pattern typically starts with someone responsible for a cloud native service coming across a staged architecture online with many pretty icons and boxes and then trying to shoehorn that architecture into their use case. Our architecture should be informed by the requirements of the application code we need to write rather than the code we write conforming to some architecture. The cause of this can be multifaceted.

A common driver for this anti-pattern is what we typically refer to as resume-driven development. This occurs when someone is more concerned about getting experience with a particular technology than about that technology's potential to solve the problem. Staged architectures can form a good starting point for potential solutions and often illustrate best practices. However, we must temper these architectures, considering their suitability across various factors. Typically, before adopting a staged architecture verbatim, we should ask ourselves some questions like the following:

- Do we operate at the scale for which this staged architecture solves a problem?

- Do we have the internal skill set to implement and maintain it?

- Does this model follow our standard architecture practices or will it be unique?

- Can we make any changes to ensure this architecture more accurately solves our problem?

The third anti-pattern we will address is manually changing deployed infrastructure or code bases outside our CI/CD pipeline. A typical example might be that our application runs a query that takes a little while to complete in production. So, the developer logs into production and quickly adds an index to the lookup column, and the problem is solved. Despite the compounding of errors that need to occur to allow the developer to make this change, fundamentally, we are introducing instability into our application. This concept is known as **environmental drift**. Our code and deployment pipelines define a model that does not correlate with what is deployed. In our example, we looked at the developer making changes to production, which means the first time that all of our subsequent changes are tested with this environmental drift is when those changes hit our production environment. It also causes an issue when we need to recreate our infrastructure; by circumventing our source model, we will create the same issue whenever we try to create a new instance of our infrastructure. The solution to this problem is relatively simple; development teams should not be able to change a non-ephemeral environment without following their CI/CD process. If they want to prototype a fix or conduct a technical spike that would be accelerated by having write access to the environment, then create a sandbox that can be destroyed once the work is done. This way, you prevent the accumulation of tests and quick fixes in any environments on the path to production. Ideally, these lower environments should be as close to the production environment as possible. On the topic of production environments, we must be careful about how we scale our code in reaction to real-world events.

Suffering from success – the downside of limitless scale

We have an upper bound for our application's throughput when working with on-premises infrastructure. Eventually, we will run out of system resources to serve requests. In a cloud environment, we often see the same thinking come into play – an anti-pattern where rate limits and service limits are ignored. The consequences of neglecting rate limits, service limits, or throttling are significantly higher in the cloud. Rather than being capped by our infrastructure, we have a virtually unlimited pool of resources to scale into. Suppose we combine this lack of physical limits with stateless servers that can interchangeably serve any request, irrespective of any service-level partitioning that we might have. In that case, we can scale to meet our customer's needs very rapidly and virtually limitlessly. In this scenario, we must set artificial caps on using our service. How these limits are partitioned (i.e., by user, tenant, customer, etc.) is up to the implementer. We set rational limits for using our theoretically limitless service to control runaway costs and ensure that we don't impact services for any other clients. Many cloud native managed services already have built-in functionality that we can use to perform rate-limiting, usage monitoring, and licensing applications. Commonly, this is applied at the **API aggregation layer**, such as in AWS **API Gateway**, Azure **APIM**, or GCP **API Gateway**. Luckily, these same API keys can be used as part of our authentication strategy, for example, tying a request to a client to enable defense in depth checking that our API key matches the tenant we're calling. As the complexity of our application grows, we might require custom authorization and rate-limiting logic on our APIs. For example, AWS allows you to add custom authorization to API Gateway through Lambda functions. Other niche API proxy players like **Apigee** (now acquired by Google) and **Kong** allow for complex logic through a comprehensive policy language.

In the on-premises monolith, things tended to fail together. Was our server overloaded or not? It's a question with a relatively simple answer. In the cloud native world, where we have services built up of many components, things tend to fail piecemeal. We need to be tolerant of these faults, but we also need to be aware that the scales the cloud lets us operate at can lead to some interesting behaviors. The next anti-pattern we will address is using bad timeout and retry practices, especially in the context of concurrent executions. Let's assume we have a process that needs to load CSV files into a database and a service that processes a single file from these buckets as they arrive. Let's assume our clients upstream, who deliver our files into the S3 bucket for us to consume, realize that they had an error in their system and haven't uploaded files for the last three days. That's fine; they have added all the files. Let's assume we have a naive architecture that sends a request to an HTTP endpoint to pull the file for processing using S3 events and SNS. If we've ignored the consequences of concurrent execution, we could suddenly begin ingesting a large amount of data simultaneously. This puts an enormous load on the database we are loading the files into. If we don't have timeouts configured for these processes, we could end up completely overloading our database. Therefore, all calls in our application code must have a timeout, and the expiration of those timeouts must be handled gracefully, cleaning up any work in progress that they have requested.

So, if a timeout fails, then what next? A naive response might be that we simply need to retry the request. If the failure results from factors other than an overloaded system, and these errors are rare, then we can probably get away with this approach. However, it's important to note that retries are compounding the issue; we are requesting more server time to solve our problem. If the system is already overloaded, then this just compounds the effect as old requests being retried are now also competing with new requests. A common tactic here is an exponential backoff algorithm, although it is advisable to cap your maximum retry period and the total number of retries. This can work; however, once your server gets overloaded, a whole bunch of calls are going to fail, and if all these calls are retried using the same algorithm, then all we've done is kick the can down the road, and we will overload the server on the next retry.

Another important aspect of retry behavior is the concept of **jitter**. We introduce **randomness** into our retry behavior to prevent a stampeding herd situation. We also need to be aware of the multiplicative effect of retries. Suppose our service makes calls that go three layers deep, and each service retries five times. In that case, the downstream system will receive 53 retries or 125 requests, which is the opposite of the behavior we want when downstream services are overloaded. Luckily, there are three effortless ways to avoid this situation:

- Decouple spiky and expensive traffic with message queues, then scale your downstream services based on queue depth

- Use cloud provider SDKs where possible, as these will already have retry behaviors built into them

- Use managed services, as these typically scale easier and have built-in retry and rate-limiting functionality you don't need to build yourself

This brings us to our last anti-pattern, using implicit properties of ephemeral resources for hardcoded dependency mapping.

Avoiding implicit ephemeral specification

When writing code, especially **infrastructure as code (IaC)**, we can easily fall into the anti-pattern of using direct specifications for partially ephemeral resources. An ephemeral specification, for example, would be applying an IaC configuration that outputs the IP address of an instance, then referring to the first configuration instance by directly using that IP address in another IaC configuration. If we change the first configuration, the IP address might change, but our ephemeral specification has created a hard dependency between them. Instead, we should use resources that aren't ephemeral, such as DNS entries that can be updated. This is the simplest form of service discovery. There are robust, full-featured service discovery platforms that extend this functionality for various cloud providers and deployment configurations. Ideally, any dependencies between our infrastructure should be explicit rather than implicit through hardcoded values to make our deployments truly agnostic of the state of the deployed environment.

Summary

We have now explored some common anti-patterns we see when shifting our application logic to the cloud. Our application code is typically the value differentiator or competitive advantage in our business, so we can move it to the cloud and, by doing so, increase its availability, resilience, and performance. Now that we understand the implications of running our application code in the cloud, how can we store all our data? This is what we will dive into in the next chapter.

Get This Book's PDF Version and Exclusive Extras

Scan the QR code (or go to `packtpub.com/unlock`). Search for this book by name, confirm the edition, and then follow the steps on the page.

Note: Keep your invoice handly. Purchase made directly from packt don't require one.

8

Don't Get Lost in the Data Jungle

Data is at the crux of everything we do. Most operations in cloud native applications relate to generating, consuming, and modifying data in myriad forms. Choosing the right places to store our data in the cloud, knowing how to ingest data, and maintaining data integrity are paramount. While much of the value of the applications we produce lives in the business logic, fundamentally, that business logic operates on data. Therefore, the way we store data is instrumental in the operation of our application. Unlike traditional on-premise services, cloud native services present new and exciting opportunities that can reduce our operational and maintenance overhead significantly. However, when used incorrectly, these services can just as quickly hamper our efforts through some insidious anti-patterns.

In this chapter, we are going to cover the following main anti-patterns that are present when persisting data in the cloud:

- Picking the wrong database or storage

- Data replication from production to development

- Backup and recovery should theoretically work

- Manual data ingestion

- No observability for data transfer errors

By the end of this chapter, you will have a solid understanding of cloud native data storage options for operational purposes and the trade-offs between them.

Picking the wrong database or storage

"When all you have is a hammer, everything looks like a nail" is a refrain commonly used to describe overreliance on the same tool for every job. Having preferences is acceptable, but when teams pick a database or storage solution, we often see the same developers repeatedly reaching for the same tools. While familiarity with a particular toolset might be advantageous for rapid onboarding and development, it can lead to suboptimal solutions and anti-patterns. Cloud native applications have a wide range of databases and storage methods, so a well-rounded cloud application should consider all the available options. Before we dive into these options, let's explore some required background knowledge to frame our conversations.

Framing the conversation

When discussing databases, it is essential to start by exploring the **consistency, availability, and partition tolerance (CAP)** theorem, normal forms, and time complexity. These three concepts explain the trade-offs and approaches to designing data models for myriad solutions.

CAP theorem

As previously mentioned, the CAP theorem stands for consistency, availability, and partition tolerance, specifically concerning distributed datastores. The consensus is that a distributed database solution can only genuinely address two of these capabilities simultaneously:

- **Consistency** ensures that when a database read occurs, it will return the database state that results from all actions committed before we request the read. Strongly consistent databases maintain this paradigm, whereas eventually consistent databases will return a state that may or may not have all applied writes propagated; it represents the state of the database from some point in the past.

- **Availability** means that every request received by a valid database node must return a non-error response. In the context of a distributed datastore, this might conflict with the guarantee of consistency. How can we ensure that our system has received all transactions from all other nodes, especially in scenarios where we might have network partitions or delays? This brings us to partition tolerance.

- **Partition tolerance** guarantees that the system will continue operating despite unreliable or late message delivery between nodes. If one of our nodes suffers catastrophic network failure, our datastore should keep operating. This is primarily an issue in distributed databases with multi-master configurations, such as some of the high-availability options discussed later in the chapter.

In an ideal world, our chosen datastore would have all three of these properties, and some recent developments in this space push the limits of this exclusivity. However, this pattern is generally closely reflected in reality.

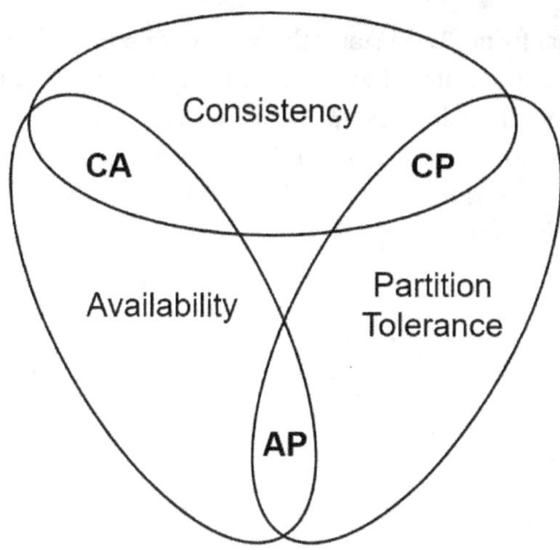

Figure 8.1 – Euler diagram for exclusivity of the CAP theorem elements

Normal forms

Normal forms refer to how we construct data in our database systems. Fundamentally, normal forms are a measure of normalization in our database. We will quickly review normal forms and use a common theme to provide examples for each. One point to keep in mind as we go through this section is that even though it may appear that the higher our normal form is, the better our database design is, in most cases, we also need to consider the performance and querying of our data and access patterns. We will only discuss the first three normal forms here as, typically, this is where most of the differences between cloud native databases lie:

- The first normal form of data (**1NF**) defines each cell as a unit that only contains a single value, and the names of columns in our data storage should be unique. Many storage solutions that support nested or unstructured data already fail this criterion. The following table shows a first normal form dataset for order information:

InvoiceItems				
InvoiceId (key)	**ItemId (key)**	**Qty**	**SalespersonID**	**Salesperson**
123	312	10	10	Aiden
123	432	5	10	Aiden
456	321	20	8	Gerald
789	432	10	8	Gerald

Table 8.1 – Invoices, items, and salespeople stored in a single table

- The second normal form (**2NF**) states that all record non-key attributes must depend on the primary key. For example, if we have a sales record with a key consisting of an invoice ID and an item ID, we store the salesperson's name against the invoice for each record. However, in our fictitious scenario, an invoice only has one salesperson attached, but we store it multiple times in the `Salesperson` column in the first table. In this scenario, our result only depends on the part of the key, the invoice ID.

InvoiceItems		
InvoiceId (key)	**ItemId (key)**	**Qty**
123	312	10
123	432	5
456	321	20
789	432	10

Table 8.2 – Invoices and items; note we have removed two columns in this table

Let's add a new table to satisfy the second normal form by storing salespeople against invoice IDs:

InvoiceSalesperson		
InvoiceId (key)	**SalespersonID**	**Salesperson**
123	10	Aiden
456	8	Gerald
789	8	Gerald

Table 8.3 – Invoices and their relation to salespeople; note that we are storing
less data now but can reconstruct the same level of detail

- The third normal form (**3NF**) states that all elements must give information about the key and nothing but the key. There should be no transitive dependencies in the data. For example, we still violate this rule in our fictitious scenario, as our `InvoiceSalesperson` table is based on the `InvoiceId` key. However, the salesperson's name depends on `SalespersonID`, which is a transitive dependency. To rectify this, let's add a `Salesperson` table (*Table 8.5*):

InvoiceItems		
InvoiceId (key)	ItemId (key)	Qty
123	312	10
123	432	5
456	321	20
789	432	10

Table 8.4 – Invoices and items; this scenario is unchanged from our previous example

We then have the same invoice salesperson mapping; however, we use an identifier rather than the salesperson's name.

InvoiceSalesperson	
InvoiceId (key)	SalespersonID
123	10
456	8
789	8

Table 8.5 – Invoices and their relation to salespeople; however,
we have removed the transitive dependency

Finally, we add a table with each of the salespeople in it:

Salesperson	
SalespersonID (key)	Salesperson
10	Aiden
8	Gerald

Table 8.6 – Maps salespeople IDs to their names; this once again reduces the data
we store but can still be reconstructed with the right access patterns

Our solution has now evolved to comply with the third normal form. As you can see, high levels of normalization require increasing dependence on relationships but provide greater consistency in our data.

Time complexity

Finally, we need to discuss time complexity and Big O notation. Big O notation describes the upper bound of a system's execution time in relation to the size of the dataset being processed. A system with a constant lookup time for a record, regardless of its dataset, is $O(1)$. A system that linearly scales its lookup time with the number of items in our dataset is $O(n)$.

A good example is a naive database implementation that checks every row in a database to see whether it matches our selection criteria. In this case, the implementation would be $O(n)$ complexity; as the number of records grows, so does the number of checks we need to make on each lookup linearly. In reality, most database solutions will lie somewhere between these values. Complexity can scale at rates greater than $O(n)$, but you should find another one if a database ever offers that complexity.

The right database for the right purpose

We see four key types of databases utilized in cloud native systems for bulk data storage: relational, NoSQL, key-value, and graph (there are many other solutions, such as ledger/blockchain databases, hierarchical databases, and vector databases, but they are outside the scope of this section). Each has advantages and is useful for different data types but requires different approaches. A common anti-pattern is developers choosing the wrong cloud databases for their applications.

Relational databases

Relational databases are the tried-and-true traditional database solution. They allow you to establish records and model the relationships between them. In this solution, the database usually conforms to a strict, predefined set of relationships and structures defined as a part of its schema. However, more and more relational database engines are providing the ability to store semi-structured and unstructured data. Due to their highly structured data models, relational databases make it very easy to maintain consistency and integrity of the data. Their inbuilt support of relationships makes it easy to query normalized data. In the cloud world, these databases are often offered as a *service* and may even have "*serverless*" offerings (more on why that's quoted in a few paragraphs); however, we run into issues when we try to scale these systems. Typically, the scaling model involves adding additional capacity to these services through vertical scaling.

Some newer solutions provide automated, transparent sharding capability priced at a premium. At vast scales, with massive datasets, this can cause issues that can result in higher cloud bills. It's also essential to note that in these systems, we're typically limited to certain index types, such as binary trees, which have a time complexity of $O(log(n))$. When we query data in a relational database, a typical pattern is to join records and perform aggregations to return the result in the format we want. This pattern can be instrumental in scenarios where you know the structure of the data you want to store but not the access patterns of how you will query that data. The flexible access patterns allow you to expand your offerings without significant changes to the underlying database. You can provide new insights with new queries.

The services that provide relational databases in the hyperscalers cover all familiar SQL flavors, such as MySQL, PostgreSQL, and SQL Server. Typically, these solutions focus on being consistent and partition-tolerant. However, many new services by hyperscalers also provide high availability.

NoSQL databases

NoSQL databases provide an alternative to traditional relational databases. They are denormalized to some degree, and rather than allowing for flexible access patterns, they rely on access patterns designed into the data model itself.

All the hyperscalers have offerings in this space: Azure has Cosmos DB, GCP has Firestore, and AWS has DynamoDB. Unlike our strictly formatted SQL tables, NoSQL databases have no enforced schema. Columns can mix data types, and data can be deeply nested. There are compelling arguments for why you should do away with separate tables and instead put all your data into one big table. These services offer extreme scalability and performance at a low price point. However, they require fundamental shifts in thinking from the traditional relational database model.

We must design our access patterns upfront to get the best value from our NoSQL database solution. This requirement can make development slightly more complicated because adding a new access pattern is more than just a case of writing a new query. We may require significant changes to our database design. Some database solutions in the NoSQL space (such as DynamoDB, Firestore, and Cosmos DB) can achieve close to $O(1)$ complexity for properly structured access patterns but incur a penalty of $O(n)$ complexity for improperly structured access patterns. Many of these solutions allow you to prioritize availability and partition tolerance or consistency and partition tolerance.

Key-value stores

Key-value stores are a straightforward type of database. Essentially, we provide a way to address (key) our stored data (value). NoSQL databases still allow for complex access patterns. Our key-value store has one access pattern: use the key to get the value stored at an address. These are typically high-performance in-memory datastores that may or may not offer some form of persistence. The typical use case for these datastores is a cache for complex queries or computational outputs from other systems. They can be helpful in our cloud arsenal when we have complex requests with low cardinality.

Graph databases

The final database type we will discuss is **graph databases**. These are useful when we have highly relational, semi-structured data. In relational databases, you can define a relation as a property on an object. For example, an `OrderID` field is referenced on the order record, the shipping manifest, and the payment record. The shipping manifest and payment record contain foreign keys to the order record; however, the actual relationship is stored on the records themselves. In a graph database, the relationships are first-class objects. We have our objects (vertices) and our relationships (edges), and the data model is optimized for extremely fast traversal of relationships, allowing us to follow paths through our dataset in a performant way. This property can be advantageous when objects interact with each other in arbitrary ways, for example, with users on a social media site, interacting with other users, posts, communities, and so on.

Other database types

Exploring other supporting services or nonstandard database types can also be advantageous. A key type of database that is often ignored is time-series databases. These might be implemented as standalone products or extensions to the previous database types. These databases are optimized for chronological access patterns and storage rather than the structures mentioned previously. Another common type of database or database extension is spatial databasing, specifically looking at geometric and geographic properties in queries. The key here is not to limit yourself to the preceding database structures but to also explore the options available for your edge cases.

In one example I worked on, the client used a Postgres database to store a list of customer addresses and identifiers. However, this system's access patterns are unsuitable for a relational database. First, the data was not relational; each record was wholly independent, and second, the Postgres keyword `LIKE` was significantly used within the database's query patterns. The client's quick solution was to put a **generalized inverted index** (**GIN**) on every column. This enabled searching on arbitrary strings but made modifying the database unwieldy. Using a search service such as OpenSearch to store the queriable documents would have been straightforward, likely resulting in a lower cloud bill and better performance.

Manual, managed, serverless, and truly serverless databases

When choosing databases, we must establish the need for the database types discussed earlier and the method by which we are going to consume the database in the cloud.

The naive approach to this from the on-premises mindset might be that we simply need to provision a cloud VM, install a database, and be good to go. While this manual approach will work, it must present a compelling value proposition. In this scenario, you are solely responsible for backups, patching the DB version and OS, and provisioning new machines. How you install, run, and maintain databases is unlikely to be a value differentiator for your business. Therefore, this manual option is generally considered an anti-pattern unless you need specific functionality or configurations that aren't available in managed services. Instead, the baseline deployment of a database is typically as a managed service.

This deployment method is where we see most companies start their cloud database adoption, as these managed services provide a way for them to use familiar tools (Postgres, MySQL, and SQL Server) while allowing the cloud provider to take care of backups, patching, and maintenance using battle tested and resilient methodologies. Many companies never find a compelling reason to leave this level, which is perfectly acceptable. We can also start to set up resilient architectures in this development mode with read replicas, automated failover, and multi-master configurations.

In the managed system, we typically see applications that have consistent, predictable patterns. However, some businesses have unpredictable traffic and usage, so you should move to a more scalable solution. This situation is where "serverless" solutions come into play. I use quotes in this scenario because they are serverless (i.e., they will automatically scale). Still, they do not scale down to zero, which many people consider true serverless. An anti-pattern we commonly see in this space is people migrating to these "serverless" solutions without considering non-relational data models.

Finally, we have truly serverless databases. These are typically NoSQL or document databases (such as DynamoDB, Firestore, and Cosmos DB in the major cloud providers in the **online transaction processing (OLTP)** space) that make trade-offs in ease of use for extreme scalability, cost-effectiveness, and performance. The anti-pattern we often see in this space is teams seeing this option and holding it as the pinnacle of achievement to build a system that utilizes this cloud native unique option without considering the downsides. Namely, your data is less portable, will be harder to hire for, and requires upfront knowledge of your access patterns. This combination can lead to bad initial experiences that cause teams to return to the familiar land of relational databases and not consider these databases for use cases where they would be a good fit.

Ignoring storage requirements

A common anti-pattern is using traditional storage mechanisms in the cloud without considering other options. Conventional filesystems evolved out of the need for on-device storage and provide considerable functionality. Network filesystems, such as FTP and NFS, became the de facto projection of these services into a multi-machine environment. The core principle in these systems is that a central server is responsible for coordinating access to the underlying storage. A common theme in this book is that centralization is usually an anti-pattern.

When we start to design a system that utilizes storage in the cloud, the first question we should ask is, *"Can we use blob storage?"* **Blob storage** is decentralized and scales horizontally, with much higher resiliency and durability than conventional network filesystems. In Azure, this service is Azure Blob Storage, GCP has Cloud Storage, and AWS has S3.

You can think of blob storage as a key-value store that can store enormous values. For most cloud native use cases, this provides more than enough capability. Do you still need metadata? Put it in your database. Do you need locks? Use your database. Need backups? Use version history. Blob storage is likely the answer to your storage needs. There are cases where specialized or traditional filesystems still provide benefits, such as in high-performance computing, low-latency applications, and conventional filesystem migrations. So, remember that no one tool is the right solution to every problem.

Ignoring the life cycle and archive policy

Storing data is easy. We send a request to our storage provider of choice and then forget about it until we need to use it. Therein lies the anti-pattern: failing to maintain the life cycle of your data appropriately can lead to severe consequences.

However, we might want to save some money here because we don't necessarily want to access this data; we just want to keep it on file. This requirement is where the concept of storage tiers comes into play.

Let's take an example: we work at a large firm that has an internal tax function. Throughout the year, people upload receipts. We must access these receipts repeatedly during tax time as various functions perform their duties. Then, after the tax period, we just need to keep a copy in case of discrepancies. In all cloud providers, we can group their storage tiers into one of three broad categories:

- **Hot** is for data that needs to be accessed regularly and available at a moment's notice. Typically, this tier strikes a good balance between cost to store and cost to retrieve. Consider this where we want our receipts to be at tax time.

- **Cold** is for data that needs to be accessed at a moment's notice but is unlikely to be accessed often. We pay a little more when we want to access items in this tier but reap the benefits of our infrequent access with lower storage costs. This tier might be where we store all of our receipts during the year as they're submitted.

- **Archive** is for data that we want to keep but do not have specific access speed requirements. This tier offers the most cost-effective storage solution with the highest access cost and slowest retrieval time (this might be on the order of hours rather than milliseconds). When we are done with all of our receipts for the year and just need to keep a record for posterity, we will move them to this tier.

Some data may need to be retained to comply with regulatory requirements, while other data may only need to be stored short-term as its validity rapidly decreases. We accomplish these use cases through data life cycles. Life cycle policy and management tools allow us to automate this process.

Typically, we take two actions in life cycle policies: we either change the storage tier of our data or delete our data. A life cycle policy might mix these two actions. For example, imagine we work for a company that creates detailed financial reports. Every month, we release a new report that is accessed frequently, then infrequently, and then it needs to be archived for six years. Our life cycle policy might look like this:

1. Create a file in the hot tier.

2. Wait 31 days (report cycle).

3. Move the file to the cold tier.

4. Wait 334 days.

5. Move the file to the archive tier.

6. Wait six years.

7. Delete the file.

If we kept our file in the hot tier, we would be paying for the convenience of frequent access without actually accessing the file. Therefore, our life cycle policy has allowed us to optimize our cloud storage spending.

Data replication from production to development

We all need data to ensure that the systems we build in our development environment match all the weird and wonderful types of data that our users generate in production.

This section is one of the few sections with an anti-pattern that is serious enough to name the entire section after. Under no circumstance should you copy user-generated data from production to development environments. While it may seem easy to get real-world use cases for your lower environment, lower environments typically have more lax security controls and broader access to developers. A few recent data breaches have directly involved this anti-pattern; real-world user data was available on test systems, and these test systems were breached. Instead, in this section, we will go through some alternatives to testing on production data and some common anti-patterns in creating data for test environments.

But we mask our production data

The first anti-pattern we will discuss is using masked data from production systems in test environments. This procedure is only marginally better than using production data directly. The fallacy in this scenario is that we are coming from an insecure position (unmasked production data), applying a transform (our masking procedure), and assuming the output is secure (masked data). To illustrate why this is a problem, let us look at a parallel example, one based on FaaS. I was working with a client who had produced an authentication and logging wrapper for lambda functions. The wrapper applied some functionality that could be enabled with flags in the lambda function code. One of the flags enabled authentication. This pattern meant that, fundamentally, any created lambda functions started as insecure functions and then had to opt in to become secure. Instead, we inverted that dependency. We made all of the functions secure by default, and you could use a flag to turn authentication off for unauthenticated functions. This change made being insecure a conscious choice rather than an unconscious mistake. When we mask data, we risk making unconscious mistakes because we start from an insecure position. The solution is to start from a secure position and explicitly make any insecure additions to our data choices. So, we have to start from a secure position, which means we need to know our schema and generate data that tests its limits.

Getting started with synthetic data

As we discussed earlier, the easiest way to ensure that the data you use is safe for lower environments is to ensure it doesn't originate from production systems. Therefore, we need a reliable way to generate fake data for our system. Luckily, we are not the first people to have this issue! A multitude of open source libraries exist with the sole purpose of generating completely fake data. Usually, for cloud projects, JavaScript is used at some point in the development cycle, be it for frontend applications or backend servers with a runtime such as Node.js, Bun, or Deno, so it usually forms a good baseline language. In this case, the Faker.js (`fakerjs.dev`) library provides a comprehensive set of generators to create fake data for testing. The other common language we see in testing frameworks is Python, which also has its own Faker library (`https://faker.readthedocs.io/en/master/`).

These libraries form an excellent foundation upon which to build. These allow us to create bulk data to see how our system handles when under heavy load. We can use our production system's utilization metrics to develop synthetic data. Synthetic data retains the schema and structure of our production data, but the contents of the records are pure fiction, making it great for functional testing. This approach allows us to load a similar amount of data present in production into lower environments, ensuring that the conditions we are testing under in our lower environments are similar to those under our higher environment. A common anti-pattern we see here is attempting to use only a small data set in lower environments. This anti-pattern is an issue because you first test the system at the production scale when you deploy it to production. Under this paradigm, scenarios and edge behaviors that only become present at the scale of the production system remain hidden during testing. These problems might be a poorly optimized SQL query or a missing index on a column. In these scenarios, small datasets are unlikely to be exposed to the issue.

Perfect synthetic data

When creating synthetic data, it can be easy to fall into the anti-pattern of developing *perfect synthetic data*. This anti-pattern only injects the data, formats, and usage patterns we expect to see in our production systems. While this might test our systems' happy path, unfortunately, users are fantastic at stressing our systems in ways we never intended. What happens if the user signs up with an address and then that address is deleted or gets subdivided into an A/B block or any other myriad of problems? We can take a leaf from the domain of chaos engineering here. Instead of creating perfect data, we make data with a certain amount of corruption, usually expressed as a percentage of the total synthetic data. Perfect data only addresses usage by perfectly homogenous users, and we all know that our user base consists of a wildly different collection of individuals.

There are some simple guidelines for creating synthetic data that I like to follow. I generally split these into two layers: one for structured data (SQL and Parquet) and one for unstructured/semi-structured data (NoSQL, CSV, JSON, and TXT). The unstructured data corruptions should be treated as an extension of the structured corruptions.

Structured data can be corrupted in the following ways:

- **Missing records**: What happens if we receive a partial object in a request to our service? What if a dependency is missing? What if the dependency existed when we created the record but manually deleted it afterward?

- **Unreachable state**: We may have transitive dependencies that are unreachable from a code perspective but permissible from a database perspective. What happens if we reach this state?

- **Corrupted records**: This is data that fundamentally does not make sense but is permissible by the system. What if the user accidentally entered their credit card number in the cardholder name field? What if one row of our CSV has an unescaped comma in a string?

- **Large records**: What happens when a user connects an infinite number of monkeys with an endless number of typewriters to your profanity filter?

Unstructured data can be corrupted in the following additional ways:

- **Duplicate records**: What happens when we try to insert duplicate records, or multiple records that represent the same object?

- **Extra fields**: What happens when our system receives extra data from the client that it wasn't expecting?

- **Missing fields**: What happens when our system doesn't receive data from the client that it was expecting?

- **Syntactically incorrect data**: This is data that doesn't agree with the rules of the data medium in use (for example, not valid CSV or JSON). Missing a column? Forgot a curly brace?

From this, we see that perfect testing data should be imperfect by design. This allows us to discover our system's edge behavior. Our test data should identify issues we might encounter before encountering them in production. However, it is impossible to be perfectly prophetic about the data issues we might see in production. The best type of corrupted data is when we find something in production. In that case, copy the methodology of the corrupted data (not the data itself!) into your synthetic data generation tool. This process allows us to find other ways in which this might impact production. For example, we have an issue where an invalid card number is entered. Then, the customer could rectify the card number, and all is good. If we add the pattern to our synthetic data, we can see how that data would have affected our system if it had been allowed to flow through to our billing run system or other application areas.

Backup and recovery should theoretically work

"The best-laid plans of mice and men oft go awry," goes the famous line from Robert Burns' "To a Mouse." The nugget of wisdom here is that no matter how carefully we plan for every eventuality, we cannot be confident of its success until we execute it. We touched on this topic in *Chapter 7* when we discussed ignoring reliability. We will go into this topic in more detail and explore how to address this anti-pattern with a specific focus on data. As discussed before, not testing your data resiliency will lead to unwanted downtime when you least expect it. Let's dive into some ways to mitigate this.

Have a plan

Having a plan is the first step toward resilient data architectures, and the key to that plan is understanding the shared responsibility model. If you are running your data solution self-hosted in the cloud against the recommendations of the first section of this chapter, then you are responsible for everything yourself. We often come across a disconnect when people shift to managed services. Inevitably, someone will find a checkbox on their managed cloud database instance that says **Enable backups** and see that it is ticked. Then, they will rest easy at night, thinking their data is safe because it is nebulously "handled by the cloud." If this sounds all too familiar (even if it doesn't), you probably need to consider putting together a recovery action plan.

Some key factors need to be considered when creating this plan, as follows:

1. Define your **recovery time objective (RTO)** and **recovery point objective (RPO)**. Respectively, these two measures are the answers to the following questions:

    - How much time can I afford for my service to be down?
    - How much data can I afford to lose when the service goes down?

    A common anti-pattern here is to answer "None" and "Nothing." Realistically, the costs of maintaining such a strategy are incongruent with reality. Typically, the question is answered in an order of magnitude, such as seconds, minutes, hours, or days.

2. Once you've outlined the parameters for your recovery plan, you must design an architectural solution to achieve this. Suppose the scales we are looking at involve second or minute granularity. In that case, you likely need to look into live read replicas that can take over as the main DB in the case of failure or even multi-master DB configurations for ultra-low downtime applications. A solid incremental backup system is enough if we look at the order of hours or days (in the first scenario, we'd still have this requirement for resilience in depth). We can test our resilience architecture by detailing stressors our system may experience, such as a failure in a database instance or an entire cloud region going down. We then draft the system response when that stressor occurs, making changes to our architecture as required. There is an interesting parallel here between the stressors we choose to simulate and the actual resilience of our system. In the research and subsequent book by Barry O'Reilly, *Residues: Time, Change, and Uncertainty in Software Architecture,* he states that often our stressors do not exist in mutual exclusivity; for example, a network failure and a tsunami wiping out a data center are likely to have commonalities in the way our architecture will respond. Therefore, our stressor list does not need to be exhaustive. We just need to list and simulate stressors until our resultant architecture no longer requires any changes to support recovery from the stressor.

3. Once we design the resilience architecture, we can start reviewing the action plan. The action plan is a detailed step-by-step manual for restoring service; think of it as the user guide to your resilient architecture. Identifying all the functional and non-functional requirements needed to complete the operation is essential. Some good questions to ask yourself are the following:

    - Who is going to act?
    - Where will they get the credentials?
    - What are the resource identifiers that they will be acting on?
    - What are the impacts on customers going to be?
    - What steps will they need to perform?

4. The final step is to run through your action plan. This dry run can be in a lower environment or a copy of production. Still, it's essential to carry out the operations in your action plan to identify any gaps in the documentation. Ideally, you would do this with team members who are not involved in designing the action plan. This process prevents the team from performing the actions based on intent rather than the documentation itself. You can do this as often as required to refine the action plan until everyone is comfortable.

Game day

When soldiers train for combat, they don't do it solely in a classroom or through reading copious, possibly outdated documentation. A core part of their readiness comes from training activities that simulate real-world scenarios as closely as possible. This regime means that when they respond to situations, they don't just know what to do in theory; they have real-world knowledge. Your team should practice responding to incidents similarly, using conditions close to real-world scenarios.

The first stage with any game day is planning. At its inception, the game day should have a clearly defined scope and boundaries to ensure the safety of the scenario. The last thing you want is a hypothetical incident response becoming an actual incident! The planning should include a scenario that tests a specific action plan. These scenarios can be as real or as fake as you want, and your list of stressors from designing your architecture might be an excellent place to start. Some of my favorites are the following:

- A senior engineer with too many permissions (does this sound familiar from *Chapter 6*?) had production database access. They accidentally dropped one of our tables. How can we get the data back?

- Your database needs critical security updates that require a database restart. How will you ensure continuity?

- Someone scheduled the deletion of the blob storage encryption key. Did we detect it? How will we prevent it?

Even though the scenarios may be fake, the tools and processes used should be the same as those we use in a real incident. The response should be as close as possible to the required real-world response.

Remember those RTO and RPO goals we defined when formulating the plan? The game day is a perfect litmus test for those goals. Going into the event, everyone should be aware of these objectives, the deadline should be enforced, and, ideally, meeting the objective should be incentivized.

A game day is a great way to build inter-team communication and break down silos within the business. Involve all affected teams, even non-technical teams. How will sales operate with missing data? Does the marketing team need to create a statement? The implications of an actual event likely spread beyond the confines of the technical team, so why not utilize your simulated event to manage the complete response? Your technical team will need additional technical-only game days, but a full-scale game day can be highly productive to test your entire business's resilience.

Executing the game day is fun: set up your simulated scenario, inform your operational team of the situation, and then watch them perform the recovery strategy. Make sure that the team is aware of the scope and boundaries of the game day before they begin executing to avoid the consequences we mentioned earlier. While testing your incident response, you should document your team's actions. This process enables you to identify gaps in your existing action plan and refine it for future game days or an actual incident.

This process should be followed by a healthy and blameless postmortem for both the simulated event (e.g., how did this theoretical event occur in the first place? How can we stop it from happening in the real world?) and the actual response itself (e.g., did we meet our RTO and RPO? Was our procedure efficient?).

We will use the documentation generated during the execution phase after the event for a post-game day retrospective. This retrospective can follow the standard Agile retrospective format:

- What went well?

- What went wrong?

- What did we learn?

- What changes can we make to do better next time?

We can usually separate the points raised through this retrospective into two distinct categories:

- Points about the execution of the recovery plan

- Points about the execution of the game day itself

Both are important to collect, but use the first set to feed into improving your recovery plan and the second set to host an even better game day next time!

The real thing

If you follow the preceding advice when an actual incident occurs, the response should be that of a well-oiled machine rolling into action. That does not absolve you of your surrounding responsibilities. You should still do the following:

- Execute according to procedure

- Document all actions taken

- Try to achieve RTO and RPO targets

- Conduct a postmortem and retrospective

You will (hopefully!) get very few of these opportunities to execute the recovery plan for real, so this is where you will get your most valuable data.

Manual data ingestion

When talking to other engineers about problems they experience when writing code, they will often say that the computer is not doing what they are telling it to do. My answer is usually the same: *"Computers will do exactly what you tell them to do."* There is an old joke that illustrates this point very well. A programmer's partner asks them to go to the shops and pick up a loaf of bread, and if they have eggs, get a dozen. The programmer returns with a dozen loaves of bread. When questioned why, they reply, "*Well, they had eggs.*" Computers are literal, but when you finally have the computer exhibiting the behavior that you want, the good news is that it will execute the actions precisely the same ad infinitum, barring some external influence. The downside is that computers are bad at performing actions that we haven't predicted. On the other hand, humans have evolved to excel at performing in situations we haven't anticipated. However, you lose the perfect execution criteria of computers.

What does this have to do with data? What would you choose if we want our data to be ingested the same way every time? A fallible human who might be able to sort out the edge cases on the fly or a significantly less fallible automated system that is deterministic in the way that the same input will always produce the same output?

The first data ingestion pipeline

The first stage of shifting to an automated data ingestion system is to define the happy path. We discussed this concept when talking about synthetic data. How would you want the system to operate if all your data was perfect? This allows you to feed perfect data into the system and receive perfect results. In an ideal world, we wouldn't need to ever progress beyond this state. In my experience, I have never encountered a data source that met the perfect criteria. So, let us start pushing data through our pipeline, and if our data doesn't hit our perfect criteria, we can deal with the issues as they arise. This might involve removing invalid records from the source dataset or manipulating the data to meet our perfect data criteria.

This has enabled us to combine the best of both worlds. Our automated system processes all of our well-formatted data to produce deterministic results, and our human operators can intervene when the computerized system cannot process the records. This allows the human element to exercise their judgment when required to allow all records to be correctly ingested. However, this setup still has one key issue: cloud services can quickly ingest our data, processing millions of records per second. On the other hand, while being more versatile, humans move at a glacial pace.

Failure granularity

When ingesting data, we want to ensure we choose the correct failure granularity for our data ingestion pipeline. A naive approach would be to fail the pipeline whenever an error is encountered. As our datasets grow and our ingestion pipelines become more complex, the chances of the pipeline not experiencing a failure rapidly approaches zero. It is an infrequent case, in my experience, that a data pipeline provides value through an all-or-nothing approach.

Typically, an incomplete dataset still offers more value than no data at all, and that is where this naive approach falls over. This is where it is crucial to consider your failure granularity. This means we need to discover the smallest unit of data that becomes non-functional when there is an error. This might mean we fail a single file, row/column, or cell in our dataset. By constraining the failure to the smallest unit of non-functional data, we can still leverage our dataset for other purposes, collect the failing units of data, and then process those failures asynchronously, enhancing the dataset as time goes on by using human judgment to deal with these edge cases.

This might consist of an automatic prefiltering stage that determines whether the data matches our specifications. Records that do match are passed onto our data ingestion pipeline, and records that do not match our specification are passed to a dead letter queue for later triaging.

Scaling the pipeline

Human labor for mundane tasks will always be the most expensive to scale. The human requirement to scale experiences hysteresis with the time required to hire, onboard, and train new resources. With the adoption of cloud native services, we barely even have to lift a finger to increase our throughput. In fact, with auto-scaling, even those few mouse clicks and keyboard strokes may be redundant!

Once the initial pipeline is built, the dead letter queue becomes a valuable resource. As we fix issues with data in the dead letter queue, we understand the types of problems we expect to see with our data. By analyzing how our human experts, with domain knowledge, rectify this problem, we can begin to provide edge case automation for these cases, codifying their knowledge into instructions that our pipeline can execute. As our pipeline scales, this automation allows it to improve its resilience, allowing our adaptable human element to deal with new problems requiring their expertise.

Automating these cases also allows us to increase the recency of our data. Rather than waiting for a human to come and rectify these errors after they have been detected as errors, we have extended our specification to include these types of data.

Making the jump to streaming

As our pipeline becomes increasingly automatic, and if our upstream data sources support it, we can increase the frequency of our data ingestion to be closer to real time. Instead of a manual ingestion process performed once a week due to human limitations, we can shift to running our pipeline much more frequently. We have seen clients achieve a shift from monthly data ingestions to hourly data ingestions with this process.

The final stage is rather than a schedule-driven process that pulls all data that has occurred in a period, we shift to a streaming model where the presence of new data kicks off the ingestion pipeline. The advantage of using cloud native services in this space is that, often, the scheduled pipelines you have already created can be run as streaming pipelines with minimal changes.

No observability for data transfer errors

I will repeat the mantra used countless times throughout this book, "*You can't fix what you can't measure.*" The same is valid for data transfer. You need to be able to view the state of your data transfers so you can make informed decisions based on the data you have. The observability method is up to the user, but it is important to note that simply getting the observability data is half the battle. The other half is getting it in front of the eyes that will most impact the quality of your data pipeline.

The data integrity dependency

Let me pose a hypothetical scenario we have seen play out at clients all too often. You have a successful app with a great dev team. To better understand your customers, you create a new data team to track how users interact with your application. To accomplish this, your developers quickly cobble together some cloud native data pipeline tools to feed data to the data team. The data team struggles to make progress because the data coming through is of poor quality, so the data team spends excessive time simply getting the data to a usable state. This causes the data team to be less effective due to both lack of time and lack of good quality data. The development team is just throwing data over the metaphorical fence and letting the data team deal with the fallout. The development team is the beneficiary of the data, as they will be the ones who can consume the data artifacts that the data team produces to understand better what they are building. Here, we see the dichotomy: the data team is rarely the team that will benefit from the data, but they are the ones who need to ensure that the data is correct to show that they are doing their jobs.

Inverting the dependency

I worked for a client previously in a company with a very large (non-software) engineering function. These engineers are tasked with ensuring that specific safety parameters are met. Part of that included ingesting sensor data from the field. One data engineer was responsible for maintaining the data pipeline. This configuration is all good in a static environment, but as we all know thanks to Werner Vogels, "*Everything fails all the time.*" What happened was that some sensors, data loggers, or even networking equipment would fail and be replaced, changing the topology of the data. The data would then show up as unrecognized, and the data engineer would go and chase down the responsible engineer for the correct parameters to ingest the data correctly. In this scenario, the data engineer did not benefit from the data but was responsible for reactively fixing the data. Alongside this client, we designed a solution that monitored pipeline health, found inconsistencies, and told the engineer responsible that the data was not being appropriately ingested. They could then log in to a UI to fix the data topology so it would be ingested correctly on the next run. As the responsibility for this data sat with the engineer, we noticed that not only did they reactively fix the data they were responsible for but they proactively went and updated the topology to prevent future pipeline failures. We had inverted the dependency!

This is the power of having the right eyes on the observability data and empowering the beneficiaries to maintain it themselves. This lets our data engineers focus instead on the bigger picture and deal with problems in the data domain rather than playing catchup with other domains.

Maintaining the dependency

Now that we have inverted the data dependency between our producers and consumers, we can start to examine how to preserve the integrity of the link. As developers move forward, they rarely stop to think about their changes' impact on the broader data ecosystem, of which their data is only a tiny part. The key to negotiating this minefield is typically through data contracts. A data contract is a specification that defines the format of the data that the application will produce. These specifications represent a mutual understanding of the underlying schema between data producers and consumers. If we use a common specification framework, such as JSON Schema, we can add tests for conformity of our data as part of the definition of done. This definition allows us to identify when we will cause breaking changes and preemptively notify downstream users that the schema is changing.

Mature operations in this space also allow for the adoption of more modern tools, such as data catalogs. These catalogs will enable us to register the data and its schema so that it can be utilized by anyone who needs it within the organization. It is also vital to centrally track these new dependencies as they grow so that we know who to notify when a data contract requires a breaking change.

So, now we have a solid understanding of how data observability is important for reacting to pipeline failures, preemptively acting, and treating our data services as first-class citizens in our application stack.

Summary

The cloud offers all new ways for us to manage one of our most important assets: our data! However, falling into the anti-patterns in this chapter can not only have implications for your bottom line but also for the durability, availability, and security of your data. By understanding the concepts in this chapter, you are well equipped to navigate the cloud native data jungle and build effective architectures. Next, we will look at how we can connect all the parts of our architecture together.

Get This Book's PDF Version and Exclusive Extras

Scan the QR code (or go to `packtpub.com/unlock`). Search for this book by name, confirm the edition, and then follow the steps on the page.

Note: Keep your invoice handly. Purchase made directly from packt don't require one.

9
Connecting It All

In cloud native environments, networking plays a critical role in ensuring the performance, scalability, and security of applications. However, as organizations embrace the cloud, they often encounter challenges stemming from misaligned strategies and outdated practices. These challenges manifest as anti-patterns—recurring issues that undermine the effectiveness of cloud native solutions.

This chapter delves into some of the most common cloud native networking anti-patterns, examining their impact and providing actionable insights to avoid them. By understanding and addressing these pitfalls, organizations can design resilient, efficient, and secure network architectures tailored for the cloud.

The anti-patterns covered in this chapter include the following:

- Ignoring latency and bandwidth
- Lack of DNS strategy
- Monolithic connectivity
- Ignoring cloud native networking features
- Zero Trust application patterns

By exploring these topics, this chapter equips you with the knowledge to recognize and mitigate these anti-patterns, fostering robust cloud native networking practices.

Ignoring latency and bandwidth

When organizations transition to the cloud, the role of networking undergoes a significant shift. In traditional on-premises setups, network engineers and administrators manage physical hardware, switches, routers, and the meticulous planning necessary to ensure low latency, redundancy, and security. This careful orchestration is crucial for optimal performance. However, as companies move to the cloud, the focus of networking shifts from physical infrastructure management to virtualized infrastructure. This shift can lead to the misconception that networking becomes a secondary concern, but in reality, it remains just as critical in cloud native environments, albeit in a different form. This is where the common cloud native anti-pattern of ignoring latency and bandwidth emerges.

The focus shifts from physical hardware to virtualized infrastructure, requiring engineers to manage components such as **virtual private clouds** (**VPCs**), subnets, security groups, load balancers, and inter-service communication. While physical constraints are reduced, the complexity of managing efficient, secure, and redundant communication across distributed systems persists. Latency and bandwidth issues can be exacerbated, especially in applications built from numerous microservices, which must communicate seamlessly across distributed environments.

In the following sections, we will examine how to plan and manage connectivity to the internet effectively, on-premises systems, and third-party services. This will include insights into designing robust, secure network architectures that facilitate seamless integration and reliable communication, whether connecting cloud resources to legacy infrastructure, external partners, or the broader public internet.

Cloud native latency

In cloud environments such as Azure, AWS, and **Google Cloud Platform** (**GCP**), network latency refers to the time a data request takes to travel from one point to another.

For example, suppose your application hosted on AWS needs to retrieve data from an S3 bucket. In that case, network latency is the delay incurred as the request traverses the network, is processed, and the response is returned. Similarly, in Azure, if your services span multiple regions, say from East US to West Europe, network latency will influence the time it takes for data to travel across these regions. Let us focus on the S3 example, as the S3 latency is something we recently encountered in an engagement. Let us use the following diagram as a reference point for the scenario:

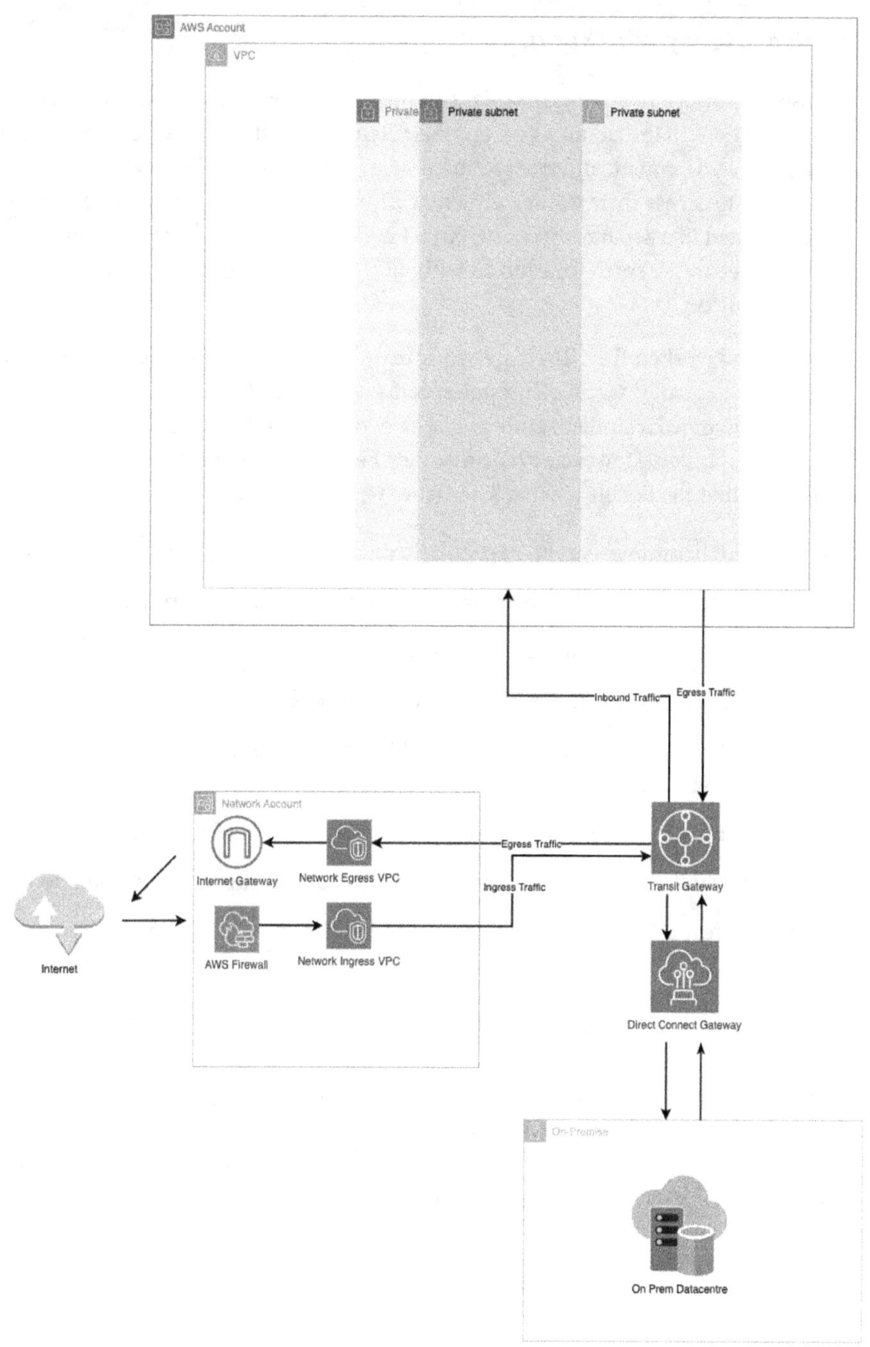

Figure 9.1 - AWS networking diagram

Cloud native latency with services

During a consulting engagement, a mid-sized e-commerce company had recently migrated a significant portion of its operations to the cloud. As part of their architecture, they stored vast amounts of product images, user-generated content, and transactional data in Amazon S3. However, instead of using S3 gateway endpoints to access their storage directly within the VPC, they routed all S3 traffic through an egress VPC hosted in a separate account. An S3 endpoint is a private connection within a VPC that allows direct, secure access to Amazon S3 without traversing the public internet, reducing latency and improving security.

Initially, everything worked fine. Their network team was familiar with egress VPCs from their on-premises days, where routing traffic through specific network exits provided centralized control and monitoring. They assumed a similar setup would be beneficial in the cloud, ensuring tighter control over internet-bound traffic. However, over time, they began noticing performance degradation. The following list goes into the details of what said issues were:

- Latency issues became apparent, particularly during peak traffic hours

- Users experienced delays while browsing extensive collections of product images

- High volumes of data uploads further exacerbated the response time issues

- Customers faced slow image loads and transaction processing delays

- The team hadn't accounted for the cost of additional network hops between their application VPC and the egress VPC

- Every request to S3 had to traverse between the two VPCs, adding unnecessary latency

- Data routing through multiple network layers before reaching S3 contributed to the delay

- API calls made to AWS services such as S3 were directed to the internet due to the absence of a gateway option

Without S3 gateway endpoints, which would have allowed for a direct, high-speed connection to S3 within the VPC itself, every request took the long way around. The solution was simple but impactful. By enabling S3 gateway endpoints within their application VPC, they could establish a direct path to S3, eliminating the cross-VPC traffic, and the traffic would stay within the AWS account rather than reaching out to the internet. Almost immediately, latency dropped and the performance issues disappeared. Their customers enjoyed a smoother, faster experience, and the engineering team learned an important lesson about the intricacies of cloud native networking. The following figure shows the usage of gateway endpoints:

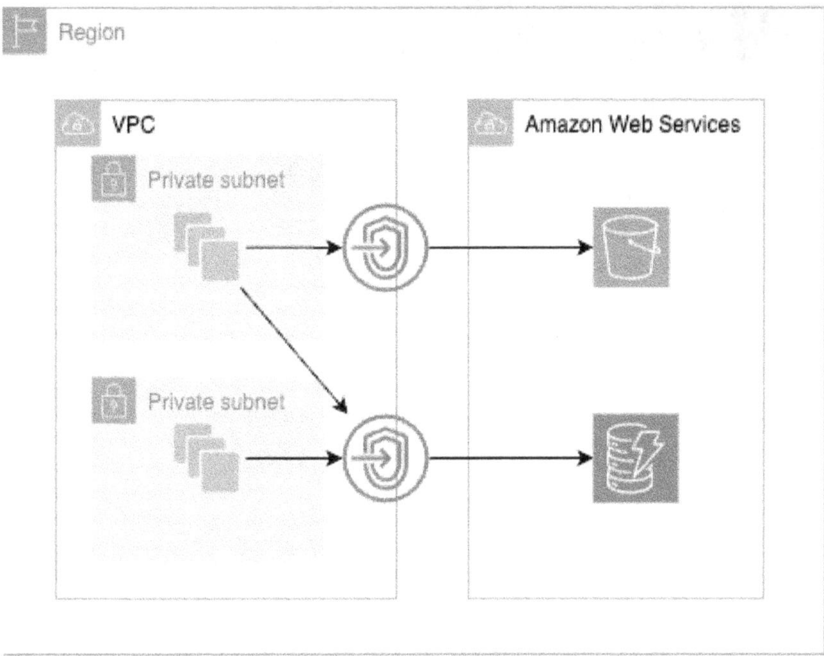

Figure 9.2 - S3 gateway endpoint and DynamoDB

It was a costly oversight that could have been avoided had they considered the native tools available within the cloud environment. Instead, they had unknowingly introduced an anti-pattern by relying on outdated network practices from their on-premises days.

Cross-zone latency

A typical pattern in the move to cloud native is found when connecting resources across multiple cloud environments or **availability zones** (**AZs**) within the same cloud provider, such as AWS, Azure regions, or GCP zones. While cloud platforms offer distributed infrastructure and the promise of high availability, organizations often underestimate the latency and bandwidth challenges that arise when resources are spread geographically. Note that geographical spread also means across zones within a specific region.

Take, for example, a typical region in AWS. You may have 3–5 distinct AZs, each of which is a grouping of data centers across different diverse locations. This allows for better fault tolerance, but latency between these zones is higher than between services/apps in the same zone.

Furthermore, data transfer costs can escalate rapidly when services communicate across regions or zones, leading to unexpected financial overhead. This anti-pattern reflects a fundamental oversight in cloud native architecture, where organizations focus on multi-zone redundancy or cross-cloud integrations without considering the performance and cost implications of networking.

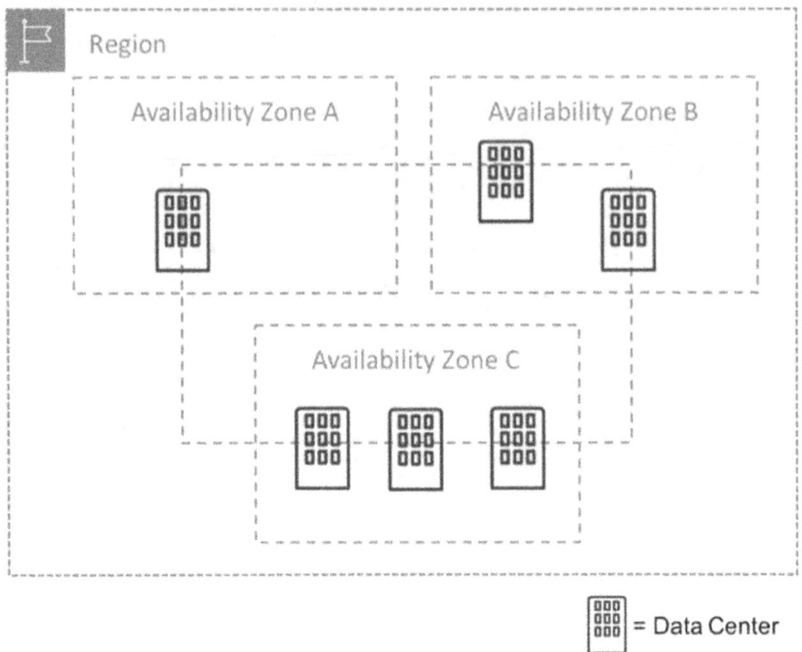

Figure 9.3 - Example of AWS AZs

It is crucial to factor in bandwidth limitations and optimize for low-latency interactions, mainly when designing architectures that span multiple zones or regions. In-region networking is optimized logically to ensure efficiency and performance, but due to the geographic separation designed to support localized high availability, it will always face inherent physical limitations. You can do the following to resolve this:

- Build your private, data, and public network layers across the same redundancy planes. If data resources are in AZ A, so should the other layers that interact.

- Account for cross-zone latency when building with **high availability** (**HA**) in mind.

- Consider latency tradeoffs for high-performance computing, as *highly available* does not mean highly performant.

Cloud native bandwidth

In cloud native environments, bandwidth limitations can significantly impact application performance, particularly as services are scaled or distributed across regions. Although the cloud abstracts much of the underlying infrastructure, bandwidth constraints still persist. Overlooking these limitations can lead to performance bottlenecks, especially in high-traffic or data-intensive scenarios.

Bandwidth limitations must be carefully addressed when scaling applications or managing large amounts of data. For instance, with the big three hyperscalers (AWS, GCP, and Azure), services like EC2 and RDS have bandwidth constraints based on instance types. Smaller EC2 instances, such as `t2.micro` or `t3.small`, offer significantly lower network bandwidth compared to larger instances like `m6a.large` or `c6a.xlarge`. Data transfers between regions or even across AZs can exacerbate latency and introduce further bandwidth bottlenecks.

Similar bandwidth constraints exist within Azure and GCP.

Ambiguity – a cause of latency and bandwidth issues

As we explored earlier, the choice of instance types in cloud environments has become far more critical than it ever was in traditional on-premises settings. The flexibility and sheer variety of options available in the cloud are both a blessing and a challenge. Consider, for example, the task of selecting an instance type in AWS for a Kubernetes node that requires four cores and eight gigabytes of RAM. At first glance, it seems we are spoiled for choice.

A quick look at AWS Pricing Calculator reveals a list of at least 10 potential instance types, each offering different combinations of network speeds, memory allocations, and pricing. The following is an example of this:

Instance name	vCPUs	Memory ▲	Network Performance	Storage	On-Demand Hourly Cost	CurrentGeneration	Potential Effective Hourly Cost (Savings %)
c6g.xlarge	4	8 GiB	Up to 10 Gigabit	EBS only	0.1776	Yes	0.0668 (62%)
c7g.xlarge	4	8 GiB	Up to 12500 Megabit	EBS only	0.1887	Yes	0.0746 (60%)
c6a.xlarge	4	8 GiB	Up to 12500 Megabit	EBS only	0.1998	Yes	0.0790 (60%)
c5a.xlarge	4	8 GiB	Up to 10 Gigabit	EBS only	0.2	Yes	0.0752 (62%)
c6gd.xlarge	4	8 GiB	Up to 10 Gigabit	1 x 237 NVMe SSD	0.202	Yes	0.0752 (63%)
c7i-flex.xlarge	4	8 GiB	Up to 12500 Megabit	EBS only	0.22145	Yes	0.0876 (60%)
c6i.xlarge	4	8 GiB	Up to 12500 Megabit	EBS only	0.222	Yes	0.0878 (60%)
c5.xlarge	4	8 GiB	Up to 10 Gigabit	EBS only	0.222	Yes	0.0835 (62%)
c6gn.xlarge	4	8 GiB	Up to 25 Gigabit	EBS only	0.226	Yes	0.0912 (60%)
c5ad.xlarge	4	8 GiB	Up to 10 Gigabit	1 x 150 NVMe SSD	0.226	Yes	0.0850 (62%)

Figure 9.4 - Extract from AWS Pricing Calculator

However, the real challenge lies in determining which instance best suits your specific use case. Do you choose `c6g.xlarge`, which is cost-effective and still provides up to 10 gigabits of network throughput? Or do you opt for the more powerful `c7g.xlarge`? It's not simply a matter of weighing performance against cost. A deeper consideration is whether your application can even run on ARM processors, both of which leverage AWS's Graviton ARM chips, which, while offering impressive performance gains, may not be compatible with all workloads.

Beyond processor compatibility, other technical specifications, such as network bandwidth and CPU architecture, require thoughtful consideration. These details aren't just abstract numbers; they directly impact your application's performance and scalability.

As we migrate from on-premises infrastructure to the cloud, the art of selecting the right instance type becomes paramount, and this choice in compute extends out to other cloud services.

Beyond VMs – bandwidth limitations for containers and serverless

It is essential to recognize that bandwidth limitations are not confined to VMs alone. Containerized services and serverless architectures can also suffer from bandwidth bottlenecks, seriously impacting application performance in cloud native environments. While abstracting infrastructure management, services such as AWS Fargate and Google Cloud Run still impose network bandwidth constraints that developers must consider when designing scalable, distributed systems.

For instance, AWS Lambda, a serverless computing service, also experiences bandwidth limitations that can affect applications. While Lambda abstracts server infrastructure, its network still faces throughput restrictions, especially when handling high-volume data transfers between services like S3, DynamoDB, or external APIs. Ignoring these limitations can lead to performance degradation in serverless applications, which rely heavily on fast, seamless communication across services. Some specific points to consider include the following:

- **VPC networking in Lambda**: When a Lambda function is configured to run inside a VPC, it may experience added latency and bandwidth constraints due to the VPC's network configuration and throughput limits. Lambda is unique in that the higher the memory allocation, the higher the background CPU count and network bandwidth. Specifically, the more CPU is available, the more accessible the full bandwidth of the elastic network interface.

- **Cold start delays**: While not directly bandwidth-related, Lambda cold starts can indirectly affect how quickly an application can process requests, especially under high loads, exacerbating bandwidth bottlenecks during initial invocations.

- **S3 and Lambda data transfers**: Large-scale data transfers between S3 and Lambda can hit bandwidth limits, especially when dealing with large files or high concurrency, leading to slower execution times or throttling. Note also the serverless limitations of Lambda, via 6 MB sync and 20 MB response size limits.

- **Outbound bandwidth to external APIs**: When Lambda functions interact with external APIs or services outside the AWS ecosystem, bandwidth constraints can increase response times or lead to timeouts if data transfer rates exceed limits.

As cloud native architectures become more complex and distributed, bandwidth considerations must not be overlooked. From VMs to containers and serverless functions, all layers of cloud infrastructure face bandwidth limitations that can introduce unexpected bottlenecks. Ignoring these limits is a common anti-pattern that can significantly degrade performance and lead to unforeseen costs, especially in high-traffic environments or applications that process large volumes of data. By proactively addressing bandwidth constraints and designing architectures with these limits, organizations can ensure their cloud native solutions are optimized for performance and scalability.

Across the big three cloud providers, applications designed without accounting for these limitations may suffer from high latency, data bottlenecks, and increased costs. Cloud native architecture must consider these factors to avoid common anti-patterns related to bandwidth and latency. The following section will show us how we can avoid the pitfalls of latency and bandwidth being overlooked. Our next section will dig into the lack of DNS strategy.

Lack of DNS strategy

"It's not DNS,

There's no way it's DNS,

It was DNS."

This now-famous haiku perfectly captures the frustration and irony of one of the most overlooked aspects of modern networking: DNS. Often dismissed as a straightforward service, DNS is one of those critical components that only garners attention when things go wrong. In cloud native environments, where services, systems, and applications rely heavily on dynamic and distributed architectures, DNS issues can quickly spiral into significant outages, performance bottlenecks, or security vulnerabilities. And yet, many organizations treat DNS as an afterthought.

The anti-pattern of inconsistent DNS management is a silent disruptor. Organizations moving toward cloud native architectures often inherit a fragmented approach to DNS. With legacy systems, hybrid environments, and third-party services all in play, DNS strategies become disjointed and poorly aligned. This leads to unpredictable issues: slow resolution times, increased latency, and intermittent failures as systems struggle to connect across varied infrastructures.

In the cloud native space, this is a recipe for disaster. Whether services are hosted on-premises or in the cloud, a lack of cohesive DNS strategy can destabilize even the most well-designed applications. The challenge is compounded when external services are involved, creating a tangled web of DNS resolution paths that can delay communication, introduce security risks, or lead to outright service failure.

This section explores the causes and consequences of lacking DNS strategy and provides a guide for creating a unified, resilient DNS strategy. We'll cover the following:

- Cloud native DNS management

- Hybrid environments

- Third-party integrations

- Undermining traffic segregation (QoS)

- Configuring low-performance backup links for high-performance primary links: considerations of QoS over backup links

Cloud native DNS management

In cloud native architectures, DNS is no longer just simply mapping domain names to IP addresses. It becomes critical to how services discover one another, how traffic is routed efficiently, and how resilience is built into the network. However, the complexity of cloud native environments and the ease of spinning new services can quickly turn DNS into a tangled mess if not managed properly.

In cloud native environments, services such as Amazon Route 53, Azure DNS, and GCP Cloud DNS provide highly scalable DNS services designed specifically for cloud native use cases. These services enable fast, reliable routing to VM instances, load balancers, API gateways, and external endpoints. When appropriately managed, they ensure low-latency access to services, seamless failover, and redundancy across regions. However, when DNS configurations are fragmented, even in cloud native environments, it can lead to severe performance and connectivity issues. These issues and their eventual solution are discussed in the example that follows.

Cloud native and on-premises DNS

We encountered a similar situation with a fintech client that used Amazon Route 53 to manage DNS for their cloud native microservices. Initially, everything worked smoothly, but as their infrastructure expanded, they began integrating services that required coordination between their cloud environment and on-premises systems. The fintech organization implemented separate DNS zones to manage internal domains, with Route 53 handling cloud native services and **Active Directory** (**AD**) DNS managing their on-premises resources. However, there was no unified DNS strategy in place, resulting in inconsistent DNS records between the two systems.

As traffic increased, these clashing DNS configurations became a problem. Services began to fail, not due to application issues but because the conflicting DNS setups couldn't handle proper traffic routing between the cloud and on-premises environments. The lack of a centralized DNS strategy led to delays in resolving internal services, causing timeouts and degrading the user experience. The fragmented approach to DNS management resulted in misrouted traffic and unnecessary latency, affecting critical financial operations.

The fragmented DNS management between AD and Route 53 led to delayed lookups, inconsistent routing, and broken connections. Services slowed down, causing latency spikes and interruptions that took significant troubleshooting time. The root of the issue? The erratic and uncoordinated DNS setup across environments.

Overcoming clashing DNS

The organization eventually resolved this issue with the help of **Route 53 Resolver**, a service designed to bridge on-premises and cloud native DNS environments. Route 53 Resolver allowed them to forward DNS queries between their AWS environment and their on-premises AD DNS servers. DNS forwarding rules created a seamless flow of DNS queries between the two systems, allowing cloud services to resolve on-premises domains, and vice versa. This approach eliminated the need for parallel DNS systems, centralizing DNS resolution under a single, cohesive architecture.

The introduction of Route 53 Resolver transformed their DNS setup into a unified system, leveraging a proper hybrid model. Internal applications could now resolve both cloud native and on-premises domain names without the delays or conflicts caused by fragmented management. By consolidating their DNS strategy, integrating AWS Directory Service with Route 53, and leveraging Route 53 Resolver, they ensured that DNS resolution was consistent, fast, and reliable across all environments. A simplified version of the solution can be found here:

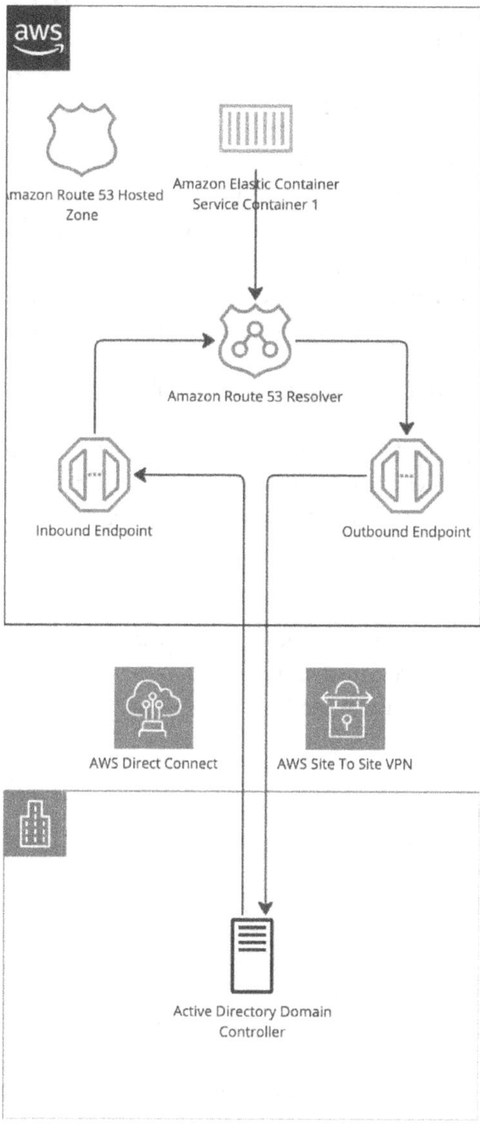

Figure 9.5 - Hybrid DNS Resolver

The next section will expand on this as we look at hybrid environments and QoS.

Undermining traffic segregation (QoS) based on application/data criticality

One of the most overlooked aspects of cloud native architecture is the importance of traffic segregation based on application and data criticality. Not all traffic in a system is equal; some workloads require high-priority, low-latency communication, while others can tolerate slower processing times. This concept is fundamental to **quality of service (QoS)**, which prioritizes traffic based on its importance to business operations. Unfortunately, a common anti-pattern in cloud native deployments is the failure to implement adequate traffic segregation, resulting in performance degradation, missed **service-level agreements (SLAs)**, and unnecessary resource consumption.

In traditional networking, QoS policies often prioritize traffic based on its type and importance. Critical applications, for example, real-time financial transactions, video conferencing, or database replication are prioritized. At the same time, non-critical tasks like backups, bulk file transfers, or routine updates are assigned lower priority. However, in cloud native environments, this approach is often neglected. Without proper QoS implementation, all traffic is treated equally, leading to significant issues when high-priority services must compete with less critical ones for bandwidth and compute resources.

The cost of ignoring traffic segregation – a fintech case study

During a consulting engagement with a large fintech company, we encountered a classic example of the pitfalls of failing to implement proper traffic segregation in a cloud environment. The company ran real-time transaction processing alongside nightly data backups, which operated in the same shared cloud infrastructure. Initially, everything seemed to work fine, but as transaction volumes grew, so did the strain on the network.

The lack of a structured traffic prioritization strategy meant that their backup operations, scheduled during peak hours, consumed a significant portion of the available bandwidth. This interference caused delays in real-time financial transactions, leading to missed SLAs and customer dissatisfaction. This is where the need for a robust QoS strategy became evident. With proper traffic segregation and prioritization, we ensured that critical services, for example, real-time transaction processing, were always given priority over less urgent tasks such as nightly backups. By isolating bandwidth-heavy operations and allocating resources based on service criticality, we helped them avoid these delays altogether.

The risks of failing to segregate traffic based on criticality

When traffic segregation based on application or data criticality is ignored, organizations are exposed to several risks, including the following:

- **Degraded performance for critical applications**: Business-critical applications, like real-time financial transactions or sensitive data transfers, may experience latency or delays if forced to compete for bandwidth with non-essential traffic.

- **Missed SLAs**: In environments where uptime, speed, and reliability are key performance indicators, the failure to segregate traffic can lead to missed SLAs, resulting in penalties or reputational damage.

- **Resource contention**: Equal treatment of all traffic can cause resource contention, where essential processes are starved for bandwidth or compute power, while less important tasks consume unnecessary resources.

- **Security risks**: Some data flows, such as those involving sensitive financial or personal information, should be segregated not just for performance reasons but also for security. Failure to isolate this traffic can expose critical data to vulnerabilities.

Best practices for traffic segregation and QoS

To avoid the anti-pattern of undermining traffic segregation, organizations should implement a structured QoS strategy tailored to their cloud native infrastructure:

Best Practice	Description
Prioritize traffic based on criticality	Define and categorize traffic based on its importance to business operations. Latency-sensitive or critical tasks should have higher priority over non-urgent processes.
Use network segmentation	Implement virtual network segmentation (e.g., VPCs or subnets) to separate traffic by priority, ensuring high-priority traffic does not compete with lower-priority flows.
Leverage cloud native QoS tools	Utilize cloud provider tools such as Amazon Traffic Mirroring, bandwidth control, Azure Traffic Manager, and Google Cloud Network Service Tiers to manage and optimize traffic flow.
Monitor and adjust QoS policies	Regularly monitor the performance of QoS policies and make adjustments as workloads change to maintain optimal performance.
Account for multi-cloud and hybrid setups	Ensure consistent QoS policies across multi-cloud or hybrid environments to prevent bottlenecks and maintain performance between on-premises and cloud infrastructures.

Table 9.1 - QoS best practices

A common anti-pattern in cloud native architectures is relying on low-performance backup links to support high-performance primary links without considering how QoS will function during failover. Backup links are implemented in many setups as a cost-saving measure, typically designed with lower bandwidth and reduced capabilities.

However, if a primary high-performance link fails, critical applications and data flows are forced onto these slower links, potentially causing severe performance degradation, increased latency, and service outages. Failing to configure appropriate QoS policies for these backup links can exacerbate the issue, as critical traffic may not be prioritized during the failover, further degrading the user experience.

Key considerations for backup link QoS

To mitigate these risks, it's essential to plan for the backup links as carefully as the primary links, ensuring that they can handle the most critical traffic if a failover occurs. Properly configured QoS can help ensure that essential services maintain priority during periods of reduced capacity and operate with minimal disruption. To ensure consistency, regular checks and testing applications via backup links are critical. Untested backups should be treated as inactive until tested in some cadence. The following points highlight how to approach backup links:

- **Prioritize critical traffic during failover**: Implement QoS policies to ensure that high-priority traffic, such as transactional data or real-time services, is prioritized over less critical traffic on backup links.

- **Test backup link capacity regularly**: Regularly test the performance of backup links to ensure they can handle the critical traffic load during a failover scenario without significant degradation.

- **Scale backup links based on needs**: Ensure that backup links are appropriately scaled to handle the most critical workloads, even if they can't match the full capacity of primary links.

- **Monitor link performance**: Continuously monitor both primary and backup links to ensure that QoS policies are functioning as intended and traffic is routed efficiently during failover events.

- **Evaluate cost vs. performance trade-offs**: Balance cost savings with critical application performance requirements. Under-provisioned backup links may reduce costs, but they can introduce unacceptable risks to business continuity during outages.

Proper planning and careful configuration of backup links with QoS policies can help ensure smooth transitions during failover, preserving the performance of critical applications and maintaining business continuity.

In cloud native environments, failing to implement traffic segregation based on application and data criticality is a serious anti-pattern that can erode system performance, increase latency, and jeopardize the reliability of critical services. By establishing a robust QoS strategy that prioritizes high-value workloads, organizations can ensure that their cloud native applications are resilient, responsive, and capable of meeting even the most demanding business requirements.

Monolithic connectivity

We briefly touched on the role of network engineers and systems admins in managing on-premises hardware such as switches, routers, and the like; with that mindset came a traditional data center way of planning networking. The individual hardware components became a single point of failure for the entire network, whereas if a core switch were to fail, the whole network stack would also crumble. The cloud native model has a very different networking setup from that of a data center of a conventional organization; a traditional data center model may set its subnets and network layers across the following:

- **Core**: The backbone of the network for core switches

- **Distribution**: This sits between the cores and handles networking policies/security

- **Access**: The access layer for servers, storage arrays, and the typical network we see from an admin perspective

The accompanying diagram offers a more detailed illustration to provide a clearer understanding of this concept.

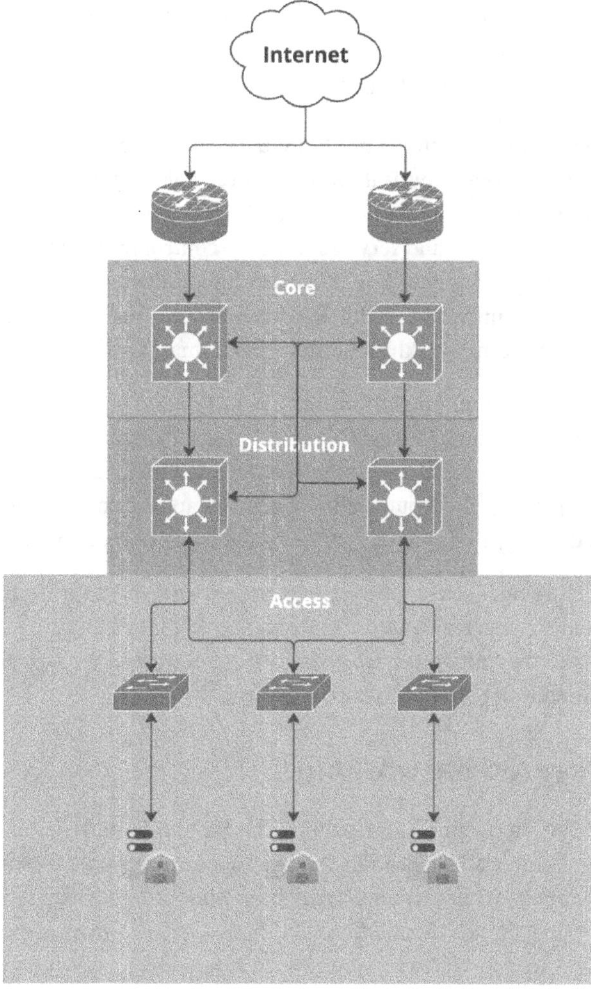

Figure 9.6 - Three-tier traditional network

Subnetting is managed differently across the three network layers. The following table details this:

Network Layer	Subnetting Approach	Function and Focus
Core layer	Minimal subnetting	Acts as a high-speed interconnect between other layers, prioritizing performance over segmentation
Distribution layer	Extensive subnetting to support diverse needs	Handles fiber channels, firewalls, and traffic monitoring between layers, requiring flexibility and control
Access layer	Traditional subnetting practices	Supports everyday network setups, tailoring subnetting to user and device

Table 9.2 - Subnetting across network layers

Monolithic friction with cloud native

While still focused on high-speed interconnectivity, the core layer may leverage virtualized networking solutions that reduce the need for physical infrastructure, making subnetting even more minimal and flexible. The distribution layer becomes highly dynamic in a cloud native context, with subnetting used to manage VPCs, security groups, and service meshes to control traffic flow between services, storage, and firewalls across multiple regions or AZs. Meanwhile, the access layer shifts toward integrating scalable resources like containerized workloads, where traditional subnetting practices give way to automated, software-defined networking solutions that dynamically adjust to workload demands.

In an ideal world, organizations transitioning to cloud native environments would leave behind the constraints of their old data centers. However, what often happens instead is that traditional networking models are simply lifted and shifted into the cloud. This creates a common anti-pattern we've encountered frequently, where outdated practices are applied to modern architectures. The result is a system weighed down by limitations, restricting the true potential of cloud native infrastructure.

This section will explore how cloud native environments transition from monolithic connectivity patterns to layered failover strategies across OSI layers. We'll focus on the challenges of synchronous versus asynchronous traffic, mitigating single points of failure and configuring packet inspection to meet the unique demands of cloud native architectures.

Monolith to layered networking

Monolithic connectivity, a common anti-pattern in legacy systems, relies on tightly coupled, single-tiered network designs where all application components communicate internally, often without clear separation or segmentation. While this model may have worked for smaller, self-contained applications, it struggles to meet the demands of modern cloud native environments, which prioritize scalability, flexibility, and resilience.

Organizations transitioning to cloud native architectures adopt layered networking models that separate services and components. This approach aligns closely with microservices, where each service operates independently and communicates through well-defined network layers. Organizations can address common issues such as lack of scalability, difficulty isolating failures, and security vulnerabilities by moving away from monolithic connectivity to a more modular, layered structure. *Figure 9.1* shows a perfect example of a modular layered network structure, with multiple private subnets segregated within a VPC.

Layered networking

Layered networking in cloud native environments introduces distinct layers, each with a specific purpose. This segmentation enhances control, isolating services based on their function, priority, or security requirements. For example, frontend services can be placed in one network layer, while backend services, for example, databases or internal APIs, reside in another. This layered approach improves scalability and security by limiting direct access to critical services. By applying network policies, organizations can ensure that only authorized services can communicate across layers, reducing the risk of lateral movement in case of a security breach.

Moreover, layered networking supports the independent scaling of services. In monolithic architectures, scaling often meant replicating the entire application, which can be resource-intensive and inefficient. In contrast, layered architectures enable individual services to scale as needed, depending on traffic and performance demands. This flexibility ensures that resources are used efficiently and allows organizations to adapt quickly to changing workloads. The following table details the benefits of the layered networking approach:

Aspect	Monolithic Connectivity	Layered Networking (Cloud native)
Scalability	Scaling requires replicating the entire monolithic application	Independent services can be scaled individually, reducing resource use
Security	All components communicate freely within the same network tier, posing potential security risks	There is a clear separation of services, enabling better security policies and isolation
Resilience	A failure in one system part can bring down the entire application	Isolated services reduce the blast radius of failures, enhancing resilience
Flexibility	It is difficult to modify or add services without impacting the entire system	Services can be added, modified, or replaced without affecting the whole architecture
Network Traffic Control	There is no clear traffic segmentation; all traffic flows freely between components	Traffic is segmented based on service layers, allowing for better traffic management and monitoring
Development Speed	Changes require complete application testing and deployment	Individual services can be updated and deployed independently

Table 9.3 - Benefits of layered networking

Monolith to microservice – networking-focused example

During a consulting engagement with a government client, we were tasked with addressing significant network challenges as part of their transition from a monolithic architecture to a cloud native environment. The company's original network design lacked segmentation, with all services, frontend applications, databases, and internal APIs residing in a single flat network. This setup led to numerous issues, including inefficiencies in traffic flow, security vulnerabilities, and scaling challenges, particularly with IP allocation due to a small subnet range.

Their monolithic network architecture made isolating services based on function or security requirements difficult. All traffic flowed through the same network, exposing critical backend services, such as databases, to unnecessary risk. Without proper network segmentation, any breach in the system could quickly spread laterally, potentially compromising sensitive data. Moreover, as traffic to their platform grew, scaling required replicating the entire system, including components that didn't need to be scaled. This approach was resource-intensive and inefficient.

The approach – three-tier network

We introduced a layered networking model on AWS, following three-tier capabilities to bring order and control to their cloud native infrastructure. This model was deployed as follows:

1. **Presentation layer (frontend)**:

    -   **Purpose**: Handles user requests and public traffic, primarily on user-facing components like web servers or APIs.

    -   **Implementation**: Place frontend services in a public subnet within the AWS VPC, accessible from the internet.

    -   **Security**: Use security groups and **web application firewalls** (**WAFs**) to protect against external threats while allowing incoming web traffic or load balancer traffic.

2. **Application layer (business logic)**:

    -   **Purpose**: Processes business logic, communicating between the frontend and the backend. This layer hosts the internal services, APIs, or microservices.

    -   **Implementation**: Deploy application services in a private subnet to isolate them from direct internet access while allowing them to communicate with both the frontend and backend layers.

    -   **Security**: Use security groups to control which frontend services can communicate with the application layer, ensuring only authorized traffic flows between these layers. Access between Kubernetes Pods was limited using security group references, eliminating IP spoofing as an attack vector.

3. **Data layer (backend):**

- **Purpose**: Stores and manages data, like databases and internal APIs, which must be secure and isolated.

- **Implementation**: Place databases and other backend services in a separate private subnet with strict access controls to ensure that only the application layer can access it.

- **Security**: Implement a VPC gateway endpoint to restrict access and configure **network access control lists (NACLs)** to further restrict any unauthorized access from other subnets.

On top of the three-tier approach here, we had distributed all three tiers across multiple AZs; the architecture was significantly more resilient and scalable, allowing the application to continue functioning even if an entire zone went offline. When an AZ was created, the application would scale to other zones, and traffic would automatically be directed to the new nodes. AZs are isolated data center locations (per zone) within an AWS region, each with independent power, networking, and cooling. They offer much greater resilience than two traditional data centers because they are geographically separate yet closely interconnected; this also consists of fully redundant dedicated fiber lines. This ensures that even if one zone fails due to a localized issue, the others remain fully operational without impacting performance. Where this multiple AZ design was leveraged best was when addressing synchronous and asynchronous traffic.

Synchronous versus synchronous traffic

Cloud native architecture fundamentally shifts how traffic and communication between services are handled. One of the most significant challenges in traditional environments is managing synchronous versus asynchronous traffic, which can become a bottleneck as systems grow in complexity and demand. Traditional organizations' services often rely on synchronous communication, meaning that one service must wait for a response from another before continuing. This approach can lead to inefficiencies, higher latency, and potential points of failure, particularly in distributed environments where network issues or service delays can halt entire processes.

Comparatively, cloud native architectures are designed to embrace asynchronous communication. This shift resolves a major anti-pattern often seen in traditional setups, where systems are tightly coupled and dependent on real-time, synchronous responses. These traditional systems struggle under high load or when services experience delays, leading to timeouts, failures, and decreased resilience. Let's look at the benefits of asynchronous traffic in a cloud native environment.

Key benefits of asynchronous traffic in cloud native

The following benefits highlight why asynchronous traffic is essential for cloud native applications:

- **Increased resilience**: Services can continue functioning even if one part of the system is delayed or unavailable
- **Improved scalability**: Asynchronous systems can handle higher loads because they don't require immediate responses, reducing the strain on services during peak traffic
- **Decoupled services**: Cloud native systems encourage loose coupling, where services operate independently, reducing the risk of cascading failures
- **Fault tolerance**: By using queues and event-driven models, systems can automatically retry failed operations without blocking other processes

From strong consistency to eventual consistency

A key aspect of this transition is the shift from *strongly consistent* to *eventually consistent* systems, which allows cloud native applications to prioritize availability and fault tolerance over immediate consistency. By adopting eventual consistency, cloud native systems can handle large-scale, distributed workloads more effectively, as they no longer rely on the entire system being perfectly synchronized. This approach increases scalability and resilience, enabling systems to operate smoothly even when components are temporarily out of sync – an essential trade-off in high-traffic, globally distributed environments.

Cloud native architectures resolve this challenge by leveraging asynchronous communication models, such as message queues, event-driven architectures, and serverless components. In these systems, services publish events or send messages without waiting for an immediate response. For example, when a user places an order on an e-commerce platform, the order might be processed asynchronously through a message queue (e.g., Amazon SQS or Kafka), allowing the frontend to continue interacting with the user while the backend processes the order in the background. This decoupling improves the application's resilience, as the failure or delay of one service does not impact the overall system's ability to respond to users or continue functioning.

Addressing monolithic connectivity

In traditional systems, the reliance on synchronous communication creates an anti-pattern of tight coupling, where services are overly dependent on each other and must be available in real time for the system to function properly. This introduces fragility, as any delay or failure in one component can ripple through the entire system.

Cloud native architectures resolve this by promoting asynchronous communication, where services interact without waiting for immediate responses. In doing so, the anti-pattern is broken, and systems become more resilient, scalable, and adaptable to change. As organizations move to cloud native, they benefit from the flexibility of being able to scale individual services independently, handle failures gracefully, and process high volumes of traffic more efficiently. This shift not only improves the system's overall performance but also lays the foundation for a more agile, adaptable infrastructure that can evolve with the business's needs.

In moving from monolithic connectivity to layered networking, cloud native architectures significantly improve scalability, security, and resilience. By adopting layered models, organizations can break away from tightly coupled, synchronous systems prone to single points of failure. Instead, services are isolated and scalable, allowing greater flexibility and control. With proper segmentation, even the most complex infrastructures can maintain high availability, and the risk of lateral movement during a security breach is minimized. These benefits make cloud native approaches far superior to traditional models, ensuring they remain robust and efficient as applications scale.

Next, we'll explore another critically overlooked anti-pattern: ignoring cloud native networking features. We'll examine how failing to leverage built-in cloud features can limit performance and security and how properly utilizing these features can maximize the benefits of a cloud native infrastructure.

Ignoring cloud native networking features

One of the most common pitfalls when transitioning to cloud native architectures is overlooking the powerful networking features inherently built into cloud platforms. In traditional on-premises environments, networking is often hardware-centric, relying on physical switches, routers, and firewalls. This leads to misconceptions and misaligned expectations when dealing with the more dynamic, software-driven nature of cloud native networking.

This section will explore how failing to fully embrace **software-defined networking (SDN)** in the cloud can lead to performance and resilience issues. We will also stress the importance of treating network configuration as code through **infrastructure as code (IaC)**, a practice crucial for successfully implementing cloud native networking. The risks associated with inadequate network boundary guardrails, especially when managing access between environments such as production and non-production are also discussed.

Each of these areas presents unique challenges, and a failure to address them can limit the potential of cloud native infrastructures, leaving organizations vulnerable to security breaches and operational inefficiencies.

SDN in the cloud – the risks from on-premises

SDN is not a concept that is limited to just the cloud native environment; the idea has been around for some time. Popularizing this concept arguably has been companies such as VMware with their VMware NSX product, released in 2013 – an early example of SDN that allows virtualization of network infrastructure, enabling the creation, management, and automation of complex networks through software rather than traditional hardware. Rather than setting up entire server racks worth of hardware from scratch, SDN tools like VMware NSX gave admins a much quicker way to deploy and extend their networks to new hardware; cloud vendors adopted this concept to do the same without needing the hardware components. SDN in traditional environments still requires hardware to deploy; it just makes templating a lot easier.

SDN thrives in the cloud, shifting control from physical hardware to software-based solutions. This transformation allows cloud providers such as AWS, Azure, and GCP to offer flexible, scalable, and dynamic networking solutions that adapt to the needs of modern applications. Here are some key examples of how SDN is applied across these platforms:

- **AWS**: Amazon VPC enables isolated networks with control over routing, firewalls, and access
- **Azure**: Azure VNet uses SDN with tools like NSGs and Azure Firewall for traffic segmentation and network policy automation
- **GCP**: Google Cloud VPC uses SDN for customizable IP ranges, firewall rules, and routing, with tools such as Cloud Armor and VPC peering for security and connectivity

Across all three platforms, SDN provides the flexibility to scale, automate, and manage network infrastructure programmatically, allowing users to build secure, optimized cloud environments without the limitations of traditional hardware.

Networking mindset changes with cloud native

One of the most common cloud native anti-patterns is the lack of understanding of SDN in cloud environments compared to traditional on-premises hardware setups. This gap in understanding often leads to unrealistic expectations around performance, resilience, and overall network behavior, resulting in misconfigurations that compromise both system reliability and scalability.

With the cloud vendors, a common misunderstanding arises when users expect cloud networking to behave like traditional hardware-based infrastructure, where dedicated physical devices dictate network performance and capacity. Network reliability is tied directly to hardware robustness, such as switches and routers in an on-premises environment. However, AWS networking, like Amazon VPC, is entirely virtualized. Performance and resilience depend on how well subnets, security groups, and multi-AZ setups are configured. Misconfigurations in this virtual environment can lead to poor fault tolerance and performance bottlenecks, starkly contrasting the expectations of physical hardware environments.

Legacy brought to the cloud native networking – a case study

We encountered a common example of a poorly configured AWS networking setup during a network uplift engagement with a banking client. However, when we refer to "poorly configured," it's essential to recognize that what was once considered best practice can, with the passage of time and advancements in technology, evolve into a suboptimal solution. This client transitioned from an on-premises infrastructure to AWS over 3–4 years. Initially, their network architects viewed the three-tier AWS network design as too simplistic and believed it introduced too much overhead for cross-domain communication and change management.

Instead of designing separate VPCs for each environment or workload, the architects implemented a design that centralized networking into a single VPC shared across multiple accounts. In this design, subnets were shared between different accounts, which seemed logical from a traditional networking perspective. It mirrored the idea of a centralized core network sharing access layers across various

AWS accounts. However, rather than solving overhead issues, this approach introduced significant complexity. When a change or flexibility was required, any alteration to the VPC structure or route table rules affected all accounts within the shared network. Instead of building a fault-tolerant, layered cloud network, they had inadvertently created a single point of failure disguised as simplicity. This design was similar to the following:

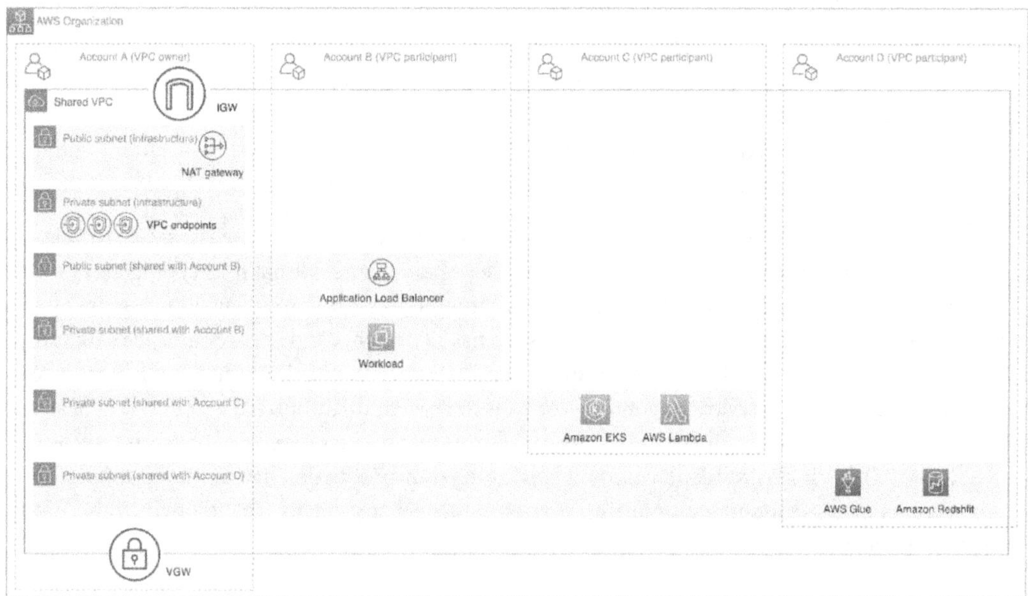

Figure 9.7 - Shared VPC design

In a risk-averse industry such as banking, this design flaw was compounded by the fact that even minor changes were heavily scrutinized during change advisory board meetings. The result was a rigid, fragile network architecture that stifled agility and introduced considerable risk.

Our solution was transitioning from shared subnets to individual VPCs for each account, interconnected through AWS Transit Gateway. To preserve the benefits of the shared subnet setup, we restructured the network, as shown in *Figure 9.1*. All outbound traffic, such as internet and third-party requests, was routed through an egress VPC, where a security appliance such as a FortiGate firewall scanned all outbound traffic. This eliminated the need for multiple NAT gateways or instances. Each VPC was configured with specific subnets, allowing cloud native features to be enabled or restricted based on the use case. For example, data/private subnets were limited to accessing only DynamoDB gateway endpoints, ensuring tighter security and minimizing unnecessary service access.

The added benefit of this rearchitected solution was a more resilient, dispersed network design. Changes were now account-specific, significantly reducing the blast radius of any failed modifications. This modular design ensured that any impact was limited to individual environments, enhancing agility and fault tolerance.

As we have touched on changes, this leads us to the next section on inadequate network access reviews and missing boundary guardrails.

Inadequate network access reviews and missing boundary guardrails

With traditional data centers, where physical boundaries naturally limit access, cloud infrastructure is dynamic, allowing for easier and potentially dangerous access escalation. Without regular, thorough reviews of access privileges, users or systems may gain unintended access to critical production environments from non-production or development systems. This lack of oversight leaves organizations vulnerable to unauthorized lateral movement, exposing sensitive data and core systems to significant threats.

The absence of solid network boundary guardrails further exacerbates these risks. Guardrails, such as security groups, firewall rules, and routing table policies, are essential for keeping access within the intended environment. Without these controls, the network becomes flat, allowing unrestricted movement across environments, which increases the risk of breaches and non-compliance with industry regulations. To secure cloud native environments effectively, organizations must implement rigorous access reviews and enforce strict boundary controls to prevent unauthorized access and escalation. A common sense approach would be to segregate resources within their groupings between environments (i.e., for AWS), having a production account containing only production networking resources and no connections to non-production or testing environments via any means. The following table outlines the risks typically found:

Risk	Description
Access escalation	Users gain unauthorized access to production systems from non-production environments
Weak security posture	The lack of boundary guardrails results in flat network structures, allowing unauthorized movement between environments
Increased attack surface	Poorly defined boundaries create vulnerabilities, enabling attackers to move laterally within the network
Compliance violations	Inadequate control and oversight can lead to non-compliance with security and regulatory standards
Operational risks	Overlapping or misconfigured access can cause outages, service disruptions, and, importantly, break compliance measures

Table 9.4 - Key risks of inadequate network access reviews and missing guardrails

Organizations can better protect their cloud infrastructure by addressing these issues through consistent access reviews and robust boundary guardrails, ensuring secure and compliant operations. To better deliver the previously mentioned IaC and automation, they are key.

IaC and automation – the networking perspective

At the heart of every cloud native organization is IaC. The specific tool you choose (Terraform, CloudFormation, or Azure Resource Manager) matters less than how you design and implement it. Every IaC tool is both terrible and terrific, but what truly defines a successful approach is the architecture and best practices behind its use. Standardization is critical to efficient infrastructure deployment across cloud native environments. This is especially true for cloud networking, where consistency is crucial for managing multiple environments, such as development, testing, and production.

Without proper standardization and best practices, cloud infrastructure can quickly become chaotic. Different teams may deploy similar resources in various ways, leading to inefficiencies, inconsistencies, and unnecessary complexity. The result is a system that becomes difficult to manage and prone to errors. Standardization is not just about keeping things tidy; it's about ensuring that every deployment follows a predictable, efficient pattern that can be repeated and scaled. So, what does effective standardization and best practice look like? Consider the following best practices:

- **Defined naming standards**: Create clear naming conventions to ensure consistency across environments. For example, using a pattern such as `{environment}-{app}-{resource}-{name}` – for example, `prod-banking-aks-node` – helps maintain clarity and avoids confusion.

- **Repeatable patterns**: For repeated deployments, such as setting up a VNet in Azure across multiple environments, use reusable modules (e.g., Terraform modules or CDK functions). This ensures consistency in how infrastructure is deployed and makes management easier.

- **Plan before you deploy**: Especially with networking resources, ensure that infrastructure changes can be made without disrupting running environments. Some changes, such as renaming resources, can trigger replacements that may bring down critical systems during change windows, and idempotency safeguards against such risks.

- **Version control**: Use Git to store and manage your IaC. Version control allows for easy tracking of changes and rollbacks and better collaboration across teams, ensuring that infrastructure deployments remain consistent and traceable.

- **Automated deployment pipelines**: Implement CI/CD pipelines for infrastructure deployment rather than relying on manual, localized processes. This reduces human error, ensures consistency, and allows for better integration with version control systems for streamlined management.

By adhering to these principles, organizations can bring order to the complexities of cloud deployments, ensuring that infrastructure is scalable, maintainable, and efficient. Standardization isn't just a best practice; it's the foundation for long-term success in the cloud. The following figure provides a simple example of what an automated and standardized pipeline looks like when deploying with CI/CD:

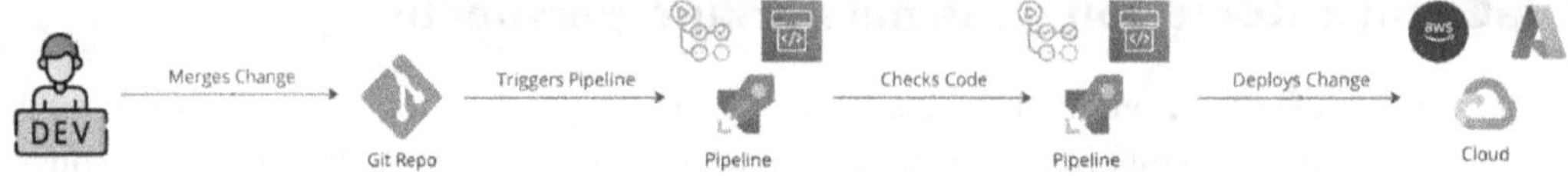

Figure 9.8 - Simple IaC change, check, and deployment pipeline

In a well-automated, IaC-driven, cloud native network, changes to routing rules or security policies are scripted, version-controlled, and deployed uniformly across environments. This ensures that every environment, whether development, testing, or production, has consistent network configurations, reducing the risk of miscommunication between services and ensuring tight security controls. Conversely, in environments where networking is managed manually, any change is subject to human error, creating discrepancies across environments that can lead to outages or data breaches.

Beyond the risk of misconfiguration, neglecting automation in networking slows down an organization's ability to scale. Cloud native environments demand agility, and without automated network deployments, provisioning new environments or scaling existing ones becomes a time-consuming, error-prone task. Teams are forced to replicate network configurations manually, often introducing inconsistencies that can cause service disruptions.

Zero Trust application patterns

As organizations transition from on-premises environments to cloud native architectures, the **Zero Trust** model is one of the most crucial security shifts they must adopt. In traditional on-premises environments, security often hinged on perimeter defenses; if you were inside the network, you were trusted. However, cloud native applications operate in a more dynamic, distributed, and potentially exposed environment. The concept of a transparent network boundary dissolves in the cloud, where services span regions, multiple VPCs, and often different cloud providers. This is where Zero Trust emerges as an essential security framework, built on the premise of *"never trust, always verify."*

In its simplest terms, Zero Trust rejects the notion of implicit trust based on location or ownership of a network. Instead, it assumes that every user, device, and application must continuously prove its legitimacy before accessing resources. The core principles of Zero Trust dictate that security should not only focus on external threats but also on monitoring and controlling access within the network, preventing unauthorized lateral movement, and reducing the attack surface. This is particularly relevant in cloud native environments, where the dynamic nature of workloads and users necessitates constant verification at every access point.

Zero Trust in cloud native versus on-premises environments

In traditional, on-premises setups, applications typically relied on network segmentation and firewalls to define security zones, sometimes called DMZs. If an application or user was inside the corporate network, they were often granted broad access to resources with little scrutiny. This approach, known as **implicit trust**, leaves significant room for error. Once an attacker gains access to the network, they can move laterally between systems without facing substantial barriers. On-premises security models have often prioritized keeping threats out rather than scrutinizing every internal interaction.

In contrast, cloud native environments treat every component as an untrusted entity, whether it's an internal microservice, user, or external client. For cloud native applications, the Zero Trust model aligns more naturally with the distributed nature of cloud services, where there are no well-defined internal and external perimeters. Applications must verify every request, whether it's between internal microservices, API calls, or user access.

Consider AWS and its implementation of the principle of least privilege. At its core, this principle aligns with Zero Trust by ensuring that users and services are granted only the permissions they need to perform their tasks and nothing more. This means leveraging services such as AWS **Identity and Access Management (IAM)**, where tightly scoped policies control every action. No service or user is inherently trusted within a single account or VPC. Each action must be authenticated and authorized, minimizing the risk of privilege escalation or misuse.

In Azure, Conditional Access policies and **Azure Active Directory (AAD)** take on a similar role, verifying each access request based on dynamic conditions, such as user location, device health, and behavioral analytics. Access is granted only when these factors align with predefined security policies. Meanwhile, Azure VNet and **network security groups (NSGs)** enable granular segmentation of traffic, ensuring that applications and services are isolated and access is controlled based on tightly defined security rules.

In GCP, the BeyondCorp model operationalizes Zero Trust by completely removing implicit trust from the equation. Google Cloud's **Identity-Aware Proxy (IAP)** ensures that each request to an application is authenticated, authorized, and encrypted based on user and device identity. No traffic is assumed trustworthy simply because it originates from a particular part of the network.

Principle	Description	Cloud native Application Example
Never trust, always verify	Every request must be authenticated, authorized, and encrypted, regardless of origin. No part of the network is trusted by default, and access is continuously verified.	Validating API requests, user logins, and inter-service communication using AWS IAM policies and AWS Secrets Manager for secure communication
Least privilege	Enforces minimal access, granting users and services only the permissions needed to perform their tasks, and nothing more. This limits the potential damage from a compromised account or service.	Azure Role-Based Access Control (RBAC) ensures least privilege access for cloud native applications, keeping internal systems isolated

Principle	Description	Cloud native Application Example
Microsegmentation	It breaks down networks into secure segments to limit lateral movement. In cloud native environments, this is achieved with virtual network constructs, which isolate workloads by default.	AWS VPCs, Azure VNets, and Google Cloud VPCs isolate resources, while security groups and NSGs control authorized traffic
Continuous monitoring and auditing	Monitors and audits all interactions within the environment in real time to detect anomalies, respond to threats	AWS CloudTrail, Azure Monitor, and Google Cloud Operations Suite provide real-time insights into access patterns

Table 9.5 - Key principles of Zero Trust

Zero Trust in practice – a cloud native example

During a consulting engagement with a financial services company, we were tasked with implementing a Zero Trust architecture for a cloud native microservice-based application deployed across multiple AWS AZs. Each microservice was deployed as an AWS Lambda function, with API Gateway serving as the communication layer between services. To ensure robust security, we implemented IAM-based authorization for each service call using AWS Signature Version 4 signing, which adds authentication details to HTTP requests. This method ensured that access to each API was tightly controlled, limiting communication strictly to authorized IAM roles.

We leveraged Amazon Cognito to enforce identity verification for user access, applying fine-grained permissions to regulate access to specific data and application functions. Additionally, network traffic between the production and staging environments was isolated using separate VPCs, preventing direct communication without explicit authorization. Real-time monitoring through CloudWatch Logs and VPC Flow Logs allowed us to track network activity and quickly flag any unauthorized access attempts. Finally, to ensure microsegmentation, we used PrivateLink and VPC gateway endpoints for client access. This comprehensive approach ensured that all interactions within the system were authenticated, authorized, and monitored, adhering to the Zero Trust principles that are critical in cloud native architectures.

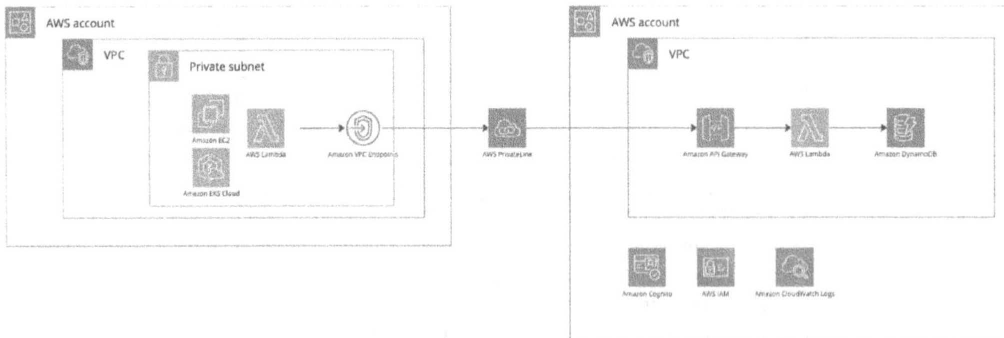

Figure 9.9 - Example of Zero Trust application in AWS

In this Zero Trust framework, the application is not only secure but also adaptable and able to scale or deploy new services without compromising its security posture. This approach contrasts sharply with on-premises models, where trust is often assumed within the network, creating vulnerabilities once an attacker breaches the perimeter.

As cloud native architectures grow in complexity and scale, adopting a Zero Trust application pattern is no longer optional, it's a necessity. By ensuring that no user, service, or device is trusted by default and that every interaction is authenticated and authorized, organizations can safeguard their cloud infrastructure against evolving threats. The Zero Trust model, supported by cloud native tools across AWS, Azure, and GCP, helps protect the distributed and dynamic nature of modern applications, ensuring security without compromising the agility and innovation that the cloud offers. The next section goes beyond Zero Trust and looks at balancing the trade-offs within cloud native.

Network defense in depth versus flat networks – balancing security and operability

The debate between network defense in depth and flat networks is critical. When trade-offs are not adequately weighed, they often reveal an anti-pattern in architectural design. On the one hand, defense in depth (a layered approach to security) prioritizes protecting resources at multiple levels, from firewalls and network segmentation to access controls and encryption. On the other hand, flat networks, which offer minimal segmentation and simpler connectivity, can enhance operability by reducing complexity and streamlining communication between services.

Defense in depth is a tried-and-true security model that applies multiple layers of protection to cloud native environments. By segmenting workloads across VPCs in AWS, Azure **virtual networks** (**VNets**), or Google Cloud VPCs, services are logically separated and protected by strict security groups, firewalls, and access control policies. This model ensures that even if an attacker breaches one layer, additional barriers, such as Azure NSGs, Google Cloud firewall rules, or AWS security groups, can prevent lateral movement and further compromise. While this layered approach strengthens security, it also increases operational overhead. However, the trade-off comes in the form of increased complexity. More segmentation means more configuration, potential points of failure, and a more significant operational overhead when managing policies across various layers.

Conversely, flat networks, which provide minimal segmentation between services, simplify the operational burden. In a flat network, communication is less restricted, making deploying and scaling services easier. The ease of connectivity reduces friction during development and deployment cycles, as developers do not need to navigate a web of security layers and access rules. However, while flat networks may enhance speed and flexibility, they sacrifice security. With fewer barriers between services, an attacker who gains access to any part of the network may move laterally with minimal resistance, potentially compromising the entire system.

The key to choosing between network defense in depth and flat networks lies in evaluating the organization's specific needs and the criticality of the data and services being managed. Security versus operability is not a binary decision but a balancing act. Critical applications may benefit from more stringent security measures in some cases, while less sensitive services may tolerate flatter, more operationally efficient architectures.

For example, when we were tasked with building microservices across an EKS cluster in a cloud native environment handling financial transactions, defense in depth was likely the best approach, ensuring that each microservice handling sensitive data was tightly secured and isolated. Beyond just the regular AWS tooling, to ensure each call was secure, we implemented a service mesh for Mutual TLS and Open Policy Agent to refine-grained access policies. Again, the trade-offs between security and operability must always be considered, with the understanding that flexibility in cloud native environments should never come at the expense of security where it truly matters. As any company that handles financial transactions needs to comply with PCI-DSS and other compliance standards, we ensured that, at all layers of the implementation, best practices have been applied.

Summary

Ignoring fundamental aspects such as latency and bandwidth can lead to significant performance bottlenecks, while a lack of a DNS strategy introduces operational inefficiencies and inconsistency in service discovery. Relying on monolithic connectivity creates a fragile network structure that is difficult to scale and secure, whereas ignoring cloud native networking features overlooks the built-in capabilities designed to optimize and secure modern infrastructures. Finally, failing to adopt Zero Trust application patterns leaves cloud environments vulnerable, as traditional perimeter-based security is insufficient for the dynamic, distributed nature of cloud native systems. To build resilient, scalable, and secure cloud native applications, it is essential to address these anti-patterns head-on, ensuring that network architectures are designed with the unique demands of the cloud in mind.

The next chapter will go over how to approach observability within the cloud native space.

10

Observing Our Architecture

In the cloud native landscape, observability and incident management are often treated as secondary concerns until they no longer are. All too often, organizations only realize the importance of proper monitoring and response processes when an unexpected outage or performance issue brings everything to a halt. The damage is usually already done by that point: trust is shaken, financial losses accrue, and teams are left scrambling to repair systems and reputations. This chapter delves into the common pitfalls, or anti-patterns, that cloud native organizations encounter when scaling their architectures without giving observability the attention it demands.

Knowing something is wrong in today's complex ecosystems is not enough. We need to know where it's going wrong, how it's affecting our services, and potential downstream impacts. Moreover, observability can no longer be purely reactive; with the advent of advanced services powered by machine learning (ML) and artificial intelligence (AI), organizations can now predict incidents before they happen and identify anomalies before they evolve into critical issues. This proactive approach is essential for organizations navigating the ever-increasing complexity of hybrid workloads, microservices architectures, and multi-cloud environments.

This chapter will explore several anti-patterns in cloud native observability and incident management and the practical remediations that can help overcome these challenges. These include:

- Incomplete Observability Coverage for Distributed Tracing
- Lack of Real-Time Monitoring
- Ignoring Out-of-the-Box ML Features
- Failure to Implement Holistic Views for Distributed Tracing
- Not Splitting Impact and Diagnostic Metrics

In the following sections, we will detail these anti-patterns, providing actionable strategies and remediations to help organizations develop a robust observability framework. Addressing these common pitfalls will give you the clarity needed to maintain operational excellence and avoid potential issues in even the most complex cloud native environments.

Let's Capture Everything in the Log Aggregator

This section begins by exploring the risks of Incomplete Observability Coverage for Distributed Tracing, followed by the critical need for Real-Time Monitoring to ensure timely detection and response. The first instinct for many organizations new to cloud native architectures is to collect as much data as possible.

"Let's capture everything," they say as if the sheer volume of logs will magically make everything clear. Unfortunately, this mindset often leads to operational chaos rather than clarity. When capturing logs, Log aggregation tools can be powerful allies, but only when used with purpose. Capturing every log entry from every system, service, and application into a single, all-encompassing aggregator may sound ideal, but it quickly becomes unmanageable. What begins as a noble attempt to enhance visibility is a quagmire of irrelevant data, burying critical signals needed to troubleshoot issues under a mountain of logs with no practical value.

Take for example a fluentbit or fluentd, great tools to capture logs but without filtering said logs, the thousands upon million logs that can be present, are impossible to discphier.

Why Indiscriminate Logging Fails

Indiscriminate logging assumes all data is equally important, but not all logs are created equal. Some data is essential for diagnosing system health or debugging issues, while other logs are merely noise. Logging every heartbeat of a service might seem helpful, but wading through thousands of heartbeat logs during an issue diagnosis is counterproductive.

Take for example logging an OK status vs WARN/FAIL status in an app. The sheer amount of OK may be considered noise to some, costing more than it's worth in cloud storage. This approach inflates operational costs, as cloud storage and processing are not free, and logging everything can quickly become a financial burden. More data means more processing power is required to analyze it, leading to escalating costs and diminishing returns.

Smart Logging: A More Effective Approach

Organizations need to be deliberate about what they log instead of capturing everything. Log retention should be front and center; however, the key is to focus on actionable data logs relevant to business-critical operations or that provide insight into system health. Setting log levels (e.g., DEBUG, INFO, WARN, ERROR) appropriately helps filter out unnecessary data, ensuring only meaningful information is captured.

Context is also key: logs should be structured to trace issues across different services and environments. Capturing metadata such as request IDs, user sessions, or transaction IDs helps stitch logs into a coherent narrative. Tools like AWS CloudWatch Logs Insights or Datadog can be used for centralized log management and visualization, reducing noise and prioritizing critical issues. This allows organizations to maintain operational efficiency and quickly resolve incidents.

Smart Logging: An Example

Consider a cloud native e-commerce application hosted on AWS. The system consists of several microservices: a user service for handling authentication, a product service for managing inventory, a payment service for processing transactions, and a delivery service. The application handles millions of daily requests, so effective logging is essential to maintain performance and troubleshoot issues quickly. Here is how smart logging can be applied:

1. **Set Log Levels Appropriately**:

   - DEBUG: During development, the engineering team enables DEBUG logs to capture detailed information about user authentication, such as API calls to AWS Cognito. In production, DEBUG logs are disabled to avoid unnecessary clutter.

   - INFO: In the product service, INFO logs capture successful actions like a user adding an item to their cart or completing an order. For instance:

     ```
     ```

     ```
     INFO: Product added to cart - user_id=12345, session_id=abc987,
     product_id=67890, quantity=1
     ```

   - WARN: When a transient issue arises, such as a timeout during a payment request to AWS RDS, a WARN log is generated:

     ```
     WARN: Payment service timeout - user_id=12345, transaction_
     id=txn001, retry_attempt=1
     ```

   - ERROR: If the payment service encounters a failure due to insufficient funds, an ERROR log is recorded, triggering an alert:

     ```
     ERROR: Payment failed - user_id=12345, transaction_id=txn001,
     error_code=PAY001, error_message="Insufficient funds"
     ```

2. **Log with Context**: Each service attaches relevant metadata to logs, such as `user_id`, `session_id`, `transaction_id`, and `request_id`. For example, the payment service logs may include:

   ```
   INFO: Payment initiated - user_id=12345, session_id=abc987,
   transaction_id=txn001, amount=49.99
   ```

3. **Aggregate and Centralize Logs**: Logs from each service are centralized using AWS CloudWatch Logs. By using `session_id` and `transaction_id`, engineers can trace a user's actions across different microservices, from logging in, adding items to the cart, processing the payment, and arranging delivery.

   For example, if a delivery fails, the error logs from the delivery service can be correlated with the initial payment logs using the `transaction_id`:

   ```
   ERROR: Delivery failed - transaction_id=txn001, delivery_
   id=delv789, error_code=DELIV_ERRORte,
   ```

In this scenario, smart logging helps reduce unnecessary noise by focusing on logs that provide actionable insights (e.g., ERROR logs for failed transactions). Each log entry includes context that enables tracing of user actions across services, allowing engineers to quickly diagnose and resolve issues.

Additionally, centralized log aggregation ensures that logs are easily accessible for analysis, providing a clear, end-to-end view of system behavior without overwhelming the team with irrelevant data. While smart logging helps streamline observability, it's important to recognize that logs alone may not be enough. Without full visibility across all system layers, particularly in hybrid environments, blind spots can emerge. Next, we will explore how incomplete observability creates these gaps and what can be done to overcome them.

The Blind Spots of Incomplete Observability and the Importance of End-to-End Distributed Tracing

Observability in cloud native environments is more than just collecting logs; it's about understanding your systems comprehensively by correlating metrics, traces, and logs across services. Many organizations fall into the trap of incomplete observability by focusing solely on specific layers, such as applications or infrastructure, while neglecting other critical components like data pipelines. This selective approach creates blind spots that obscure the true source of issues, making troubleshooting time-consuming and frustrating. For instance, a smoothly running application may actually be suffering from bottlenecks in its data pipeline. Still, if observability is focused only on the application layer, the problem may go unnoticed until it visibly impacts performance or availability.

To address these blind spots, organizations need to adopt comprehensive end-to-end distributed tracing. **Distributed tracing** follows the flow of requests across different services, applications, and hybrid environments, providing a detailed view of how systems interact and where potential bottlenecks or failures occur. This is especially crucial in microservices architectures, where a single user request may touch dozens of services before completion. Distributed tracing becomes even more critical for organizations running hybrid workloads, where cloud and on-premises systems must work together. Without it, latency issues, transaction failures, or inconsistencies between cloud native and legacy systems can go undetected until they cause significant disruptions.

Each of the major cloud providers offers unique tools to implement end-to-end distributed tracing:

Cloud Provider	Distributed Tracing Tool	Key Features
AWS	AWS X-Ray	Trace requests across AWS services like Lambda, API Gateway, and DynamoDB. Provides detailed visibility into system performance and failures. Supports hybrid workloads by tracing requests across on-premises and cloud-based systems.
GCP	Cloud Trace (Google Cloud Operations Suite)	Tracks latency and performance across services such as Google Kubernetes Engine (GKE), Cloud Run and Cloud Functions. Identifies bottlenecks and supports hybrid workloads with OpenTelemetry integration for tracing requests between cloud and on-premises environments.
Azure	Azure Monitor (Application Insights)	Tracks request flows across services like Azure App Services, Azure Functions, and Azure Kubernetes Service (AKS) offer deep visibility into microservice interactions and integrate with on-premises environments through SDKs and Azure Hybrid Cloud services for end-to-end traceability.

Table 10.1 - Cloud providers and tracing tools

By leveraging these tools, organizations can gain a holistic view of how their systems perform, tracing errors and latency across multiple services and addressing issues before they cause significant disruptions. End-to-end distributed tracing is essential for diagnosing problems in complex cloud-native architectures. Nonetheless, it is crucial in optimizing performance and ensuring seamless interaction across hybrid environments.

The ability to trace requests across all layers of your infrastructure provides deep insights into where failures may occur, allowing for proactive adjustments. This enhances system reliability, reduces downtime, and improves user experiences across increasingly complex architectures.

Hybrid Workload Integration and Unified Observability

To ensure complete observability, organizations must adopt tools that handle hybrid workloads, providing visibility across boundaries between cloud native and on-premises environments. A unified approach to observability brings together logs, metrics, and traces into a cohesive framework, offering comprehensive insights across the entire infrastructure. The key components of hybrid observability include:

- **Cross-Environment Tracing**: Tools like OpenTelemetry standardize tracing across cloud and on-premises systems, following requests across boundaries for a complete view.

- **Unified Metrics Collection**: Metrics should be consistently collected across environments using tools like AWS CloudWatch or Prometheus and centralized for real-time analysis.

- **Log Aggregation and Correlation**: Logs from cloud and on-premises systems must be aggregated into a single repository (e.g., Splunk, Datadog) for analysis and event correlation.

- **Unified Monitoring Dashboards**: A single dashboard (e.g., Datadog, Grafana) should provide real-time insights across cloud native and on-premises systems, simplifying management.

- **Alerting and Incident Management**: Alerts must trigger real-time notifications across both environments, ensuring consistent incident response with tools like PagerDuty or Opsgenie.

While hybrid workloads provide flexibility and scalability, they also introduce challenges like inconsistent data formats, latency, and monitoring gaps, which can lead to data silos. However, adopting a unified observability approach improves visibility, speeds up troubleshooting, and enhances system reliability across hybrid environments.

Real-Time Monitoring: A Necessity for Transactional Systems

In industries like financial services, where real-time transactions are crucial, monitoring must be as close to real-time as possible. Delays of even a few minutes can have severe consequences, including financial losses, compliance failures, and damage to customer trust. Take for example SaaS providers, these organizations have Terms And Conditions with their API responses to meet specific customer requirements. In the case of Payment providers, response time needs to be within a specific period of time, otherwise, payments drop. Event-based alerting systems that trigger notifications when critical events occur (e.g., transaction failures, latency spikes, or security breaches) allow teams to respond swiftly, preventing minor issues from escalating into more significant incidents.

However, the effectiveness of real-time alerting is often diminished by alert fatigue, a common challenge in cloud native environments. **Alert fatigue** occurs when operations teams are overwhelmed by the sheer volume of alerts generated by monitoring systems, often leading to desensitization and missed critical signals. As teams struggle to keep up, they may begin ignoring or dismissing notifications, increasing the risk of missing real threats. To combat this, smarter alerting strategies are essential, such as leveraging AI to prioritize critical issues, reduce noise, and ensure that alerts are both meaningful and actionable.

Real-time monitoring is also essential for security. It allows teams to detect anomalies (e.g., unauthorized access attempts or unusual transaction behavior) and respond proactively. When paired with real-time logging, event-based alerts help teams maintain system performance and security without being overwhelmed by unnecessary notifications. The table below details which cloud native services from the big three cloud providers can help execute a proper real-time monitoring setup.

Category	AWS	Azure	Google Cloud Platform (GCP)
Real-Time Metrics	CloudWatch: Monitors transaction latency, error rates, and throughput in real-time. Detects spikes in failed transactions instantly.	Azure Monitor: Tracks real-time metrics across microservices, including transaction completion times and error rates.	Cloud Monitoring: Observes latency, error rates, and transaction metrics in real-time. Flags abnormal spikes for investigation.
Instant Alerts	SNS: Triggers notifications via SMS, email, or Slack when alarms are raised.	Azure Action Groups: Sends notifications through email, SMS, push notifications, or Microsoft Teams.	Pub/Sub: Triggers alerts, notifying teams via email, SMS, or Google Chat.
Automated Responses	Lambda: Automatically reroutes traffic to backup services during failures.	Azure Functions: Automates responses like scaling instances or handling increased load.	Cloud Functions: Automates failover responses, redirecting traffic to alternate regions for high availability.
Security Monitoring	CloudTrail: Tracks and analyzes API activity for suspicious behavior.	Azure Security Center: Monitors and analyzes API activities for unauthorized access attempts.	Security Command Center: Tracks and analyzes suspicious API activities and logs.
Anomaly Detection	CloudWatch Anomaly Detection: Identifies unusual patterns in transactions, triggering alerts.	Azure Monitor: Uses ML-based anomaly detection for irregular transaction patterns.	Cloud Monitoring: Leverages anomaly detection to flag abnormal transaction behavior.
Automated Security Protocols	AWS Systems Manager: Automates security responses like disabling accounts.	Azure Logic Apps: Automates responses to security threats, such as flagging suspicious transactions.	Cloud Automation: Automatically triggers actions like quarantining suspicious transactions or disabling accounts.
Real-Time Logging for Deep Visibility	CloudWatch Logs: Collects real-time logs from all microservices and infrastructure components for deep analysis.	Azure Monitor Logs: Collects real-time logs from all services, offering detailed visibility into vstem events.	Cloud Logging: Provides realtime logging across services, enabling forensic analysis and event tracing.

Table 10.2 - Cloud Vendors and monitoring services

Implementation Checkpoints and Guardrails for a Corporate Strategy

A solid corporate strategy backed by crucial implementation checkpoints is needed for cloud native observability to be effective. These should ensure observability practices are applied consistently across the organization. Key elements include:

- **Defining Critical Events**: Identify which events (e.g., transaction failures, security incidents) are most critical to the business and prioritize them in monitoring and alerting systems.

- **Regular Audits of Observability Gaps**: Conduct audits to identify and address gaps in observability, especially as new services and architecture changes are introduced.

- **Automated Guardrails for Enforcement**: Automated guardrails enforce consistent logging, tracing, and monitoring standards across all systems, ensuring every deployment adheres to best practices.

Automating these best practices reduces human error, ensures consistency across the organization, and reduces operational overhead. Instead of manually configuring observability for every new service or deployment, guardrails take care of this automatically, freeing engineers to focus on higher-level work.

For instance, when deploying new applications through a CI/CD pipeline with integrated guardrails, these guardrails actively enforce compliance by blocking any deployment that fails to meet the established requirements.

Cloud native observability is critical for maintaining control over increasingly complex systems. By avoiding the pitfalls of overlogging and incomplete observability, adopting real-time monitoring, and enforcing consistency through automated guardrails, organizations can gain the visibility they need to prevent disruptions and improve their operational resilience. Success in cloud native environments depends not on capturing everything but on capturing the right insights at the right time and ensuring that these insights drive actionable outcomes. However, beyond traditional observability methods, organizations can unlock even greater potential by leveraging the built-in machine learning (ML) and artificial intelligence (AI) capabilities offered by modern observability platforms to proactively detect anomalies and predict incidents before they escalate. The prior will be discussed in the next section, Ignoring ML and AI capabilities.

Ignoring ML and AI capabilities

In the previous section, *Let's Capture Everything in the Log Aggregator*; we explored the common cloud native anti-pattern of overwhelming logging systems by collecting every possible data point without a strategic approach to filtering or prioritizing valuable insights. This scattershot method often results in data overload, making it difficult to extract actionable information when it's most needed.

Building on that concept, another critical oversight in cloud native architectures is the tendency to ignore the out-of-the-box machine learning (ML) and artificial intelligence (AI) capabilities offered by leading cloud providers like AWS, Azure, and GCP. These platforms provide potent tools such as AWS's Anomaly Detection in CloudWatch, GuardDuty, Azure Monitor's AI-powered insights, and GCP's Cloud Operations suite, which includes advanced log analysis and anomaly detection features.

This section will go over:

- Leveraging Cloud AI/ML for Anomaly Detection

- Improving Log Aggregation with AI Insights

- Centralized Monitoring with Automated Intelligence

- Reducing Operational Complexity through ML Automation

Leveraging Cloud AI/ML for Anomaly Detection

While real-time alerting and monitoring have become essential components of cloud native operations, they are no longer enough to keep pace with the growing complexity of modern systems. Traditional monitoring techniques often rely on static thresholds and manual rule-setting, which can result in missed critical events or unnecessary noise from false positives. In an environment where applications are increasingly distributed and dynamic, organizations need more intelligent solutions to detect subtle issues before they become full-blown problems. This is where *anomaly detection*, powered by AI and machine learning, becomes indispensable. Anomaly detection provides proactive insights that allow teams to address issues early, often before users even notice a degradation in service, shifting from reactive monitoring to intelligent, predictive observability.

Cloud providers like AWS, Azure, and GCP offer advanced AI/ML capabilities that transform traditional monitoring and observability. In AWS CloudWatch, for example, Anomaly Detection uses machine learning models to detect deviations from expected performance patterns automatically. Azure Monitor incorporates AI-driven insights to predict issues before they arise, while GCP's Cloud Operations provides anomaly detection to pinpoint unusual behavior across logs and metrics. By utilizing these capabilities, organizations can gain a proactive edge in detecting potential issues before they become full-blown incidents, enabling teams to address problems in real-time.

However, despite the availability of these tools mentioned prior, many organizations fail to adopt them fully, sticking to manual monitoring methods that often fall short. Ignoring AI/ML-powered anomaly detection means missing out on a layer of protection that traditional rule-based alerting simply cannot provide. The power of machine learning lies in its ability to identify subtle patterns in massive data streams, patterns that may be missed by even the most experienced operators. By leveraging these cloud native AI/ML tools, organizations can enhance their monitoring efforts, reducing downtime and improving system resilience. The following example of Leveraging Cloud AI/ML for Anomaly Detection provides strong context on why its a tool that should not be ignored.

Anomaly Detection: An example

An example of AI/ML anomaly detection can be found in AWS CloudWatch Anomaly Detection. This feature uses machine learning to automatically establish a metrics baseline and detect deviations from this expected behavior.

For instance, in a web application, CloudWatch Anomaly Detection could monitor the number of requests to the server and establish an expected pattern based on historical data. Suppose the traffic suddenly spikes or drops outside the expected range, such as a sudden flood of requests indicative of a DDoS attack or a sudden drop in traffic suggesting a failure. In that case, it flags this as an anomaly and triggers an alert. The image below illustrates what that would look like:

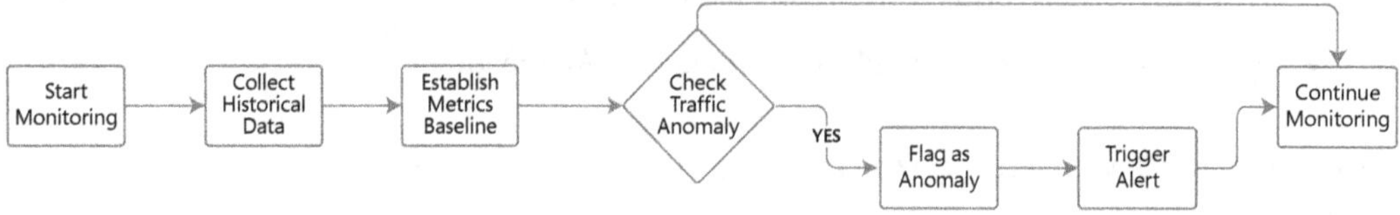

Figure 10.1 - Typical Flow of Anomaly detection (Redraw please)

This flowchart outlines a monitoring process that begins with data collection and baseline establishment, continuously checks for traffic anomalies, flags and triggers alerts for anomalies detected, and loops back to ongoing monitoring if no anomalies are found.

As we progress, we must understand that effective monitoring doesn't stop at anomaly detection. The next layer of observability involves Improving Log Aggregation with AI Insights, where machine learning continues to enhance how we filter and interpret vast amounts of log data.

Improving Log Aggregation with AI Insights

Log aggregation is critical to any observability strategy but is not enough to collect data. The true challenge lies in filtering through the immense volume of logs to extract actionable insights. AI and ML capabilities embedded in cloud platforms like AWS, Azure, and GCP are invaluable here. These tools offer smart filtering and categorization, enabling organizations to focus on the most relevant data.

For instance, AWS CloudWatch Logs Insights and Azure Log Analytics use machine learning to identify patterns and anomalies, helping teams make sense of vast amounts of log data more efficiently.

While many organizations are content to rely on manual searches and predefined queries, these methods often result in information overload or missed signals. AI-enhanced log aggregation helps reduce noise, highlights critical issues, and predicts future system behavior. By integrating these capabilities into the log aggregation pipeline, companies can improve their troubleshooting efficiency and prevent potential incidents by acting on predictive insights. This approach brings a level of sophistication to logging that manual methods simply cannot match. By integrating AI and ML capabilities into log aggregation, cloud native environments can significantly improve how logs are processed, analyzed, and acted upon. Below are some key ways in which AI enhances log aggregation:

- **Smart Filtering and Categorization**: AI models automatically sort logs based on relevance, reducing the time spent manually filtering through non-essential data.

- **Pattern Recognition in Large Data Sets**: Machine learning identifies patterns in logs that would be too subtle or complex for manual detection, enabling teams to uncover hidden issues or trends.

- **Anomaly Detection in Log Data**: AI detects anomalies within logs that indicate potential failures, security threats, or performance bottlenecks, allowing teams to act before problems escalate.

- **Predictive Insights for Future Behavior**: Machine learning analyzes historical log data to predict future behavior, offering teams proactive recommendations for avoiding incidents or optimizing system performance.

- **Noise Reduction**: AI-enhanced log aggregation reduces the noise by filtering out irrelevant or duplicate entries, making it easier to focus on critical log events and streamline incident response.

- **Automated Insights and Recommendations**: AI tools directly provide actionable insights and recommendations from log data, helping teams prioritize their efforts and resolve issues faster with data-backed guidance.

Looking ahead, it becomes clear that centralized monitoring is the backbone of enhanced observability, bringing together vast data streams for intelligent analysis at scale. In the next section, Centralized Monitoring with Automated Intelligence, we'll uncover how AI and ML are the catalysts that elevate this approach from routine oversight to predictive power.

Centralized Monitoring with Automated Intelligence

Centralized monitoring has become the foundation of modern observability, allowing organizations to manage complex systems more easily. However, with the advent of AI and ML, centralized monitoring has evolved beyond merely consolidating data into dashboards.

Today, cloud providers like AWS, Azure, and GCP offer sophisticated monitoring platforms that do more than aggregate metrics; they:

- Analyze data in real time to deliver intelligent alerts and recommendations powered by machine learning.

- Visualize the performance of distributed systems to simplify the management of cloud native workloads.

- Centralize logging across all resources, enhancing visibility and enabling more efficient monitoring.

These platforms, such as AWS CloudWatch, Azure Monitor, and GCP Cloud Operations, allow teams to visualize the performance of distributed systems and reduce the complexity of managing cloud-native workloads, making monitoring more efficient and actionable.

In addition to performance metrics, all major cloud vendors now offer solutions to centralize logging across all resources, further enhancing observability. For instance, AWS provides AWS CloudWatch Logs and AWS Organizations, which enable centralized log aggregation and policy management across multiple accounts. This ensures that data from various services and resources, whether distributed or complex, is collected and accessible in one unified location.

Similarly, Azure Log Analytics and Google Cloud's Logging offer comparable capabilities, aggregating logs from across regions and services while incorporating AI/ML-driven analytics to highlight significant trends, anomalies, and potential issues before they escalate.

Centralized Monitoring: An AI Example

These AI and ML-driven tools go beyond traditional monitoring by moving from reactive to proactive observability. Instead of simply responding to events as they occur, these platforms provide predictive insights that help teams identify issues before they manifest.

For example, AWS GuardDuty integrates with AWS Organizations and uses anomaly detection powered by machine learning to flag suspicious activity, such as unusual network traffic or unauthorized access attempts. Similarly, machine learning models across these cloud platforms can detect emerging patterns that indicate impending resource constraints or application bottlenecks, enabling operators to take preemptive action. The result is a more intelligent, responsive monitoring system that lightens the load on operations teams while ensuring better performance, security, and overall reliability of cloud workloads.

Reducing Operational Complexity through ML Automation

In cloud native environments, operational complexity can quickly spiral out of control. The sheer scale of data, distributed architectures, and dynamic infrastructure create monitoring challenges that are difficult to manage manually.

Fortunately, machine learning automation offers a solution by simplifying tasks like anomaly detection, alerting, and capacity planning. Cloud platforms like AWS, Azure, and GCP provide ML automation tools to handle these repetitive and time-consuming tasks, allowing operations teams to focus on higher-value activities.

For example, Azure offers a suite of machine learning automation tools specifically designed to streamline operational complexity. Azure Monitor's Autoscale feature dynamically adjusts resources based on real-time demand, automatically increasing or decreasing capacity without manual intervention. With Azure Machine Learning's anomaly detection capabilities, organizations can proactively address potential performance bottlenecks and resource constraints before they impact the end-user experience. Azure Automation, another powerful tool, automates routine operational tasks such as patch management, compliance checks, and system backups. These automated processes ensure that operations teams are no longer bogged down by repetitive tasks, allowing them to focus on strategic initiatives that drive business value.

ML Automation: Working Example

In a recent consulting engagement, clients facing growing operational complexity are often overwhelmed by the sheer volume of alerts and manual tasks that consume their team's time. In these situations, leveraging Azure's ML-driven automation tools can significantly transform their operations. For example, during a recent engagement, we worked with a client struggling with frequent scaling issues due to their fluctuating user base. By implementing Azure Monitor's Autoscale and integrating predictive analytics from Azure Machine Learning, the client was able to reduce manual oversight, optimize resource allocation, and prevent costly downtime. The shift to ML automation enabled their team to reclaim time spent on firefighting and instead focus on innovation and growth.

By embracing ML automation, organizations can reduce the need for constant manual intervention, ensuring faster response times and more reliable systems. Automation increases efficiency and reduces the potential for human error, often the source of operational failures. In this way, AI and ML-driven automation act as a force multiplier, enabling operations teams to do more with less effort while maintaining robust system performance. As cloud native architectures evolve, ML automation will only grow in importance, becoming an essential component of successful observability strategies.

To get to the point where a traditional organization can utilize ML automation when moving to cloud-native, the table below provides a set of considerations:

Step	Description
Assess Your Current Operational Processes	Identify repetitive, time-consuming tasks that can benefit from automation (e.g., anomaly detection, scaling, system maintenance).
Set Clear Objectives	Define specific goals for ML automation, such as reducing manual intervention, improving response times, or enhancing resource optimization.
Evaluate Existing Cloud Automation Tools	Review ML automation features in your cloud platform (e.g., AWS GuardDuty, Azure Monitor, and GCP Operations) for potential integration.
Prioritize Use Cases	Select the most impactful areas to automate first, like auto-scaling during peak loads or automating patch management.
Integrate Machine Learning Models	Implement cloud native or custom ML models for anomaly detection, predictive analytics, and resource optimization.
Develop Automation Pipelines	Build pipelines that integrate ML models with operations, triggering actions like resource scaling or issue resolution based on ML insights.
Test and Monitor Automation	Run simulations and monitor performance to ensure ML automation meets objectives, refining models and workflows as needed.
Scale Automation Across Operations	Expand ML automation to additional processes once initial use cases are successful, incorporating more complex workflows and models.
Implement Feedback Loops	Continuously gather data from automated processes to improve models and automation strategies, ensuring continual learning and refinement.
Train Your Teams	Ensure teams receive effective training to manage and optimize ML automation, maintaining performance and adaptability.

Table 10.3 - ML Automation Considerations

As we've seen, AI/ML-driven anomaly detection in cloud native environments is not just an enhancement to observability; it's a critical tool for maintaining system resilience. Whether it's identifying unusual traffic spikes, unexpected performance drops, or subtle patterns that could indicate emerging issues, these capabilities give organizations a proactive edge in managing complex, distributed systems. By failing to leverage the intelligent, automated insights provided by AWS, Azure, and GCP, many companies are unnecessarily exposing themselves to more significant operational risks and inefficiencies. Embracing these tools is not just about reducing downtime; and it's about building a more intelligent, adaptive infrastructure.

Yet anomaly detection is only one piece of the observability puzzle. As systems grow more distributed, tracking issues across multiple services and microservices becomes even more challenging. This is where distributed tracing is a critical technique for following a request's journey across different components and identifying performance bottlenecks or errors in complex, interconnected systems.

In the next section, we'll explore how *Neglecting Distributed Tracing* can leave gaps in your observability strategy, making it harder to diagnose issues and optimize performance in cloud native architectures.

Neglecting Distributed Tracing

Neglecting distributed tracing is a classic cloud native anti-pattern. It undermines one of the core principles of cloud native architecture: *end-to-end observability*. When tracing is overlooked, it disrupts the flow of visibility across distributed systems, leading to hidden performance bottlenecks, misdiagnosed issues, and a loss of accountability in critical pathways. This anti-pattern breaks the promise of transparency and agility that cloud native environments are supposed to deliver, leaving teams scrambling to diagnose issues without the whole picture.

This section will explore the importance of cloud native log aggregation within a security data lake and highlight how failing to integrate logs across distributed systems compromises security insights and operational awareness. Additionally, we will explain why splitting impact metrics from diagnostic metrics is not just a best practice but a necessity for precise, actionable insights.

Here's what to expect:

- **The Fragmentation Problem**: How overlooking distributed tracing leaves gaps in visibility across microservices.

- **Metrics that Matter**: The importance of distinguishing impact metrics from diagnostic metrics for better incident response.

- **Real-World Consequences**: Case studies of what can go wrong when distributed tracing is neglected.

- **Best Practices for End-to-End Tracing**: A guide to implementing comprehensive tracing across complex systems

The Fragmentation Problem

Cloud native architectures thrive on the promise of agility, resilience, and scalability. By decoupling applications into independently deployable microservices, businesses gain flexibility and speed. However, as these systems grow in scale, so does the complexity of managing them effectively. When distributed tracing, the key to visibility within microservices, is neglected or improperly implemented, a dangerous anti-pattern known as fragmentation emerges.

Fragmentation occurs when tracing is applied inconsistently or only in parts of the system, leaving critical gaps in visibility. Instead of a clear, end-to-end view of transactions, teams are left with a disjointed mess, akin to navigating through a fog of partial data.

Distributed tracing exists to provide transparency throughout a system, capturing the full journey of requests as they flow between microservices, databases, and third-party APIs. When applied correctly, it offers a holistic view, enabling teams to pinpoint bottlenecks, identify errors, and optimize performance. However, when tracing is not implemented consistently across the entire architecture, teams are forced to rely on fragmented data, piecing together logs from disparate services without seeing the whole picture. This lack of cohesion doesn't just compromise visibility, it introduces significant operational risks.

Fragmentation: An Example

Consider the case of an e-commerce retailer grappling with slow checkout times during high-traffic sales events. Their logs from individual microservices appeared normal without a unified tracing system, suggesting everything was running smoothly. Yet the customer experience told a different story: lagging transactions and failed checkouts, causing customer frustration and lost revenue. The real culprit, a third-party payment processor throttling requests, remained hidden from view, only uncovered after hours of expensive investigation. Had comprehensive distributed tracing been in place, the issue could have been identified in minutes, preventing financial loss and safeguarding customer trust.

Fragmentation as a cloud native anti-pattern breaks one of the core tenets of microservices: the ability to maintain observability across the entire system while still managing services independently. The tension between autonomy and operational oversight becomes unsustainable without distributed tracing. The solution is straightforward:

- **Treat Distributed Tracing as a Foundational Element**: Integrate distributed tracing into the architecture from the outset, ensuring it is a core part of the design rather than an afterthought.

- **Implement End-to-End Tracing**: To avoid blind spots, ensure every transaction is fully traced across all microservices, third-party APIs, databases, and other system components.

- **Avoid Fragmented Visibility**: Consistently apply tracing across the entire system to prevent teams from compiling incomplete data from isolated logs.

- **Monitor All Critical Paths**: Focus on critical user journeys, such as checkout processes or key transactions, to immediately detect and resolve bottlenecks, errors, or latency.

- **Foster a Proactive Approach**: Address potential risks before they become problems by continuously monitoring and tracing critical services, ensuring the system remains resilient under pressure.

- **Enhance Observability**: Integrate tracing with logging and metrics to provide a comprehensive observability stack, enabling faster diagnostics and incident response.

This approach builds a more reliable, agile, and resilient system that can scale effectively while maintaining operational visibility.

Metrics that Matter

Not all metrics are created equal in effective distributed tracing. To ensure a robust incident response and maintain a high-performing cloud native system, it is crucial to distinguish between impact metrics and diagnostic metrics. This distinction allows operations teams to prioritize alerts based on an issue's severity while offering deeper insights for troubleshooting and resolution. The table below goes into further detail as to what the metrics types are:

Metric Type	Description	Examples	Purpose
Impact Metrics	Focus on user experience and overall system health. Measure the direct impact on customers or business outcomes.	**Latency, Error Rates, Request Failures**	Quickly detect and address issues that affect end users, such as slow response times or failed transactions.
Diagnostic Metrics	Dive deeper into system internals to uncover the root cause of issues. Provide detailed technical information for troubleshooting.	**CPU Usage, Memory Consumption, Network Traffic, Database Query Performance**	Diagnose and resolve issues identified by impact metrics by analyzing system performance and resource

Table 10.4 - Metric split

It is one thing to know the metrics types, but to utilize them is another. In the example below, we use OpenTelemtry to pull useful metrics from an application here using the OpenTelemtry SDK, directly tying to the code itself, instead of relying on an agent:

```python
from opentelemetry import metrics
from opentelemetry.sdk.metrics import MeterProvider
from opentelemetry.sdk.metrics.export import ConsoleMetricExporter,
PeriodicExportingMetricReader

# Set up MeterProvider and Metric Exporter
provider = MeterProvider()
metrics.set_meter_provider(provider)

exporter = ConsoleMetricExporter()
reader = PeriodicExportingMetricReader(exporter)
provider.add_metric_reader(reader)

# Create a meter for recording metrics
meter = metrics.get_meter(__name__)

# Define metrics: Impact and Diagnostic
impact_latency = meter.create_histogram("impact_latency", unit="ms",
description="Request Latency")
diagnostic_cpu_usage = meter.create_observable_gauge("diagnostic_cpu_
usage", description="CPU Usage")

# Function to simulate recording of impact metrics
def record_impact_metrics(latency_value):
    impact_latency.record(latency_value)
    print(f"Recorded impact latency: {latency_value}ms")

# Function to observe diagnostic metrics
def observe_diagnostic_metrics():
    import psutil
    return psutil.cpu_percent(interval=None)

# Register diagnostic metric callback
meter.create_observable_gauge("diagnostic_cpu_usage",
callbacks=[observe_diagnostic_metrics])

# Simulating metric recording
record_impact_metrics(120)   # Simulating a latency of 120ms
```

Key Points to observe in the code are:

- **Impact Metrics**: The `impact_latency histogram` tracks the length of a request, a key metric for user experience. In this example, we record a latency of 120ms.

- **Diagnostic Metrics**: The `diagnostic_cpu_usage` observable gauge monitors CPU usage. We use the `psutil` library to gather CPU statistics, a proper diagnostic metric to understand system resource usage during incidents.

By collecting and analyzing impact and diagnostic metrics, teams can quickly detect performance issues while gathering the information necessary to diagnose and resolve root causes. This combined approach ensures that cloud native systems remain resilient and performant, even under pressure.

Proper metrics dictate the relevance of results; the next section will go into a real-world scenario of what happens when we neglect distributed tracing.

Real World Consequences

During a recent engagement with a leading e-commerce retailer, we were called in to address significant performance issues that emerged during a high-traffic sale. The retailer's microservices architecture managed critical operations like inventory management and payment processing, but their observability was fragmented. Relying solely on logs and metrics from individual services, they couldn't trace transactions end-to-end, making it impossible to quickly identify the source of latency when checkout times began to slow down under the increased load. Hours into the incident, we implemented distributed tracing, immediately revealing a third-party payment API as the bottleneck causing the delays.

Introducingm distributed tracing gave the retailer real-time visibility into the entire transaction flow across all microservices. The integration of this tracing allowed the operations team to pinpoint and resolve issues much faster, avoiding prolonged outages that could have been identified within minutes instead of hours. Our intervention reduced downtime and restored customer trust by ensuring that future peak traffic periods would be handled with better performance monitoring and faster response times. The image below shows a simple Kubernetes microservice followed by a list of issue we had discovered

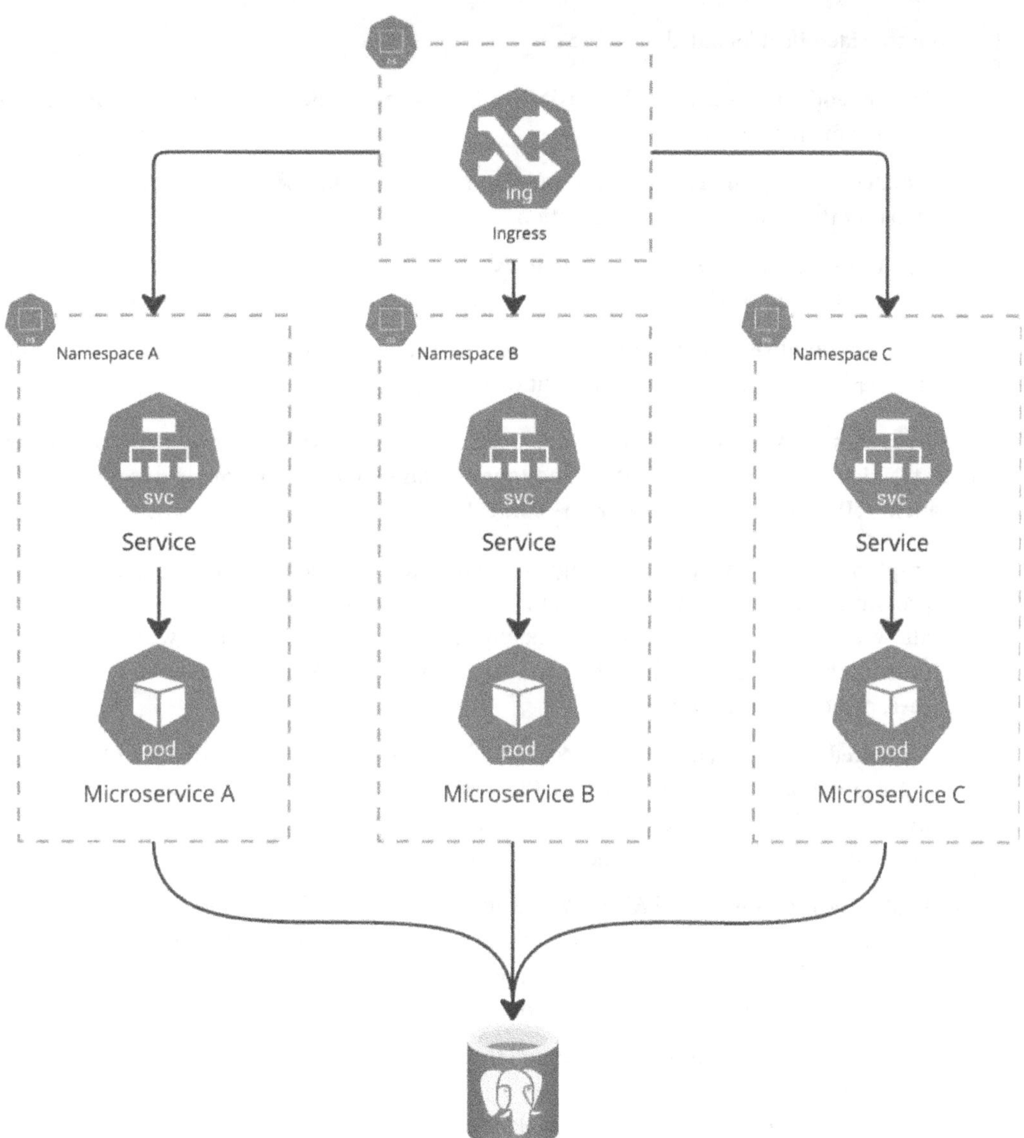

Figure 10.2 - Simple Kubernetes Microservice

Key issues we identified included:

- **Lack of end-to-end transaction visibility**: The system couldn't trace the customer journey through microservices.

- **Isolated logs and metrics**: Metrics were limited to individual services and offered no insight into how they interacted in a transaction.

- **Unmonitored third-party dependencies**: The third-party API causing the delays was not adequately monitored, making it invisible until distributed tracing was implemented.

- **Slow incident response times**: Without distributed tracing, the team relied on manual troubleshooting, prolonging the resolution of critical issues.

To address these challenges, organizations need a comprehensive observability strategy that integrates distributed tracing, centralized logging, and robust monitoring across all system components. The list below provides more context:

- **Implemented Distributed Tracing**: We deployed OpenTelemetry as our tracing solution, providing end-to-end visibility of transactions across the microservices architecture. This allowed the team to detect bottlenecks immediately, including the slow third-party API causing checkout delays. The key to consistency was to package OpenTelemtry SDK (in this case, python) with all code.

- **Enhanced Log Aggregation**: We integrated the tracing system with CloudWatch for centralized log aggregation, ensuring all logs from the various microservices were collected and searchable in one place. This improved the team's ability to correlate logs with tracing data, making incident detection and diagnosis faster and more accurate.

- **Real-Time Monitoring and Alerts**: We set up monitoring dashboards and real-time alerts using Prometheus and Grafana, configuring them to display system health, performance metrics, and traces. This gave the operations team proactive insights into system performance, reducing their reliance on reactive troubleshooting during high-traffic events.

- **Monitoring of Third-Party Dependencies**: We established specific monitors for third-party APIs, which included setting latency thresholds and failure rate alerts. This ensured that external dependencies were continuously tracked for performance degradation, preventing them from silently becoming bottlenecks in the future.

By leveraging these tools and strategies, we improved the retailer's system visibility and reduced their response times to critical incidents. These solutions can be replicated using equivalent services in the major cloud providers, such as AWS XRay + CloudWatch, Azure Application Insights, and Google Cloud Operations Suite.

Next, we will discuss best practices and what to consider when building distributed tracing to tie together all we have learned up to this point.

Best Practices for Resolving Tracing Neglect

Neglecting distributed tracing is like trying to navigate a complex city with incomplete maps; inevitably, you'll get lost. End-to-end tracing acts as your GPS, connecting the dots between microservices, identifying bottlenecks, and illuminating paths that might otherwise remain hidden in the shadows of fragmented logs. Distributed tracing must be treated as a foundational practice, not an afterthought, to ensure a cloud native system remains agile, scalable, and responsive.

Consider the following when applying building tracing:

- **Start Early and Be Consistent**: One of the most critical best practices is implementing tracing from the beginning. Retroactively adding tracing to an existing architecture is akin to patching holes in a sinking ship; it is inefficient and prone to leaving gaps. Consistency is key; every microservice, dependency, and path that requests take through your system should be covered by tracing. This ensures that no part of the system is left in the dark.

- **Trace the Entire Journey**: Successful tracing doesn't stop at the surface. It needs to span the entire request lifecycle, from the user-facing frontend through the backend services and to external dependencies like third-party APIs. This complete visibility ensures that any latency or failure can be tracked down to its root cause, whether it is inside your system or external to it. The result is faster diagnostics, quicker resolutions, and fewer headaches when incidents arise.

- **Integrate with Metrics and Logs**: Tracing is robust, but it becomes a force multiplier when combined with metrics and logs. Use impact metrics to identify when user experience is degrading and diagnostic metrics to figure out why. Aggregating all three pillars of observability, tracing, metrics, and logs creates a comprehensive view of your system, empowering teams with the insights they need to stay proactive rather than reactive.

- **Automate and Set Guardrails**: Manually instrumenting every service for tracing can be daunting, especially in dynamic, cloud native environments. Automation tools and frameworks like OpenTelemetry simplify this process, ensuring that tracing is baked into every new microservice or deployment by default. Setting automated guardrails for latency thresholds, error rates, and critical service performance can trigger alerts before incidents spiral out of control.

- **Monitor What Matters Most**: Not every trace, log, or metric needs to be treated equally. Prioritize tracing for the critical paths within your system, such as user transactions, payment flows, or any service that directly impacts customer experience. This focus ensures that your team's attention is on what matters most while still keeping an eye on the broader system's health.

Adhering to these best practices can help traditional organizations transform distributed tracing from a reactive tool into a proactive asset when shifting to cloud native. When tracing is holistic and integrated, the result is a cloud native architecture that is resilient, transparent, and able to meet the demands of modern applications. While tracing forms the backbone of a well-functioning cloud native system, the actual test of resilience lies in how an organization responds when things go wrong. Even with the best tracing practices, the system's ability to recover and maintain stability is compromised without a mature process for handling alerts and incidents.

In the final section of this chapter, we will explore how immature processes for alerts and incidents can undermine even the most robust architectures and how addressing these shortcomings is essential for sustaining operational excellence in cloud native environments.

Immature processes for alerts & incidents

While offering agility and scalability, cloud native organizations can often suffer from immature processes when handling alerts and incidents. In environments that manage thousands of microservices, the noise from redundant alerts, incomplete observability setups, and ineffective incident response protocols can overwhelm teams. As organizations modernize their infrastructure, they often forget a fundamental truth: **alerting and incident management are not about gathering all available metrics but focusing on the right metrics, responding to the right signals, and ensuring these processes function smoothly across all environments, not just in production.**

At the heart of many cloud native failures is a *"collect everything"* mindset, gathering every possible metric and sending alerts for every anomaly. This approach often leads to chaos, leaving engineering and operations teams drowning in data without actionable insights. The issue is not a lack of metrics; it's the absence of purposeful, well-aligned metrics and alerts. By understanding the dangers of metric dumping, we can become more cautious and aware, ensuring that every alert has a clear purpose, and each metric gathered should address a specific use case tied to both business and technical objectives.

This section will provide a guide through building a mature, effective system for alerting and incident response, highlighting common pitfalls and strategies for overcoming them.

In this section, we will cover:

- Purpose-driven metrics and alerts

- The trap of metric dumping

- Shifting left in observability

- Alert fatigue

- Incident response maturity

These topics will help develop a resilient, proactive approach to alerting and incident management, enabling teams to respond swiftly and intelligently when challenges arise.

Purpose-driven Metrics and Alerts

The sheer volume of metrics available can be overwhelming. However, not every metric is useful, and collecting everything without a clear purpose, leads to noise, alert fatigue, and inefficiency. Purpose-driven metrics focus on gathering data that aligns directly with specific business or technical objectives, ensuring that every metric serves a tangible purpose.

Metrics should be chosen based on their ability to provide actionable insights, not just because they're easy to collect. For example, instead of gathering CPU usage for all instances, consider: *"What are we trying to achieve by monitoring this? Are we looking to understand performance under load? Predict infrastructure scaling needs? Optimize resource utilization?"* Once the goal is clear, we can design metrics and alerts that align with it.

Purpose-driven Metrics and Alerts: An Example

For instance, let's consider a microservices-based e-commerce platform. One critical business objective is ensuring a seamless customer checkout experience. In this case, purpose-driven metrics could include:

- **Latency of the checkout service**: This metric tracks the time it takes for the checkout process to complete, directly impacting user experience. The business goal is to ensure customers aren't abandoning their carts due to slow performance. The associated alert could trigger when latency exceeds a defined threshold, prompting engineers to investigate slowdowns before they impact many users.

- **Error rate during payment processing**: Monitoring this metric helps ensure that failed payment transactions don't disrupt sales. Instead of sending alerts for every failed transaction, an alert might be triggered when the error rate surpasses a certain percentage over a specific time window, allowing teams to differentiate between minor blips and real issues.

- **Inventory update delays**: If inventory updates after sales are delayed, this can result in overselling, impacting revenue and customer satisfaction. A targeted metric around the time it takes to sync inventory after an order is placed serves a business goal of operational accuracy. Alerts are triggered if these delays exceed acceptable limits.

By defining metrics like these, we do not just collect data for the sake of it. Instead, we ensure that each metric serves a well-defined purpose, allowing teams to focus on what truly matters to the business. Now that we've seen the value of purpose-driven metrics, we must avoid the opposite approach, which we call the "metric dumping" trap.

Next, we will examine the trap of metric dumping and how it can derail even the best-intentioned cloud native monitoring strategies.

The Trap of Metric Dumping

In the rush to embrace monitoring tools and gather insights, many organizations fall into the trap of metric dumping. This occurs when every possible metric is collected without considering its value or purpose. On the surface, this might seem like a way to guarantee complete visibility. However, it leads to data overload, alert fatigue, and reduced system performance, making it harder for teams to respond to critical issues promptly. **Metric dumping** is the process of collecting every available metric, whether it's CPU usage, memory, network latency, or disk I/O, without considering how these metrics will be used or whether they contribute to achieving business goals. Teams may believe that collecting more data gives them more control and insight.

Metric Dumping: An Example

For example, imagine an organization that monitors the CPU usage of every instance across hundreds of microservices, regardless of whether CPU usage is relevant to the service's performance. They collect this data at a highly granular level (every second), even though the service has no history of CPU-related performance issues. Over time, this approach generates vast amounts of data that clog dashboards, increase storage costs, and create an alert system constantly firing off non-critical warnings. This is a classic case of metric dumping, collecting more data than is necessary or actionable.

Metric dumping creates two significant problems that slow down operations: operational inefficiency and alert fatigue. Here's how these issues manifest:

- **Operational Inefficiency**:

  - The flood of unnecessary metrics slows down monitoring systems, as every metric must be processed, stored, and analyzed.

  - This results in massive data pipelines that consume more resources than needed.

  - Engineers and operations teams must sift through irrelevant data, making it harder to find important insights.

  - Critical alerts may be delayed, buried, or missed, potentially allowing issues to escalate into outages.

- **Alert Fatigue**:

  - Monitoring too many metrics leads to excessive alerts, overwhelming teams with a stream of non-critical notifications.

  - Over time, teams become desensitized, increasing the risk of missing or ignoring truly important alerts.

  - This reduces team effectiveness and increases the likelihood of system downtime, longer recovery times, and a negative impact on customer experience.

Here's how you can move away from metric dumping and toward a more focused, efficient monitoring strategy:

Action	Description
Define Clear Business and Technical Goals	Ensure every metric has a well-defined purpose. Start by asking, "What business or operational problem are we trying to solve?" Collect metrics supporting these objectives.
Prioritize Actionable Metrics	Focus on metrics that provide actionable insights. Avoid collecting data just because it's available. Ensure metrics help the team make decisions or take action.
Regularly Review and Prune Metrics	Periodically audit the metrics being collected. Retire those that are no longer relevant, reducing noise and keeping the monitoring system efficient.
Create Threshold-based Alerts	Design alerts that trigger only when critical thresholds are crossed. This reduces unnecessary alerts and helps teams focus on the most important issues.
Use Aggregated Metrics	Aggregate metrics to get a high-level view, avoiding excessive granularity. Monitor averages over time to identify meaningful patterns and reduce noise.
Focus on Key Performance Indicators (KPIs)	Align metrics with KPis that measure the health and performance of critical systems, like user experience, transaction success rates, and service latency.

Table 10.5 - Metric dumping resolution table

By following these steps, you can eliminate the inefficiencies of metric dumping and create a streamlined monitoring system that delivers clear, actionable insights. This will improve response times, reduce alert fatigue, and enable teams to focus on the most critical aspects of your cloud native environment. The next section will dive into the observability side by addressing *Shifting left in Observability*.

Shifting Left in Observability

One of the most overlooked aspects of cloud native observability is the failure to extend monitoring and alerting into the early stages of the software development lifecycle(SDLC). This oversight leads to an anti-pattern where full observability is treated as a production-only concern. In cloud native environments, where microservices sprawl and deployment velocity are high, waiting until production to catch issues is akin to letting the fuse burn down on a bomb. This is where the practice of shifting left comes into play.

Shifting left in observability means embedding monitoring, alerting, and diagnostics into earlier environments, such as development, testing, and **UAT (User Acceptance Testing)**, instead of waiting until the code reaches production. By doing so, organizations can catch performance bottlenecks, scaling issues, or misconfigurations earlier, long before they disrupt production services or, worse, customers.

Imagine a scenario in which a cloud native e-commerce application is being deployed. In production, the company uses a robust observability platform like Prometheus and Grafana for monitoring and alerting system health. However, in pre-production environments, like staging or UAT, there's only a basic setup: maybe some logs or simple uptime monitoring.

This means that while the application undergoes various stages of testing, critical performance metrics such as API latency or resource saturation are not being monitored. The development team is unaware that under load, a particular microservice starts exhibiting high latency after a specific number of concurrent users. This issue only surfaces once the application is live in production, where latency spikes impact real users, leading to a scramble to mitigate the issue under the stress of a live incident.

Had observability been shifted left, this problem could have been identified much earlier. With the right metrics in place, developers would have seen that API latency gradually degrades with increasing load during the load-testing phase, allowing them to resolve the issue before production deployment.

The key to shifting left in observability is realizing that monitoring is crucial in all environments, not just production. Here's how to start:

Action	Description	Benefits of Shifting Left
Instrument Early	Add monitoring and tracing from the start, ensuring every feature or service has observability baked in during development across all environments (development, CI, staging).	- Early issue detection- Improved developer ownership
Monitor Load Tests	Treat pre-production load tests like production. Use tools like Grafana or New Relic to monitor API performance, memory, and throughput to identify bottlenecks early.	- Early issue detection- Reduced cost of failure
Set Alerts in Lower Environments	Implement alerts for critical issues (e.g., rising error rates, abnormal latency) in testing phases to address issues before they hit production.	- Faster time to resolution- Reduced cost of failure
Use Distributed Tracing	Apply distributed tracing in non-production environments to identify inefficient paths and bottlenecks, providing developers insights for fixing issues before they escalate.	- Faster time to resolution- Improved developer ownership

Table 10.6 - Starting with Instrumentation

In summary, shifting left in observability transforms it from a reactive, production-focused practice into a proactive, holistic approach that safeguards the entire lifecycle of cloud native applications. By investing in observability early, you significantly reduce the likelihood of surprises in production, ensuring that your cloud native architecture can scale and perform reliably under any conditions.

Alert Fatigue & Incident Response Maturity

In cloud native environments, alert fatigue is the silent enemy, creeping in when teams are bombarded with endless notifications, many of which signal minor issues or false alarms. This constant noise desensitizes even the most vigilant engineers, causing critical alerts to be overlooked or delayed. In the worst cases, teams may become so accustomed to low-priority alerts that they miss the ones that matter most. Incident response maturity, on the other hand, is the antidote, a reflection of a team's ability to manage alerts efficiently, triage effectively, and resolve issues with precision and speed.

But how do you avoid drowning in a sea of alerts? And more importantly, how do you transform alert chaos into a streamlined, mature incident response process?

How to Combat Alert Fatigue

- **Prioritize Critical Alerts**: Focus only on the alerts that genuinely matter, those that directly impact system performance and customer experience. If an alert doesn't require immediate action, it's just noise. Keep the signal clear.

- **Set Thoughtful Thresholds**: Alerts should trigger only when critical thresholds are crossed. A minor fluctuation in CPU usage shouldn't send your team into a frenzy. Design alerting rules that capture significant changes and filter out the minor blips.

- **Group Related Alerts**: When multiple alerts fire for the same underlying issue, it's easy to get overwhelmed. By grouping related alerts into a single, actionable notification, you reduce the clutter and give your team a clearer picture of the problem.

- **Tune and Retune**: Alerting rules aren't "set it and forget it." Regularly revisit and adjust them to keep pace with evolving system behavior. What was important six months ago may not be relevant now. Prune the dead weight.

- **Automate the Repetitive**: For known, recurring issues, automate the resolution. If a problem can be fixed by a script, there's no need to wake a human at 3 a.m. Automation reduces the volume of alerts and keeps your team focused on what really matters.

- **Post-Incident Review**: After an incident, analyze which alerts helped and which ones added noise. Use these lessons to refine your system further, ensuring that next time, your alerts are sharper and more accurate.

By focusing on what truly matters and continuously refining your alerting processes, you shift from reactive firefighting to proactive, thoughtful incident management. This is the path to incident response maturity: where every alert has a purpose, every response is swift, and the system becomes resilient. As alert fatigue fades, what's left is a finely tuned machine, one that runs smoothly, efficiently, and with the confidence that when something does go wrong, you'll know about it, and you'll know exactly how to fix it.

Summary

In this chapter, we've peeled back the layers of common cloud native anti-patterns—logging everything indiscriminately, overlooking the potential of ML and AI, neglecting the importance of distributed tracing, and stumbling through immature alert and incident processes. Each of these missteps chips away at the stability and efficiency of a cloud native architecture, leaving teams grappling with noise, blind spots, and unnecessary firefighting. However, by refining our approach—using targeted log aggregation, harnessing AI-driven insights, embracing distributed tracing for visibility, and maturing our incident response processes—we lay the groundwork for a more resilient, agile system. As we sidestep these anti-patterns, we transition from reactive crisis management to proactive operational excellence.

Now that we've tackled the hidden pitfalls, it's time to ensure the system runs smoothly under pressure. In the next chapter, we'll delve into strategies for maintaining stability and performance as cloud-native workloads scale and evolve.

11

Running It Without Breaking It

In this chapter, we'll explore the operational challenges that come with managing cloud environments and how to keep systems running smoothly, no matter what. We'll cover everything from understanding cloud provider SLAs to building resilience through multi-region deployments, failover architectures, and automated scaling. We'll dive into the importance of proactive planning, redundancy, and automation to minimize downtime and ensure business continuity. Whether it's preparing for cloud provider outages, updating runbooks and documentation, or adapting to the cultural shifts required for successful cloud operations, this chapter will arm us with the strategies and tools needed to keep our cloud infrastructure strong and reliable.

We'll address this within the following topics:

- Assuming the Cloud is Just 'Business as Usual'
- Inadequate Disaster Recovery & Backup Plans
- Out-of-Date Runbooks and Documentation
- Ignoring the Cultural Shift
- Developing Around CSP SLAs

Assuming the Cloud is Just 'Business as Usual'

When businesses shift to the cloud, it's all too common to overlook the complexity and steep learning curve that comes with it. Cloud operations need a whole different skill set compared to traditional IT, and without the right planning, teams can quickly find themselves in over their heads.

In this section, we will gain a deep understanding of the complexities that come with cloud adoption and learn how to prepare our team for the challenges ahead. We'll dive into the nitty-gritty of cloud infrastructure, automation, scaling, and cost management, so we can plan and avoid common pitfalls.

Understanding Cloud Complexity

When making the decision to move to the Cloud, we've generally got a very good reason to do so. We want to;

- Avoid replacing expensive legacy hardware on premise

- Modernize our product to use more up-to-date technologies.

- Take advantage of the flexibility in varying technologies.

- Infinitely scale our storage solution

- Have an offsite backup

This list is neither exhaustive nor limited, but for whatever reason we decide to move to the Cloud, we can expect there to be a learning curve.

When businesses transition to the cloud, they often assume it's just another IT upgrade. But the truth is, it's a whole new ballgame. Let's break down some of the things that catch teams off guard.

- **Infrastructure as Code (IaC)**: In traditional IT, setting up infrastructure might have involved physically installing servers or clicking through a UI to provision resources. In the cloud, we're potentially dealing with Infrastructure as Code (IaC). This means we're writing scripts—using tools like AWS CloudFormation, Terraform, or Azure ARM templates—to define our entire environment. If our team isn't used to thinking about infrastructure as something we version control and manage like software, we're already behind. The flexibility IaC provides is powerful, but it also requires developers and ops teams to be on the same page, understanding every line of code that affects the environment.

- **Automation and CI/CD Pipelines**: Another area that's often underestimated is the role of automation and continuous integration/continuous deployment (CI/CD) pipelines. In the cloud, manual deployments are not scalable. We need pipelines that automatically build, test, and deploy our applications. Teams that aren't experienced in setting up automated workflows will quickly find themselves drowning in manual processes, facing delays, and risking inconsistencies between environments. What seems like a quick deployment can end up being a troubleshooting marathon when it's done manually.

- **Multi-Region Redundancy and Scalability**: Cloud environments give us the ability to run our applications in multiple regions, ensuring uptime even if one location goes down. But setting this up isn't as simple as flicking a switch. It requires careful planning and a deep understanding of how our application and data need to be replicated across regions. If our team doesn't have the experience or hasn't thought through the design properly, we could be left vulnerable during an outage, with data that's inconsistent or difficult to recover.

- **Cost Management**: Cloud services are pay-as-you-go, which can be a double-edged sword. While we're not paying for hardware upfront, poor resource management can quickly lead to unexpected costs spiraling out of control. Teams that aren't used to thinking about cost optimization—like scaling down non-essential services when they're not needed—can find themselves hit with massive bills at the end of the month. It's not just about building a solution; it's about building one that's cost-efficient from day one.

In short, cloud operations are an entirely different beast compared to traditional IT. If our team isn't equipped to deal with this complexity, we're setting ourselves up for a rough ride. Proper planning, training and a deep understanding of the tools at our disposal aren't just *"nice to haves"*—they're critical if we want to succeed in the cloud.

Training and Upskilling

When a business is planning to move to the cloud, it's not as simple as flipping a switch. We need a solid plan that covers everything, from the technical side to getting the whole organization on board. Here's how we do it:

1. **Start with a Cloud Readiness Check**: Before we dive in, we've got to figure out where we stand. A cloud readiness check is all about understanding what we have in our current setup—what can move easily, what might need some work, and what the potential costs and risks are. And it's not just IT that should be involved. Business leaders need to understand how this move could impact their departments—operations, budgets, everything.

    Example: When we did our cloud readiness check, we found some of our legacy systems needed major reworking to even consider running in the cloud. But on the flip side, our databases? They were practically begging for a lift-and-shift, which saved us both time and money from the get-go.

2. **Education and Training for Everyone**: The skills gap is real when it comes to the cloud. Sure, our IT staff will need to get cloud certifications but don't stop there. Finance, marketing, risk teams, and even legal teams need to understand what the cloud means for them—cost structures, compliance, security, and so on. Invest in workshops, training programs, and external consultants to make sure everyone's on the same page.

    Example: We didn't just train IT. Finance learned how cloud billing really works and set up alerts to avoid those nasty surprises at the end of the month. Meanwhile, marketing got a crash course on cloud compliance, making sure they didn't trip over data privacy in our shiny new environment.

3. **Set Clear, Measurable Goals**: We need to know why we're making this move. Are we doing it to cut capital expenditure costs? Improve scalability? Improve on our disaster recovery plan? Whatever our goals are, make them measurable and align them with our business priorities. This way, we will know if we're on track, and our teams will have something concrete to aim for.

    Example: One of our big goals? Cutting infrastructure costs by 30% within the year. We made sure it was tied to the business and tracked it every quarter, holding ourselves accountable to make sure the cloud was pulling its weight.

4. **Build a Solid Migration Strategy**: Once we've got our goals set, we need a strategy that outlines how we're going to get there. What's the approach—lift and shift, re-platform, or something else? Who's responsible for what? Do we go with a single cloud, multi-cloud, or hybrid model? These are the decisions that will shape our migration. Make sure our strategy accounts for things like vendor lock-in, interoperability, and security.

   Example: Our migration strategy wasn't a one-size-fits-all. We started with a phased approach, lifting and shifting non-critical apps while re-platforming the core services to tap into cloud-native features like auto-scaling. We also kept one eye on the future by planning a multi-cloud approach to avoid vendor lock-in.

5. **Communication is Key**: This isn't just an IT project—it's a shift for the entire business. We need to keep everyone in the loop. Explain why we're moving to the cloud and how it's going to benefit the business. Regular updates can help avoid resistance and ensure everyone knows what's coming and how it affects them.

   Example: Every two weeks, we ran company-wide updates, explaining where we were in the migration and what was coming next. This open dialogue helped reduce resistance and kept everyone on the same page, no surprises, just progress.

6. **Set Up Governance and Compliance Early**: The cloud gives us flexibility, but without the right governance, things can spiral. Set up policies from the start to define who can access resources, how data is handled, and how everything is monitored. Get our legal, compliance, and security teams involved early to make sure everything is in line with regulations.

   Example: We got the legal team involved early, working side by side with IT to set up access policies and make sure data handling met specific client required standards. Regular audits were built into the process so compliance was baked in as we scaled.

7. **Test Everything**: Before we flip the switch, make sure we've tested everything—performance, security, backup and recovery processes. Run pilots or proof of concept projects to iron out any kinks before the full migration. This is our chance to catch potential issues, so don't skip it.

   Example: Before we pulled the trigger on migrating our customer-facing app, we ran it in parallel with our on-prem system for a month. That gave us time to iron out a few latency kinks and ensure everything was solid before switching users over.

8. **Post-Migration Support**: The work doesn't end when we've moved our data or apps. We will need a plan for ongoing support—monitoring, cost optimization, and troubleshooting. Make sure we've got a team or partner ready to handle the day-to-day cloud management and keep things running smoothly.

   Example: After the migration, we had a cloud operations team ready to go, handling monitoring and troubleshooting. Automated cost alerts were set up to catch any spikes, and a weekly review kept us in check, making sure our environment stayed optimized.

In short, moving to the cloud requires more than just technical planning. It's about getting the whole business on board, setting clear goals, and having a solid strategy in place. If we cover all our bases, we will make the transition smooth and avoid surprises down the line.

Collaborative learning is key

In summary, encouraging collaboration is key to closing the skills gap and keeping our team sharp. Set up internal training sessions, invest in cloud certifications, and make sure documentation is easy to access and up to date. When everyone shares knowledge and works together, we will avoid the bottlenecks and confusion that can come from working in silos. Make sure the whole team is moving forward with the same understanding—it'll pay off in the long run.

In the next section, we will discuss how your team should be working together to form the appropriate disaster recovery plans and ensure your data is backed up safely.

Inadequate Disaster Recovery & Backup Plans

Disaster recovery (**DR**) often gets pushed to the back burner in cloud operations, with many businesses thinking their cloud provider will handle it all. But that's a dangerous assumption. While cloud providers offer some built-in redundancy, the responsibility for disaster recovery falls on you. Without a solid DR plan that's regularly tested, we're opening the door to massive downtime and potential data loss. We can't just hope our cloud setup will bounce back after a failure, we need a clear, tested strategy in place.

We'll walk through the essential components of building a comprehensive disaster recovery and backup plan, the critical difference between **Recovery Point Objective** (**RPO**) and **Recovery Time Objective** (**RTO**), and strategies for tackling data loss, instance failures, and availability zone outages. The goal is to ensure our systems can bounce back faster and keep running, even when things go wrong.

Building a Comprehensive Backup Plan

Our DR strategy isn't just a nice-to-have; it's essential to keeping our business running when things go sideways. We need to think beyond basic backups and start building redundancies across multiple regions. Use cloud native tools like AWS Elastic Disaster Recovery, Azure Site Recovery, or GCP Backup & Restore to ensure that if one region fails, our services can seamlessly switch to another. Think about failover mechanisms, automatic scaling, and how fast we can get critical systems back online.

There are many considerations to be made when formulating a comprehensive backup plan.

RPO vs RTO

Firstly, let's start with the definition of both terms:

- **Recovery Point Objective (RPO):** This is the maximum amount of data loss that we can sustain in the event of some sort of failure. Ask yourself, *"how much data can my business afford to lose?"*.

    A retail store can probably afford to have a high RPO. That is, in the event of a failure, they can support a data loss going back to the previous day's close of business.

    A financial institution, on the other hand, cannot afford the loss of data and needs the RPO to be as low as possible, into the minutes, or even zero in some cases.

- **Recovery Time Objective (RTO):** This is the maximum amount of time that can elapse whilst we are restoring our environment.

  Ask ourselves, "How much business do I want to lose in the event of a failure?". And really, we don't want to lose any but in the event of a failure, time is a factor.

  Looking back at our two examples above, a retail store that may trade Monday - Friday, 9:00 am until 5:00 pm may be able to sustain an RTO of 24 - 48 hours (about 2 days). After all, system failures only happen on a Friday afternoon right, just as we're about to go for a relaxing weekend? Joking aside, in our retail example, a large RTO can be absorbed.

  Our financial institution, on the other hand, will need a very low RTO, in some cases lower than an hour.

There are many ways we can build on our RPO and RTO strategy:

- Customer **Service Level Agreements (SLA)** / **Service Level Objectives (SLO)**
- Technical objectives and constraints
- Industry-level compliance and regulatory requirements

However, it would not be recommended to decide our disaster recovery plan on just one of these factors. It's important to ensure that all three factors are considered in a collaborative approach.

- The Customer SLA / SLO's are decided at a high level and placed into contracts by executives and sales representatives. However, these cannot be honored if the technical objectives are not aligned.

- The technical team can set up a disaster recovery plan and configure backup plans, however, these cannot be effective without a set of clear goals. There may also be technical constraints binding the technical team from delivering the correct result.

- The technical and executive teams also need to be across industry-level requirements for fear of commercial penalties or loss of certain accreditations.

Collaboration is key to building a comprehensive, clear, concise disaster recovery plan.

Disaster Recovery Strategy

Having a DR plan is only half the battle, testing it is where the real work begins. We can't just set it and forget it. Run regular disaster recovery drills and simulate outages to see how our team and infrastructure respond. Test our backups, run failover scenarios, and make sure everything works as expected. It's better to find out now that something's broken rather than when an actual disaster hits. If our backups are out of date or corrupted, we will be in for a nasty surprise when we need them most.

It's important to ensure that we are planned and practiced across some of the most common scenarios. Testing disaster recovery strategies are critical for making sure our workloads can bounce back when things go wrong. It's not just about having a plan—it's about reducing downtime and getting everything back online faster when issues hit. Consider the following three main scenarios and ask yourself the rhetorical question of, *"How am I going to recover from this?"* as you form your strategy:

Accidental data loss

If someone drops the wrong table in the database or a customer record is corrupted in production, how do we recover the data? Data loss isn't just constrained to databases either. Think about object storage in Amazon S3, Azure BLOB Storage or Google Cloud Storage. What about file storage on server-attached volumes such as Amazon EBS, Azure Disk Storage, or a Google Persistent Disk?

For databases, we need to consider some level of **Point In Time Restore** (**PITR**). This can help protect against accidents, deletes, or writes on our database, allowing us to restore to a particular point in time, to a granularity of minutes. PITR uses database features such as transaction logs within the relevant database technology to achieve this.

Enabling PITR on our database can bring our RPO down to as minimal as possible, in the range of 0 - 15 minutes, depending on the choice of database engine.

For object storage, protecting against accidental deletion or writing of data has a simple but powerful setup. Enabling versioning on our object store and enabling multi-factor authentication on deletion of objects are just two ways to protect our data. If someone accidentally overwrites a copy of our object, we can revert to the previous version. This has a very similar effect to PITR with databases, lowering our RPO for object store to practically zero.

Block storage is far more difficult to protect than objects or databases. As it's a block system based on snapshots in time, we're restricted to just what's available in the last snapshot in time. For this reason, it would be recommended to offload persistent data into managed shared data services such as Amazon EFS or FSX, Azure Files, or Google Cloud File Store. These act in a similar way to NAS devices attached to our servers which can then be backed up separately with more granular backup policies. Block storage should only be used for ephemeral applications.

Instance Loss

Within your architecture, you probably have a number of compute or database instances. This section applies to any of the below instances, but is not limited to:

- Amazon Web Services

  - EC2 Instances

  - ECS Containers

  - EKS Nodes

  - Lambda Functions

  - RDS Instances

- Microsoft Azure

  - Virtual Machine

  - Kubernetes Service (AKS)

  - Container Instances (ACI)

  - Azure Functions

  - Azure Database

- Google Cloud Platform

  - Compute Engine Instances

  - Kubernetes Engine (GKE) Nodes

  - Cloud Run Containers

  - Cloud Functions

  - Google Cloud SQL

Consider in our architecture what happens when any of these items go down.

It's always a good idea to plan this in detail. Draw out the architecture in a diagram and start to consider what happens if we take out a single resource. What's the impact on our architecture? Do we have a single point of failure?

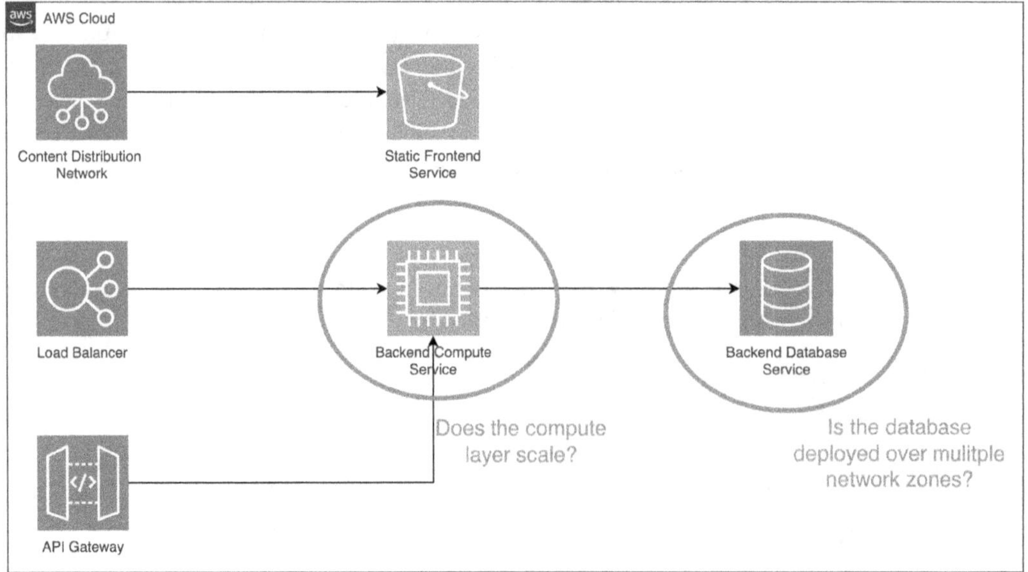

Figure 11.1-Reviewing an architecture for single points of failure

For most compute-level services there are a couple of simple but effective ways of protecting against the loss of an instance.

- **Load Balancing**: By placing a Load Balancer in front of our workload, we can take advantage of many features that can help protect our workload.

  - Separating load across multiple instances.

  - SSL offloading

  - Edge-level network protection (WAF, DDoS protection, etc)

  By using a load balancer, even in a single instance situation, we are shielding our instance from direct internet traffic, applying protection in layers.

- **Auto Scaling Groups**: If our service is ephemeral by design then placing it into an auto scaling group can really help our disaster recovery efforts. An auto scaling group (provided by Amazon EC2 Auto Scaling, Azure Virtual Machine Scale Sets, Google Compute Engine Autoscaler) can add an extra instance as required should our instance become overwhelmed with load. It can also monitor the health of our instance whilst it's launched and then in the event it is considered unhealthy, will replace it with a fresh instance providing a level of auto-healing.

  Like the load balancer, using an autoscaling group, even in a single instance environment, can provide essential protection.

Combining both services together can provide a strategy that can apply our workload across multiple network subnets or availability zones.

For database instances, this should be less complicated. Most managed database instances can be protected:

- **AWS RDS**: Uses multi-AZ configurations to automatically replicate our database across multiple Availability Zones for high availability and automatic failover.

- **Azure SQL Database**: Offers Zone Redundant Configurations to replicate data across Availability Zones, ensuring resilience and high availability. For more advanced setups, we've got geo-replication and failover groups with Azure SQL Managed Instance and Azure Database for MySQL/PostgreSQL.

- **Google Cloud SQL**: Provides high availability configurations by replicating our database across multiple zones within a region. If one zone goes down, failover kicks in automatically. For distributed workloads, Cloud Spanner and Bigtable offer built-in replication across zones and even regions for global resilience.

Each provider has its own approach to multi-zone and multi-region setups, but the goal's the same: *keeping our databases running even when things go sideways.*

Availability Zone failure

The third and final type of scenario to be considered is the major failure without the local data center or provider.

> **Global Cloud Infrastructure Explained**
>
> **Amazon Web Services (AWS)**: AWS has Regions, which are geographically separated areas, and each region has multiple Availability Zones (AZs). These AZs are isolated data centers that give us high availability and redundancy.
>
> **Google Cloud (GCP)**: GCP follows a similar setup with Regions that are geographically distinct, and inside those regions, we've got Zones, which work just like AWS's AZs. Each zone is its own isolated location for failover and redundancy.
>
> **Microsoft Azure**: Azure also has Regions and Availability Zones (AZs), just like AWS and GCP, to ensure our workloads stay resilient. But Azure also adds something called Availability Sets. These help us spread our VMs across different hardware clusters within a data center, giving us an extra layer of protection against localized failures.

When we're building our architecture, we will need to consider how we spread the workload across varying locations. Ensuring that we have at least the ability to fail over to another Zone / AZ is important and some services account for this in their feature sets.

Database services allow for Multi-AZ or Redundant zone configurations. This means that if a zone fails our database will fail over within the shortest possible time. This is an optional configuration and often has cost implications, but the cost is to cover the extra instances that are configured in the background and then replicated in real-time. In most cases, this is a transparent configuration, once the option is selected, it then just happens and is often easy to take for granted and consider disabling to save costs. This is the insurance policy we didn't know we needed and sometimes didn't realize got utilized, as there are many reasons to use Multi-AZ configurations.

- Automatic failover of an AZ

- Less downtime during configuration changes by applying them to the standby instance first and then switching over

- The ability to take backups without impacting the performance of the primary node by taking them from the standby instances

Other options to consider for databases could be a read replica instance instead. This is an instance that we would purposefully configure and use as a read-only data source for things like Business Intelligence reporting or backups, or maybe even customer access. These can be promoted to primary nodes in the event of a failure, so it makes sense to run our read replica in another AZ/Zone too.

For compute instance types, the methods discussed in instance loss are generally the same for AZ/Zone failure. Just make sure we configure our Load Balancers and Scaling groups to be spread across 2 or more Zones. This will ensure they are highly available and don't create a single point of failure.

Wrapping up Disaster Recovery and Backup

In short, disaster recovery is something we can't afford to leave unplanned or untested. It's about more than just data backups—it's ensuring that when things fail, our services can recover quickly and seamlessly. By focusing on a comprehensive strategy that covers RPO, RTO, and multi-zone redundancy, we will be far better prepared to handle any disaster that comes our way.

Whilst a disaster recovery plan is important, it's also just as important to ensure you have up to date runbooks and documentation available for your team at the right time. We go into that in more detail in the next section.

Out-of-Date Runbooks and Documentation

Cloud environments evolve at breakneck speed. Infrastructure changes, new services are added, scaling happens on the fly, and security updates roll out frequently. With so much in motion, it's easy for documentation and runbooks to fall out of date. When that happens, we open the door to operational inefficiencies, miscommunication, and mistakes during critical moments. Outdated documentation can lead teams down the wrong path when troubleshooting, wasting time, and possibly causing even bigger problems. Keeping runbooks and documentation up to date is crucial to maintaining smooth operations and ensuring everyone is on the same page when issues arise.

Through this section, we will review the main best practices for ensuring we maintain maximum operational efficiency by looking after our documentation and runbooks. We will review both the concept of and then some practical steps we can take to help keep things well documented.

Maintaining Updated Documentation

Documentation isn't something we write once and forget about, it's a living, breathing asset that needs regular care. As infrastructure changes happen, whether it's new deployments, scaling, or changes in architecture, our runbooks and documentation should reflect those updates immediately. When documentation is out of sync with the current environment, teams are more likely to follow outdated procedures, which can lead to slow incident response times or, worse, operational failures.

One of the best ways to manage this is by setting up a documentation review schedule, tied directly to key operational events. After every major infrastructure update, teams should review relevant runbooks and technical documents to ensure they align with the current setup. This review process can be built into change management procedures, ensuring that updates to our infrastructure automatically trigger documentation reviews. It's about creating a habit of continuous review and alignment across teams to avoid confusion down the line.

Another more engaging method of ensuring that documentation is up to scratch is to utilize a "Game Day". This could be considered a tabletop exercise or even fictional scenarios that are played out in a safe environment. *Chapter 8* references Game Day's in more detail.

> **Important note**
>
> Implementing ISO 9001 can greatly enhance the process of keeping runbooks, SOPs, and documentation up to date in cloud environments. By focusing on document control, regular reviews, and continuous improvement through the Plan-Do-Check-Act (PDCA) cycle, ISO 9001 ensures consistency and accountability. With its emphasis on risk-based thinking and audits, it helps mitigate the risks of outdated documentation, aligning well with automation tools like AWS CloudFormation and Azure ARM Templates to streamline updates and maintain accuracy.
>
> ISO 9001 is an international standard for quality management systems (QMS). It provides a framework for organizations to ensure that their processes consistently meet customer and regulatory requirements. Focused on improving efficiency and maintaining high-quality standards, ISO 9001 emphasizes principles like customer focus, leadership, risk-based thinking, continuous improvement, and document control, making it a valuable tool for ensuring reliable, repeatable outcomes across any industry.

Automating Documentation

Manual documentation updates? That's a fast track to disaster. In fast-moving cloud environments, manual updates just won't cut it. When someone comes to fix an incident, that's time critical, they need to understand why the architecture is in the current state it is, before trying to fix something that may make things worse. That's where automation comes in. Tools like AWS CloudFormation, Azure ARM templates, and GCP Deployment Manager automatically keep our documentation in sync with infrastructure changes, cutting down on human error and ensuring we're always working with up-to-date information.

Take AWS CloudFormation, for example. When we use CloudFormation templates to manage our infrastructure, the templates themselves serve as a form of documentation, showing exactly how our resources are configured. Similarly, Azure ARM templates and GCP Deployment Manager perform the same function. These tools generate real-time infrastructure updates, and by using them, we ensure that our documentation is never lagging.

Automating documentation also reduces the human error that comes with manual updates. As our cloud infrastructure grows in complexity, keeping track of every change manually becomes unmanageable. Automation tools help us streamline this process and keep our documentation accurate, up to date, and aligned with our current infrastructure.

Standard Operating Procedures (SOPs)

Our **Standard Operating Procedures** (**SOPs**) are critical to keeping our cloud environment running efficiently, but they are only as good as their relevance. Like runbooks, SOPs should not be written once and forgotten—they need to evolve alongside our infrastructure and workflows. This is especially true in cloud environments where rapid changes to architecture or services can render old procedures obsolete.

A regular SOP review process is essential. Every time our cloud architecture evolves, whether it's new services being deployed or scaling changes, our SOPs should be revisited to ensure they are still relevant. Procedures that were effective when we were managing a smaller infrastructure might no longer apply as we scale up. Regularly reviewing and updating SOPs ensures that our teams are working with the most current information and can execute tasks quickly and efficiently.

Also, when updating SOPs, make sure to include any lessons learned from incidents or outages. If a failure occurs because of a procedural gap or oversight, update our SOPs to prevent that from happening again. SOPs aren't just about handling day-to-day operations, they reflect our organization's continuous improvement process.

> **Important note**
>
> The AWS Well-Architected Framework was born out of lessons learned from a large-scale outage, where early cloud adopters faced significant challenges in designing resilient, scalable architectures.
>
> The AWS Well-Architected Framework constitutes a set of documented best practices (or SOPs) to get the most out of our cloud architecture.

Let's look at this more practically.

Documentation and Runbooks in practical terms

So, we've talked about the common principles around documentation and SOPs, but what practical steps can we take in order to ensure we are following best practices around documentation? What technical guidance can we follow?

- Implement Infrastructure-as-Code (IaC)

  - **Tooling**: Use tools like AWS CloudFormation, Azure ARM Templates, and Google Cloud Deployment Manager to define and manage our infrastructure as code. These tools automatically create templates that serve as live documentation for our environment.

  - **Version Control**: Store these templates in version control systems such as Git to track all infrastructure changes over time, allowing for easy rollback if necessary and providing an accurate record of changes.

  - **Benefits**: Infrastructure-as-Code keeps our documentation aligned with the current state of our infrastructure and eliminates the need for manual updates.

- Automate Documentation Updates

  - **Tooling**: Integrate tools like Terraform Cloud or CloudFormation Drift Detection to automatically detect changes in our infrastructure and update our documentation in real-time.

- **Scripts**: Set up automated scripts that pull changes from infrastructure and update documentation in platforms like Confluence or SharePoint.

- **Benefits**: Automation ensures our documentation is always current without relying on manual processes, reducing the likelihood of outdated information causing errors.

- Use Monitoring and Alerting Systems

  - **Tooling**: Leverage AWS CloudWatch, Azure Monitor, or Google Cloud Operations Suite to monitor infrastructure health and changes.

  - **Automation**: Automatically trigger reviews of documentation when infrastructure changes or alerts are detected. This can be tied into our IT service management (ITSM) tools like ServiceNow or Jira.

  - **Benefits**: Continuous monitoring ensures that teams are aware of any critical changes in infrastructure, providing a chance to proactively update documentation or SOPs as needed.

- Centralized Knowledge Management

  - **Tooling**: Implement centralized documentation tools such as Confluence, Notion, or Azure DevOps Wiki to store and organize all runbooks, SOPs, and technical documentation in one place.

  - **Searchable Database**: Ensure that all documentation is easily searchable and accessible to teams.

  - **Benefits**: Centralizing documentation ensures all teams are referencing the same up-to-date information, which reduces confusion and miscommunication during operations.

- Embed Documentation into Change Management

  - **Change Management**: Ensure every infrastructure change includes a review of the associated documentation, so updates happen as part of the change process. This can also be useful to ensure there is no unintentional drift from the original design.

  - **Ownership**: Assign responsibility for documentation updates to specific team members to create accountability.

  - **Benefits**: Embedding documentation into change management ensures that no change is made without the necessary updates to runbooks and SOPs, preventing misalignment between infrastructure and documentation.

Keeping runbooks, documentation, and SOPs up to date is about more than just following best practices. It's about avoiding costly mistakes, reducing downtime, and ensuring that our teams can respond effectively in real-time when things go wrong. In cloud environments, where things change rapidly, outdated documentation is a ticking time bomb that can lead to slow responses, confusion, and even failure to resolve critical issues.

By regularly reviewing and automating updates to our documentation, we're not only improving operational efficiency but also making sure that our teams have the right information at their fingertips when they need it most. It's an investment in resilience, agility, and long-term cloud success.

Runbooks and documentation should start to form part of your culture as you shift to the cloud, ignoring this could be devasting to your cloud adoption efforts. We talk more about the cultural shift in the next section.

Ignoring the Cultural Shift

Operating in the cloud isn't just about adopting shiny new tech—it's about getting teams to work together in a whole new way. Too many organizations dive headfirst into cloud projects, thinking it's all about the tools, but the real challenge lies in changing the way people collaborate. If we're not encouraging cross-functional teamwork, our cloud strategy is going to hit a wall fast. Success in the cloud hinges not only on infrastructure but also on embracing a fundamental shift in how teams interact, share knowledge, and align their efforts to a common goal.

In this section, we'll get a clear understanding of why collaboration is key to making the cloud work. We'll learn how breaking down silos and getting dev, ops, and security teams working together can prevent mistakes and speed things up. We'll also dive into why cross-functional teams and a DevSecOps mindset are essential for improving efficiency and security. Plus, we'll talk about the importance of knowledge sharing and keeping everyone in the loop as our cloud setup evolves. Lastly, we'll see how to manage resistance to change and make sure our shift to the cloud is smooth and effective.

Encouraging Collaboration

Cloud environments thrive when teams are talking to each other. In traditional IT setups, development, operations, and security are often siloed. Developers push code, ops handle infrastructure, and security keeps an eye on vulnerabilities—everyone's in their own bubble. But in the cloud, we can't afford that kind of separation. Dev, Ops, and Security must always be in sync. Open those lines of communication and ensure these teams are working together from the start.

Why is this so important? Cloud environments are dynamic, and things change fast. Code gets deployed quicker, resources scale up or down, and security threats evolve constantly. If our teams aren't collaborating, one group can make changes that might inadvertently cause issues for another. A developer might introduce new code that inadvertently weakens security. The operations team might roll out changes without knowing how they affect the overall infrastructure. When teams are isolated, these changes can slip through the cracks, leading to inefficiencies, downtime, or worse—security breaches.

Collaboration isn't just a "nice to have." It's the backbone of effective cloud operations. Teams need to break down barriers and work as a unit, aligning around shared objectives. One of the most effective ways to foster this kind of collaboration is through regular check-ins, cross-team meetings, and collaborative problem-solving sessions. By creating these open lines of communication, we're giving the teams the space to discuss issues early, share knowledge, and catch problems before they become major headaches.

Breaking Down Silos

Silos within an organization are a major barrier to collaboration. In the traditional IT world, it's common for teams to have rigidly defined roles and responsibilities. Development teams focus on writing code, operations teams handle the deployment and maintenance of infrastructure, and security teams monitor for threats and vulnerabilities. While this division of labor made sense in the era of on-premises infrastructure, it doesn't align with the flexibility and speed of cloud environments.

In the cloud, we need everyone working together throughout the lifecycle of a project. The development team can't just throw code over the wall to operations and walk away. Security can't afford to stay out of the loop until the end of the process. Cloud environments require constant coordination. The flexibility and scale that the cloud offers are great, but they also increase complexity—and with complexity comes risk. Silos only compound these risks because they lead to miscommunication, disjointed workflows, and duplication of effort.

So how do we break down these silos? Start by fostering a DevSecOps culture, where development, security, and operations work together from day one. The key here is shared responsibility. Each team should understand how their work impacts the broader system and how they can contribute to a shared goal. We can also implement more formal processes like integrated project management systems and regular cross-functional team meetings. Breaking down silos takes time, but once teams start collaborating more closely, we'll see fewer bottlenecks, faster problem resolution, and a much smoother cloud operation.

> **Think back - Conway's Law**
>
> As we dive into breaking down silos and pushing for more collaboration across teams, it's worth keeping Conway's Law in mind (which we covered back in Chapter 1). This idea reminds us that the way our teams communicate will directly shape how our systems turn out. If we're not working together as one, our cloud architecture is going to reflect those gaps. So, getting development, ops, and security on the same page isn't just a nice-to-have, it's essential if we want to build systems that are truly resilient.

Cross-Functional Teams

The creation of cross-functional teams is one of the most effective ways to promote collaboration in cloud operations. These teams bring together members from development, operations, and security, ensuring that all aspects of the project are covered right from the start. No more waiting until the last minute for the security team to weigh in on vulnerabilities, or for ops to figure out how to scale a new deployment. Everyone is involved from day one, which leads to better alignment, faster decision-making, and fewer surprises down the road.

Cross-functional teams aren't just about getting things done faster—they're about doing them better. Each team member brings their unique expertise to the table, and by working together, they can address challenges more holistically. For instance, developers know the code, but they may not be aware of the infrastructure limitations. Ops knows how to scale, but they might not understand the security implications of certain configurations. Security understands vulnerabilities but may not be aware of the newest development frameworks. By combining these perspectives, we create a more resilient, well-rounded cloud operation.

This approach also fosters a DevSecOps mindset, which is key to cloud success. DevSecOps is all about continuous integration and continuous delivery (CI/CD), where development and operations work hand-in-hand to automate and streamline deployments. This mindset eliminates the friction between development and deployment, making it easier to roll out updates and reduce downtime. Security needs to be baked into this process from the start, so a DevSecOps approach—where security is integrated into development and operations—is essential for protecting our cloud environment.

Knowledge Sharing

Cloud technology is always evolving, and keeping up can feel like a never-ending race. If our teams aren't sharing knowledge, we'll quickly fall behind. Every new tool, every update to our infrastructure, and every security threat needs to be understood by everyone involved. That's where knowledge sharing comes in.

It's not enough for one person or team to be an expert. Information needs to flow freely between teams so that everyone stays up to speed on what's happening. This can be done through formal channels like training sessions, but it's often more effective to create a culture of informal knowledge sharing. Regular team meetings where people can talk about the challenges they're facing, the new tools they've found, or the lessons they've learned are invaluable.

The cloud is complex, and nobody knows everything. But by encouraging our teams to share what they know, we can build a stronger, more cohesive operation. When one team learns something new, make sure they pass that knowledge on to others. This not only helps the team grow but also ensures that knowledge silos don't form. The more our teams share, the more resilient our cloud operations become.

Promoting a DevSecOps Mindset

The DevSecOps mindset is all about breaking down barriers between development and operations. In a traditional IT setup, these two teams often work in isolation, which can lead to delays, miscommunication, and inefficiencies. However, in a cloud environment, development and operations need to work together continuously. This approach fosters collaboration, improves efficiency, and allows for faster, more reliable deployments.

In a DevSecOps world, developers don't just write code and hand it off to ops—they're responsible for how that code performs in production too. And ops aren't just there to maintain infrastructure—they're involved in the development process to ensure that everything runs smoothly once it's deployed. This shared responsibility helps catch issues earlier and ensures that the entire team is aligned on the goals of the project.

Automation plays a huge role here. By automating repetitive tasks—like testing, deployment, and monitoring—we free up our teams to focus on higher-level problems. Automation also reduces the risk of human error, which is critical in fast-moving cloud environments. When everything is automated, we can move faster and deploy updates more frequently without worrying about things falling through the cracks.

Overcoming Resistance to Change

Even when we know collaboration is essential, it's not always easy to implement. Teams that are used to working in silos might resist the shift toward collaboration. They may feel like it's more work or that their expertise isn't being respected. This resistance is natural, but it needs to be addressed if our cloud strategy is going to succeed.

To overcome resistance to change, we need more than just words—we need to demonstrate the benefits in real time. One of the most effective ways to do this is by rolling out a pilot project. A pilot allows us to test the waters on a smaller scale while showing everyone how cross-functional teams can drive real results. By choosing a key project, we bring development, operations, and security together from day one, breaking down silos and showing how collaboration leads to quicker deployments and fewer headaches down the road.

As we see faster problem resolution and smoother operations, it's easier to get buy-in from the rest of the organization. The beauty of a pilot project is that it's low-risk but high-impact—giving us the evidence we need to prove that working together isn't just more efficient, it's essential for building resilient systems. Once the pilot proves successful, we can expand this approach across more teams, making collaboration the new standard.

Leadership also plays a key role here. Leaders need to set the tone for collaboration, showing that it's not just a passing trend but an essential part of how the organization operates. They need to encourage open communication, provide the necessary tools and support, and be patient as teams adjust to the new way of working. The cultural shift doesn't happen overnight, but with the right approach, it can transform the way our teams operate.

Ignoring the cultural shift when moving to the cloud is one of the biggest mistakes an organization can make. It's not enough to just have the right tools in place, we need our teams to work together seamlessly if we want to succeed in the cloud. Collaboration, cross-functional teams, continuous learning, and a DevSevOps mindset are all crucial to building a resilient cloud operation. Break down silos, foster communication, and make sure everyone is aligned on the same goals. Only then will we unlock the true potential of the cloud and ensure long-term success.

As we bring this chapter to a close, we finally look around some of the pitfalls and misunderstandings around cloud service providers service level agreements and why they should not be your first crutch to lean on.

Developing Around CSP SLAs

Cloud Service Provider (CSP) SLAs might promise high availability, but relying solely on these guarantees can leave us vulnerable. Developing resilient architectures beyond what the SLAs offer is critical for maintaining uptime and ensuring business continuity.

In this section, we'll dive into why relying solely on cloud provider SLAs isn't enough for real resilience. We'll break down how to build redundancy with multi-region deployments, failover systems, and load balancing to keep everything running smoothly, even when the provider hits a bump. We'll learn how to protect our systems with multi-cloud strategies, third-party redundancy, and offsite backups, ensuring our data is safe and our operations stay live. Finally, we'll explore how automating failover, load balancing, and autoscaling gives us an edge, minimizing downtime and keeping our infrastructure responsive without relying on manual fixes.

> **What is a CSP SLA?**
>
> A **Cloud Service Provider** (CSP) SLA is essentially the contract between us and our cloud provider, laying out what kind of performance, availability, and uptime we can expect from their services. It's the provider's way of saying, "Here's what we guarantee," but with plenty of fine print. These agreements typically cover metrics like uptime guarantees, say 99.9% availability, and define the limits of the provider's responsibility. It's important to understand exactly what's in an SLA because anything outside those boundaries becomes our responsibility, not theirs. So, if things go south, we need to know where the line is between their liability and what we're expected to handle.

Building Redundancy Beyond SLAs

Just relying on our cloud provider's SLA isn't enough if we want true resilience. Sure, they promise high availability, but even a 99.9% uptime guarantee still leaves room for downtime, over eight hours a year, in fact. For mission-critical systems, we can't afford to leave it at that. We need to build our own layers of redundancy on top of what the CSP guarantees. That means having backup plans for when things inevitably go wrong because the question isn't if, but when. Redundancy ensures that our systems stay up and running, even when our provider's services aren't living up to their promises.

Here are some key steps on how we can build true redundancy and ensure our systems stay up, even when our provider's SLAs fall short:

- **Deploy Across Multiple Availability Zones**: Start by spreading our resources across multiple availability zones within a single region. This gives us protection against zone-level failures, like hardware issues or localized outages.

- **Go Multi-Region**: Take it a step further by deploying across multiple regions. If one region goes down, our services can automatically failover to another, keeping our global operations running smoothly.

- **Set Up Failover Architectures**: Implement failover systems like hot or cold standbys. These systems kick in automatically when a failure occurs, so we don't lose valuable time trying to fix things manually.

- **Use Load Balancers**: Distribute traffic across multiple instances using load balancers to avoid overloading any one server. If an instance goes down, the load balancer will shift traffic to healthy instances, maintaining service availability.

- **Implement Auto-Scaling**: Use auto-scaling to ensure we always have enough resources. When demand spikes or systems fail, auto-scaling kicks in, adding more instances or resources as needed.

- **Leverage Backups for Critical Data**: Regularly back up data, and store copies in different regions. If the primary storage fails or becomes corrupted, we can quickly restore it from another location without losing vital information.

- **Monitor and Alert Proactively**: Use tools like CloudWatch or Azure Monitor to keep an eye on systems. Set up alerts so we get notified immediately when something goes wrong, allowing for faster response times.

- **Test Failover and Redundancy Plans**: Regularly test failover and redundancy setups. Don't wait for an actual outage to see if systems work, run drills to make sure everything functions as expected when failure happens.

When it comes to building reliable cloud systems, we can't just rely on the provider's SLA and hope for the best. True resilience means layering in our own redundancy, deploying across multiple availability zones, setting up failover systems, and ensuring our infrastructure can handle failures without skipping a beat. By taking these practical steps, load balancing, auto-scaling, multi-region deployments, etc, we are not just reacting to problems, we are proactively building an architecture that can withstand them. The key is to anticipate failure and be ready before it happens. That's how we keep our cloud environment running smoothly, no matter what.

Preparing for Provider Downtime

Even the biggest cloud providers face outages from time to time, and when that happens, we don't want to be caught flat-footed. Preparing for downtime isn't about waiting for something to go wrong, it's about building an architecture that can handle failure and keep running no matter what. This is where multi-cloud architecture, third-party redundancy, and offsite backups come into play. These strategies help ensure that, when our provider experiences downtime, our operations don't.

Multi-Cloud Architecture

Relying solely on one cloud provider is convenient but can sometimes be seen as risky when it comes to requiring a tight set of high availability conditions. With multi-cloud architecture, we end up spreading our resources across multiple cloud providers, think AWS, Azure, and GCP. If one provider goes down, the others can pick up the slack, keeping our services live. The key here is not just duplicating everything across different clouds but designing the applications to be cloud-agnostic, so they can run smoothly on whichever platform is available. It's not a one-size-fits-all approach, but for mission-critical services, it's a safeguard we can't afford to skip.

> **Multi-Cloud Technologies**
>
> When thinking about going multi-cloud, we will need to consider building on frameworks and technologies that are not vendor locked, such as:
>
> Compute: Terraform/OpenToFu, Docker, Kubernetes
>
> Monitoring: Grafana, Prometheus, ELK Stack
>
> Devops: Github actions, Gitlab, Jenkins
>
> Identity: Auth0, Okta
>
> Most database technologies are transferable between Cloud providers, especially those using more open standards like MySQL and postgresql that are not license bound.

Third-Party Redundancy

Another way to protect against provider downtime is by integrating third-party redundancy. This means using external services or vendors to back up critical functions. For example, if our primary cloud provider manages the database, consider using a third-party service to handle backups or key pieces of infrastructure. This way, even if the provider goes down, the data remains secure and accessible. The goal is to reduce reliance on any single vendor so that all critical operations are always covered from multiple angles.

Offsite Backup in Other Cloud / Hybrid Solutions

For ultimate peace of mind, look beyond just one cloud provider and assess the viability of offsite backups in another cloud or a hybrid solution. This is the last line of defense, storing data or essential resources in a different environment altogether. By maintaining backups on a separate cloud provider or even on-premises, we ensure that if our main provider suffers a major outage or loss, our data and systems are still recoverable from a separate location. Hybrid solutions can also come into play here, giving us a mix of on-prem and cloud resources to work with.

The key takeaway? Never rely on just one provider to keep everything running. By implementing a multi-cloud strategy, integrating third-party redundancy, and maintaining offsite backups, we are preparing for the inevitable hiccups in cloud availability. That way, when provider downtime hits, our systems won't even flinch.

Trade Offs

Like any solution or strategy, there are some pros and cons of running a highly available multi-cloud architecture:

Pros	Cons
Increased Resilience and Availability By leveraging multiple cloud providers, we reduce the risk of downtime since a failure in one provider can be mitigated by resources from another.	**Increased Complexity** Managing workloads across multiple providers adds layers of complexity, especially in terms of architecture, monitoring, and security.
Avoid Vendor Lock-In Using multiple cloud platforms prevents us from becoming too dependent on a single provider, giving us more flexibility to switch services or negotiate pricing.	**Higher Learning Curve** Teams need to be proficient in multiple cloud platforms, which can mean additional training and expertise are required.
Optimized Performance We can choose the best provider for specific tasks, optimizing for speed, latency, or other performance metrics based on the strengths of each platform.	**Challenging Integration** Integrating services and ensuring seamless communication between different platforms can be difficult, especially when using cloud native tools that aren't universally compatible.
Cost Management Different providers may offer more competitive pricing for specific services, allowing us to optimize costs by spreading workloads based on pricing models.	**Higher Operational Costs** While multi-cloud may reduce costs in certain areas, the added complexity can increase operational overhead, requiring more tools, staff, and management.
Compliance and Geographic Flexibility Multi-cloud allows us to meet regional compliance requirements by distributing data and services across various geographic locations and providers.	**Latency and Performance Variability** Running applications across multiple clouds may introduce latency or performance issues when services from different providers need to communicate in real-time.

Table 11.1 - Pros and Cons of a Highly Available Multi Cloud Architecture

> **Real-World Example**
>
> By way of example, a popular highly regulated Australian financial institution attempted to balance their architecture across two cloud providers and ended up with a cost factor of 10.4x more than being in a single cloud and, also, created latency issues that impacted their RPO and RTO.
>
> It's important to assess the trade-off in these situations.

Automation for Resilience

Resilience in the cloud isn't just about preparing for the worst, it's about automating key processes, so our systems stay ahead of potential issues. By integrating failover, load balancing, and autoscaling into our architecture, we ensure that services keep running without manual intervention. Here's how we can blend automation with smart architecture choices to build a truly resilient cloud environment.

Automate Failover

When a service or instance goes down, the last thing we want is to scramble for a fix. Automating failover allows traffic to reroute seamlessly, minimizing downtime and keeping things running smoothly.

- **Health checks for proactive monitoring**: Services like AWS Route 53 health checks, Azure Traffic Manager, and Google Cloud Load Balancer continuously monitor the health of critical endpoints.

  These tools detect when a service is down and automatically reroutes traffic to healthy instances. This instant failover means no disruption in service, something manual intervention can't guarantee.

  We should set up health checks for all mission-critical services. For example, configuring Route 53 in AWS to reroute traffic to a backup instance if the primary fails. Regularly testing these checks ensures they're working as expected.

- **Automated DNS failover**: Leveraging DNS failover ensures that traffic automatically shifts to backup regions or resources when issues arise.

  Automated failover keeps traffic flowing, even if an entire region goes offline. Instead of manually switching DNS records during an outage, automation reroutes traffic instantly.

  Setting up DNS failover policies that shift traffic to backup resources when needed. In AWS, we can configure weighted routing policies in Route 53 to distribute traffic evenly between primary and secondary resources.

Load Balancing and Autoscaling

Balancing traffic and scaling resources automatically is crucial for preventing overloads and maintaining performance during spikes in demand. Let's unpack each option:

- **Load balancing for seamless traffic distribution**: Load balancers, such as Elastic Load Balancing (ELB) in AWS, Azure Load Balancer, and Google Cloud Load Balancer, spread traffic across multiple instances to ensure no single instance is overwhelmed.

  By distributing traffic, load balancers keep systems running smoothly, even during high-traffic periods. They prevent bottlenecks and ensure better availability by routing requests to healthy instances.

  We should implement load balancers in our cloud architecture. For example, configuring AWS ELB to distribute traffic across multiple availability zones. This way, if one instance goes down, traffic is automatically routed to another.

- **Autoscaling for dynamic resource management**: Autoscaling ensures that resources adjust to demand, scaling up during traffic spikes and scaling down during quieter periods.

  Autoscaling optimizes both performance and cost-efficiency. When demand increases, it automatically adds resources to handle the load. When things calm down, it scales back to avoid unnecessary costs.

Setting up autoscaling rules based on traffic or resource thresholds. In AWS, configuring Auto Scaling Groups to add instances when CPU usage exceeds a certain percentage. Regularly reviewing these thresholds ensures they align with our actual needs.

Why Automation is Key for Resilience

Automation gives us a proactive edge. By setting up failover and autoscaling in advance, we ensure that systems react instantly to issues, minimizing downtime.

Automated systems can detect issues and reroute traffic or scale resources instantly. This not only reduces the risk of human error but also ensures that the response time is faster than any manual fix.

Autoscaling helps manage costs by only using the resources needed, while load balancing prevents performance issues by evenly distributing traffic.

By automating failover, load balancing, and autoscaling, we build a resilient cloud architecture that handles challenges in real time. The combination of proactive monitoring, automatic traffic distribution, and dynamic resource management ensures our systems stay responsive and efficient, no matter what happens.

Summary

In this chapter, we took a deep dive into the operational challenges of managing cloud environments and learned how to keep systems running smoothly under pressure. We covered everything from breaking down cloud provider SLAs to building resilience with multi-region deployments, failover setups, and automated scaling. We also looked at the value of proactive planning, redundancy, and automation to cut downtime and keep the business ticking. Along the way, we explored how to handle provider outages, keep documentation up to date, and adapt to the cultural shifts that cloud operations demand. Now, we're equipped with the strategies and tools needed to keep our cloud infrastructure resilient and reliable.

In the next chapter, we will be looking at migration strategies from on premise architecture to the cloud and even from one cloud provider to another and the risks of not addressing cloud security in a cloud native way.

Get This Book's PDF Version and Exclusive Extras

UNLOCK NOW

Scan the QR code (or go to `packtpub.com/unlock`). Search for this book by name, confirm the edition, and then follow the steps on the page.

Note: Keep your invoice handly. Purchase made directly from packt don't require one.

12

Migrating from Legacy Systems to Cloud Native Solutions

In this chapter, we're going to dive into how cloud migrations can go off the rails, and more importantly, how to steer clear of those traps. We'll break down the most common mistakes that lead to cloud adoption failures, like jumping in without a solid strategy, lack of buy-in from key stakeholders, and trying to force outdated on-prem security practices into the cloud.

Here's what we'll cover:

- How to craft a clear migration strategy that aligns with your business goals, so you're not just moving workloads but actually adding value.

- The critical role of stakeholder engagement throughout the cloud journey, ensuring everyone is on the same page and committed to success.

- Why on-prem security practices don't translate to the cloud, and how to shift to cloud native security models that fit today's dynamic environments.

- How to identify and close skill gaps, making sure your team is equipped for a smooth and efficient transition.

By the end of this chapter, you'll have a roadmap for avoiding the pitfalls that can sabotage cloud migrations and be better prepared for a seamless move to the cloud.

Planning for an effective migration

One of the biggest reasons cloud migrations hit roadblocks or fail entirely is the lack of a clear strategy and proper planning. Too many businesses dive in headfirst without considering the full scope, leading to confusion, unexpected costs, and inefficiencies. A successful migration requires careful thought and alignment with business goals right from the start.

In this section, we'll start by discussing why a solid migration plan is essential to keep things on track. We'll explore how setting clear priorities for applications, choosing the right cloud platform, and deciding on a treatment approach—whether it's lift-and-shift or a complete re-architecture—can make all the difference. By understanding these foundational elements, we can approach migration with clarity, focus, and a stronger chance of success.

Jumping in Without a Plan: Why planning is important

A common mistake seen time and again is treating cloud migration like a quick fix for aging infrastructure. Teams often rush the process, assuming they can just move applications or whole servers to the cloud without much thought. This lack of planning leads to:

- Applications are not being optimized for the cloud environment.

- Misaligned workloads with the right cloud services.

- Unanticipated costs due to poor resource scaling.

- Unrealized return on investment due to not leveraging cloud native services.

- Failure to address compliance and security requirements early on.

- Each of these can be a root cause of increased operational costs, delays in migration and cloud adoption and even degraded performance of workload.

- Without proper planning, we can find ourselves in a tangled mess, a patchwork cloud setup that's inefficient, expensive, and prone to failure. It's the classic case of *"act in haste, repent at leisure."*

Developing a Clear Migration Strategy

The key to a successful cloud migration starts with a rock-solid strategy. Shifting to the cloud isn't just about moving workloads; it's a major shift that needs careful planning and a clear direction. Without a strong plan, the process can quickly spiral into unexpected costs, delays, and unnecessary complexity. This section dives into what it takes to build a migration strategy that aligns with business goals and keeps your team focused. From assessing your current setup to choosing the right cloud model, we'll cover the foundational steps that set you up for a smooth, future-ready migration

Assessing Your Current Environment

Before anything else, get a handle on what you're working with. Identify critical applications, dependencies, and integrations. Figure out what can be retired and what needs significant reworking. Don't forget to look at network dependencies and latency needs too.

To properly assess our current environment, we will need to leverage cloud migration assessment tools from the cloud provider of choice or a third party. For example:

- AWS Migration Evaluator can help us break down the on-prem infrastructure by mapping workloads, dependencies, and integrations. It'll give a detailed cost analysis and show us how things might look in the AWS environment.

- Similarly, Azure Migrate can map out the dependencies and network interactions, showing what's cloud-ready and where potential latency issues might crop up.

- Google Cloud's Migrate for Compute Engine works in much the same way, giving insights into VMs, apps, and the infrastructure, making sure we have a clear path for each workload.

Using one of these tools provides a detailed breakdown of critical applications, how they interact, and any network or latency requirements. This kind of visibility allows us to make more informed decisions about what can be retired, reworked, or kept as-is, helping avoid the common pitfalls that often cause migrations to fail.

In each of the above cases the output should provide you with a useful list of assets to be migrated and the resources they may require. Below shows a sample of this data, not limited nor an exhaustive list:

HostName	CPU Cores	OS	OS.Version	RAM Total
app-server01.local	4	Windows Server 2019	1809	8192
linux-db01.local	4	Ubuntu 20.04	Focal Fossa	16384
mssql-db01.local	8	Windows Server 2016	1607	32768
app-server02.local	2	Windows Server 2019	1809	8192
backup-server.local	4	Windows Server 2012 R2	9600	8192
web-server01.local	2	RHEL 8	Ootpa	4096
dev-server.local	4	Windows 10 Pro	21H1	16384
linux-app01.local	2	CentOS 7	Core	8192
storage-server.local	16	Windows Server 2019	1809	65536
dns-server.local	1	Ubuntu 18.04	Bionic Beaver	2048
mail-server.local	4	Windows Server 2016	1607	8192
log-server.local	8	Ubuntu 22.04	Jammy Jellyfish	16384

Table 12.1 - Migration Assessment Data

Prioritizing Applications: Using a Lighthouse

We don't have to move everything all at once. The smart move is to prioritize applications based on their business impact, how easy they are to migrate, and what will gain the most from the cloud. We start with the low-hanging fruit, those simpler applications, and as we get more comfortable, we take on the more complex ones. We sometimes refer to this concept as a *"Lighthouse"*.

> **Choosing a lighthouse**
>
> A lighthouse application is your first step in proving the value of cloud adoption. It's a smaller, low-risk app that sets the tone for everything else. When picking one, go for something important enough to show real impact, but not so complex that it bogs down your team. The perfect lighthouse app is easy to migrate, clearly benefits from cloud native features like auto-scaling or serverless and gives you a quick win to build momentum. It's all about starting smart, setting the foundation for larger, more complex moves later on.

Not every workload needs the same approach, and grouping them by size, "small," "medium," and "large"—helps us streamline planning and resource allocation. T-shirt sizing gives us a quick, practical way to categorize workloads based on complexity and migration effort.

- Small Workloads

  These are simple, low-impact applications that can be easily lifted and shifted. Ideal for early migrations, they require minimal changes and can help build momentum quickly.

- Medium Workloads

  Applications here might need some re-platforming or tweaking to perform optimally in the cloud. They tend to have specific latency or integration requirements and benefit from a bit more planning.

- Large Workloads

  Large, mission-critical applications usually require significant re-architecture to fully leverage cloud benefits. Their migrations are phased in and involve detailed planning to ensure alignment with business needs.

By sizing workloads upfront, we gain clarity on resources, timelines, and dependencies, allowing us to focus on quick wins while preparing for more complex migrations in a manageable way.

By leveraging tools like AWS Application Discovery Service or Azure Migrate's Assessment, we can automate the process of figuring out which workloads are ready for the cloud and which will need more work. These tools give us a clear view of where to start and what to save for later.

This phased approach helps us reduce risk, keeps the team from getting overwhelmed, and lets us build momentum as we go. Starting with easier migrations ensures smoother transitions and sets us up for long-term success when it's time to tackle the more critical applications.

Defining Your Cloud Model

Before we dive into the migration, one of the most important decisions we need to make is which cloud model fits our needs: *single cloud*, *multi-cloud*, or *hybrid*. Each has its own strengths and trade-offs, so it's crucial we choose wisely, based on what we're trying to achieve with each workload.

Single Cloud

If we stick with a single cloud provider, whether that's AWS, Azure, or GCP, it keeps things simple. Managing one environment makes things easier for the team, as we only have to focus on one set of tools, APIs, and services. For less complex or internal applications, this approach often provides all the reliability and performance we need.

However, we have to consider the risks of vendor lock-in and the potential impact of outages. If our entire operation is reliant on one provider, any downtime they experience could hit us hard. That's the trade-off, simplicity versus flexibility and risk mitigation.

> **Global Infrastructure of Cloud Service Providers**
>
> As we decide on our cloud model, it's important to evaluate the global infrastructure of the **Cloud Service Provider** (CSP) we're considering. This includes understanding how many points of presence they have and their capacity to ensure high availability.
>
> Choosing a single cloud provider doesn't mean sacrificing high availability, as most CSPs offer multiple availability zones and regions that can be leveraged for redundancy and failover.
>
> For more on how to approach high availability, refer to *Chapter 11*, where we dive deeper into this topic.

Multi-Cloud

When it comes to mission-critical applications, multi-cloud strategies give us that extra layer of resilience. By spreading our workloads across multiple cloud providers, we reduce the risk of being affected by a single point of failure.

For example, we might run our main application on AWS while having a secondary backup on Azure, ready to take over if needed. This way, if one provider goes down, our operations don't. Multi-cloud can also help us navigate compliance requirements across different regions or industries. However, we need to be prepared for the added complexity, managing different tools, APIs, and configurations across multiple platforms. It requires our team to be well-versed in all the platforms we use, and we need to keep up with updates and changes across the board.

Hybrid Cloud

A hybrid approach allows us to combine the best of both worlds, mixing on-prem infrastructure with cloud resources, or even blending multiple cloud providers. This is especially useful if we can't fully move to the cloud because of legacy applications, data residency laws, or strict regulatory requirements.

In a hybrid setup, we might keep sensitive data on-prem while moving less critical workloads to the cloud. Tools like AWS Outposts, Azure Arc, and Google Anthos make it easier for us to bridge the gap between on-prem and cloud environments. The challenge, though, is ensuring everything works seamlessly across both environments, especially when it comes to networking, security, and maintaining consistent data.

A hybrid cloud could also be represented as a transitory phase when migrating between two cloud service providers or on premise to the cloud. It's very common that these sorts of migrations can take months to years, depending on size or complexity.

In summary, the model we choose needs to reflect both the technical and business goals we're aiming for. Mission-critical apps may call for the redundancy and availability of multi-cloud, while simpler applications could sit comfortably in a single cloud. And if we've got legacy systems or specific compliance requirements to consider, a hybrid model might be our best bet. Ultimately, the choice we make has to align with both our operational capabilities and our long-term objectives.

Using a Treatment Plan for Migration

The first question to ask here is, "What is a treatment plan?" in the context of Cloud Native migrations. In short, a Treatment Plan is a framework or model to help organizations make important decisions about how to migrate each workload. It can be seen as a decision making tool to categorise and prioritizr workloads to determine the best approach for migrating infrastructure, applications and data to the cloud.

When we're making decisions about workloads, it's crucial to use the right framework, whether it's AWS's 7 Rs, Azure's Cloud Adoption Framework, or GCP's 6 Rs. These help us stay aligned with our goals and make sure we're taking the best approach for each app.

Whilst the differing CSP's have different names for their Treatment Plans, they all revolve around the same basic principals, below:

- **Rehost (Lift and Shift)**: Move workloads to the cloud with minimal changes. This is our go-to when time is tight or we need to keep things simple, and it's an option across AWS, Azure, and GCP.

- **Replatform**: Make small tweaks to optimize for the cloud without a full overhaul. We might use AWS Elastic Beanstalk, Azure App Services, or GCP App Engine to give our apps a better platform while keeping things familiar.

- **Repurchase (SaaS)**: Swap out on-prem software for SaaS solutions where it makes sense. Think Microsoft 365 or GCP's Workspace, less management, more efficiency, and someone else is handling the heavy lifting.

- **Refactor**: When we need to redesign an app to make it truly cloud native, we turn to tools like AWS Lambda, Azure Functions, or Google Cloud Functions for serverless, or break things down into microservices with Kubernetes.

- **Retire**: This is about cutting loose the apps we no longer need. Whether it's to reduce complexity or save costs, shutting down obsolete systems is key to keeping our cloud environment lean.

- **Retain**: Sometimes it's best to keep certain apps on-prem, especially if they're not cloud-ready or compliance demands it. We can manage that through hybrid solutions like AWS Outposts, Azure Arc, or Google Anthos.

- **Relocate**: Move workloads between clouds as needed. Flexibility is everything, and shifting between providers lets us optimize for performance, cost, or compliance as the business evolves.

> **Note**
> We also briefly touched on the 7 R's, specifically lift and shift, in *Chapter 7*, section 1.

Choosing Your Cloud Platform

Whether we're looking at AWS, Azure, GCP, or a mix of them, it's essential that the platform fits our business and technical requirements. Each cloud provider has its strengths, so understanding what we need is crucial to avoid mismatches that could limit performance or drive-up costs. The following are some of the considerations to take before choosing your cloud platform.

Evaluating Services and Features

We need to start by reviewing the core services each provider offers, particularly in areas critical to our business. For example:

- AWS is known for its extensive and mature ecosystem, especially in areas like compute (EC2), serverless (Lambda), and data lakes (S3).

- Azure, on the other hand, might be the better choice if we're already in the Microsoft ecosystem due to its seamless integration with tools like Active Directory, Office 365, and Windows Server.

- GCP often excels with its AI/ML capabilities, Kubernetes (GKE), and Big Data solutions like BigQuery.

Deciding which provider suits our needs involves assessing how well these core services line up with our current and future workloads.

Cost Considerations

While cloud providers are typically pay-as-you-go, pricing models differ significantly between platforms. We need to evaluate not just the upfront cost of services, but also the long-term financial impact based on scalability, storage, and data transfer fees. AWS, Azure, and GCP each have unique pricing structures for things like compute, networking, and storage tiers.

In a multi-cloud scenario, pricing gets even more complex. We'll need to factor in the cost of data egress between providers, making sure any data transfers between platforms don't lead to unexpected charges.

It's also worth noting that a hybrid-cloud strategy could incur varying costs as well from direction connectivity from private data center into the CSP or VPN costs and extra data transfer costs.

> **Pricing Tools**
>
> Tools like AWS Pricing Calculator, Azure Pricing Calculator, or Google Cloud Pricing Calculator will help us estimate these costs based on our usage patterns.

Compliance and Security

If compliance is a major factor, (e.g. GDPR, HIPAA, PCI-DSS, etc) we need to ensure that the platform we choose has the necessary certifications and data residency options. AWS, Azure, and GCP all have strong security and compliance offerings, but the depth and regional availability of these services can vary.

For instance, if we're working with sensitive data in Europe, AWS and Azure offer specific regions with stronger GDPR alignment. Google Cloud might be more appealing if we're heavily focused on AI/ML workloads with privacy requirements.

> **Note**
>
> As discussed in *Chapter 6*, compliance and certification is a shared responsibility between the cloud service provider and yourself.

Multi-Cloud and Hybrid Cloud Strategies

If we're planning to adopt a multi-cloud strategy, we'll need to carefully evaluate interoperability. How easily can services between AWS, Azure, and GCP work together? We'll need to decide whether to standardize using cloud-agnostic tools like Terraform for infrastructure-as-code or Kubernetes for container orchestration. This ensures we're not locked into any one platform, giving us the flexibility to migrate workloads or scale operations between clouds.

For hybrid cloud setups, solutions like AWS Outposts, Azure Stack, and Google Anthos allow us to extend the cloud into our on-prem data centers, enabling us to manage workloads across environments seamlessly. Choosing one over the other depends on how we want to manage the connection between on-prem and cloud, and the specific workloads we're running.

Latency and Regional Presence

Another key factor in our decision-making process is the geographic footprint of the cloud provider. If low latency is critical for user experience, we'll want to select a platform with a strong regional presence near our customer base. AWS has the most extensive global infrastructure, but Azure and GCP also offer robust coverage. We'll need to analyze the available regions and availability zones for each provider and determine how well they align with our geographic needs.

Ultimately, choosing the right cloud platform comes down to understanding both the technical requirements and the broader business goals. Whether we're going all-in on one provider or spreading workloads across multiple cloud providers, each decision should be backed by an in-depth evaluation of services, costs, compliance, and scalability options.

Setting Clear Timelines and Milestones

When planning out a cloud migration, setting realistic timelines and clear milestones is the backbone of keeping things on track and ensuring no steps get overlooked. Here's how we can break it down, adding the technical depth needed to keep this process tight and predictable.

Assessment Phase (Discovery and Planning)

Before we move a single workload, we need to allocate enough time for a deep assessment of our current environment. This means running discovery tools like AWS Migration Evaluator, Azure Migrate, or Google Cloud Migrate to map out all our dependencies, app connectivity, and performance metrics. These tools give us the full picture of what we're dealing with, no surprises later.

If we review our table from the section "Assessing Your Current Environment" we see that this sets our clear requirements to ensure we can start to plan out our Instance Types or requirements.

HostName	CPU Cores	OS	OS.Version	RAM Total
app-server01.local	4	Windows Server 2019	1809	8192
linux-db01.local	4	Ubuntu 20.04	Focal Fossa	16384
mssql-db01.local	8	Windows Server 2016	1607	32768
app-server02.local	2	Windows Server 2019	1809	8192
backup-server.local	4	Windows Server 2012 R2	9600	8192
web-server01.local	2	RHEL 8	Ootpa	4096
dev-server.local	4	Windows 10 Pro	21H1	16384
linux-app01.local	2	CentOS 7	Core	8192
storage-server.local	16	Windows Server 2019	1809	65536
dns-server.local	1	Ubuntu 18.04	Bionic Beaver	2048
mail-server.local	4	Windows Server 2016	1607	8192
log-server.local	8	Ubuntu 22.04	Jammy Jellyfish	16384

Table 12.2 - Migration Assessment Data

At this stage, technical audits are crucial. We'll identify network configurations, databases, security policies, and storage setups that could be impacted by the migration. Setting a milestone for completing this discovery phase ensures that we have all the critical data in hand before making any decisions. Think of it like setting a two-week window to run the migration assessment and holding a review session with the key stakeholders when the data's in.

Proof of Concept (PoC) / Pilot Testing

After we finish assessing, we can't just jump headfirst into the full migration. We need a **Proof of Concept (PoC)** or pilot test. Here, we'll take a non-critical app or two and run the migration process as a trial. For instance, we might lift and shift a small app using AWS Application Migration Service or try refactoring a component using Kubernetes on Azure or GCP.

The key milestone here is completing the PoC successfully. This shows us whether the tools and processes we've chosen will work at scale. Depending on the complexity of the app we're testing, we're likely looking at a 2 – 4-week timeline. Check-ins are important here to track how well the migration works and resolve any issues before scaling it up.

Full-Scale Migration

Once the PoC is signed off and running smoothly, we move into a full-scale migration. This is where things get technical fast. We'll have checkpoints like making sure our IAM roles, network settings, and security groups are properly configured before we start moving anything. This is where tools like AWS Database Migration Service, Azure Database Migration, or GCP's Data Transfer come into play to handle database migrations seamlessly.

At this stage, our milestones should involve migrating in batches. We're not dumping everything into the cloud at once. Instead, we'll set targets, say, migrating 20% of our apps over 4–6 weeks, then reassess, review performance, and fine-tune before pushing forward.

Optimization and Fine-Tuning

The job doesn't end when the apps are in the cloud. This phase is about reviewing performance, right-sizing our resources, and implementing auto-scaling to meet demand efficiently. Monitoring tools like CloudWatch (AWS), Azure Monitor, or GCP Operations Suite are key here to track performance and identify any inefficiencies in our setup.

We'll set milestones for this stage to ensure our cloud architecture is optimized for both performance and cost. That means regular performance reviews and keeping an eye on resource utilization so we can adjust as needed. A post-migration review with all stakeholders lets us evaluate what worked, what didn't, and how we can streamline future migrations.

Regular Stakeholder Check-Ins

Throughout the entire process, regular check-ins with stakeholders, both technical and non-technical, are essential. We'll schedule weekly or bi-weekly updates to ensure everything aligns with the broader business goals, and technical teams are hitting their key milestones. Detailed migration runbooks, architecture diagrams, and regular progress updates keep everyone on the same page and allow us to make adjustments if needed.

By setting clear milestones for each phase, assessment, PoC, migration, and optimization, we stay organized, prevent issues before they become bigger problems, and make sure the whole process moves according to plan. Regular check-ins with stakeholders mean no one's left in the dark, and we can adjust timelines or processes to ensure a smooth migration from start to finish.

Cloud migration without strategy is asking for trouble. A solid, thought-out plan ensures you don't just throw everything into the cloud and hope for the best. Prioritize your applications, use frameworks like the AWS 7 Rs, and pick the right cloud model to set yourself up for success. With a clear plan, you'll avoid unnecessary delays, inefficiencies, and the costly mistakes that come with diving-in unprepared.

Another part of the strategy is ensuring stakeholders across the business are all informed as to the migration activities. We cover this in more detail in the next section

Minimum Stakeholder Commitment

When it comes to cloud adoption, there's a common misconception that it's a purely technical exercise, something the IT team can handle on their own. The reality, though, is far from that. Cloud migration isn't just another tech project, it's a fundamental shift in how the business operates. And for it to be successful, it requires full engagement from stakeholders at every level, from C-suite executives to department heads and technical leads.

> **Note**
> *Chapter 5* covers the shift in culture in more detail.

But what we often see is minimum stakeholder commitment, a hands-off approach where decision-makers are only engaged when problems arise. They might be present at the start, offering high-level support, but then fade into the background, assuming the technical team will handle everything. This disconnect leads to delays, misaligned objectives, budget overruns, and in worst cases, migration failure. If stakeholders aren't actively involved from the beginning, the whole project can lose direction, and before you know it, the migration has veered off course.

Let's break down why this is an anti-pattern and how stakeholders should take ownership of cloud adoption.

Understanding the Anti-Pattern: Minimum Stakeholder Commitment

It's important to understand what can go wrong as much as what can go right in these situation. Below we review some key call outs with minimum stakeholder commitment

The Problem with Passive Stakeholder Involvement

Here's the thing, if stakeholders aren't fully engaged, it creates all kinds of headaches. The IT team may be focused on operational efficiencies or cost savings, while the business side might be looking at scalability or customer experience. Without regular involvement from stakeholders, these objectives can end up clashing.

When key decision-makers aren't involved, delays start creeping in. Decisions about workload prioritization, resource allocation, or changes in migration scope end up stalled. This is because no one is actively steering the ship.

What happens then? The project drags on, and nobody feels a sense of ownership when challenges arise. This lack of responsibility causes a vicious cycle of slow responses and poor accountability.

Reactive Instead of Proactive Approaches

Minimal stakeholder involvement leads to a reactive approach, where decisions are made only when something breaks.

The result? You end up with rushed *"lift-and-shift"* migrations, where workloads are moved to the cloud without being optimized for it. This is a missed opportunity, and you end up paying more for a cloud environment that's no better than the one you left behind.

Without proactive planning, migration efforts are often focused on short-term gains, like moving workloads to avoid hardware refresh costs or meeting a regulatory deadline. But this misses the bigger picture, optimization, scalability, and long-term cloud benefits. We lose out on the full potential of cloud native features, and our cloud setup ends up as inefficient and costly as the one we left behind.

These two approaches have been common practice in a lot of failed migrations, causing increased costs, delays and businesses reverting back to legacy technology due to lack of direction.

How Stakeholders Should Engage in Cloud Adoption

For cloud migration to truly succeed, it's not enough for stakeholders to just be on the sidelines. Active, ongoing involvement is key. Here's how stakeholders can play a critical role in driving the success of cloud adoption from the very start.

> **Who are "Stakeholders"**
>
> In a cloud migration, stakeholders are individuals or groups with a vested interest in the migration's success. These could be Executive leadership team, IT management and architects, application owners or developers, operations teams, finance teams or end users. This list is niether exhaustive or final, anyone can be a stakeholder if they interface with the applcation, data or infrastrcture.

Clear and Regular Communication Channels

Stakeholders need to be in the loop from the start. We're talking about setting up regular meetings where both the technical and business sides come together to discuss progress, challenges, and upcoming decisions. By doing this, everyone stays aligned, and we avoid the siloed communication that slows projects down.

Try the following:

- **Steering Committees**: Create a steering committee with representatives from technical and business teams. This way, decisions are made collaboratively, ensuring the migration aligns with both operational goals and business objectives.

- **Check-ins**: Weekly or bi-weekly check-ins help keep the migration moving. These shouldn't be just status updates but a chance to adjust strategy if needed and address potential roadblocks before they become bigger problems.

Define Business Goals

Cloud adoption needs to be seen as a business transformation, not just a technical migration. Stakeholders should define clear, measurable business goals tied to the migration, whether that's improving agility, cutting costs, or enabling faster product rollouts.

Stakeholders need to own these business goals, ensuring that they are revisited regularly throughout the migration process to confirm the project is still on track. Some practical steps may include:

- **Align Goals**: Make sure the cloud migration ties directly into broader business objectives, like improving customer experience or streamlining operations.

- **KPIs**: Establish measurable KPIs for success, whether that's reduced downtime, faster deployments, or cost savings. These metrics should guide decisions throughout the migration process.

Resource Allocation and Prioritization

Resource allocation is where stakeholders really need to roll up their sleeves. Delays and budget issues often arise because there isn't enough oversight on where resources are going. Stakeholders need to be involved in prioritizing workloads, ensuring that critical applications get the attention they need. Key steps here may include:

- **Budget Oversight**: Stakeholders should actively manage the migration budget, ensuring that financial resources are allocated appropriately, especially for critical workloads and cloud optimization post-migration.

- **Workload Prioritization**: Involve stakeholders in decisions about which workloads to migrate first. This helps the technical team focus on high-impact applications that will deliver immediate value to the business.

Regular Review and Flexibility

Cloud migration isn't a straight line, it's iterative. Stakeholders need to review progress regularly and be ready to make adjustments as needed. This isn't a "set it and forget it" situation. There will be challenges, and stakeholders need to stay engaged to make course corrections quickly. Practical Steps that can help here are:

- **Quarterly Strategy Reviews**: In addition to regular check-ins, stakeholders should hold quarterly reviews to assess whether the migration is hitting the intended business outcomes.

- **Post-Migration Optimization**: The work doesn't stop once the migration is done. Stakeholders should stay involved during post-migration optimization to ensure the cloud setup is fine-tuned for performance and cost efficiency.

With this kind of engagement, we can finally align cloud projects with real business goals, bringing the agility and innovation we missed in the old, hands-off way of doing things.

Technical Considerations for Stakeholders

When it comes to stakeholder involvement there are some considerations to be made at the stakeholder level.

Use Cloud Native Governance Tools

Governance is critical in a cloud environment. Stakeholders should push for the use of cloud native tools to enforce policies, manage multiple accounts, and ensure security and compliance are always in check. For example:

- **AWS Control Tower or Azure Blueprints**: Tools that help manage accounts and apply governance policies across environments, ensuring we're always compliant and secure.

- **GCP Organization Policies**: This ensures centralized control over resources, making governance easier across multi-cloud setups.

Set Security and Compliance Benchmarks

Cloud migration brings new security challenges, and stakeholders need to be on top of this. Security features like IAM, encryption, and logging should be implemented from day one, and compliance benchmarks need to be part of the migration plan. Think about applying:

- **Regular Compliance Audits**: Ensure the cloud environment is compliant with industry standards by running regular audits.

- **Security Reviews**: Security should be baked into the migration process, not an afterthought. Stakeholders should ensure security reviews happen at every stage of the migration.

No matter what approach you take, active stakeholder commitment is essential for success.

Minimal stakeholder involvement is a recipe for delays, budget overruns, and missed opportunities. For cloud migration to succeed, stakeholders must be engaged from start to finish, ensuring that decisions are aligned with business goals, resources are allocated effectively, and adjustments are made as necessary. By staying involved and proactive, stakeholders ensure that cloud adoption delivers its full value and sets the business up for long-term success.

If the stakeholders are not involved and informed, it's very easy to slip into replicating on premise concepts into the cloud due to lack of directon or minimal rushed direction.

Replicating On-Prem Security Controls

One of the biggest mistakes organizations make during cloud migration is trying to transplant their old on-prem security controls into the cloud. It might feel like a safe move, after all, those controls worked fine in your old environment, so why reinvent the wheel?

But the reality is, that the cloud operates in a completely different way, and dragging those traditional controls along for the ride can cause more harm than good. Not only does it create security gaps, but it also adds operational overhead that slows your team down and eats up resources.

On-prem security models are based on static environments, hard network perimeters, and tools that need manual configuration. But cloud environments are dynamic, constantly shifting as resources spin up and down to meet demand. Security has to be as flexible and scalable as the cloud itself, and that's where cloud native tools come in. Sticking to what's familiar might feel like the safe bet, but it's an anti-pattern that can cost you in terms of security, efficiency, and operational complexity.

Let's dive into why replicating on-prem security controls is such a bad idea and explore how to adapt your security strategy to leverage the full power of cloud native solutions.

Understanding the Anti-Pattern: Replicating On-Prem Security Controls

When moving to the cloud, it's easy to fall back on what we know, using the same security controls we've relied on for years in on-prem environments. But the reality is that what works in a traditional setup doesn't fit in a cloud-first world. Trying to replicate those old controls in the cloud usually leads to inefficiencies, vulnerabilities, and operational headaches. Instead of enhancing security, we end up with a patchwork of outdated controls that don't fully leverage the cloud's strengths.

In this section, we'll unpack why this approach falls short and explore the real value of shifting to cloud native security practices.

The Problem with On-Prem Security in the Cloud

In traditional on-prem security, the assumption was simple, once you're inside the network, you're trusted. Everything behind the perimeter was considered safe. But in the cloud, that model doesn't hold up. With workloads spread across regions and resources scaling up and down on demand, the old way of thinking quickly falls apart. This is where **Zero Trust** steps in.

In a cloud environment, we can't trust users, devices, or applications simply because of their network location. Zero Trust flips that assumption on its head, requiring verification every time, whether it's users, devices, or workloads. Everything has to prove it's secure before it gets access. This shift to a Zero Trust model is essential for embracing true cloud native security.

Key Pillars of Zero Trust include:

- **Identity verification**: Always confirm who or what is requesting access.

- **Least privilege access**: Limit access to only what's absolutely necessary for each user or service.

- **Continuous monitoring**: Track activity in real time to detect threats and mitigate risks as they arise.

- **Micro-segmentation**: Break down your network into smaller segments to isolate resources and limit the attack surface.

- **Device security**: Ensure that all devices meet strict security standards before granting access.

By adopting these core principles, we move away from the outdated idea that anything inside the network perimeter is automatically safe. Zero Trust ensures that every component within your cloud environment is continuously verified, offering stronger protection against internal threats, misconfigurations, and breaches that might otherwise slip through in a traditional on-prem setup. It's the mindset shift we need to stay secure in an increasingly complex cloud landscape.

Trying to apply traditional security controls in the cloud often means missing out on the flexibility and scalability that the cloud offers. Legacy tools can't keep up with the pace of change in cloud environments and often require manual adjustments that slow operations down. Worse, they can leave your cloud infrastructure exposed if they don't integrate well with cloud native services.

For example, while on-prem environments rely heavily on firewalls to block unauthorized traffic, cloud environments demand more granular security controls. This is where Identity and Access Management (IAM) comes in. In the cloud, it's not just about keeping bad traffic out; it's about ensuring that only the right users, services, and applications have access to the resources they need—nothing more, nothing less. Relying solely on traditional network-based security tools can leave dangerous gaps in access management.

The Shared Responsibility Model, often overlooked and misunderstood

One of the most important things to understand when moving to the cloud is the shared responsibility model. In a traditional on-prem environment, you control everything, from the physical hardware to the applications running on it. But in the cloud, the security responsibilities are split between you and your cloud provider. The provider takes care of the infrastructure, like the physical security of data centers and the network between them, but you're responsible for securing what you build on top, your applications, data, and identity management.

Failing to grasp this distinction often leads to weak security configurations. For instance, thinking that your cloud provider will handle encryption or access controls for you can result in data breaches or unauthorized access. On-prem security models don't account for this shared responsibility, and organizations that try to copy them directly into the cloud often end up with serious gaps in their security posture.

How to Shift from On-Prem to Cloud Native Security

Replicating on-prem security in the cloud just doesn't cut it. To get the most out of cloud infrastructure, we need to shift gears and adopt cloud native approaches. In this section, we'll break down exactly how we can move away from those outdated security models and start taking full advantage of cloud-native tools and practices.

Consider the below tips when reviewing your implemention of Cloud Native Security

- **Embrace Identity-Based Security Models**: In the cloud, security revolves around identity, whether it's a user, an application, or a service. **IAM** (**Identity and Access Management**) is your first line of defense. By assigning specific roles and permissions to every user and resource, you can control who has access to what, and under what conditions. Practical steps that you could consider here are:

  - **Adopt the Principle of Least Privilege**: Make sure that users and services only have the permissions they absolutely need. In AWS, this means defining fine-grained IAM policies. In Azure and GCP, similar identity-based controls allow you to manage access at a granular level.

  - **Implement Multi-Factor Authentication (MFA)**: MFA should be mandatory for all access to sensitive resources. This extra layer of security ensures that even if credentials are compromised, attackers can't gain access without the secondary factor.

  - **Regular Audits**: Keep an eye on permissions. Cloud environments change rapidly, and roles that made sense last month may be too permissive today. Regular audits help you stay on top of who has access to what.

> **Note**
>
> For more information on this review *Chapter 6* and the usage of temporary credentials

- **Use Cloud Native Security Tools**: Rather than forcing on-prem security tools to work in the cloud, take advantage of the cloud native tools that are built for this environment. Every major cloud provider offers a suite of security services that are designed to monitor, protect, and scale your infrastructure.

The following tools can help you implement a good foundation of cloud native security.

- **AWS Shield & AWS WAF**: Protect your applications from DDoS attacks and other malicious traffic using AWS Shield and **AWS Web Application Firewall (WAF)**. Azure and GCP offer similar services, like Azure DDoS Protection and GCP Cloud Armor.

- **Centralized Security Dashboards**: Use centralized platforms like Azure Security Center or Google Cloud Security Command Center to gain a full view of your security posture and quickly identify any vulnerabilities or misconfigurations.

- **Automated Threat Detection**: Tools like AWS GuardDuty, Azure Advanced Threat Protection, and Google Cloud Security Scanner continuously monitor for suspicious activity and can alert you to potential threats before they escalate.

- **Automate Security Management and Monitoring**: Cloud environments are constantly evolving, which makes manual security management impractical. Fortunately, the cloud gives us the following tools to automate many aspects of security monitoring and incident response, reducing operational overhead and ensuring a faster response to potential threats.

  - **CloudTrail/CloudWatch**: In AWS, use CloudTrail and CloudWatch to log and monitor all activity in your cloud environment. Similarly, Azure Monitor and GCP's Operations Suite provide real-time cloud native insights and alerts.

  - **Automate Responses to Threats**: Configure automatic workflows for threat responses. For example, if AWS GuardDuty flags suspicious activity, you can automatically revoke credentials or trigger a security group change to block unauthorized access.

  - **Security Audits and Compliance**: Schedule regular, automated security audits with tools like AWS Config, Azure Policy, and GCP Policy Intelligence. This ensures that your environment stays compliant with security policies and industry regulations.

- **Minimize Operational Overhead with Cloud Native Solutions**: Sticking to on-prem security tools not only limits your security capabilities but also introduces significant operational overhead. Manually configuring firewalls, managing static IPs, or constantly adjusting VPN settings in a cloud environment is time-consuming and prone to error. Cloud native solutions reduce the need for manual intervention, automating much of the security management process. Keep the below in mind as you plan your migration:

  - **Reduce Manual Configurations**: Replace manual firewall and VPN setups with dynamic, identity-based access controls. This reduces the need for constant updates and monitoring.

  - **Centralized Governance**: Use cloud native governance tools like AWS Control Tower, Azure Blueprints, or Google Cloud Organization Policies to manage policies across multiple accounts, enforce best practices, and automate compliance.

  - **Automate Incident Response**: With cloud native automation tools, you can eliminate much of the manual work involved in responding to security incidents. Automatically revoke compromised credentials, adjust firewall rules, or launch backup instances as needed—without the need for human intervention.

In summary, you need to embrace Cloud Native security to eliminate legacy overhead. Replicating on-prem security controls in the cloud is not just inefficient, it's risky. Legacy tools and manual processes can't keep up with the fast-paced, dynamic nature of cloud environments, leading to security gaps and operational inefficiencies.

By embracing cloud native security models, automating key processes, and leveraging the full suite of tools offered by AWS, Azure, or GCP, you can build a security posture that's stronger, more scalable, and more efficient than ever before.

The bottom line is this: cloud security is not just a copy-paste job. It requires a fundamental shift in thinking. With the right approach, stakeholders and technical teams can transition smoothly from outdated, labor-intensive security models to a cloud native environment that maximizes both security and operational efficiency.

In our last section of this chapter we'll review how important education and knowledge transfer is to a succesful migration.

Underestimating Skill Gaps

When moving to the cloud, one of the most critical and often overlooked factors is the skill gap within teams. Many organizations jump into cloud adoption with the belief that their existing technical teams will seamlessly adapt to the new environment. But cloud infrastructure operates on different principles compared to traditional IT, and assuming the same skill set will carry over is a recipe for delays, inefficiencies, and sometimes failure. Underestimating the skill gap can lead to issues like misconfigurations, missed opportunities to optimize, or, worst of all, security vulnerabilities that go unnoticed until it's too late.

Cloud migration isn't just a technical shift, it's a mindset shift. Without proper training, support, and a realistic understanding of the skill sets needed, organizations often find themselves struggling to take full advantage of cloud capabilities. Let's dig deeper into this anti-pattern and explore practical strategies to close the skill gap effectively.

Understanding the Anti-Pattern: Underestimating Skill Gaps

When it comes to cloud adoption, many businesses assume that if someone is proficient in traditional IT or data center management, they'll naturally be able to handle cloud operations too. However different CSPs operate on completely different paradigms.

Terms like infrastructure as code, serverless, and container orchestration aren't just buzzwords; they require a deep understanding of new tools and approaches. Without the right skills, cloud migrations can quickly get off track. Let's break down this section a little more by focussing on tradition skills vs cloud skills and then the impact on cloud adoption.

Traditional Skillsets vs. Cloud Skillsets

In traditional on-prem environments, managing infrastructure meant physically deploying hardware, installing software, and managing everything manually. Cloud environments, on the other hand, require mastery over automation, dynamic scaling, and a deep understanding of cloud native services. Concepts like elasticity, auto-scaling, and security models are often new to many technical teams, and without focused training, gaps quickly emerge.

Impact on Cloud Adoption

Failing to address skill gaps doesn't just result in slower migration timelines; it can have a direct impact on the success of cloud adoption. Teams lacking the necessary skills might replicate old on-prem processes that aren't optimized for the cloud, leading to inefficient workflows and misconfigurations. Even worse, poor security practices can open vulnerabilities that compromise the integrity of the entire cloud environment.

How to Close the Skill Gap

Acknowledging that there's a skill gap is the first step, but that's not enough. You need a solid plan to close it. Here is how we do it.

Invest in Cloud Training and Certifications

The quickest way to close the skill gap is through structured training and certifications. Each major cloud provider offers a range of certifications that are designed to equip teams with the knowledge needed to handle cloud architecture, operations, and security. AWS, Azure, and GCP all have learning paths tailored to different roles, from architects to developers to DevOps engineers.

- **Identify Key Training Areas**: Don't just send your teams to generic cloud training. Identify the specific areas where your team needs upskilling. Is it around automation? Security? Container management? Focus on what will give your organization the most value.

- **Encourage Certification**: Push for formal cloud certifications. AWS Certified Solutions Architect, Azure Administrator, and Google Cloud Engineer certifications provide teams with both foundational and advanced knowledge. Not only do they validate skills, but they also keep your teams on top of cloud best practices.

- **Continuous Learning**: Cloud platforms evolve quickly. Make learning an ongoing process, encouraging teams to regularly engage with webinars, hands-on labs, and new certification exams.

Foster a Culture of Cross-Functional Collaboration

Underestimating skill gaps often come from isolating technical teams into silos. Cloud operations thrive when teams—developers, operations, and security—work together toward a common goal. Creating a culture of cross-functional collaboration not only closes skill gaps but also ensures smoother cloud operations overall. Consider the following.

- **Cross-Training**: Encourage cross-functional training where developers learn about infrastructure, and operations learn more about code and automation. This helps create a DevOps or even DevSecOps mindset within the team.

- **Collaborative Projects**: Run projects where cross-functional teams come together to solve real-world problems. For example, building a cloud-based application from scratch could involve development, security, and operations all working in unison. This fosters teamwork while upskilling in real time.

- **Mentorship Programs**: Pair senior engineers familiar with cloud environments with those who are still getting up to speed. Mentorship accelerates learning while promoting collaboration across departments.

Balancing Technical and Soft Skills

It's not just about the technical know-how. Teams also need the ability to communicate, collaborate, and problem-solve in a cloud environment. Cloud adoption is a company-wide initiative, not just a technical project, and it requires business and technical teams to work closely together. Bridging skill gaps often involves fostering better communication between these groups. The following guidance is essential to ensuring balancing technical and soft skills

Develop Cloud Fluency Across the Organization

Cloud adoption affects everyone in the organization, not just the IT department. To make the most out of cloud migration, stakeholders across the business need to have a basic understanding of cloud principles. Whether it's finance tracking cloud costs, security managing compliance, or legal navigating cloud contracts, cloud fluency across all departments is key. Keep the following in mind:

- **Stakeholder Workshops**: Set up cloud fundamentals workshops for non-technical teams. Help them understand how cloud affects their roles and why cloud is critical for the business.

- **Cloud-Specific KPIs**: Define cloud-specific key performance indicators (KPIs) for different departments. This helps ensure that all business units understand the impact and benefits of cloud adoption and keeps everyone aligned on the goals of the migration.

Establish Clear Ownership and Responsibility

One of the biggest contributors to skill gaps is the lack of clear ownership in cloud projects. When roles and responsibilities are vague, people fall back on what they know, which can result in technical debt and operational inefficiencies. Establish clear ownership of cloud initiatives to ensure accountability and expertise grow where needed. In order to achieve clear ownership;

- **Define Roles**: Clearly define who is responsible for what during cloud migration. Whether it's the infrastructure, security, or deployment, assign clear ownership so nothing falls through the cracks.

- **Create Cloud Champions**: Appoint cloud champions within the organization—people who will own specific areas of cloud expertise and drive best practices across teams.

> **Closing the Knowledge Gap is Key to Cloud Success**
>
> Underestimating skill gaps in cloud adoption is a common anti-pattern, but it's also one of the most fixable. By investing in targeted cloud training, fostering a collaborative culture, and building cloud fluency across the organization, you can bridge these gaps and ensure a smooth migration. Cloud adoption is more than just technology, it's about building a team with the skills and mindset to succeed in a rapidly evolving environment.

Summary

Cloud migration is far more than just moving workloads, it is a complete transformation that requires careful planning, strong stakeholder engagement, and a shift to modern, cloud native practices. In this chapter, we tackled some of the most common anti-patterns that can hinder progress, from inadequate planning and weak stakeholder involvement to outdated security practices carried over from on-prem environments.

Using frameworks like AWS's 7 Rs or equivalent options from Azure and GCP, we can make smarter decisions about each workload, ensuring that every step aligns with both technical and business objectives. By prioritizing applications strategically and choosing the right cloud model—whether single cloud, multi-cloud, or hybrid—we can reduce risks and create a migration roadmap that delivers real value. Addressing skill gaps is also critical, as it equips teams to embrace the tools and methodologies needed to succeed in the cloud.

This isn't just about migrating systems; it's about laying the groundwork for agility, scalability, and innovation. With a clear strategy, collaborative teamwork, and modernized approaches, we're well-positioned to not just move to the cloud, but thrive there.

13

How Do You Know It All Works?

Testing our code is how we ensure that our changes are both fit for purpose and that they don't regress any existing functionality. In a cloud native environment, our complexity increasingly lives in areas beyond the scope of our code, so testing our application in a meaningful way can become complex. Let's explore how we can test cloud native code in ways that are both time-efficient and meaningful while avoiding some common anti-patterns.

In this chapter, we're going to cover the following main topics:

- General testing anti-patterns
- Lack of contract testing
- Manual testing
- Trying to recreate the cloud
- Poorly structured code

General testing anti-patterns

Before we explore the types of tests commonly used in cloud native applications, we must first explore some general testing anti-patterns that we must avoid. These anti-patterns typically result from the evolution of the application's testing strategy as it is migrated to the cloud. While most of these anti-patterns apply to unit tests, it's essential to be mindful of them when testing other patterns as well.

First, we will look at some testing anti-patterns and how they surface in a cloud native environment. The specific anti-patterns we will explore are the following:

- Tests that have never failed
- Coverage badge tests
- Testing implementation details
- Tests that intermittently fail
- Tests with side effects or coupled tests
- Multi-stage tests

Tests that have never failed

When we think about testing, we might think that a test that has never failed is good. That means our code and changes have always complied with our expected behavior, right? Without the test failing, how can we be sure that the test fails when its contract is breached?

To illustrate this situation, I will use my experience with some of our teams in a previous role. The teams had just finished writing their functionality and were in the process of writing tests. They were working with an asynchronous code base in Node.js, and a quirk of asynchronous programming in Node.js is that when an asynchronous function is called and it contains asynchronous code, without a top-level await on the function call in the test, the test will exit before the asynchronous code executes. This means any assertions in the asynchronous code would only throw errors after the test, and because no assertions were thrown during test execution, the test passes. From an untrained perspective, the test appears to test the functionality expected. However, in practice, the test is useless. Unsurprisingly, many tests started failing when we sprinkled in some `async` and `await` syntactic sugar.

In this example, a lack of understanding of asynchronous programming principles contributed to functionally useless tests that gave the impression everything was okay.

This anti-pattern is an easy trap to fall into in cloud computing. As systems become asynchronous, decoupled, and eventually consistent, our testing strategy must match the system's complexity. You will notice that the entire situation could have been avoided had the team followed **test-driven development (TDD)**. The common TDD approach I like to utilize is *Red*, *Green*, and *Refactor*:

- **Red**: First, create the minimum structure required to support your test. This might be an empty function block, method, or object. Second, write a test (or tests) that you believe tests your expected behavior. When you run your tests, they should fail, showing red.

- **Green**: Fill out your empty placeholder with the logic to make your test pass, showing green.

- **Refactor**: Create new tests and functionality to handle edge cases. In these scenarios, it is best to create positive and negative test cases and purposefully break the test a few times to ensure it behaves as expected.

In the cloud native world, typically, these tests would form part of our automated integration pipeline, such as in AWS CodePipeline, GCP Cloud Build, or Azure DevOps Pipelines.

Coverage badge tests

Another anti-pattern that often comes up is **coverage badge tests**. When attempting a cloud migration or refactoring of existing cloud code, a common goal we see added to the agenda is to increase test coverage. This mentality is putting the cart before the horse. Good test coverage should arise from writing good, comprehensive tests. It is perfectly possible to have high test coverage but poor-quality tests. A test that simply checks that an HTTP server returns a 200 status code might give you good test coverage, but is it a good test? What about the semantic structure of the data? Does the output match the expected input? The behavior of the endpoint is completely untested in this scenario. We haven't guaranteed that any future changes won't result in unexpected behaviors, just that they will return a status code of 200.

Incentivizing code coverage in isolation will not give you greater certainty of the emergent behaviors of your application. Instead, you must incentivize writing proper tests that have been peer-reviewed to describe the expected behavior of the system. A simple litmus test for good testing practice is whether the test ensures that the emergent behavior of the system more closely aligns with the behavior in our mental model of the system.

Testing implementation details

Requiring developers to hit a code coverage threshold set too high can also lead to another anti-pattern: testing implementation details. This anti-pattern can be particularly insidious in the cloud native domain as we are more concerned with the result and emergent system behaviors than the method used to achieve them, as implementation details can be very fluid as we leverage new architectural and technological patterns. For example, if we need to sort an array, we might first check that the input is an array of numbers, then call a bubble sort function if it is. Let's say we write two tests here:

- Check that the bubble sort function is not called when the array is not an array of numbers and the result is an error
- Check that the bubble sort function is called when the array is an array of numbers and the result is a sorted array

Later, someone removes the initial check to see whether the array is an array of numbers and replaces the bubble sort with a merge sort function that already has built-in type checking. This is what happens to our test:

- Our first test passes, even though we now call the sort function on every execution because our merge sort function differs from our bubble sort function
- Our second test fails because we did not call the bubble sort function

In this case, we have not changed the emergent behavior of the system; we have only changed the implementation details. Instead, we could design our test to look like this:

- Check that we get an error on anything other than an array of numbers
- Check that we correctly sort an array of numbers

These tests check solely the exhibited behavior, not how we achieved it. Under this new testing framework, both tests will pass when we perform our refactor.

Intermittently failing tests

I have often asked clients about a failing test pipeline only to be told, *"Yeah, it does that sometimes. Just rerun it."* Intermittently failing tests breed ambiguity.

When a test pipeline fails, our first instinct is to rerun it. This ambiguity means that our mean time to identify failures in our pipeline goes through the roof, as we don't know whether the culprit is a failing test or whether the pipeline is just acting up. It is essential to be not only confident in the success of your passing tests but also in your failing tests.

Let us imagine a hypothetical intermittently failing series of tests. These tests would block production deployments, PR reviews, and local testing. It always seems to sort itself by the next run, it only happens a few times a year, and it's an infrequently updated micro-frontend, so why bother fixing it?

After triaging the issue, we found the culprit pretty quickly: someone asserted in a test that the current UTC minute of the hour was less than 59 instead of less than or equal to. This change, in line with probability, was pushed and merged successfully. The expectation was buried deep in a block that prevented a precursory glance from diagnosing the problem from the test output. This also creates a compelling argument for verbose and well-formatted test outputs. As you can imagine, someone's pipeline failed after working locally; they decided to rerun it, and it passed. It became known that that particular pipeline was flaky and we could fix it with a rerun. What effect do you think that has on developers?

When I ran into this situation in my work, we found that the number of failed reruns significantly outpaced the actual number of *flaky* runs due to a lack of confidence in the failures of the underlying pipeline. Cloud native delivery allows us to push incremental changes to our code base rapidly. This process means that a high-performing team will run these pipelines multiple times daily.

Therefore, in a cloud native environment, having faith in your pipelines, both in success and failure, is imperative. Another common way that tests become flaky is by relying on test side effects or coupled tests.

Tests with side effects or coupled tests

Relying on side effects or coupling tests is an easy trap, especially as we refactor code and add existing tests, as other tests may already cause side effects that our new tests may unknowingly come to depend on.

For illustrative purposes, let us consider tests that ensure user behavior. We have two endpoints: one to create users and one to delete users. We have one test that generates a random email, creates a user with that email, and saves it as a global variable in the test file. Then, another test reads the global variable and deletes the user, checking whether the user is deleted correctly. We have broken both rules here. Not only do we have a side effect by modifying the global state but we have also coupled two tests through that side effect. It's essential to understand what we have lost here:

- **Isolated testing**: Because of the coupling, if we want to run only the *user delete* test, it will always fail because it needs to be run in concert with the *user create* test. We can now only run the entire test file.

- **Ability to refactor**: If we move the tests to different files or change their execution order, they will fail. This makes refactoring harder, as we now need to understand its coupled tests to refactor the test for the functionality we are interested in.

- **Parallel execution**: As our test base grows, it becomes apparent that we need to optimize our pipeline execution. The first tool people will usually reach for is parallel execution. When we couple tests, parallel execution can cause you to lose the deterministic execution of your test suite. This lack of determinism means that your tests may intermittently fail, contributing to "flaky" pipelines as the tests may or may not execute in the correct order.

How can we remove the coupling and side effects from our example? A simple indicator for a single test is to run our test in isolation and check that it still passes. This check ensures that our test has no upstream coupling; it does not test for side effects or downstream coupling.

The next step is to refactor our test files. Ideally, there should be no global variables. This concept can be controversial as many test implementations will have static data in global variables. Still, strictly controlled generated data will always beat static data.

The driving force behind this is simple: having generated data means that you are testing the bounds of your system to a greater extent. It can contribute to intermittently failing test pipelines, but if you hit an intermittent failure, take it as a blessing, not a curse. Hitting an intermittent failure means the data you generated to match your expected production data does not behave as expected! If you had used static data, you would never have found this edge case before production.

The other issue with static data is that teams tend to get lazy. The usual culprit is UUIDs. I've seen production systems go down because someone had used the same UUID to index two different values and then created a correlation in code where no correlation existed in the production data. The cause was that rather than generate a new UUID, a developer saw a UUID generated for a different entity and decided to copy the already compliant UUID to save about 20 seconds of development effort. As you can imagine, saving those 20 seconds was massively outweighed by the impacts of the eventual downtime.

Most testing libraries have pre-test and post-test hooks to set up your data and application components. A level of granularity is also usually provided. You can run before and after *all* tests or before and after *each* test. The deciding factor on when to use them is based on the application component.

If the component has an internal state modified by tests, then that component should be created and disposed of before and after each test. Examples include local caches and persistence layers. If the component does not have an internal state, it is probably safe to optimize by setting it up once for all tests and tearing it down when all tests have finished.

Examples might include authentication layers (unless you're storing sessions in this layer!), request routing layers, or utility components. When we look at avoiding side effects and ordering in tests, we might think of putting our entire flow in a single test. Then, we're not breaking the boundaries between our tests! However, this leads us to our next non-functional antipattern: multistage tests.

Multistage tests

Multistage tests often come about because we see actions as being related. However, we need to keep in mind that the purpose of testing is usually to test a unit of behavior, even in integration tests, albeit with a broader definition of our unit of behavior. To understand why this is an anti-pattern, we need to look at our failure modes. When we have many atomic tests, we can easily see which functionality is broken. With a smaller number of multistage tests, we might cover the same amount of behavior, but we lose fidelity in our reporting.

Early errors in a multistage test can also cause the test to fail early, masking errors from later in the multistage test. It might be a logical fallacy, but if we replaced all our tests with one large multistage test, we would have either a pass or fail for the entire system, which makes the search area on failure very broad. At the other extreme, where we make our tests as atomic as possible, we get extremely high fidelity and know precisely which units of behavior are broken. A pattern to follow in this area is to use **arrange, act, and assert (AAA)**:

- **Arrange**: Set up everything required for the test to run (data, authentication, application instances, etc.).

- **Act**: Perform the behavior under test. This action might be calling an endpoint or method, or performing an integration flow.

- **Assert**: Check that the results of your behavior match what you expect.

The key here is that this pattern should only occur in order once in a test. For example, a test that does not follow this pattern might go like this: arrange, act, assert, act, assert, act, assert. Failures in higher asserts mask all actions after the first assert. Therefore, our tests should have the correct level of atomicity to provide as much detail as possible.

So far, we have mainly focussed on unit testing, but we should not unit test to the exclusion of all else. Next, we will look at another critical type of testing to ensure semantic correctness: contract testing.

Lack of contract testing

In a cloud native environment, we often have loose coupling between components, with functionality exposed through a combination of APIs and events while consumed by other microservices, user interfaces, third parties, and every combination and permutation. When developing system components, worrying about the immediate application is no longer enough. Instead, we need to provide confidence about the communications between our services. This is where contract testing comes into play.

Contract testing

At the core of **contract testing** is the concept of a contract. A **contract** is a specification that explains precisely how data will be shared between services and its format, and it may even make some assurances around non-functional requirements. This contract may exist as an OpenAPI specification, JSON Schema, Protobuf definition, Smithy interface, or similarly in any **interface definition language (IDL)**.

The other piece of the data contract puzzle is that it should also give the semantic meaning of the data being transferred. The key is providing consumers with a clear definition of what to expect. Now that we have a contract, we can examine our application's output and ensure it agrees with our published schema. In other words, we test our application against the contract.

We can now decouple the development of different parts of our application. By defining our communication patterns in advance and defining tests that allow us to check our compliance with that pattern, we can build multiple parts of the application if we agree on the contracts we align to. As teams grow and functionality development grows beyond the scope of one developer, these types of tests become increasingly important. If one developer is working on a vertical slice of application functionality, they might iteratively design the communication patterns between the application components as they progress. This allows for agile development; however, it falls over when that developer needs to collaborate on that functionality with other parties. The iterative changes they are keeping in their head suddenly become impediments to the system's progress as a whole, as these frequent changes need to be communicated.

While it may sound slightly waterfall-like to define your communication patterns up front, it's important to note that the level of upfront planning is minimal. We're operating at atomic units of functionality here, one or two API endpoints at a time, not a monolithic definition of a system. Putting in the time up front to build a shared understanding of the communication model will pay dividends in the future, as rather than iterative, rapid changes to data exchange models, we are now only making changes to the model as functionally required by and agreed upon by both parties.

Beyond the initial contract

As we build out these contracts for data exchange methods, we can start publishing these artifacts for other parties to consume. By ensuring that we remain faithful to our data contracts through contract testing, we ensure that our current and future consumers can enjoy the continued operation of their dependencies. New users can easily onboard as consumers of the system as it is documented.

The question then becomes, what happens when we need to change a contract? This is where two other anti-patterns present themselves. The first anti-pattern is not maintaining a service dependency map. A service dependency map tells us exactly which services consume functionality from the service we have built to the contract specification.

This allows us to assess the blast radius of the service we are making a contract change to and ensure that any changes we make to the contract are compatible with other services that consume it. Many cloud service providers will have distributed traceability of transactions through inbuilt observability tooling, or we may be able to build one through any of the third-party tools that offer a similar service. Without a service dependency map, we don't have any visibility into the blast radius of changes we plan on making. Let's look at an example of a simple service diagram.

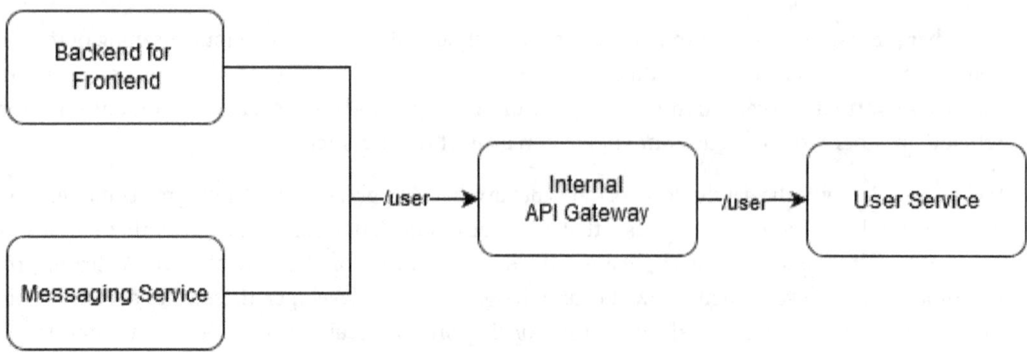

Figure 13.1 - A simple example of a user service, exposed through an API gateway, called by two upstream services

In this example, we have a user endpoint called by both the messaging service and the backend for frontend services.

From the preceding example, we can see that a change to the contract of /user on the user service will impact two upstream services that may also have to be updated to ensure continuity of service. When we define the new contract, we can use it to test the upstream services and, if they all pass, safely make the change. How can we make contracts that don't break upstream services when we change them?

This brings us to our second anti-pattern, which directly manipulates the existing data contract. We can extend the data contract to include new functionality instead of modifying the semantic meaning of existing fields or functionality. Consider an object used by the preceding messaging service that returns a name field from the /user endpoint. Our data contract specifies that this field is the first name of the person, for example, Alice. The messaging service might also want to provide a salutation, for example, Ms. Alice. With no changes to the messaging service, we could change the semantic meaning of the /user endpoint data contract so that *name* now means *salutation plus name*. However, this might have unexpected effects on other consumers of the service. Let's say the **backend for frontend** (BFF) service gets information about multiple users and sorts their names alphabetically. Now, we sort by salutation instead of name. We have unintentionally modified behavior by changing the semantic meaning.

This contrived example may seem easy to avoid; however, even simple changes to data contracts can have unintended consequences. There are two options here: either we change the data contract and deal with the fallout (usually hard to predict, discover, and rectify), or we extend our data contract. When we extend our data contract, we rely on services not involved in the change to ignore the extensions. For example, rather than changing the semantic meaning of the name field, we add a new field called salutation. The messaging service can consume this field to provide the required functionality, and the BFF service can continue using the name field as expected, ignoring the salutation field.

If we really must change the underlying semantics of the data contract, then we can still follow our principle of not modifying the behavior expected by other systems. This may seem counter-intuitive. However, by utilizing API versioning, we can fundamentally change the structure and semantics of our data contract by adding a v2 of our API. This preserves the data contract between our old systems while allowing us to make considerable changes to support new functionality. We can retroactively update the dependent services by aligning them with the new data contract by utilizing contract testing. Eventually deprecating the original endpoint without any material impact, we have essentially decoupled the modification of data contracts from the adoption of the new data contracts, which, in turn, changes a highly synchronous deployment exercise and likely downtime into an asynchronous process that can be undertaken as the business needs arise.

Contract enforcement

It's all good to define the data contract we use between services, but the next stage is contract enforcement. It is not enough to define the contracts that our services communicate in. Ideally, at both ends, we should check that the data we transfer aligns with our understanding of the contract. An important aspect here is to validate what we know and discard what we don't; this leaves us the option of contract expansion, as we discussed earlier. Contract validation at runtime can save us from unexpected data behaviors and alert us to mismatches between contracts.

A good practice here is to complement our contract testing with fuzzing, injecting corrupted or invalid data to ensure our application rejects it. In the cloud environment, rejecting the wrong data is just as important as accepting the right data!

To provide a good user experience, enforcing our data contract at the application layer is often useful before sending it to our services. Not only does this provide faster feedback to the users but every error we catch in the application is a request we don't need to serve, reducing the load on the underlying resources. The cheapest computer you can use is usually at the closest edge to the user.

On the flip side, though, we want to validate our data when we receive it for both correctness and security purposes. Anyone could send anything they want to our endpoints, and it is our responsibility to work out what to do with it. If we enforce contracts on both the backend and frontend, though, we require our data contract to be portable.

Portability

In these scenarios, it should go without saying that the format of your data contracts should aim to be as technology-agnostic as possible. Framework- and language-specific libraries often have valuable features. However, locking us into a framework can make it challenging to operate across technologies. In like-for-like execution environments, say a frontend in React and a backend in Node.js, both run JavaScript under the hood, so it might be tempting to use a specialized solution. However, what if your company acquires a product with a code base in C#? How will they access contracts and ensure data integrity? Hence, the requirements for portability, which are a feature of all formats mentioned earlier in the chapter, should always be at the forefront of the mind.

A mature standard (if you are using JSON, which feels like the de facto cloud native standard, except for perhaps Protobuf in GCP!) is JSON Schema. It is maintained through the **Internet Engineering Task Force (ITEF)**, and any precursory web search will reveal them as the stewards of many standards we take for granted today. You can typically find very mature libraries to generate, validate, and test JSON schemas in the language and framework of your choice. It also allows for clear delineation between the data schema to test against (JSON Schema) and the interface definition through a standard such as OpenAPI or AsyncAPI. If the schema is the definition of the data, the interface definition is the metastructure that defines the relationships between our schemas and service endpoints.

Code generation

If we have both our schemas and our interface definitions predefined, then there exist multiple open source projects that allow for this information to be used to generate code. Typically, this code generation consists of three discrete components:

- **Type generation**: Generating types from our schemas for consumption in our code. This generation is typically a prerequisite for the other two types.

- **Client generation**: From our interface definitions and our generated types, we can automatically build SDKs to interact with our services, without having to worry about needing to make API requests, marshal and unmarshal data, and so on.

- **Server stub generation**: From our interface definition, we can generate server stubs that allow us to conform to our interface definition, only requiring us to build out the business logic.

When we look at the big three cloud providers, they use this methodology to maintain the SDKs that they provide for such a wide range of languages. AWS uses the Smithy IDL 2.0, which was custom-made for defining interfaces and code generation for AWS but is open source. Azure uses OpenAPI specifications, which we have discussed in depth already. Finally, GCP uses Protobuf definitions for all its services, which can encode in both JSON or a custom and compact binary format. By using code generation, they can make a change to the underlying contract and apply it across all their subsequent client SDKs by regenerating them.

So, contract testing ensures we don't break functionality and semantics for upstream services and ensures we have confidence in calling our downstream services. But how do we ensure continuity in our user interface? This is where an anti-pattern is so prevalent that it deserves its own section: manual testing.

Manual testing

When beginning this section, a quote of disputed origin springs to mind: "*I didn't have time to write you a short letter, so I wrote you a long one.*" As counter-intuitive as this may seem, people often have the same mentality about manual testing. They are so caught up in the process of testing the long way that they do not pause to consider the possibilities of automation. This anti-pattern is typically heavily ingrained in organizations right down to the team structure. This section will look at the case for transitioning to test automation in a cloud native environment and the practices you can use to migrate your manual testing processes to automated tests.

Typical company testing archetypes

Usually, companies are convinced that unit testing will provide tangible benefits and agree that these can be automated. If you are a company that manually performs unit testing, your engineers must have unlimited patience.

Integration tests form the middle ground, and companies approach this differently. Some companies believe that integration tests are optional if they write enough unit tests (more on that in the next section). Some companies have some integration tests, but they don't form part of the deployment pipeline or are only run manually once in a blue moon.

Finally, we have the companies that have integration tests, have them automated, and they form part of the deployment pipeline. There are other approaches/levels of maturity, but these are some common integration testing archetypes we see. At the final tier, we have our end-to-end tests, which may be automated and form part of the deployment process; if this is the case in your company, this section may be preaching to the choir. However, these tests are much more likely to exist in the form of a dedicated QA function, clicking through user interfaces, following steps in a spreadsheet or document, and then reporting back on the result, either pre- or post-deployment.

So, at the crux, we are looking at three separate kinds of tests:

- **Unit tests**: Testing atomic units of functionality within a single service or component

- **Integration tests**: Testing the interactions between components

- **End-to-end tests**: Testing the system's functionality from the end user's context

The case for test automation

With these three forms of test in mind, I would also like to call back to the top of your working memory the DORA metrics:

- Deployment frequency

- Lead time for changes

- Change failure rate

- Time to restore service

Tests involve optimizing one metric: *change failure rate*. The more testing we do before we deploy a change, the lower our change failure rate. Note that this eliminates an entire swath of the testing archetypes we discussed earlier in this subsection.

If your testing does not occur on your deployment path, you are not protecting your change failure rate! You might have a faster time to restore service as you may uncover errors or their source earlier with post-deployment tests, but this is an entirely different area of expertise (see Chapter 10 for observing your deployed architecture). So, we have established the requirement that for tests to have a meaningful impact on the performance of your software teams, they need to be on the critical path for deployment to production.

When we have manual processes, we end up batching together our changes so that they can keep up with the pace of change in our code bases. This protects the change failure rate. However, in reality, batching changes together increases our change failure rate because the chances of any of the changes we have batched together negatively impacting the application significantly increased compared to if we deploy those changes individually.

Let's say 5 of our changes fail if we deploy 100 changes individually. Then, we have a 5% change failure rate. If we deploy batches of 10 changes 10 times, we might get lucky, and those 5 failures across those 100 changes are all batched into 1 segment, but that's still a 10% change failure rate. More than likely, those 5 failures spread throughout those 10 segments, and now, up to half of those segments fail, resulting in a change failure rate of up to 50%. If we just do one significant change, then what ends up happening is every change has a failure. It's just a matter of magnitude, so batching things together, even though tests are on our critical path, can still cause issues with our change failure rate.

So, we have established that batches are bad for our change failure rate. Let's now look at our other metrics: our deployment frequency and lead time for changes. Both of these functions depend on our total pipeline time. Introducing manual stages into our pipeline significantly increases the time it takes to complete. Longer pipeline cycle times mean developers are less likely to deploy small incremental changes; instead, they are more likely to batch together changes, leading to the same problem we discussed before batching together changes for testing. This impacts our deployment frequency.

Our other metric, lead time for changes, is a function of all the linear steps that must occur before a change Is deployed to production. By increasing the pipeline time, even if we kept our changes atomic and deployed frequently, the lead time for changes would still be more significant because one of its components takes a long time to complete. So, manual testing is destructive for our change failure rate and affects our other metrics, lead time for changes, and deployment frequency. We discussed earlier on in the book that introducing stages on the deployment path that have long cycle times or increase the times that deployment also means that we are unlikely to perform the same checks when the service is heavily impacted, so changes that are hotfixes or are intended to be fixes for urgent issues in production tend not to be as rigorously tested as of the code that initially caused the problem in the first place.

So, if we follow our process to the letter, we will see that we negatively impact our time to restore services as well. We can improve our time to restore service only through workarounds and avenues outside of our standard operating procedures. This negates any benefit that might be achieved through the earlier detection of issues through testing production or outside the critical deployment path.

As soon as we introduce humans into our process, we introduce variability. Humans are very good at taking the unknown, applying their knowledge and heuristics, and solving problems they have not encountered before. Testing is the exact opposite of this process. We know the issues we want to test for and how to test for them. Therefore, humans are poorly suited to the task of manual testing. We can accelerate this process significantly through automation. As soon as we take humans out of the equation and introduce automated over manual processes, the function of how much testing we can perform does not become a question of *human* resources but of *compute* resources. With the advent of the cloud, on-demand compute resources can quickly be provisioned and deprovisioned as needed to perform testing. This process accelerates our feedback cycle, allowing us not only to have certainty that the changes we are applying will not cause failures but also to have all of our developers empowered to perform adequate testing on all of the code they push into a production environment.

Now, this may sound like humans don't add value to the testing process in any way; however, I would like to postulate that humans add unique value in how they can define and envision test suites rather than the execution of those test suites. The definition and creation of test suites is a unique skill; they are variable and nuanced, and humans are great at that task. A great joke goes like this: a developer walks into a bar and orders 1 beer; a tester walks into a bar and orders 1 beer, 10,000 beers, negative 1 beers, a sofa, and so on. Still, the part of testing that we value is the creative side, understanding the problem space, and coming up with unique edge cases to ensure consistency in behavior. The actual execution of these tests is something that testers are wasted on. This section won't tell you to make your entire testing team redundant. This section tells you to put your testing team to the best use possible by allowing them to exercise their creativity.

Migrating manual testing processes

As discussed, manual testing processes typically exist in the end-to-end space. The migration process for manual integration tests puts them on the critical path, as they likely already exist as code-driven tests. If they don't, then the integration tests can be created using the existing skill set of your development teams. Manual end-to-end tests, on the other hand, can seem like a much more daunting task to migrate. Our testing function may not have coding skills. However, that does not mean we must revamp our entire testing department. Instead, we can perform three key actions:

- Lean on our development function

- Utilize tooling to accelerate the migration

- Upskill our testing teams

As I said before, humans can deal with variability. Our development function may have exploited this not maliciously but inadvertently by relying on visual cues to the tester performing the manual testing. When we migrate to automated testing, typically, we must depend on properties in our user interface that are invisible to the tester but visible to our testing framework. For example, when we change a button in our interface to a hyperlink but keep the same styling, the tester is unlikely to register a change. Still, this is a significant change for an automated test suite looking for a button element.

Therefore, our development function needs to improve its working methods to ensure that the artifacts it produces are testable. In the web world, this may look like leveraging ARIA labels to provide meaning to specific elements. In this way, a hyperlink and a button that share an ARIA label can be treated similarly. Regarding aria labels, not only will your testers thank you for making your UI more testable but suitable aria labels also make your site more accessible. Hence, it's something you should be doing anyway. Our development function is already likely well versed in adding tests to the pipeline to production. So, we can lean on our development teams to help integrate this new test suite into the path to production, removing the requirement for this capability within our testing teams.

We still need help writing the tests. However, it's unlikely that our development teams will want to go through all of the documentation produced in the past by a manual testing team and convert them into automated tests. This is also not future-proof; any new test we want to add will depend on the development team. This is where we can utilize tooling to accelerate the migration. Many testing suites we would use for end-to-end testing include functionality allowing us to record tests directly from the browser. Using this functionality, we can do one last manual run of our tests, record them, and then save them for use in our automated testing framework.

Our source of truth is no longer copious pieces of documentation but codified tests with no ambiguity. This process gets us significantly closer to automated end-to-end testing without involving the development team. For this initial migration, interfacing with the development team may be beneficial in getting the project off the ground. However, in the long run, the testing team must complete this process autonomously.

We must upskill our testing teams in the framework that we use for creating tests. This does not mean that every tester needs to become a developer. However, every tester needs the capability to define, record, and integrate tests into the test suite autonomously. This process is a much smaller ask, but utilizing tooling and leaning on our development function prevents us from needing to change the structure of our teams. The one case in which I recommend changing the structure of your teams is to shift toward the structure we mentioned earlier in the book that allows teams to be self-sufficient.

If your testing function is a standalone unit of your business, consider integrating them into your delivery teams to enable them to be fully autonomous. Not only will this break down the adversarial nature between a standalone testing function and a development function but it will also allow end-to-end ownership of the delivery of the team's outcomes. This closer alignment means that testers can lean upon the development resources within their teams as they upskill to become fully self-sufficient.

Trying to recreate the cloud

In the previous section, we discussed the overuse of unit tests to compensate for the lack of integration tests. Good coding practices drive good testing. Our business logic, the part of our code that drives value, should be unit-tested. However, unit testing for this part of our code should not involve extensive mocking of the environment in which it runs. The anti-pattern we typically see in this space is that people try to recreate the cloud on their local environment through third-party tooling, extensive mocking, or some other method.

To dissect this anti-pattern, we will look at the traditional testing paradigm, what testing looks like in a cloud native world, and how we can best leverage cloud services to test our code. Previously, we focused on end-to-end, contract, and unit tests, so it should be no surprise that this section will focus heavily on integration tests.

The traditional testing paradigm

The traditional testing paradigm typically consists of a large number of unit tests because they're cheap, a few integration tests because they're a little bit harder to write and a little bit harder to run, and just a couple of end-to-end tests because, as discussed previously, this is often a manual function. This typically gives us a pattern referred to as the testing pyramid.

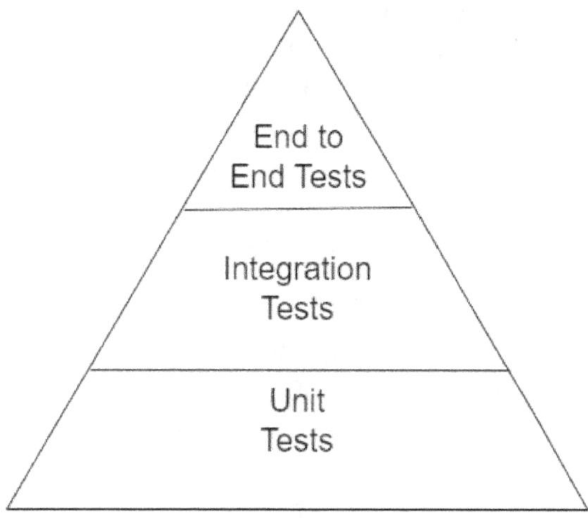

Figure 13.2 - The testing pyramid

In the initial premise for this section, I mentioned that our unit test should focus on testing the parts of our code that are unique to our business: our business logic. In the cloud world, resources are cheap, and much of the complexity that used to live inside our application can now be farmed out to the cloud service provider itself. This presents an interesting problem: if our logic is pushed out to the cloud service provider, less and less of our functionality becomes testable through unit tests. Typically, we see developers start relying on extensive mocking in this scenario. It's not uncommon to enter a code base at a client and see eight or more cloud services mocked out to test a piece of business logic. Third-party tools have also sprung up and promise to provide cloud-like functionality inside your test pipelines or local environment.

If we continue in our traditional mindset of unit tests first, then these all look like attractive propositions. When we look at the testing pyramid, it may feel that resorting to an integration test is a failure on behalf of the developer: *"I wasn't good enough to write a unit test for this."* We may feel that integration tests are reserved explicitly for very complex cross-service behaviors, but this leads us to integrated test territory, not integration test territory. Much like the producers of a popular nature documentary, we want to observe the behavior of our system in its natural habitat. In our case, its natural habitat just happens to be the cloud.

The testing honeycomb

Spotify R&D published an excellent article in 2018 examining the testing honeycomb (`https://engineering.atspotify.com/2018/01/testing-of-microservices/`). In this honeycomb, we remove our overdependence on unit tests as the base level of testing and rely instead on integration or service tests. Spotify specifically talks about the removal of integrated tests, which are tests that span multiple services. However, we believe that end-to-end tests can still produce value even if they span numerous services. They should not be taken as an indication of an individual service's health but as an overall system health check before deployment.

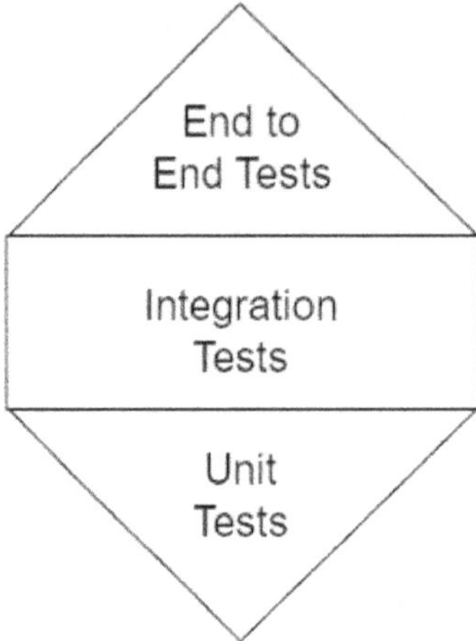

Figure 13.3 - The testing honeycomb

Using integration tests, we more accurately represent the real-world deployed environment than in unit tests. Instead of testing against a simulacrum of the cloud, we deploy our services to the cloud and then test them in their natural habitat. This was fine in the traditional model, where a large amount of our functionality existed within the context of our application.

However, as we have said, more of the common parts of our application are being outsourced to managed services in the cloud. Therefore, it can be easy to produce tight coupling between cloud services and the logic we want to test. In the next section, we will go into more detail on structuring our code, but for now, let's focus on integration testing.

Testing in the cloud versus testing for the cloud

Earlier in this book, we discussed development in ephemeral environments. The same concept can be used in our testing pipeline. Using the structure of the testing honeycomb, we have many integration tests that specify how our application interacts with the cloud environment. These tests can be run in a temporary cloud environment. This allows us to test our code in the cloud, using actual cloud services rather than mocking them. When we mock out services in the cloud, we are testing our code against our mental model of the cloud. When we use actual cloud services, there is no transitive mental model that our code needs to pass through to be tested.

There are some core concepts that we need to have implemented to be able to test our code in ephemeral environments:

- We must have solid **infrastructure as code** (**IaC**) foundations to spin up and tear down environments as required

- We need to understand which parts of our infrastructure take longer to provision and supply pre-provisioned resources for testing purposes to keep cycle times low

- Our testing pipeline must have access to a cloud environment

When discussing solid IaC foundations, we mean following good practices when implementing IaC. To test our applications effectively, we need to pull up just the part of our infrastructure required for testing instead of our entire application. Typically, we need firm domain boundaries between different application areas to test our system effectively with the cloud in isolation from other application components. For more information on providing firm boundaries between application components and strong cohesion within application components, we recommend reviewing the *Tight coupling, low cohesion* section.

The other interesting part of IaC that is typically exposed through this practice is the solidification and codification of specific IaC properties. When we need to deploy multiple copies of our application to run tests, sometimes numerous copies simultaneously, we can quickly highlight any areas of our infrastructure that have solidified around a single deployment. Hence, testing this way can also highlight gaps in our resiliency plan and ability to bring up new application instances.

Some parts of IaC configurations can be provisioned very quickly. Things such as serverless functions or API gateways can be provisioned in minimal time. On the other hand, more traditional resources such as relational database instances or virtual machines may require more time to be created. Typically, we can use common resources between our test environments and partition them by namespaces or any other supported partitioning method. For example, suppose we had a relational database service. In that case, each test environment might use the same database instance, which takes a long time to provision. However, create a separate database within that instance to perform its test and then delete it upon completion. An in-memory key store might use a single instance with keys prefixed with namespaces unique to the test suite execution. This process ensures that we keep our cycle times low and provide fast feedback to our developers while also allowing us to maintain a high deployment frequency and low lead time for changes.

Fundamental to all of this is that our testing environment needs to be a real cloud environment. This requirement might mean linking our testing pipeline with cloud credentials, infrastructure pipelines, and CI/CD processes. This increases complexity; however, the benefit is increased certainty in our deployments. Applying the same best cloud practices described elsewhere in this book to the cloud environment used for testing is also essential. We can still apply the practices of good cloud governance, FinOps, DevSecOps, and platform engineering to make this cloud environment a first-class citizen in our cloud estate. By practicing good hygiene in this cloud environment, we not only make it easier for the developers who need to run tests in this environment but also gain increased certainty in the tests we run, avoiding the issues of flaky pipelines, long pipeline runtimes, and long lead times for changes.

Testing non-functional requirements

Now that we are testing in a real cloud environment and have mature integration tests, we can also test for properties that were previously unfeasible. Some of the key properties that are great to test for in this space include the following:

- **Latency**: This ensures our requests are completed in a reasonable amount of time

- **Consistency**: Many cloud systems operate on the principle of eventual consistency, but we might have non-functional requirements regarding time to consistency

- **Scalability**: We might want to perform load testing to ensure that our services can handle the expected traffic shapes

- **Resilience**: Assuming we have resiliency strategies, we will want to test them based on the reasons we discussed earlier in the book

At this point, you need to apply your judgment. Previously, we talked about testing needing to be on the critical path to be useful. Testing non-functional requirements is not always feasible to perform on the critical path and often deals with slowly changing properties of our application. Therefore, running this sort of testing on a schedule can occasionally be better due to its complex nature. Typically, these tests are used to test for regression from previous executions. We can also apply the same rigor of checking for regressions of non-functional requirements on our other tests.

We can certainly check test execution times for regressions on the critical path. In a recent case, a manually discovered regression uncovered a vulnerability in XZ, a popular compression utility. A developer noticed regressions in SSH execution times, which, in the subsequent investigation, revealed a complex multi-year-long plot to backdoor the utility. The full story sounds like the plot of a spy movie and is worth additional research by any interested readers.

Even though these were manually discovered regressions, had they not been found, they could have had potentially catastrophic effects for many projects built on these tools.

Poorly structured code

One of the key anti-patterns we see in writing cloud native software is a false equivalency between 100% code coverage and code quality. It's important to remember that high code quality and good coding practices should naturally result in sufficient code coverage to guarantee the behavior we want to test. As professionals, we must ensure that we adhere to these practices. One of the main impediments to writing good tests is poorly structured code, or, to put it another way, low-quality code. Therefore, in this section, we will explore some common anti-patterns that can arise when writing cloud native software and how that impacts our ability to test.

Key terms

Before we discuss code structure, we need to define some key terms to understand the topic at hand:

- **Business logic** is anything our application does that transforms the information between our user and the persistence layer. Business logic might consist of evaluating custom rules to determine whether a customer is eligible for a product or assigning inventory to a new order that has just entered a purchasing system. Fundamentally, business logic is the part of our application that presents our unique business proposition. If we connect the user directly to the persistence layer, are we adding any value for the customer? Other non-business logic areas of the company still derive value by providing things such as a good user experience, reliability, and fulfillment. But, in a software sense, the codifying and repeatability of processes through business logic is usually one of the core elements through which we derive value.

- **Side effects** are anything our application does that affects other parts of the system and relies on behavior outside the defined function. For example, a side effect might be creating a new record in the database or sending a notification to a user's phone. Anything that our function does other than returning a value based on its arguments is a side effect. Side effects are not inherently wrong. Instead, they are an essential part of our application, allowing us to perform actions such as persistence, evolution, and eventing.

The monolith

Just because we escaped the monolithic application through microservices or serverless functions does not mean we've escaped the conceptual idea of the monolith within our code. I defined the previous two terms because they represent two significant but very different actions an application must perform. The critical difference is that a pure function can typically represent our business logic. This function has no side effects and relies solely on its arguments to produce a return value. To maintain the results of this function, we must rely on side effects to communicate with other parts of our system, such as our database.

This is where we can once again fall into the monolithic trap. It can be tempting to intersperse our business logic with side effects as we require them. This makes sense from a logical perspective, and from structuring our code, we add effects as we need them where we need them. However, this leads us down the path of high coupling and low cohesion, which we had previously in the monolithic structure. Instead, what we should look to do is separate our concerns from our business logic. The rules that define how we operate should be written as pure functions. They shouldn't have any side effects, making our company's unique value proposition directly testable.

When we start introducing side effects directly alongside our business logic, we suddenly run into the requirement to provide mocking that mimics these side effects simply to test the rules by which we run our business. This can turn the practice of testing our business logic from a 10-minute exercise testing a pure function into a multi-hour exercise where most of our time is spent setting up the environment to run our tests by mocking out the side effects. Recalling the testing honeycomb from the previous section, we can test our side effects through a different type of test. In that case, we should use integration tests and test our code in the cloud rather than extensive mocking and unit tests. The logical extension of this is writing our business logic as a pure function and testing only our business logic to ensure correctness against our business rules and expectations. Then, when we want to test our system's side effects, we can begin integration testing against the deployed service.

So, now we've managed to separate the concerns of our business logic from the side effects required to make it useful. A lot of functional glue still binds our business logic with our side effects. While this could be tested through integration testing, other alternatives allow us to increase our code coverage without replicating the cloud in our unit tests. This is advantageous because unit tests have lower complexity, faster execution, and faster feedback cycles than integration tests.

Hexagonal architecture

In 2005, Alistair Cockburn introduced the concept of hexagonal architecture. Broadly speaking, hexagonal architecture provides a methodology for decoupling the implementation of our side effects from their usage. I'll provide a diagram for hexagonal architecture and then we can go into it in more detail.

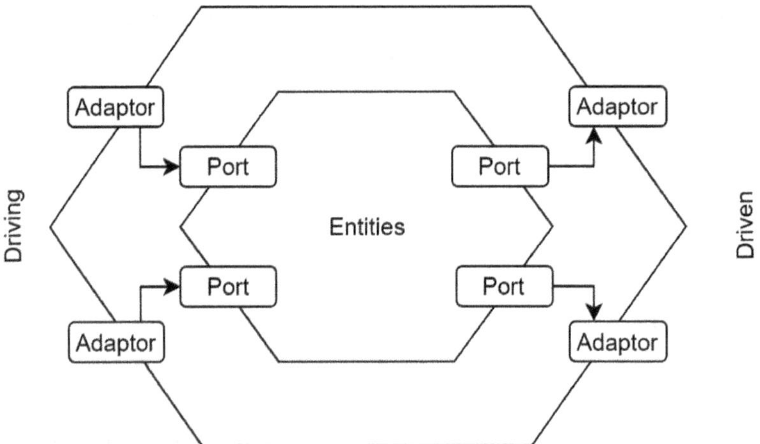

Figure 13.4 - Conceptual diagram of the hexagonal architecture model

At the core of our application, we have our application code that glues our side effects and business logic together; this bundle is our entity. The side effects are exposed through standard interfaces referred to as **ports**. For example, we might have a persistence port or a notification port. What's important is that the entity is agnostic of the implementation of these ports. All it knows is the interface by which this functionality is exposed. Adapters implement these interfaces or ports. The adapter contains all the knowledge to interact with the external system. For example, our database port may connect to an adapter that provides a database through a PostgreSQL-compatible service. Our entity is unaware of Postgres; it could be DynamoDB, SQL Server, MySQL, or any other database engine. What's important is that it exposes the functionality expected by the entity and defined in the port. Likewise, our notification port could use SMS email push notifications or carrier pigeons; it doesn't matter to the entity.

Similarly, we have ports driven by external adapters for incoming traffic to our entity. Whether our entity is triggered by an event from an event queue or by a direct HTTP request, we have ports that represent the interface of the request and then adapters that connect those ports to our entity. This is a crucial distinction: we have driving ports, external forces that act upon our entity, and driven ports, which our entity uses to act on external systems.

This might seem unrelated to testing; however, one of the key benefits of this architecture pattern is that it makes our entities, our application code, agnostic of where it's being run. The complexity of actually interacting with actual services is hidden away in the adapters. Mocking our side effects becomes much easier through the simplified interface presented through our ports, as we can produce a new adapter that implements the expected behavior rather than trying to mock out cloud native services. This also prevents us from tying our unit testing and application code to specific libraries or SDKs, as all of that is taken care of in our adapters and will eventually be tested through our integration tests.

So, here, we not only get a benefit in the testability of our code but we also gain portability of our code if we need to change an integration with an external system; it is a simple matter of writing a new adapter that agrees with the interface for the existing port. This negates one of the key arguments against writing cloud native software: it will cause vendor lock-in. By utilizing hexagonal architecture, we can ensure the code we are writing is agnostic of where it's being run, increasing the portion of our code base that will be utilized if we decide to migrate cloud providers.

Structuring your code correctly from day one

We have covered test-driven development in a few sections of this chapter, but I want to discuss it in a different context. When we talk about structuring our code to be testable and about good structure in general, TDD can help us achieve this outcome. If the first thing we write in our code base for new functionality is a test, then, by default, the code we write to fulfill this test will be testable implicitly.

I will use Java to paint a picture of testable versus untestable code, as it has some insidious anti-patterns. Let's assume we're testing some business logic, and we have a class that contains everything we need for our feature to run. We might be tempted to implement our business logic as a private method in this class to call it from within our application logic that is exposed to the outside world as a public method. If we're already following some of the practices in this section, we might also mark our private business logic method as static to indicate that it doesn't rely on this class's internal state.

Now, it comes time to test our code; of course, the main function we want to test is our business logic to ensure that the business rules we are solidifying in the code are correctly implemented. However, due to the structure of our class, this is one of the least testable parts of our code because it's private and only exposed to our class's internals.

What can happen in this scenario is that the developer can be tempted to do one of the following:

- Make the method public
- Test the application code in a way that tests all bounds of business logic

The first method is not preferable because we're changing the visibility of class internals specifically for testing purposes. Other people relying on this business logic may call it directly from this class, which is not its primary purpose, violating the single responsibility principle.

The second is not preferable because we are testing the code through a proxy, which makes the test brittle to application changes. It also causes us more work on the testing side as we have to mock out everything required for the application code to run.

Now, consider if we had written a test that expected a method that would implement our business logic. What might our code look like in this scenario? We're free from the constraints of the application so it's unlikely that we would try to test it through the application code. We could make a public method, but it's also likely our application code doesn't exist yet because we want to refine the business logic. So, rather than add it to the class for the application code, we instead produce a static class that solely implements our business logic, is directly testable, has a single responsibility, and is consumable within our application code.

Therefore, TDD is not only a tool for writing productive tests but also for helping drive well-structured code. This doesn't mean you need to write every test before starting to write code, just that you define the core behavior that you want to achieve in advance.

Summary

Testing is one of the greatest tools we have in the cloud native toolbox. It prevents regressions, ensures compatibility, and allows us to have more confidence that the behavior of our system closely matches the behavior of our mental model. Hopefully, you have picked up some tips on how to build meaningful tests without blowing your development timelines. Good testing practices are critical to scaling cloud native applications, and by avoiding the anti-patterns in this chapter, you will be well on your way to deploying quickly and with confidence. We have covered a lot so far. Next up, we will look at how to get started on your cloud native journey.

Get This Book's PDF Version and Exclusive Extras

Scan the QR code (or go to `packtpub.com/unlock`). Search for this book by name, confirm the edition, and then follow the steps on the page.

Note: Keep your invoice handly. Purchase made directly from packt don't require one.

14

How to Get Started with Your Cloud Native Improvement Journey

By now, you will have absorbed a lot of information. We have discussed many anti-patterns and focus areas so far. In the two remaining chapters, we want to prepare you to commence your cloud improvement journey and transition into best practices.

In this chapter, we will focus on the first part: starting your cloud native improvement journey. We will go through the following areas:

- How to identify anti-patterns

- Defining a target state

- Performing a gap analysis

- Structuring a business case

It looks like we have another information-packed chapter ahead, so let's get started with identifying anti-patterns.

Identifying anti-patterns

In the previous chapters, we have gone through a detailed process of identifying anti-patterns. We now want to keep it at a higher level to identify alarming behaviors we must look out for. We will group the anti-patterns by area. This will help us stay focused rather than get lost in detail.

Once we know what behavior or observation could be an alarming sign, we can go back to the individual chapter and look up detailed information about anti-pattern recognition, the risks it brings, and how to remediate it. Let's see how we can spot anti-patterns; we will go through them and group them by problem spaces.

General indicators

There are general giveaways for anti-patterns. The following mistakes typically impact several areas:

- A very obvious sign that we will be in trouble is if we have to cut corners to meet deadlines. We will produce average or below-average quality and build up tech debt. If there is no time later on to remediate the tech debt, we will drown in operational complexity.

- Underestimating the cultural impact and learning curve of a cloud native and DevSecOps transformation is also a trap that can impact all areas, from strategy to security, compliance, data quality, operational complexity, and so on. A common giveaway is a lack of training budget and allocated training time. A lack of pairing with external consultants indicates that the knowledge is not embedded in our organization.

- A lack of standardization of building blocks and operational procedures is a red flag that we can easily see. Inconsistency will increase technical debt operational complexity, decreasing resilience and a self-service experience that helps us achieve fast release cycles. Giveaways for this anti-pattern include a lack of a service catalog or opinionated CI/CD pipelines, little changes that take a considerable amount of time, and an operating model that has never been agreed on, is outdated, or does not have clear demarcations.

- If we skip phases in our SDLC, our outcomes will have gaps. For example, if we don't work out requirements and start with the design, we miss out on requirements in our solutions. Typically, those are operational, security, resilience, testing, data consistency, and non-functional requirements. The same is the case when we start with implementing without a design. This does not stop us from using Agile practices. We just need to consider the holistic SDLC picture.

After those general indicators, we will now look into particular problem spaces, starting with cultural and automation-related anti-patterns.

DevSecOps culture and automation

We will examine several key indicators here and reference the chapters that describe them in greater detail:

- If developers accidentally delete instances, containers, or databases or manually create certificates or secrets, that is a sign that we have an immature CI/CD pipeline and do not have sufficient guardrails in place. It also means we are not enforcing the principle of least privilege and must set up the required permission scans to scale back permissions accordingly. We discussed these in *Chapters 5* and *6*.

- If we heavily rely on penetration tests before a go-live and severe findings are identified in an audit, then we lack a continuous assurance process, which we discussed in *Chapter 6*.

- If we don't have good test coverage, we will either have outages or our testers will become a bottleneck when we try to achieve fast release cycles. To leverage all the cloud benefits, we need functional and non-functional tests embedded in our pipelines. This includes contract tests, performance tests, and security tests such as secrets scanning and vulnerability scanning. We explored those test types in *Chapter 13*.

We can see that some of the described anti-patterns, such as taking shortcuts, can be linked to some of the general indicators. As a next step, we will summarize strategic and cloud adoption-related indicators.

Strategy and cloud adoption-related anti-patterns

This group of anti-patterns seems particularly hard to spot by members of a centralized architecture team, and the consequences have a long-term negative impact on our transformation journey. Let's look into them now:

- If our cloud strategy has not been updated over a year or our actions are not aligned with the strategy's articulated goals, then we have a problem. It means we are either heading in the wrong direction or don't even know which direction our organization should take. If priorities change frequently during a sprint, that is also a giveaway for reactive behavior, and we explored this anti-pattern remediation in *Chapter 2*.

- If we rely on a very decentralized governance model that does not allow for team autonomy, we cannot scale our business sufficiently, and we probably struggle to meet our customer needs. On the other hand, if we do not have any governance in place, we will struggle with compliance, reliability, self-service experience, and other challenges. A red flag is if our implementations do not reflect security policies and compliance requirements. We will need the right balance of guardrails, cultural transformation, and training, which we explored in *Chapter 3*.

- If we lack cost accountability and do not have a mature charge-back model in place, then there is no incentive for the product teams to optimize their cloud value. The result will be resource underutilization, a lack of cost-related architecture decisions, and regular cloud overspending. We discussed this in *Chapter 4*.

- When we run cloud migrations and do not replatform or refactor our applications to leverage the full cloud native benefits, we will experience increased operational complexity and security procedures. Minimum stakeholder commitment and a lack of migration planning are revealing factors here, and we investigated this in *Chapter 12*.

Of course, these anti-patterns have flow-on effects on other problem spaces. One of them is operations and observability, which we will explore next.

Operational and observability anti-patterns

This category will impact the reliability of our applications and is likely to result in team frustrations and potential SLA penalties:

- If a user reports an incident but the incident team does not receive any alerts, we know that our logging and monitoring coverage is not as good as it should be. Logging and monitoring must span the entire stack, from network to operating system, application logic, and database, as discussed in *Chapter 10*.

- If we get too many alarms, we will end up with alarm fatigue. The result is that there will be an alert, but no one will respond because these alerts happen continuously. We must ensure we use the correct log severity levels and not use info or debug levels in higher environments, as we discussed in *Chapter 10*.

- If we breach performance SLAs due to slow response times, we need to pinpoint the bottleneck. Without traces and spans, we will not have the insight to improve our architecture, and we explored this in *Chapter 10*.

- If we do not have a DR strategy and have not tested a recovery in a while, we know we are not in good shape for a real-world recovery scenario. Just because we are taking backups does not mean we can recover. The backups might be corrupt, the deployment might not be as automated as we think, and the runbooks could be outdated. We discussed this in *Chapter 11*.

Now that we have summarized indicators for operations and observability, we are ready to move on to the final group: technology indicators.

Technology anti-patterns

Within the technology-related indicators, we will focus on the areas of applications, data, and networking:

- Stateful applications often indicate that we have been carrying technical debt for a while and have not refreshed our architecture. That could be due to a technical limitation of a **custom off-the-shelf** (**COTS**) product or because we have not allocated enough time to improving our architecture continuously. Stateful applications will hold us back when adopting cloud native features such as FaaS, blue-green deployments, and auto-scaling. We explored this in *Chapter 7*.

- When we use tight coupling in our application, we cause long waiting times and also burn through compute and data expenses due to increased CPU, memory, or function call times. Mechanisms such as asynchronous calls and using queues mean we can decouple our architecture and scale more efficiently. We discussed this in *Chapter 7*.

- If we use only relational databases for every single use case, we are probably on the wrong track. Purpose-built databases such as NoSQL or time series databases exist for a reason. They perform quick lookups for particular use cases. They also have features relational databases do not offer, such as event streams or time-based analytics, which we explored in *Chapter 8*.

- If we don't have active-active or failover routing, our network link is a single point of failure. Cloud native networking constructs, which we discussed in *Chapter 9*, can avoid that scenario and cater to resilience.

Anti-patterns can occur across a wide range of areas, from culture to CI/CD, strategy, cloud adoption, operations, and observability. Spotting those anti-patterns is not always easy, especially if we have applied them for a while. After internalizing the anti-patterns, it is time to move on to defining where we want to be and identifying the gaps between our current state and the target state.

Defining the best outcome and identifying gaps

Once we have identified pain points in our cloud native adoption journey, we must identify the root cause. We have investigated the cause in depth throughout this book and have a good understanding of possible problem areas, such as cultural aspects, a lack of strategy, or operational excellence. By now, we also know that some of the remediations will require significant undertaking. Often, there are dependencies, which means we need to solve other issues before we can tackle the problem we are trying to solve. For instance, if we want to improve our CI/CD pipeline to establish a better security posture and quicker time to market, we might first need to establish a mature DevSecOps culture. During this chapter, we will frequently use the terms *current state*, *target state*, and *gaps*. Our definitions deviate from the TOGAF to align more with a cloud native context.

> **Definitions – current state, target state, and gaps**
>
> The **current state** is our current situation. It can refer to our current architecture, ways of working, operating model, security, or compliance posture. Some architecture frameworks assume that this is a specification that has been formally approved, but this does not necessarily reflect the reality, in our experience.
>
> The **target state** is the description of the situation or architecture we aim for. This is not necessarily 100% aligned with all best practices since we deal with the constraints described in the project management triangle.
>
> A **gap** is "*A statement of the difference between two states. It is used in the context of gap analysis, where the difference between the Current State and Target State is identified.*" [source: TOGAF – `https://www.opengroup.org/togaf`].

We will now explore our current state and what our target state should look like.

Defining the current state

We want to establish a helicopter view of everything we should tackle to get a holistic picture while still being resourceful with our time and budget. This doesn't mean we can tackle them all, as we will deal with constraints and, therefore, we have to make trade-off decisions. The constraints are depicted in the following project management triangle diagram.

Figure 14.1 – The project management triangle (source: https://
en.wikipedia.org/wiki/Project_management_triangle)

The triangle represents the key factors that impact a project's success: **scope, time**, and **cost**. It shows that changes in one constraint will affect the others. For example, increasing a project's scope will likely require more time and money. We have to balance these constraints to meet project goals while maintaining quality. The triangle emphasizes that optimizing all three aspects simultaneously is challenging, which creates the need for trade-offs. These are the steps that will help us articulate the helicopter view:

1. **Defining focus areas:**

    Looking into every single issue that we could solve quickly becomes overwhelming. Therefore, we need to pick some focus areas to start with. This will later help us limit the scope to address cost and time constraints. Internal and external factors can drive the priorities of our focus areas. Internal examples are an unreliable environment or immature DevSecOps practices. External factors may be a new regulatory framework we must address or a recent data breach. Depending on the severity of the driver, we need to choose our focus areas. We probably also want to balance strategic uplifts with quick wins to gain momentum.

2. **Assessing existing documentation:**

    We will have documentation that can help us get a clearer picture of the current state. This sounds great in theory, but quite often, the documentation is incomplete and out of date. Documentation that is out of date can be misleading since it doesn't reflect the actual current state. Therefore, it will be good to validate the documentation with the key stakeholders, which will bring us to the next step. Suppose we struggle to find the corresponding documentation because it is scattered across Google Drive and several Confluence spaces, including personal spaces. In that case, we might add standardization of documentation to our target state.

3. **Identifying stakeholders:**

We need to identify our stakeholders from various business units, such as customer engagement, strategy, operations, security, development, and testing. The stakeholders are the **subject matter experts (SMEs)**. A product or service owner will know what the application is capable of and what enhancements are required to be more competitive in the market. Someone involved in the operations will be able to tell us what the operational shortcomings are, such as an unstable runtime, lack of patching, or observability, which makes incident management challenging. There are different variations of stakeholder matrices. Some of them illustrate the power and interest of stakeholders. At a minimum, we want to create a list that shows us the business unit, the job function, and the representative's name.

4. **Planning our workshops:**

Workshops with the identified stakeholders will help us provide more details about our problem spaces. We want to be mindful of our stakeholders' valuable time at this stage. We do not have funding for our change initiative, and our stakeholders must perform their jobs. Therefore, we need to be diligent about who needs to be in what conversation. It is always good to have a short kick-off meeting so that everyone hears the same story about what we want to achieve. Let's say we want to improve our network reliability. Therefore, we must engage our network, security, and cloud platform SMEs. We could run two 1.5-hour workshops, with the first one exploring the current state:

5. **Current state discovery workshops:**

The first workshop captures the current state and all the challenges that come with it. We need to make sure that we create a safe environment where everyone can bring up their views and problems. We should also bring relevant documentation since it will help us start the conversation. Capturing previous incidents is very helpful to gain insights into where the problems are.

For example, during a previous incident, we could not fail over since our active-passive topology did not work, or we could not troubleshoot because the logging did not capture all the information we required. Ideally, this is a highly interactive session, and the outcome could be high-level network and data flow diagrams, current response SLAs, and throughput requirements. We also want to cover any remediation ideas that the SMEs will raise. We must capture all information and take detailed notes. Additionally, we should record the meeting after everyone has consented to look up the details when we analyze the findings, which we will do next.

We have now collected all the information about our current state. We can now analyze the findings and prepare a target state proposal, which is what we will discuss next.

Defining the target state

Having a holistic and validated picture of the current state and all the pain points will help us to articulate a target state and gaps. This is how we get started:

1. **The target state strawman**:

   After the current state discovery workshop, we need to analyze our findings. We captured great meeting notes. For each finding, we should document the problem statement, impact, gap, remediation steps or options, business benefit, and priority recommendations.

   The remediation options are short statements of what could be done to bridge the gap and get us from the current to the target state. If we identify dependencies, we need to call them out. At this stage, we only need high-level statements. Depending on how many areas we covered during the workshop, we will have findings across several problem areas. If that is the case, it is worthwhile grouping those findings. That way, we can better structure the following workshop, which will help us define work packages later.

2. **Target state discovery workshop**:

   We need to prepare a short and crisp visual presentation for this workshop. This could be a spreadsheet, slides, or diagrams in our drawing software, such as Lucidchart or Miro.

   For instance, it can be a combination of a spreadsheet for the facts and diagrams for the solution recommendation. It is critical to keep the workshop well structured, get everyone's feedback, and provide clarifications as needed. At the end of the workshop, we should have our proposal validated. This includes identified gaps and an agreement on the proposed solutions and priorities. Since the effort estimate is our next step, we must assign the right SME for each remediation. By now, it should be obvious who the right SMEs are for each remediation. It is essential to remind the SMEs of two things:

   - Firstly, do not assume that they are not necessarily the individual who performs the change. If the person is the most knowledgeable, the estimate will be relatively low, but they might not be available to perform the change.

   - The second call-out considers the organizational complexity, especially for regulated industries. Now that we have allocated two estimators for each remediation, we are ready for the activity.

3. **Gathering effort estimates**:

   The next step is a high-level effort estimate. Sometimes, this is referred to as T-shirt sizing when we only categorize the magnitude of change between small and extra-large or higher. However, we want some representative numbers.

   An approach that has worked well over the years is having two individuals provide their effort per remediation. Some SMEs underestimate tasks, and others estimate conservatively because they know potential hold-ups and complications. Every person must provide their confidence level as a percentage. If we have just done a required task and know the exact time it took, the confidence level will be close to 100%. If we are unsure, the percentage will be low, such as 50%.

Rather than doing this completely offline, we usually get better results when SMEs pair up for a video call to review their assigned remediations and discuss the complexity of the required change. As a rule of thumb, we will discuss a medium complex change for 2 to 5 minutes.

The following table illustrates a simplified version of remediation actions and estimates. The first column contains an ID to make sure we can reference the items more easily; the `Task` column describes the required action followed by a clarification comment column. We probably want to align the action to a benefit or risk category we address, which we do in the next column. The remaining four columns capture the first effort estimate in days (`EE-1`) and the first confidence level (`CL-1`), and then the same again for the estimate of the second SME:

ID	Task	Comments	Benefit	Risk	EE-1	CL-1	EE-2	CL-2
S-01	Remove human access for Test, UAT, and Prod	Update IAM roles and/ or service control policies	Security and compliance uplift Promote automation best practices	CI/CD knowledge gaps might delay developers CI/CD pipelines need to be created for legacy apps Training might be required	7	80%	5	90%
S-02	Enforce encryption at rest	Update service control policies	Security and compliance uplift	Increased cost for certain encryption keys Latency overhead	15	90%	12	80%
S-03	Enable packet inspection for third-party integration	Deploy network firewall and update routing in all accounts	Security uplift	Additional monitoring and alerting scope Increased cost for the new capability	120	60%	100	50%
T-01	Enable self-service DNS creation	Enable subdomain creation for business units	Improved user experience and time to market	DNS records might not align with Internal standards unless guardrails are established	20	80%	15	60%

Table 14.1 – Remediation actions and effort estimates

4. **Finalizing the time estimates**:

Next, we take the average of the two individual effort estimates per remediation. Then, we look at the confidence level. We will add an appropriate contingency percentage to the average time estimate depending on the confidence level. For high confidence levels above 90%, we will add 5%; for low confidence levels at 50%, we can add 25%, and go higher, the lower the confidence level. Of course, those numbers can be adjusted; the most important thing is to keep them consistent. We can estimate the contingency per line item or as a bulk percentage.

5. **Getting ready for the business case:**

    As a next step, we need to validate the effort estimate with the SMEs involved in the previous two workshops. The SMEs will not challenge their own effort estimate, but it increases the buy-in if we can walk everyone through the holistic picture. This is an excellent opportunity to provide visibility to what has been produced as a team effort. We know that change is challenging for individuals, especially when it impacts ways of working and requires the adoption of new skills or letting go of responsibilities. This is a great time to thank everyone for their dedication, input, and open-mindedness in getting our organization into better shape.

Now, we have a solid picture of our current state, the target state, the gaps, and the remediations required to bridge those gaps. We also have priorities assigned to the remediations, and we grouped them by problem spaces. We are in a knowledgeable position. *"Knowledge is power"* is a well-known quote, and in this case, it puts us in a solid position to start a business case that can improve our organization. Let's look into this now.

Defining the best outcome and identifying gaps

Up to now, we have created a solid skeleton that helps us articulate a high-level design, benefits, and rough effort estimate for the initiative we want to propose. But there are still a couple of steps ahead of us until we can start on the business case and get it into a shape that gives us confidence that it will be endorsed. We will also need different views for different target groups, and more importantly, we need to add more details about the business benefits. In this last section of this chapter, we want to focus on the following areas:

- Socializing our planned initiative across the organization

- Getting to the next level of detail

- Creating a work break-down structure

- Crafting the business case document

- Navigating the organization to get an endorsement

For each of these areas, we will explain why it is essential and what we must consider to make it a successful start to our best practice journey. Let's start by engaging the wider group.

Socializing the high-level plan with the broader group

We know that humans are resistant to change. Therefore, we need to provide early visibility and insight into what we want to achieve. That way, others can reflect longer about changes that might impact them. That gives them more thinking time, and they might even provide valuable feedback that could lead to a better outcome. Continually engaging with the broader group will also help us earn trust. We will need that not only for the business case approval but also for the implementation.

When others believe in our actions, they are prepared to help. These are the actions we need to take during this phase:

1	Continuing the core stakeholder engagement:
	<ul><li>Maintain ongoing conversations with the stakeholders involved in our previous two workshops to stay aligned with evolving requirements.</li><li>Use existing cadence meetings for updates or regular one-on-one meetings depending on the stakeholder's personality. Some individuals don't raise concerns in front of a group.</li><li>We need to address all insights to turn our proposal into a success.</li></ul>
2	Identifying the broader stakeholder group:
	<ul><li>Use existing governance forums for new proposals.</li><li>Examples are an architecture working group, engineering working group, architecture review board, change approval board, technical review board, and strategic governance forum.</li><li>Larger organizations usually have hierarchies. For example, the architectural fit might need to be endorsed by one forum before the cost and risk can be supported by another forum.</li></ul>
3	Engaging the broader stakeholder group:
	<ul><li>We want to present our proposal to the required forums first, and we need to make sure they have the proper target group representation.</li><li>The governance structure can be very different from company to company.</li><li>We need someone to help us navigate the governance process if we are new to an organization, such as our manager or peer contact.</li><li>When we present our proposal, we need to be mindful of two aspects:<ul><li>Not everyone has the in-depth knowledge of the problem space that we have been focusing on for a while. Therefore, we must adjust our language and consider the target group with visuals, such as architecture diagrams.</li><li>We must watch for body language tonality and proactively listen to feedback. Observing the room will help us to identify concerns and set up follow-ups with the individual stakeholders.</li></ul></li></ul>

Table 14.2 – Socializing the high-level plan

The activities we just explored will help us get to the next level of detail, which we will discuss next.

Adding organization-specific details

We want to get to the next level of detail and will tackle this from several angles. We will start with internal factors that will impact cost and timelines. How detailed we need to be will depend on the nature of the organization, which we will discuss next:

- **The right level of detail:**

  Kicking off new initiatives is usually easier for start-ups that just got seed funding. We must prove a robust due diligence process for regulated industries and government organizations that outlines pros and cons and a neutral vendor selection process.

  The latter might require a **request for quote (RFQ)** or **request for proposal (RFP)**, and the procurement department can assist with templates and guidelines. If many business units compete for a budget, we must prepare well. This includes good visuals, sound data that backs up our proposal, realistic estimates for the implementation, ongoing license fees, and other operational expenses. The required level of detail will vary depending on the organizational context, and we need to factor that into the artifacts we create.

- **Producing new views:**

  We must create different views for different stakeholders, such as architecture views, process flows, or RACI matrices. We will need high-level views for enterprise architects and describe the benefits, opportunities, risks, reliability, and so on. We will need detailed network diagrams illustrating data flows and routing for the network team.

  The security team will want to see the security controls we put in place, such as traffic inspection, network access control lists, DDoS protection, secrets management, and so on. The risk team might require a risk matrix. The list gets longer, depending on the organizational context we discussed earlier.

- **Identifying skill gaps:**

  Since we have gone through a more detailed effort estimate, we have a clearer picture of the skills that will be required. We need to address skill gaps in our costing and time estimates if there are skill gaps. The upskilling is usually done using several different channels. They can be classroom courses, lowering the chance that our team members get distracted by ad-hoc requests, as long as they don't keep monitoring their email, Slack, or Teams channels.

  Classroom courses offer more flexibility since they can be done anytime from anywhere. In addition to courses, we should use team augmentation. With this approach, we bring in experts from a consultancy who work with our teams to complete the job. But most importantly, we must ensure that knowledge transfer to our teams is happening. We need to address this in our time estimate. We will capture all training-related expenses because we need them for our business case.

- **Identifying cultural and change management gaps**:

  If our proposal involves a cultural transformation, we need to address this. We might need to hire a change manager and have conversations with the **human resources** (**HR**) department to update job descriptions.

  We also need to factor in the lower productivity during the transition phase while our teams adjust to the new ways of working and dedicate time to training initiatives. The time it takes to transform an organizational culture is typically underestimated. During this phase, it will be helpful to have conversations with HR. If we have a change manager in our company, they can provide high-level estimates. HR and change management can provide more insight into what organization-specific activities will be required and what notice periods we need to factor into our roadmap.

- **Operating model**:

  Does our current operating model support all the aspects of the new initiative? Are we introducing any new components or third-party solutions? If there is a new vendor that we have to onboard, who will do that? Who will manage the licenses and monitor license limits? Is there a new maintenance activity required, such as patching or creating new container images that need to be rolled out frequently? If we have gaps, we need to define who is accountable, responsible, need to be informed, or consulted. If we have an existing RACI matrix, we can add those new activities. If we do not have one, we should start creating one and involving our stakeholders to mature the current operating model.

Now that we have explored our organizational context and their combined impacts, we can move on to external factors and technology impacts.

Addressing external factors and technology impacts

External factors will depend on the industry and market we operate in, the skill market, and the economic cycle. Architectural changes or a volume increase will drive technology impacts, and we will look into that category first:

- **Architecture and volume increase impacts**:

  When we modify our architecture, we need to consider whether we need to upscale any downstream systems. If we expand to a multi-region deployment, our application will create more logs, such as audit logs. We will need to ingest those logs, and there might be a license impact, or we might need to upgrade our storage. The cost of logging is often underestimated, and it is worthwhile to look into current log volumes. A multi-region deployment will also incur cross-region data transfer fees, which we must consider. We will also need more TLS certificates. We will incur increased expenses if we acquire them from a third party. We need to capture those downstream impacts for the total cost because we need those numbers to create the business case document. If our new solution is successful, it will likely lead to increased traffic, and our infrastructure will need to scale out more. This will lead to increased data transfer fees and additional costs for our infrastructure resources, which we discussed in *Chapter 4*.

- **Existing tech debt and strategic uplift**:

  There is always tech debt that will slow us down. As part of the new initiative, we need to consider what can be remediated to achieve a better outcome. We need to consider gaps in our CI/CD landscape. Do we have code scanning in place and automated testing? Do we have all the guardrails for our CI/CD toolchain and the cloud platform? Do we need to improve our *Landing Zone* because it does not consider security or compliance segregation enough? These gaps will hold us back, and they will either slow down delivery timelines or increase the overall risk. Therefore, we should remediate them, as we discussed in *Chapter 4*, and we need to re-architect on-premises applications for a cloud migration, which we explored in *Chapter 12*.

- **Regulatory considerations**:

  If our new solution needs to address regulatory requirements, we need to make sure we factor this into the complexity, delivery timelines, and effort involved. We must put the required controls in place and validate them. We must also consider the audit effort involved due to regulatory requirements. Compliance frameworks like PCI require a thorough collection of evidence for least privilege enforcement, data protection, encryption, firewall rules, logging of critical events, access logging, vulnerability scanning, and much more. The effort will take several months, and we must dedicate resources to these audits. We discussed regulatory requirements in *Chapter 3*.

- **Changing markets and technology trends**:

  Changing market trends can impact our solution thinking. Consumer websites offer more photos, sometimes 3D renderings and videos of their products, and we need to consider these changes to stay competitive. Technology keeps changing as well. More and more service offerings get commoditized and FaaS and serverless storage solutions are examples of that. We want to make sure we utilize those commodities to reduce our operational effort. We discussed Wardley Mapping in *Chapter 2*.

- **Technology and partnerships**:

  New technology trends and standards also need to be considered. If a new standard, for example, OpenTelemetry, helps to reduce vendor lock-in, we should consider it and assess its impact. If we are selecting new software, for example, a deployment tool, then we should evaluate the ecosystem, such as user groups and partners in our region, and see whether we can get free training if we establish a good partner relationship. We talked about this in detail in *Chapter 2*.

- **Other external factors**:

  Other factors include legal and contractual considerations. We will review relevant SLAs, including RTOs and RPOs, and ensure our architecture and processes align with them. Geopolitical factors such as trade restrictions and regional political stability can impact the success of our initiative, especially if we are operating globally. We talked about the network-related aspects in *Chapter 9* and RPOs and RTOs in *Chapter 8*.

At this stage, we have a solid understanding of our organizational context and the internal and external factors we need to consider. Equipped with this knowledge, we are ready to revisit our effort estimates and build our roadmap.

Building a roadmap and keeping the stakeholders informed

During this phase, we will reference Agile terminology that we will use to build our roadmap. For this purpose, use the definitions from the Agile Alliance (`https://www.agilealliance.org/agile101/agile-glossary/`).

> **Definitions – Agile terminology**
>
> **Epic**: An epic is a large user story that cannot be delivered as defined within a single iteration or is large enough that it can be split into smaller user stories.
>
> **Story**: In consultation with the customer or product owner, the team divides up the work to be done into functional increments called "user stories."
>
> **Product backlog**: A product backlog is a list of the new features, changes to existing features, bug fixes, infrastructure changes, or other activities that a team may deliver in order to achieve a specific outcome.
>
> **Product owner**: The product owner is a role on a product development team responsible for managing the product backlog in order to achieve the desired outcome that a product development team seeks to accomplish.

The preceding terms are frequently used, but since there are different agile delivery frameworks, we mean the same thing when we use those terms.

We previously produced a high-level effort estimate. After assessing internal and external factors, it is time to validate these estimates and progress to the next level of detail:

1. **Assess previous effort estimates**:

    With the insight gained, we have to validate whether our previously captured effort estimate captures all required activities. If steps are missing, we need to add them. It is always good to keep a version of the initial estimate to compare them later. We can involve the same SMEs that provided the initial estimates to revalidate the effort estimate. We can kick this revalidation off with a meeting where we provide all the context. This will be a short refresher on the initiative, previous estimates, and new findings since the initial effort estimate. We will need to spend some time on the findings because any new internal or external findings can impact the effort estimates. The team can then go back to the initial estimates and add them. Now is the time to add a column to the initial time estimate to capture the job function(s) that should perform a particular task. This will help us validate whether we have all the necessary skills and resources. The outcome will be updated time estimates and added responsibilities.

2.   **Create a backlog**:

Based on the updated time estimates, we will create a backlog. Ideally, this is done in an agile management solution such as Jira or Wrike. If we don't have a license, we could use a free tier offering such as Trello, but we need to ensure our organization endorses the software to avoid shadow IT. Commercial solutions have useful planning features, like managing dependencies between tasks, creating overarching epics, mapping stories to epics, and grouping them into sprints. Once this structure is created, we can generate a roadmap.

The following screenshot illustrates a roadmap example in Jira by Atlassian. Jira uses the word *issues* instead of *stories* and *timeline* instead of *roadmap*, but the concept is the same, as we can see:

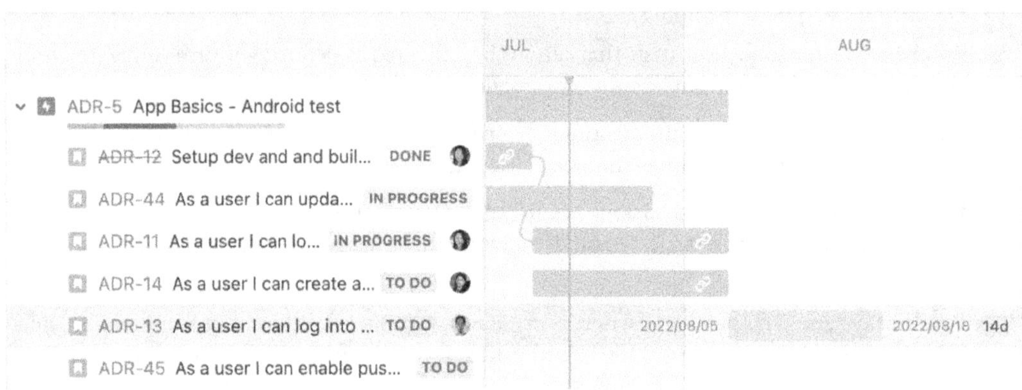

Figure 14.2 – Roadmap in Jira (source: https://www.atlassian.com/software/jira/guides/basic-roadmaps/tutorials#filter-and-view-settings)

3.   **Keep the stakeholders engaged**:

We must keep our stakeholders informed while we progress with our planning activities. We have previously provided visibility and presented at the architecture and engineering forums. We have new insights, and the scope or approach might have changed since our initial high-level proposal. We can now present to those forums and provide more details. Keeping everyone informed will reduce resistance, as people have been kept in the loop and had opportunities to raise concerns.

So far, we have collected many data points and kept our stakeholders informed. We have many inputs that we reuse for our business case, and we can start documenting them next.

The business case document

We need to understand our target audience to ensure that the document uses the right terminology. CSP-specific terminologies including Lambda, Apigee, or Azure Blob Storage might not mean anything to the stakeholders who need to endorse the business case. Therefore, we should avoid technical jargon, and if we have to use technology terms, we need to explain them and the benefits they bring. If we work for a larger organization, we will likely have a business case template to leverage.

Typically, the strategy and architecture team maintain this. If we don't have a template, that is not a problem either because we will go through a structure that can be used:

#	Section title & description
1	Executive summary
	This section will provide a brief overview of the cloud transformation initiative. We have produced different views so far, and we can leverage one of the high-level views in this section. We need to explain strategic objectives and expected business outcomes. We will also document a high-level cost summary, the benefits, and a high-level view of the roadmap we produced earlier.
2	Business drivers and strategic alignment
	Here, we can describe current business and technology challenges. We will call out pain points and current inefficiencies. We can also reference market, industry, and technology trends relevant to our organization. We need to outline how our initiative aligns with the corporate strategy and how our solution will help to gain a competitive advantage, such as quicker product release cycles.
3	Vision and goals
	In this section, we will describe the long-term vision for our cloud initiative and capture key goals and metrics, such as KPIs and success criteria. Examples are improved time-to-market, security or compliance uplift that reduces overall risk, or improved resilience, which will reduce the number of outages.
4	Current state
	We will provide an overview of current challenges here, including infrastructure, applications, data, challenges, and limitations, including technical debt, performance, scalability, and security challenges. We must address all gap areas, including skills, resources, culture, operations, governance, security, compliance, change management, CI/CD, lack of guardrails, and technical debt, which should have been documented in previous workshops.
5	Target state
	This section will describe the proposed initiative. We will cover the same areas as in the current state and point out how the target state will differ from it. If we keep the structure the same as in the previous section, it will be easier for the stakeholders to see the differences. The workshop documentation should provide all the input we need here.

6	Financial analysis
	Here, we will provide a cost breakdown showing the initial investment, migration costs, and operational expenses. We also capture additional staff or external consultants that we need. If we move from on-premises to the cloud, there will be a shift from CapEx to OpEx. We are planning this initiative because our organization will benefit from it, and we need to show that in an ROI calculation. We will illustrate the expected ROI, payback period, and long-term savings. Benefits include reduced operational effort, quicker delivery of new solutions, and reduced SLA breaches, which reduce penalty payments. Unless we are already 100% in the cloud, we will explain the cloud pricing model (for example, pay-as-you-go) and committed spending plans.
7	Value proposition and benefits
	Here, we will describe the quantitative benefits, for example, cost savings and increased business agility, and outline the qualitative benefits, such as improved innovation, customer satisfaction, employee experience, and competitive advantages.
8	Risk assessment and mitigation
	This section is particularly important in regulated industries. We will describe key risks addressing operations, technology, delivery, and financial obligations. We will also outline the risk mitigation strategies and contingency plans, such as staggered deployment and small change increments, staff upskilling, implementing guardrails, managing cost overruns, and so on.
9	Implementation plan
	Here, we will provide the roadmap that we produced earlier. We need to outline key milestones, phases, and timelines. This section will also include a resource plan that shows internal teams, consultants, and SMEs from our CSP. We will also describe who our stakeholders are, including change management and governance. This information will be required for upcoming stakeholder conversations, including sharing the business case document.
10	Organizational impact
	In this section, we will describe the skills and workforce transformation, including training, hiring, and upskilling needs. We will also describe process changes, such as moving from manual to automated testing, and cultural aspects, for example, establishing a DevSecOps culture and moving toward a cross-functional team approach.
11	Partner and vendor strategy
	If we purchase a new SaaS solution, we will outline how it integrates with our current ecosystem and describe our partnership strategy. Can the SaaS provider assign a key account manager and SMEs? Can they provide training tailored to our organization?
12	Compliance, security, and legal considerations
	Here, we will describe whether the third party fulfills all compliance requirements, such as SOC-2, HIPAA, or PCI. We also need to describe whether the vendor meets data protection and privacy requirements. We will also describe SLAs, including availability and performance SLAs, and the vendor can provide this information.

13	Summary and recommendations
	In this last section, we will summarize key findings and conclusions, call out final recommendations, and outline required actions. This section summarizes the document. Some stakeholders will only read the first section, the last section, and a section they directly relate to, such as the legal section or the financial analysis. Therefore, we need to use clear business language in the first and last sections of the document.

Table 14.3 – The business case document

The document must be reviewed by various team members and the stakeholders involved in the workshops. If time capacity is an issue, we can split the review between stakeholders. If we make apparent mistakes, for example, financial calculation errors, we lose credibility, and we want to avoid that by all means.

We need to find the right balance for our documentation to provide enough information to convey the necessary information without going into unnecessary details and becoming hard to read. The document reviews will help find that balance. While working on the document, we continue engaging the broader stakeholder group and communicating timelines for the next steps, which we will discuss next.

Next steps and other considerations

We are coming to the tail end of our business case journey. The only "minor" thing missing is the endorsement before transitioning into best practice. But how do we achieve this last step that is so significant and needed to get the implementation started? Let's look into a few aspects we need to consider and actions we need to take:

- **Perfect timing for requesting budget**:

  Is there a perfect time to ask for a budget? Larger organizations have financial cycles, and budget requests must be submitted several months before a new financial year starts. For this request, we do not need a finalized and endorsed business case, but we need at least the high-level benefits. Most of the time, a cloud architect can provide this information by reaching out to key stakeholders or providers to get some cost input. If we just had an incident, such as a data breach, getting funding for a security uplift will be a no-brainer and can happen out of the financial cycle, unless the breach puts us out of business.

- **Perfect timing for a business case**:

  Is there a perfect time for a business case? If we have previously requested a budget, we must ensure that the business case sign-off aligns with our planned implementation kick-off. We need to factor in unplanned delays, such as stakeholders not being available or emergency initiatives taking priority and we do not get an immediate presentation slot at the next governance meeting. Some companies have a quarterly or half-yearly priority assessment process. If that is the case, then having the business case ready will be helpful if we make good points to leave the organization in a better state. The short answer to the question of whether there is a perfect time is that it depends, but the best thing is to be prepared and be well-connected to stakeholders.

- **The approval process**:

  The approval process is very organization-specific. If we haven't raised a business case before and are not fully aware of the process, we need to engage with our manager or a peer contact who has done it before. They can provide some coaching and point us to the individuals running the governance forums who will endorse the business case. We must ask them what we need to look out for and the critical areas for a sign-off. It might be security, compliance, or procurement, and that will depend on the industry and organization. We will also need a presentation that summarizes our business case, and we will talk about that next.

- **The presentation**:

  We need a presentation that uses the right artifacts for our stakeholders in the governance forum to endorse our solutions. Depending on the organization's size, we might need approval in several forums. For example, one forum challenges all architecture and engineering aspects. Once we get an endorsement, we can present at a forum that challenges risk and offers organizational benefits. In that case, we need two presentations: a technical one and one focused on business and risk. The time we spend working out these presentations is as valuable as the time we spend on the actual business document. The presentations are the sales brochure of a product we believe will be a success story.

At this point, we wish you good luck with the presentation and move on to summarize the key takeaways from this chapter.

Summary

We started by exploring how to spot anti-patterns and the signs we needed to look out for. That included general indicators and specific focus areas such as culture, automation, strategy, operations, observability, and technology. Then, we moved on to defining the current and target state and exploring gaps we need to bridge and how important it is to keep our stakeholders engaged. We also explored how to add the organizational context and consider internal and external factors that might shape our solution. We explored how to build a roadmap, a business case document, and presentations that support our business case while keeping our stakeholders engaged. By now, we should have an endorsed business case and be ready to start our transformation, which we will discuss in the following and very last chapter.

Get This Book's PDF Version and Exclusive Extras

Scan the QR code (or go to `packtpub.com/unlock`). Search for this book by name, confirm the edition, and then follow the steps on the page.

Note: Keep your invoice handly. Purchase made directly from packt don't require one.

15

Transitioning to Cloud Native Good Habits

Transitioning to a cloud native architecture is more than a technical undertaking; it is a strategic transformation that touches every corner of an organization. It involves shifting from legacy mindsets and processes to a modern approach prioritizing agility, resilience, and innovation. This chapter goes beyond the technical steps of cloud adoption and dives into the crucial elements that make a transformation successful: aligning stakeholders, defining a strategic and flexible roadmap, and establishing a culture of continuous improvement. It is not just about leveraging the latest technologies; it is about integrating them into a cohesive strategy that supports and prepares our organization's goals for the future.

As we navigate this transition, we must ensure that every piece of the puzzle fits together seamlessly, from stakeholder engagement to execution. We'll explore how to rally support and unify our team around a shared vision, transforming buy-in into momentum. This chapter is meant to act as a guide in crafting a detailed yet adaptable roadmap that keeps our organization moving forward with precision and purpose. Finally, we'll emphasize the importance of building a feedback loop and fostering a culture of continuous improvement, ensuring that the organization not only adapts to change but thrives in an ever-evolving cloud landscape. Here's what we will cover in this chapter:

- Stakeholder alignment

- Your roadmap

- Continuous improvement

Let's start by exploring the crucial step of stakeholder alignment, the foundation upon which a successful cloud native transformation is built.

Stakeholder alignment

Building on the stakeholder alignment fundamentals we established in *Chapter 14*, transitioning to a cloud native organization involves more than just technical changes; it requires transforming how people and teams collaborate, make decisions, and align with the overall vision. In this section, we explore the critical aspects of stakeholder alignment, emphasizing the importance of engaging the right people, managing dependencies, and ensuring that teams are structured for success. This section builds on the insights from *Chapter 2, Strategizing Your Shift to Cloud native*, focusing on practical strategies for aligning stakeholders effectively.

Stakeholder management considerations

A successful cloud native transformation hinges on effective stakeholder management. Without it, misalignment, conflicts, and failed initiatives are likely outcomes. To navigate these challenges, it is essential to understand the needs and expectations of each stakeholder group and manage them accordingly.

Stakeholder Group	Considerations
Executive leadership	As discussed in *Chapter 14*, engage early to secure sponsorship and resources. Demonstrate ROI and strategic advantages.
Technical teams	Involve architects, developers, and SREs to ensure buy-in on technical decisions and implementation.
Operations and security	Integrate operations and security teams to align with DevSecOps practices, fostering collaboration.
Business stakeholders	Ensure business leaders understand how cloud native solutions align with the goals and metrics. This extends beyond senior leadership and encompasses change management and HR domains for cultural changes.

Table 15.1 - Stakeholders and considerations

Establishing consistent communication is crucial for successful stakeholder engagement. Regular updates through various channels, such as meetings, newsletters, dashboards, or project management tools, keep stakeholders informed and involved throughout the transformation process. Transparent insights into cloud native initiatives' progress, challenges, and achievements foster trust and create a sense of shared ownership, making stakeholders feel integral to the journey. By building this level of engagement, we encourage a collaborative atmosphere where stakeholders provide valuable insights and feedback, which are crucial for refining strategies and overcoming obstacles.

Additionally, interactive workshops and training sessions are essential for building a shared understanding of cloud native principles, particularly for non-technical stakeholders who may be less familiar with the complexities involved. These sessions aim to demystify cloud native concepts such as microservices, containerization, and CI/CD, while illustrating the business value in practical terms, as can be found in *Chapter 7, Expressing Your Business Goals as Application Code*. Workshops also focus on aligning different departments around shared objectives, promoting early cross-functional collaboration. Supporting this alignment further requires clear roles and responsibilities using frameworks like **RACI** (which stands for **Responsible, Accountable, Consulted, Informed**), which help manage expectations by specifying responsibilities and decision-making authority. Establishing these boundaries upfront reduces ambiguity, enhances coordination, ensures that efforts are structured toward a unified goal, and establishes a solid trust foundation. This foundation of clear communication and mutual understanding sets the stage for the next crucial step: identifying the right people to drive the transformation.

Identifying the required people

Building an effective cloud native team goes beyond filling roles; it requires assembling individuals with the skills, mindset, and collaborative spirit necessary to navigate the transformation's complexities. This process involves creating a balance of technical experts, strategic thinkers, and cross-functional collaborators who work together seamlessly. Each role should be filled by individuals who possess not only technical expertise but also the adaptability to learn and grow as the organization evolves, such as the following:

- **Cloud architects and platform engineers**: Vital for designing and managing cloud native architectures that align with business needs, as discussed in *Chapter 7*.

- **Security engineers**: Play a critical role in embedding security measures throughout the lifecycle, as emphasized in *Chapter 5*

- **Product owners and business analysts**: Ensure that implementations align with business objectives and deliver measurable outcomes, covered in *Chapter 3.*.

Understanding these specific skills and responsibilities is crucial to building a cohesive team capable of addressing the challenges of the transformation. The following are the key roles needed for a successful cloud native journey and the organization's required skills:

Role	Description	Key Skills
Cloud architect	Designs the cloud architecture and ensures it aligns with cloud native best practices	Solution design, cloud platforms, and automation
Platform engineer	Manages cloud infrastructure, focusing on automation and infrastructure as code (laC) practices	laC (Terraform, CloudFormation/ CDK, ARM/Bicep), automation, and scripting
Developer/ SRE	Builds, deploys, and maintains cloud native applications with a focus on scalability and reliability	CI/CD, containerization, and microservices
Security engineer	Implements continuous security controls and monitors cloud native environments for threats and vulnerabilities	DevSecOps, automation, and threat detection
Product owner	Ensures technical implementations align with business objectives, bridging the gap	Business analysis and stakeholder management

Table 15.2 - Critical roles for the cloud native journey

Once these roles are established, it is vital to anticipate and manage potential challenges that may arise when trying to align these stakeholders effectively.

Common challenges in stakeholder alignment

Even with a structured approach, cloud native transformations often encounter significant challenges in aligning stakeholders. These challenges typically arise from varying levels of familiarity with cloud native technologies, resistance to change, or conflicting departmental goals. *Chapter 2* highlights the importance of aligning strategies with business objectives. Building on that foundation, here, we explore specific challenges that emerge when bringing stakeholders together and provide strategies for overcoming them.

Resistance to change

Resistance is a frequent challenge in cloud native transformations, particularly when stakeholders are unfamiliar with or hesitant about new approaches. Concerns often stem from disruptions to established workflows or perceived risks associated with cloud native practices. To address this, leverage evidence-based case studies and data to demonstrate tangible benefits such as improved time to market, enhanced agility, and overall business value. By aligning these success stories with the organization's strategic goals, as emphasized in *Chapter 2*, we can mitigate resistance and build confidence among stakeholders.

Conflicting priorities

Conflicting priorities are common, especially between departments with different goals. Development teams may prioritize rapid releases, while operations teams emphasize system stability. These conflicts can create friction and slow progress. The solution is to facilitate collaborative workshops where stakeholders align on a balanced approach that addresses both technical and business needs. The following table details workshops designed to align these priorities:

Workshop	Focus	Outcome
Objectives and key results (OKR) alignment workshop	Align development and operations teams around shared goals and metrics	A unified set of OKR that balance speed and stability, providing a clear, measurable path forward
Cross-functional planning session	Bring together development, operations, security, and business unit representatives to map out the cloud native roadmap	An agreed-upon action plan that integrates technical and business needs for a smoother implementation
Release strategy and deployment workshop	Establish a common understanding of deployment practices, including blue-green deployments, CI/CD, and automation techniques	A deployment strategy that aligns development and operations for efficient, reliable, and secure rollouts
Risk management and stability workshop	Develop strategies to mitigate risks associated with rapid deployments while ensuring operational stability	A risk mitigation framework that balances the need for speed with the focus on minimizing disruptions
Cultural integration and collaboration workshop	Address cultural differences between development and operations teams, promoting communication, shared responsibility, and collaboration	Improved team cohesion and a culture that supports cross-functional collaboration for cloud native success
Technical and business alignment session	Engage technical and business stakeholders to discuss how cloud native practices meet business and technical requirements	A balanced strategy that ensures technical efficiency while delivering business value across departments

Table 15.3 - Collaborative workshops

Without executive support, cloud native initiatives risk stalling due to insufficient resources or unclear direction. As outlined in *Chapter 2*, securing executive sponsorship early is a critical factor for success. Emphasize the strategic value of cloud native adoption and demonstrate how it aligns with business goals, such as increased scalability, resilience, and cost efficiency. Present these advantages in terms that resonate with executive leaders to secure the necessary backing and resources.

Role dependencies and impacts of hiring strategies

A successful cloud native transformation requires assembling the right team and understanding dependencies between roles to ensure coordination. This section explores the impacts of hiring strategies, skill gaps, and team organization to build a cohesive and adaptable structure. We begin by assessing skill gaps. Evaluating our team's skills is essential before launching the transformation to identify any gaps. This helps determine where upskilling or hiring is needed. Key areas include the following:

- **Cloud architecture**:

    - **Current assessment**: Evaluate whether teams are familiar with cloud native architecture patterns (e.g., microservices, serverless, and CI/CD skills for test automation)

    - **Actions needed**: Provide training programs and certifications, such as AWS Certified Solutions Architect or domain-specific technologies such as Kubernetes or serverless

- **Security expertise**:

    - **Current assessment**: Assess whether security teams know cloud native security practices (e.g., zero trust and automated threat detection)

    - **Actions needed**: Hire DevSecOps specialists or offer focused training sessions to build internal expertise

- **Collaboration skills**:

    - **Current assessment**: Review the team's readiness for cross-functional work as required by DevOps and platform engineering models

    - **Actions needed**: Implement workshops and team-building activities to encourage collaborative behavior

Understanding the dependencies between roles and teams is critical for ensuring the cloud native transformation is cohesive and well-coordinated. The following are the key dependencies and their impact on team structure:

- **Cross-functional collaboration**: As emphasized in *Chapter 2*, effective collaboration between development, operations, and security teams is central. Organize product-oriented squads to reduce silos and foster efficiency.

- **Decentralized governance**: Decentralized governance, discussed in *Chapter 3*, empowers teams to make quick, effective decisions while aligning with objectives and minimizing bottlenecks.

- **Shared responsibility model**: Define clear responsibilities between cloud providers and internal teams to manage security, compliance, and operations effectively. More on this can be found in *Chapter 1, Benefits of Cloud native and Common Misunderstandings.*

Impacts on hiring and organizational structure

The shift to cloud native often necessitates rethinking organizational structure and hiring strategies. Moving from traditional silos to product-centric models can optimize for cloud native best practices.

To align with cloud native best practices, organizations should move away from traditional siloed structures and instead adopt product-centric teams. These teams own the entire life cycle of a product or service, enhancing accountability and responsiveness. Here's how the shift affects the organizational structure:

Traditional Model	Product-Centric Model
Siloed departments (e.g., development, operations, and security)	Cross-functional teams with shared product ownership
Specialized skills focus	Generalist skills that adapt to changing needs
Longer decision-making cycles	Decentralized, faster decision-making

Table 15.4 - Model comparisons

The following are the benefits of **product teams**:

- **Enhanced ownership**: Teams own the entire life cycle, enabling quicker decision-making
- **Alignment with objectives**: Close alignment with business goals and customer outcomes
- **Collaborative culture**: Promotes continuous learning and innovation

Hiring considerations

The move to a product-centric, cloud native environment often requires hiring new talent or developing existing employees. The following strategies can guide this process:

Skills diversity: Hiring for cloud native roles should focus on a diverse skill set. Candidates with backgrounds in network engineering, security, data management, and automation bring essential expertise that strengthens the team's capabilities.

Cultural fit: Cloud native environments thrive on collaboration, agility, and a mindset that encourages continuous learning. Prioritize candidates who embrace these values, ensuring they can adapt to the fast-paced and evolving nature of cloud native practices.

Balancing specialists and generalists: While generalists are valuable for their adaptability and broad knowledge base, having specialists in critical areas like security, FinOps, and platform engineering ensures that deep expertise is available when needed.

Upskilling and training programs

When hiring externally isn't feasible, upskilling existing team members can be a highly effective strategy. Developing a comprehensive training program that builds both technical and soft skills is key:

- **Certification programs**: Offer certification pathways such as a certification from the big three cloud service providers to help team members gain the necessary cloud native skills. These programs provide a structured way for staff to develop expertise in critical areas.

- **Internal cloud academies**: Establish internal academies where experienced cloud engineers mentor other team members, sharing their knowledge through hands-on experience. This approach fosters a learning culture and ensures knowledge transfer within the organization.

- **Hands-on workshops and labs**: Facilitate practical workshops and labs where teams can apply their knowledge in simulated cloud native scenarios, building CI/CD pipelines or deploying serverless applications. These sessions reinforce learning and improve team confidence and competence.

Achieving stakeholder alignment is foundational for any cloud native transformation. Organizations can set up a smooth transition by managing stakeholders effectively, assembling the right team, and addressing hiring impacts and people dependencies. Drawing on strategies from *Chapters 2* and *7*, this section provides the tools needed to build a coalition of support, ensuring a unified approach across all levels of the organization. With these foundations in place, organizations are well prepared for the next phases of their cloud native journey. Next, we will look at establishing a roadmap and how to approach these.

Your roadmap

A successful cloud native transformation doesn't happen by chance; it results from a well-thought-out and meticulously designed **roadmap**. Just as a building needs blueprints before construction begins, a cloud native transformation requires a detailed plan that aligns technical initiatives with strategic business goals. Expanding on *Chapter 14*, this roadmap is a guide, helping us navigate complex changes while ensuring that every step is purposeful and aligned with our organization's objectives.

This section will outline building a practical roadmap that drives our cloud native transformation. We will explore the essential components of a successful plan, including the following:

- Migration planning

- Transition architectures

- Delivery initiatives

Each of these is necessary to turn strategy into reality. By the end of this section, we will clearly understand how to create a roadmap that supports and accelerates our journey to becoming a cloud native organization.

Understanding the migration path

Every cloud native transformation begins with a **migration plan**. This plan is not a simple checklist but a dynamic strategy that evolves based on business needs, technical requirements, and the organization's willingness to change. The migration plan should address which workloads and applications will be moved to the cloud and how they will be adapted to fit cloud native architectures. This section builds on previous chapters, emphasizing the importance of a well-structured migration approach.

To build a successful migration plan, follow these steps:

- **Assess and classify applications**: Comprehensively assess your existing applications and systems. Determine which are best suited for a cloud native environment and classify them as the following:

  - **Rehost (lift and shift)**: For applications that can be moved with minimal changes

  - **Refactor/replatform**: For applications that need modification to run efficiently in the cloud

  - **Rebuild**: For legacy systems that may require significant redevelopment using cloud native technologies

  - **Retire or replace**: For applications that are obsolete or can be replaced by SaaS or PaaS solutions

Chapter 2 goes into much more detail.

- **Define prioritization criteria**: Not all applications must move to the cloud simultaneously. Develop a prioritization framework based on business impact, technical complexity, regulatory requirements, and current system dependencies. Applications that offer the most value with the least risk should be prioritized early in the migration. The AWS **Cloud Adoption Framework (CAF)**, *Microsoft Cloud Adoption Framework for Azure*, and Google's own CAF are great input and reference structure points.

- **Establish a phased approach**: Adopting a phased migration strategy allows us to manage risks and learn from each stage before moving on to the next, as follows:

  - **Phase 1**: Migrate non-critical applications to gain familiarity with cloud native processes

  - **Phase 2**: Move critical applications that require moderate refactoring

  - **Phase 3**: Address complex legacy systems that need significant reengineering or replacement

By structuring the migration into phases, organizations can build momentum, refine processes, and manage changes systematically. This phased approach aligns with the incremental nature of cloud native adoption discussed in earlier chapters, ensuring flexibility and controlled risk management.

A solid migration plan must be supported by transition architectures that guide the organization through each journey phase. Transition architectures act as intermediary states between the current and target cloud native state, ensuring that each phase of the migration is controlled and manageable. This aligns with the strategies outlined in *Chapter 17, Expressing Your Business Goals in Application Code*, where adapting applications to cloud native environments is emphasized.

These are the vital elements of transition architectures:

Element	Description
Interim state design	Develop architecture blueprints for each migration phase, showing how applications and systems will function temporarily before reaching the final cloud native state
Temporary services	Utilize temporary services or hybrid architectures (e.g., a mix of on-premises and cloud resources) to ensure continuity during the transition
Integration points	Establish integration points between legacy systems and cloud native components, such as API gateways or data synchronization tools, to maintain consistency and minimize disruption

Table 15.5 - Transition architectures

If we cannot move from current state to target state architecture in a single release, we require transition architectures. They enable us to mitigate risks and solve technology dependencies as we plan ahead. Transition architectures should be tailored to the specific needs of each migration phase. For instance, in the early phases, a hybrid cloud model may maintain legacy systems while testing new cloud native capabilities. Later, as applications become fully cloud native, they can decommission these temporary setups.

Building for flexibility and agility

A critical aspect of the migration plan and transition architectures is ensuring flexibility and agility. Cloud native environments are dynamic, so the roadmap must allow for adjustments as new requirements, technologies, and insights emerge. Embrace the following practices to create a resilient roadmap:

- **Modular planning**: Break down the migration into modular components that can be executed independently. This approach minimizes disruption and enables teams to work in parallel, accelerating the overall migration timeline.

- **Feedback loops**: Establish feedback loops where teams review progress and outcomes from each migration phase. Regular retrospectives and performance reviews help refine the plan and adapt future phases based on lessons learned.

- **Automation and orchestration**: Use **infrastructure as code (IaC)** and orchestration tools to automate deployments and transitions. Automating key elements reduces manual effort, mitigates risk, and speeds up migration activities, ensuring that each transition is efficient and consistent.

Planning ahead for your migration beyond the technical is critical; the delivery initiatives must also be addressed.

Planning delivery initiatives

Much like we started with developing a comprehensive migration plan and transition architectures in *Chapter 14*, the next step is defining and executing delivery initiatives. These initiatives translate strategy into action, ensuring that cloud native principles and practices are embedded into the organization's operations and culture. This step is where the roadmap transitions from planning to execution, aligning with the delivery strategies covered in previous chapters.

Delivery initiatives should be structured to cover various aspects of the cloud native transformation, including development, infrastructure, security, and operations. To ensure a holistic approach, consider the following delivery initiatives:

- **Infrastructure modernization:**

  - **Objective**: Transition from legacy infrastructure to a fully automated and scalable cloud native environment, as discussed in *Chapter 7*

  - **Actions**:

    - Implement IaC using tools like Terraform, AWS CloudFormation, ARM templates, or Azure Bicep

    - Build CI/CD pipelines to automate the deployment and scaling of infrastructure components

    - Introduce container orchestration platforms (e.g., Kubernetes) for managing microservices and workloads at scale

- **Development practice enhancement**:

  - **Objective**: Establish cloud native development practices to improve agility and reduce time to market, as discussed in *Chapter 5*

  - **Actions**:

    - Adopt microservices architectures to break down monolithic applications

    - Implement CI/CD practices for automated testing, integration, and deployment

    - Leverage serverless computing where appropriate to increase development speed and reduce operational overhead

- **Security integration (DevSecOps):**

  - **Objective**: Embed security practices throughout the development life cycle to minimize vulnerabilities, as discussed in *Chapter 11, Running It Without Breaking It*, and *Chapter 5*

  - **Actions**:

    - Automate security scans and compliance checks as part of the CI/CD pipeline

    - Implement a zero-trust architecture to secure cloud native applications and infrastructure; *Chapter 9, Ignoring Latency and Bandwidth*, provides an in-depth overview of the zero-trust architecture

    - Develop a security monitoring strategy using cloud native threat detection and response tools

By structuring these initiatives, we can ensure that cloud native principles are implemented and operationalized, setting a foundation for a robust and resilient cloud environment.

Phased delivery – aligning initiatives with migration phases

To maintain coherence between the migration plan and delivery initiatives, the initiatives have to be aligned with the phases of the migration. This approach ensures that each phase migrates systems and builds the necessary capabilities to support cloud native operations. By aligning each delivery initiative with a specific phase, we create a structured, systematic progression that minimizes risks, maximizes efficiency, and allows for iterative learning and adaptation. This phased delivery approach echoes the incremental strategies discussed in earlier chapters, ensuring a smooth transformation journey. The following is a detailed table of reference for a phased move to cloud native:

Phase	Key Activities	Details and Actions	Outcomes
Phase 1	Establish foundational cloud infrastructure	IaC implementation: Deploy foundational infrastructure using IaC tools such as Terraform, automating network setup, security groups, and VPCs CI/CD pipeline setup: Build CI/CD pipelines to automate deployments for infrastructure components, ensuring consistency and repeatability Container orchestration: Set up a container orchestration platform (e.g., Kubernetes) for managing workloads, supporting microservices, and providing scalability Security controls: Integrate basic security controls, such as firewalls and identity management, to establish a secure baseline environment.	A scalable, automated environment using IaC and CI/CD pipelines, providing the base for deploying applications and scaling resources efficiently

Phase	Key Activities	Details and Actions	Outcomes
Phase 2	Refactor and deploy business-critical applications	Application refactoring: Adapt critical applications for cloud native environments, breaking monoliths into microservices where appropriate Platform redesign: For suitable workloads, implement cloud native architectures to reduce operational overhead and enhance scalability Enhanced security: Integrate advanced security practices such as zero-trust architectures and automate security scans within CI/CD pipelines (refer to *Chapter 5*) Observability setup: Deploy monitoring and logging tools (e.g., Prometheus or Grafana) to ensure visibility and real-time tracking of application performance and health	Cloud native applications with improved agility, deployed through automated pipelines and monitored securely, providing immediate insights into system performance and stability
Phase 3	Rebuild or replace legacy systems entirely	System rebuilds: For legacy systems unsuitable for simple refactoring, address the rehost in the cloud or managed/SaaS offerings (i.e., utilizing DocumentDB for AWS – a managed MongoDB-like database – instead of self-hosting MongoDB) Data migration: Migrate databases to managed cloud services like Amazon RDS or Google Cloud databases, ensuring data consistency and availability Infrastructure optimization: Optimize infrastructure usage with auto-scaling groups, load balancers, and caching mechanisms, ensuring efficient resource utilization and cost management (building on insights from *Chapter 4*, How to Avoid a Bill Shock)	Fully integrated cloud native systems that leverage microservices, serverless computing, and cloud native security, achieving enhanced performance, scalability, and cost efficiency
Phase 4	Optimize and automate cloud native operations	Full automation: Automate the management and scaling of applications using advanced orchestration tools like Helm for Kubernetes, enabling hands-off operations DevSecOps integration: Expand DevSecOps practices, embedding security controls deeper into CI/CD pipelines and automating compliance checks Cloud cost optimization: Implement FinOps practices to continuously optimize cloud spend by using tools such as AWS Cost Explorer to identify savings opportunities and establish cost guardrails, as discussed in *Chapter 4* Performance tuning: Perform application performance tuning, leveraging insights from monitoring tools to adjust resources dynamically and ensure optimal application performance	Highly automated cloud native operations with a focus on efficiency, security, and cost optimization, enabling continuous delivery and rapid scaling in response to business needs

Table 15.6 - Phased delivery example

To ensure a seamless evolution from current-state systems to the target architecture, it is crucial to embed structured transition strategies within delivery initiatives.

Building transition architectures into delivery initiatives

Transition architectures play a vital role in the execution of delivery initiatives. We can manage dependencies and mitigate disruptions by integrating transition designs into the delivery process. Here's how to incorporate these architectures effectively:

- **Temporary integration layers**: Use API gateways or middleware solutions as temporary layers between legacy systems and new cloud native components. This approach ensures continuity of service while systems are incrementally migrated and refactored. The **facade approach** or **strangler fig pattern** by Martin Fowler are well suited here. *Chapter 7* provides further insights.

- **Hybrid deployment models**: For workloads that cannot be moved immediately, implement hybrid deployment models where components operate across on-premises and cloud environments. These models allow for gradual shifts without compromising the availability of critical systems.

- **Iterative rollouts**: Instead of migrating everything simultaneously, implement iterative rollouts where components or services are moved in controlled batches. We can adjust subsequent phases based on performance and insights from monitoring each rollout phase and capturing key metrics.

Transition architectures should be viewed as temporary solutions that evolve as the migration progresses, eventually phasing out as the organization reaches its cloud native target state.

Measuring success and adjusting the roadmap

The success of our roadmap hinges on the ability to measure progress, capture important metrics, and make necessary adjustments. Establishing measurable outcomes that align with our organization's business objectives is part of our delivery initiatives. Common metrics include the following:

- **Deployment frequency**: How often can new features or updates be deployed? Increased frequency indicates a successful transition to cloud native practices.

- **Time to recovery** (TTR): Measure the time it takes to recover services from an incident. Faster recovery times demonstrate improved resilience and cloud native maturity.

- **Application performance**: Monitor application response times, throughput, and resource usage to assess whether cloud native refactoring has optimized performance.

By tracking these metrics, we can identify areas of improvement, refine our roadmap, and ensure that each phase and initiative delivers measurable value.

As cloud native environments are dynamic, our roadmap should incorporate continuous feedback loops to adapt to changes, innovations, and lessons learned. These loops involve regularly assessing the outcomes of each phase and initiative, ensuring that adjustments can be made based on real-world performance data.

Good habits for continuous feedback

The following are good habits you can follow to get continuous feedback:

- **Retrospectives**: Hold retrospective sessions after each phase to review successes, challenges, and areas for improvement. Use this feedback to refine upcoming phases and adjust the roadmap as necessary.

- **Automated monitoring and alerts**: Implement automated monitoring systems that provide real-time data on application performance, security incidents, and infrastructure health. Automated alerts help teams quickly respond and adjust strategies based on emerging trends or issues.

- **Cross-functional review boards**: Establish review boards of representatives from development, operations, business, and security teams. These boards provide holistic insights, ensuring that technical and business goals remain aligned throughout the transformation.

Building a cloud native roadmap requires careful planning, strategic alignment, and the flexibility to adapt. Developing a comprehensive migration plan, designing effective transition architectures, and structuring delivery initiatives, we create a path that supports and accelerates our cloud native journey. This section has laid out the foundational elements needed to craft a roadmap that transforms our organization methodically and efficiently.

Now that the roadmap has been established, the focus shifts to ensuring continuous improvement throughout the cloud native journey. The following section will delve into strategies for creating a culture of ongoing evolution and refinement to maximize the benefits of our transformation.

Continuous improvement

The journey to becoming a cloud native organization doesn't end with migration or a well-structured roadmap; it is an ongoing commitment to continuous improvement. In a dynamic cloud environment, processes, technologies, and organizational goals evolve constantly, requiring teams to adapt quickly. **Continuous improvement** is the mechanism that keeps the cloud native environment optimized, resilient, and aligned with both operational needs and business objectives. By embedding continuous improvement, a cloud native organization can consistently innovate and respond to changing demands, ensuring sustained success in the cloud native landscape.

This final section explores how to embed a culture of continuous improvement into cloud native practices. We will address the following:

- **New or modified building blocks**: Essential technical and operational components that support continuous optimization and cloud native success

- **Cultural impact on teams and ways of working**: The shift in team dynamics and mindset needed for fostering a continuous improvement culture

- **Technology dependencies**: Understanding and managing interdependencies to maintain an adaptable, high-performance cloud environment

These components create an ecosystem where cloud native practices can mature and evolve, keeping the organization competitive and agile.

Establishing new or modified building blocks

A cloud native environment is only as strong as the building blocks it is built on. As the organization transitions, modifying existing building blocks or introducing new ones may be necessary to support continuous improvement effectively. Building blocks refer to technical and operational components, like tools, infrastructure, processes, and governance frameworks, that enable cloud native success.

The essential tools and infrastructure during the initial migration phase may require adjustments or replacements to meet the demands of a mature, continuously improving cloud native environment. New tools may need to be introduced to address automation, observability, or security gaps.

The following are examples of key building blocks for continuous improvement:

- **Enhanced CI/CD pipelines**: As discussed in *Chapter 5*, cloud native environments expand, and CI/CD pipelines need to evolve to support higher deployment frequencies, integrated testing, and improved rollback capabilities. Advanced automation and orchestration tools, such as Argo CD and Flux for Kubernetes, can help make pipelines more efficient, secure, and resilient while supporting a GitOps-native approach. For more on GitOps strategies, see *Chapter 3*.

- **Observability and monitoring tools**: Real-time observability is essential. Upgrading or implementing tools like Prometheus, Grafana, and New Relic enables teams to monitor metrics, trace requests across distributed systems, and capture logs, providing a comprehensive view of system health. *Chapter 10, Observing Your Architecture*, offers more profound insights into building an effective observability strategy.

- **Automated policy enforcement**: Policy enforcement ensures ongoing compliance with security, cost management, and operational standards. Tools such as AWS Config and Kubernetes OPA Gatekeeper can streamline this process, minimizing the need for manual intervention. *Chapter 4* and *Chapter 2* explore preventative guardrails in more detail, highlighting ways to maintain compliance proactively.

Each new or enhanced building block plays a role in reducing friction and increasing iteration speed. This adaptability ensures that the environment can seamlessly handle new applications, services, and workloads.

Creating and modifying governance frameworks

A **governance framework** provides oversight and structure, ensuring that cloud native practices align with organizational objectives. However, as the cloud native environment develops, the governance framework must adapt to changing needs. Early governance efforts might have been focused on establishing compliance and security standards; now, they should shift toward supporting innovation and flexibility. In a continuously evolving environment, the ability to adjust governance practices in response to new tools, processes, and services is crucial. Adapting the governance framework allows teams to work autonomously, make agile decisions, and leverage innovative solutions without facing constraints.

Additionally, adaptive governance frameworks create a more inclusive environment where team feedback is integrated into governance adjustments. By encouraging regular feedback loops, teams can highlight gaps or opportunities for policy improvement, enhancing the relevance and impact of governance practices. To foster a governance framework that aligns with continuous improvement, consider the following key practices, each designed to promote flexibility, autonomy, and responsiveness in a maturing cloud native environment:

Consideration	Description
Dynamic guardrails	Leverage flexible guardrails, as discussed in *Chapter 5*, that adapt to new tools, processes, and services, enabling teams to innovate within organizational boundaries without restrictive policies
Decentralized decision-making	Encourage autonomous decision-making within a defined framework, reducing bottlenecks and accelerating innovation cycles, as discussed in *Chapter 3*
Feedback-driven adjustments	Gather regular feedback from teams on governance policies and refine frameworks accordingly, ensuring alignment with evolving needs and fostering continuous improvement

Table 15.7 - Governance framework practices

Governance frameworks that adapt to continuous improvement not only promote operational efficiency but also support a culture of innovation and experimentation.

Embracing a culture of continuous improvement

A successful cloud native transformation relies as much on culture as it does on technology. Without a continuous improvement mindset, the teams may struggle to keep up with the pace of change that cloud native environments require. Embedding a culture of continuous improvement helps ensure that teams are proactive, engaged, and committed to refining both processes and the technology stack.

A cloud native organization thrives on cross-functional collaboration, which promotes faster decision-making and better alignment with business goals. In a continuously improving environment, collaboration across **development, security, and operations (DevSecOps)** becomes even more critical.

The following are strategies for building a collaborative culture:

- **Cross-functional squads**: Create product-oriented squads that include members from development, operations, and security teams. These squads allow for shared responsibility and foster a culture where teams collaborate closely to solve challenges and deliver value. More on this can be found in *Chapter 1*.

- **Regular retrospectives**: Conduct regular retrospectives to evaluate successes and identify areas for improvement. Retrospectives provide a safe space for team members to voice concerns, celebrate wins, and generate ideas for refining processes.

- **Knowledge sharing sessions**: Encourage knowledge sharing by hosting internal workshops, lunch-and-learns, or tech talks. These sessions build a collective knowledge base, ensuring teams stay informed about new tools, best practices, and evolving cloud native concepts.

Embedding a collaborative culture helps reduce silos and supports continuous learning and innovation. This collaborative foundation not only accelerates decision-making and streamlines workflows but also fosters a culture where team members feel empowered to contribute ideas and improvements, further driving innovation and adaptability across the organization.

Empowering teams for autonomy and accountability

Along the cloud native journey, empowering teams to make decisions and take ownership of domains becomes essential. Autonomy not only speeds up processes but also fosters accountability, as team members feel directly responsible for the success of initiatives. The following approaches can be utilized to foster team autonomy:

- **Decentralized decision-making**: Allow teams to make decisions within the domains without waiting for centralized approvals. For example, teams can own CI/CD pipelines, choosing tools and processes that best meet the organization's needs. Another approach can be found in *Chapter 2*, which approaches decision-making via top-down and bottom-up adoption.

- **Clear ownership models**: Assign clear ownership for applications, services, or components within the cloud environment. Ownership can extend to maintenance, updates, and improvements, ensuring that every system has a dedicated team monitoring and enhancing its performance.

- **Define success metrics**: Establish specific success metrics for each team, such as DORA metrics (deployment frequency, change failure rate, and time to restore service) that align with business goals. Metrics encourage teams to improve processes to meet or exceed expectations continuously and identify bottlenecks where possible.

Creating an autonomous and accountable environment reduces dependencies on other teams and drives continuous improvement from the ground up.

Addressing technology dependencies

In a continuously evolving cloud native environment, technology dependencies are a critical factor. Dependencies between tools, platforms, and services can impact performance, scalability, and flexibility. Effectively managing these dependencies is essential to enable seamless improvements and ensure that cloud native systems remain agile.

As the cloud native environment matures, dependencies between services, databases, and infrastructure components become more complex. A clear understanding of these dependencies helps avoid issues when updating or introducing new elements to the system. The following steps can be used to manage dependencies:

- **Dependency mapping**: Create a visual map of dependencies between services, databases, APIs, and third-party tools. Use dependency mapping tools such as service discovery tools (e.g., AWS Cloud Map, GCP service discovery, or Azure API Center).

- **Regular dependency audits**: Conduct regular audits to identify outdated, unsupported, or underperforming components. Dependencies that are no longer compatible with the cloud native architecture should be upgraded or replaced.

- **Establish dependency owners**: Assign owners to critical dependencies, such as databases or external APIs. Ownership ensures that dependencies are monitored, updated, and optimized regularly, minimizing the risk of performance degradation.

By mapping and managing dependencies, we can reduce unexpected failures, improve system resilience, and streamline updates across the environment.

Proactively managing third-party integrations

Many cloud native environments rely on third-party serviceslike SaaS applications or data providers. Managing these integrations effectively is essential for maintaining system performance, ensuring data consistency, and avoiding disruptions. The following are important considerations for third-party dependencies:

- **Service-level agreements (SLAs)**: Review SLAs for third-party services to understand their performance guarantees, availability, and support levels. Ensure that SLAs align with operational requirements, especially for mission-critical integrations.

- **Proactive monitoring**: Implement monitoring tools that track the performance and availability of third-party services. If an integration starts to underperform, automated alerts can help teams respond before users are affected.

- **Fallback mechanisms**: For essential services, establish fallback mechanisms, such as failover instances or backup providers, to ensure continuity during outages. This is particularly important for services that support high-availability applications or critical functions.

Proactively managing third-party integrations ensures that dependencies do not become points of failure, supporting continuous improvement in performance and reliability.

Embedding feedback loops for continuous improvement

Feedback loops are vital to continuous improvement, providing data-driven insights that inform decisions and drive enhancements. By embedding feedback mechanisms across processes, infrastructure, and applications, the teams gain insights to make informed, real-time adjustments.

Continuous monitoring is essential for capturing real-time feedback on system performance, security, and user experience. An observability stack, including monitoring, logging, and tracing, offers a complete view of the cloud native environment, allowing teams to detect and address issues proactively. The following are key components of an observability stack:

- **Real-time monitoring**: Use tools like Prometheus and Datadog to monitor infrastructure and application health. Real-time monitoring provides instant alerts for issues such as increased latency or CPU usage.

- **Centralized logging**: Implement a centralized logging solution such as the **Loki, Grafana, Tempo, and Mimir (LGTM)** Stack (a popular open source monitoring stack) to aggregate and analyze logs. Centralized logging enables teams to identify patterns, troubleshoot errors, and gain insights across the environment. This extends to the big three cloud service providers who have their own cloud native solutions like Amazon CloudWatch, Azure Monitor, and the GCP operations suite.

- **Distributed tracing**: Tools such as Jaeger or OpenTelemetry enable end-to-end tracing across microservices. Tracing provides visibility into request flows, helping teams identify bottlenecks and optimize application performance.

Real-time observability enhances the feedback process, equipping teams with actionable insights to maintain high availability and performance standards.

Leveraging DORA metrics for performance insights

DevOps Research and Assessment (DORA) metrics are invaluable for measuring the success of continuous improvement efforts, as they provide quantifiable insights into software delivery and operational performance. These metrics include the following:

- **Deployment frequency**: This measures how often code is deployed, reflecting agility and responsiveness

- **Lead time for changes**: This tracks the time from code commit to deployment, indicating pipeline efficiency

- **Change failure rate**: This represents the percentage of changes that lead to failures in production, showing the quality of testing and validation

- **Mean time to restore (MTTR)**: This measures the time to recover from production failures, highlighting resilience

Here is how DORA metrics can be used to drive improvements:

- **Set performance baselines**: Use DORA metrics to establish performance baselines and track improvements over time
- **Identify areas for optimization**: High change failure rates, for instance, may suggest the need for more robust testing or code review processes
- **Celebrate successes**: When metrics show improvement, celebrate these milestones to reinforce a culture of continuous improvement and motivate teams

The cloud native technology landscape evolves rapidly, with new tools, frameworks, and methodologies emerging frequently. As part of continuous improvement, regularly evaluate and optimize the technology stack to take advantage of advancements and ensure that the environment remains efficient and competitive. The following strategies can be used for stack optimization:

- **Evaluate new tools**: Periodically review the latest tools and technologies that could enhance productivity or performance. For example, service meshes like Linkerd or newer CI/CD tools may offer improved features that support continuous improvement.
- **Optimize resource allocation**: Regularly analyze resource usage to identify areas for cost savings. Leveraging auto-scaling, reserved instances, or spot instances can reduce cloud spend without compromising performance.
- **Refine CI/CD pipelines**: As pipelines evolve, look for ways to optimize them, such as integrating new testing frameworks or adding quality gates that reduce the need for manual intervention.

By embracing continuous improvement in the technology stack, we can ensure that the environment remains agile, efficient, and capable of meeting business demands.

Summary

Executing continuous improvement in a cloud native organization is an ongoing, iterative process requiring a commitment to enhancing technical and cultural practices. By establishing new or modified building blocks, embracing a culture of collaboration and autonomy, managing technology dependencies, and embedding feedback loops, organizations can create an environment where cloud native practices evolve alongside business needs.

With continuous improvement embedded into the organization's DNA, our cloud native journey remains flexible, resilient, and capable of driving sustained growth and innovation. This chapter concludes the foundational strategies and insights for building, executing, and optimizing the cloud native transformation, empowering teams to lead with agility and confidence in a constantly evolving digital landscape.

Get This Book's PDF Version and Exclusive Extras

Scan the QR code (or go to `packtpub.com/unlock`). Search for this book by name, confirm the edition, and then follow the steps on the page.

Note: Keep your invoice handly. Purchase made directly from packt don't require one.

16

Unlock Your Exclusive Benefits

Your copy of this book includes the following exclusive benefit:

- Next-gen Packt Reader
- DRM-free PDF/ePub downloads

Follow the guide below to unlock them. The process takes only a few minutes and needs to be completed once.

Unlock this Book's Free Benefits in 3 Easy Steps

Step 1

Keep your purchase invoice ready for *Step 3*. If you have a physical copy, scan it using your phone and save it as a PDF, JPG, or PNG.

For more help on finding your invoice, visit `https://www.packtpub.com/unlock-benefits/help`.

> **Note**
>
> If you bought this book directly from Packt, no invoice is required. After *Step 2*, you can access your exclusive content right away.

Step 2

Scan the QR code or go to `packtpub.com/unlock`.

On the page that opens (similar to *Figure 16.1* on desktop), search for this book by name and select the correct edition.

Discover and unlock your book's exclusive benefits

Figure 16.1: Packt unlock landing page on desktop

Step 3

After selecting your book, sign in to your Packt account or create one for free. Then upload your invoice (PDF, PNG, or JPG, up to 10 MB). Follow the on-screen instructions to finish the process.

Need help?

If you get stuck and need help, visit `https://www.packtpub.com/unlock-benefits/help` for a detailed FAQ on how to find your invoices and more. This QR code will take you to the help page.

> **Note**
>
> If you are still facing issues, reach out to `customercare@packt.com`.

Index

Symbols

12-Factor App methodology 6

A

account manager 59
Agile 5, 36
Agile Alliance
  reference link 371
Agile compliance 172
Agile Manifesto 5
AI for operations (AIOps) 7, 13, 61
AI insights
  used, for improving log aggregation 270, 271
AI/ML anomaly detection
  example 270
alert fatigue 266, 287
  combat, considerations 287
alerting 47
alerts & incidents
  immature processes 282
  metric dumping 284
  purpose-driven metrics and alerts 283
  shifting left in observability 285, 286

aliases 204
all-or-nothing deployment strategies 203
Amazon Relational Database
    Service (RDS) 9, 42
Amazon Web Services (AWS) 5, 33, 145
anomaly detection 38
  cloud AI/ML, leveraging 269
anti-pattern indicators
  cultural indicators 49, 50
  external indicators 52, 53
  in documents and systems 50, 51
  lack of cadence 56
  operational and delivery indicators 52
  passive behavior 56
  undocumented vendor onboarding 56
anti-patterns 31, 187
  cloud adoption-related anti-patterns 359
  DevSecOps culture and automation 358
  general indicators 358
  identifying 357
  knowledge outsourcing, to consultancies 49
  observability anti-patterns 359
  operational anti-patterns 359
  strategic anti-patterns 359
  strategic related anti-patterns 359
  technology anti-patterns 360

anti-patterns, cloud adoption runaway train
blueprints, ignoring 63
CI/CD best practices, ignoring 63
coding best practices, ignoring 65
operational best practices, ignoring 64

anti-patterns, lack of clear objectives and strategy
bottom-up strategy trap 32
top-down strategy trap 33

anti-patterns, lack of migration strategy
cloud footprint, growing organically 40
guidance 40, 41
lack of service catalog 41

anti-patterns, lack of partnership strategy
panic-driven partner selection 54

anti-patterns, outsourcing of cloud knowledge and governance
knowledge outsourcing, to consultancies 48
knowledge outsourcing, to freelancers 48

anti-patterns, tagging
lack, of tagging enforcement 103
lack, of tagging standards 103

API aggregation layer 208
API Gateway 190
Apigee 190
API Management 190
API proxy layer 190
application code 187
application configuration
as state 196

application function 106
application logging 164
application performance 390
application performance monitoring (APM) 202
application role 106
arrange, act, and assert (AAA) 340
artificial intelligence (AI) 4

asynchronous traffic
benefits 250
versus, synchronous traffic 249

attribute-based access control (ABAC) 10
automated intelligence
used, for centralized monitoring 271, 272

automated pipeline 139
automated testing 99
automation, for resilience 311
automate failover 311
autoscaling 311, 312
features 312
load balancing 311

Autoscale feature 272
Auto Scaling groups 195
availability zones (AZs) 10, 33, 235
AWS API Gateway 208
AWS Cloud Adoption Framework (CAF) 60, 61, 385
AWS EC2 42
AWS Heroes and Community Builders 57
AWS Identity and Access Management (IAM) 257
AWS Migration Acceleration Program (MAP) 44
AWS Migration Evaluator 315
AWS Prescriptive Guidance 61
AWS Security Hub 169
AWS Security Token Service (STS) 163
AWS Server Migration Service 42
AWS Step Functions 195
AWS Trusted Advisor 116
AWS Web Application Firewall (WAF) 330
AWS Well-Architected Framework 61
AWS X-Ray 265
Azure 33
Azure Active Directory (AAD) 257
Azure APIM 208

Azure App Service 195

Azure Automation 272

Azure Blob Storage 194

Azure Blueprints 62

Azure Cache 193

Azure CAF 61

Azure Event Grid 199

Azure Logic Apps 195

Azure Migrate 42, 315

Azure Migration and Modernization
Program (AAMP) 44

Azure Monitor 265

Azure Policy 62

Azure Resource Manager (ARM) 15, 107

Azure Security Center 169

Azure Service Bus 199

Azure SQL 42

Azure Synapse 194

Azure VMs 42

B

backend for frontend (BFF) 198, 342

backup and recovery 223
game day 225, 226
plan 223, 224

behavior-driven development (BDD) 149

benefits, cloud native 8
CI/CD 11
cost benefits and paradigm change 12
elasticity 9
faster time to market 8, 9
global deployments 11
managed services 9
portability 12
reliability and availability 10
scalability 9
security and compliance 10

BigQuery 194

blob storage 219

blue-green deployment 204

bottom-up strategy trap 32

building blocks, for continuous
improvement
examples 392

business account manager 59

business agility 35, 46

business as usual (BAU) 68, 106

business case, of cloud native adoption 366
document 372-375
external factors, addressing 369-371
high-level plan, socializing with
broader group 366, 367
next steps and other considerations 375, 376
organization-specific details,
adding 368, 369
roadmap, building and keeping
stakeholders informed 371, 372
technology impacts, addressing 369-371

business drivers 46

business goals 47

business logic 187

business outcomes 60

business strategy 31

C

calcified bureaucracy 82
strategies, for disrupting 83
symptoms 82

canary deployment 204

capital expenditure (CapEx) investment 12

CAP theorem 212
availability 212
consistency 212
partition tolerance 212

centralized governance 79-82
centralized logging 47, 396
centralized monitoring
  AI example 272
  with automated intelligence 271, 272
change advisory board (CAB) 95
change failure rate (CFR) 14
chaos engineering 205
chief information officer (CIO) 35
CI/CD standardization articulation 36
CI/CD toolchain 47
cloud 5
  non-functional requirements, testing 352
  recreating 348
  testing honeycomb 350
  traditional testing paradigm 349
cloud adoption framework (CAF) 44
  communalities 62
cloud adoption-related anti-patterns 359
cloud AI/ML
  leveraging, for anomaly detection 269
cloud business office (CBO) 84
cloud center of excellence (CCoE) 80, 83
  recommended strategies, for creating 84
  structure 84
cloud complexity 290, 291
  collaborative learning 293
  training 291, 292
  upskilling 291, 292
cloud development kit (CDK) 107
cloud engineering 84
cloud factories 189
Cloud Firestore 194
cloud governance
  change management, integrating
    into operating model 96
  proactive culture, creating 98
  role of change management 95, 96

cloud migrations
  applications, prioritizing 316
  assessment phase 321, 322
  cloud model, defining 317
  current environment, assessing 315
  effective migration, planning 313
  full-scale migration 322
  optimization and fine-tuning 322
  pilot test 322
  platform, selecting 319
  Proof of Concept (PoC) 322
  regular check-ins, with stakeholders 322
  significance, of effective
    migration planning 314
  timelines and milestones, setting 321
  treatment plan, using 318, 319
cloud model
  defining 317
  hybrid cloud 317, 318
  multi-cloud 317
  single cloud 317
cloud native 3, 6, 32
  benefits 8-12
  evolution 4
  misunderstandings 23-28
  operational aspects 47
cloud native adoption
  cultural impact 73, 74
  current state, defining 361-363
  effective strategies, for cultural change 79
  target state, defining 364-366
cloud native application protection
    platform (CNAPP) 7, 52, 201
cloud native bandwidth 236
  ambiguity 237
  limitations, for containers and serverless 238
Cloud Native Computing
    Foundation (CNCF) 7

cloud native DNS management 240
  clashing DNS, overcoming 240
  on-premises DNS 240
Cloud-Native Governance Tools
  using 326
cloud native IaC 15
cloud native initiatives
  people and organizational aspects 46
  technology aspects 47
cloud native latency 232
  cross-zone latency 235, 236
  with services 234, 235
cloud native networking features
  IaC and automation 255, 256
  inadequate network access reviews 254, 255
  missing boundary guardrails 254, 255
  SDN in cloud 251
cloud native principles 35
cloud native problems
  solving, without cloud native
    experience 206, 207
cloud native security
  tips, for reviewing implementation 329-331
cloud platform, considerations
  compliance 320
  cost 319
  hybrid cloud strategy 320
  latency and regional presence 320
  multi-cloud strategy 320
  security 320
  services and features, evaluating 319
cloud provider-managed networks 201
Cloud Run 195
Cloud Service Provider (CSP) 4, 32, 317
Cloud Service Provider (CSP) SLAs 307
  automation, for resilience 311
  multi-cloud architecture 309
  provider downtime, preparing 308
  redundancy, building 307, 308

Cloud Spanner 194
Cloud Storage 194
Cloud Trace 265
cloud transformation value chain 60
code generation
  type generation 344
code scanning 37
cohesion 196
cold recovery 205
collaborative culture
  strategies, for building 394
commander's intent 153
commercial off-the-shelf (COTS) 42
committed use discounts (CUDs) 117
community of practice (COP) 35, 80
compliance audits 40
Comprehensive Backup Plan 299
  building 293
  RPO, versus RTO 293
comprehensive coverage 171
consulting partner
  selecting, considerations 57, 58
container orchestration 37
containers 6, 47
content delivery network (CDN) 145
**content distribution network
    (CDN) 6, 40, 127**
Continuous Compliance 169
continuous compliance validation 172, 173
continuous improvement 391, 392
  building blocks, establishing 392
  culture, embracing 393, 394
  DORA metrics, for performance
    insights 396, 397
  feedback loops, embedding for 396
  governance frameworks, creating 392, 393
  governance frameworks, modifying 392, 393
  teams, empowering for autonomy
    and accountability 394

technology dependencies, addressing 395

third-party integrations, managing 395

continuous improvement and continuous delivery (CI/CD) 140

continuous improvement, tagging

cloud native tools, for regular audits 108

tagging automation and enforcement 107

continuous integration and continuous delivery (CI/CD) 5, 16, 99

structure, defining 16

continuous monitoring 171

contract 340

contract testing 340, 341

client generation 344

code generation 344

enforcement 343

initial contract 341-343

portability 343

server stub generation 344

conversation, framing 212

CAP theorem 212

normal forms 213-215

time complexity 216

Conway's law 4, 197

corporate strategy

checkpoints and guardrails, implementing 268

correlation ID 200

Cosmos DB 194

cost management 47

cost of ignoring learning 68, 69

addressing 69-72

cost optimization controls 38

cost savings, over driving value 127, 128

anti-patterns 128, 129

impacts 130

indicators 131

problems, tackling 131, 132

coupled services

decoupling 199

coupling 196

coverage badge tests 336

CSP partnership

improving, considerations 59

CSP selection 35

considerations 57

cultural change 40

cultural shift, managing 303

collaboration, encouraging 303

cross-functional teams 304, 305

DevSecOps mindset, promoting 305

knowledge sharing 305

resistance to change, overcoming 306

silos, breaking down 304

current state 361

Customer SLA / SLO 294

custom off-the-shelf (COTS) 360

D

databases 216

graph databases 217

key-value stores 217

life cycle and archive policy, ignoring 219, 220

NoSQL databases 217

other database types 218

relational databases 216

serverless databases 218

storage requirements, ignoring 219

data best practices 47

Databricks 194

data egress fees 33

data integrity dependency 229

inverting 229

maintaining 230

**data replication, from production
    to development** 221

  production data, masking 221

  synthetic data, creating 222, 223

  synthetic data, working with 221, 222

data sovereignty 37

data warehouse (DWH) 121

DDoS (distributed denial-of-service) 10

dead letter queues (DLQs) 41, 199

decentralized governance 81

  lack of decentralized governance,
    challenges 80

deployment best practices 47

deployment frequency (DF) 14, 390

destructive changes anti-pattern 144

detective guardrails 87, 146

  benefits 88

DevOps 5, 6, 13

**DevOps Research and Assessment
    (DORA) metrics** 137, 396

  for performance insights 396, 397

**DevOps Research and Assessment
    (DORA) team** 14

DevSecOps 6, 13, 14, 33, 138, 139, 393

  culture and automation 358

DevSecOps culture 50

disaster recovery (DR) 11, 204, 293, 294, 299

  accidental data loss 295

  availability zone failure 298

  instance loss 295-297

distributed applications 4

distributed tracing 264, 396

documentation generation 37

Domain Driven Design 140

domain name service (DNS) logs 18

**dynamic application security testing
    (DAST) framework** 146

DynamoDB 194

E

edge computing 6

edge locations 11

ElastiCache 193

Elastic Cloud Compute (EC2) 5

Elastic Load Balancing 195

encryption 37

end-to-end distributed tracing tools

  AWS X-Ray 265

  Azure Monitor 265

  Cloud Trace 265

end-to-end tests 345

environmental drift 207

epic 371

EventBridge 199

external audits 173

external state storage 193

F

facade approach 390

Faker.js

  URL 221

Faker library

  reference link 221

fallback mechanisms 395

fault tolerance 35

feature flags 143

feature release

  decoupling 143

feedback loops 91

  cost of time and effort 93

  need for 92

  slowed development cycle and
    increased pressure 93, 94

FinOps 7, 101
  anti-patterns 109-111
  anti-patterns, impacts 111
  cost management, through SDLC 112
  deploy phase 114, 115
  implement and test phase 114, 115
  maintain and improve phase 115-118
  plan and design phase 112-114
firewalls 189
Forrester 58
fragmentation
  example 275, 276
  issues 275
function as a service (FaaS) 6, 34, 97

G

G2 58
gaps 361
Gartner 58
GCP API Gateway 208
GCP CAF 62
GCP Cloud SQL 42
GCP Migrate for Compute Engine 42
GCP Rapid Migration and Modernization
    Program (RaMP) 44
generalized inverted index (GIN) 218
Git branch 17
  pruning 141, 142
GitHub Actions 36
git pull command 17
global reach 35
Google Cloud Innovators 57
Google Cloud Platform (GCP) 5, 33, 232
Google Cloud Security Command
    Center (SCC) 169

Google Kubernetes Engine 195
Google Pub/Sub 199
Google's GCE 42
Google Workflows 195
governance 67, 68
governance framework 392
governance, risk, and compliance
    (GRC) policies 85, 90
  challenges 90, 91
  enforcing, significance 90
  key elements 90
graph databases 217
guardrails 37, 38, 85, 145
  benefits 86
  case, for guardrail observability 146, 147
  detective guardrails 87, 146
  example 147, 148
  preventative guardrails 146
  proactive guardrails 87

H

hardware 189
hardware security module (HSM) 127
Harvey ball 38
hexagonal architecture 354, 355
high availability (HA) 236
high-privilege accounts
  securing 158, 159
holistic due diligence 60
hot recovery 205
human resources (HR) 369
hybrid workload integration 266
  components 266
hypervisors 189

I

identity and access management (IAM) 10, 201, 329

Identity-Aware Proxy (IAP) 257

ignoring cultural change 74

  lack of buy-in 75, 76

  lack of buy-in, overcoming 76, 77

  poor communication 77, 78

  poor communication, overcoming 78

  resistance to change 74

  resistance to change, overcoming 75

ignoring observability anti-pattern 202, 203

ignoring reliability anti-pattern 203-205

ignoring security anti-pattern 200-202

implicit ephemeral specification

  avoiding 209

implicit trust 257

incident response maturity 287

indiscriminate logging

  failure, reasons 262

infrastructure as a service (IaaS) 23, 36

infrastructure as code (IaC) 15, 96, 107, 143, 209, 251, 351, 387

  advantages 16

insecure hash algorithms 191

integrated development environment (IDE) 17

integration tests 345

interface definition language (IDL) 340

internal DNS 204

Internet Engineering Task Force (ITEF) 344

Internet of Things (IoT) 6

ISO 9001 300

isolated development 150

IT service management system (ITSM) 95

J

jitter 209

JSON Web Token (JWT) 193

K

key-value stores 217

Kong 208

Kubernetes 6, 190

L

lack of standardization 40

Lambda function 197

Lambdalith 197

layered networking 247

leadership team (LT) 111

lead time for changes (LTFC) 14

least privilege enforcement 37

lift and shift 187, 188

  building in cloud, versus building for cloud 188

  cloud factories 189

  cloud native, through strangler fig pattern 189-192

Lighthouse 316

limitless scale

  downside 207-209

linting 37

load balancers 195

Log4Shell 167

log aggregation

  improving, with AI insights 270, 271

Log Aggregator 262

logging 47, 164

  application logging 164

  security logging 164

logs 18

    quality 19, 20

**Loki, Grafana, Tempo, and Mimir
(LGTM) Stack 396**

low cohesion 200

low-quality code 352

    hexagonal architecture 354, 355

    key terms 353

    monolithic application 353, 354

    structuring 355, 356

M

machine learning (ML) 4

    services 123

manual data ingestion 226

    failure granularity 227

    first data ingestion pipeline 227

    pipeline, scaling 228

    pipelines, streaming 228

manual testing 344

    case, for test automation 345-347

    processes, migrating 347, 348

    typical company testing archetypes 345

maturity level 39

mean time to recovery (MTTR) 14

mean time to restore (MTTR) 144

Memorystore 193

metric dumping 284

    example 284, 285

microservices 6, 47

Microsoft Learn training platform 62

Microsoft Most Valuable Professionals 57

migration acceleration initiative 44

    assessment, reading 44

    change, quantifying 46

    funding 44

    migration planning 45

    organizational context 45

    proof of concept 45

    simplified treatment plan example 45

    treatment plan 45

migration plan 385

    agility, building 386

    building 385

    continuous feedback 391

    delivery initiatives, planning 387, 388

    flexibility, building 386

    phased delivery 388, 389

    success, measuring 390

    transition architecture elements 386

    transition architectures, building
        into delivery initiatives 390

migration readiness assessment 44

migration strategy 37

migration strawman 43

**minimum stakeholder
commitment 323, 324**

minimum viable product (MVP) 77

Miro 44

ML automation

    operational complexity,
        reducing through 272

    working example 273, 274

Momento 193

monitoring 20, 47

monolith 353, 354

monolithic connectivity 244-246

    monolithic friction, with cloud native 246

    networking-focused example 248

    three-tier network 248, 249

    to layered networking 246, 247

    to microservice 248

multi-cloud 33

Multi-Factor Authentication (MFA) 10, 162

multistage tests 340

Mural 44

mutable artifacts anti-pattern 144

N

NAT gateway (NAT-GW) 128
National Cyber Security Center of
    Excellence (NCCoE) 7
National Institute of Standards and
    Technology (NIST) 7
neglecting distributed tracing 274
  best practices, for resolving 281, 282
  fragmentation problem 275
  metrics 276-278
  real world consequences 278-280
network access control list (NACL) 10, 148
network address translation
    (NAT) gateway 23
network security groups (NSGs) 257
non-disclosure agreement (NDA) 56
non-obvious CSP cost
  anti-patterns 119-122
  factors 122-124
  ignoring 118
  indicators 125, 126
  missing non-obvious cost, impacts 124, 125
  remediations 126, 127
no reverse definition for a change
    anti-pattern 144, 145
normal forms 213
  1NF 213
  2NF 214
  3NF 214, 215
NoSQL databases 217

O

observability 18, 20, 264
observability anti-patterns 359
observability platform 139
ongoing security assessments 171
  comprehensive coverage 171
  continuous monitoring 171
  proactive defense and continuous
      compliance 171
  vulnerability scans and penetration tests 171
online transaction processing (OLTP) 219
Open Policy Agent (OPA) 7, 38, 107
  policies 114
OpenSearch 206
OpenTelemetry 7, 20
OpenTofu 15
operational anti-patterns 359
operational complexity
  reducing, through ML automation 272
operational expenses (OpEx) 25
organizational transformation 60
organizational unit (OU) level 115
outsourcing
  drivers 47
over-privileged users and services 159
  permissions for humans 160
  permissions for services 160
  principle of least privilege 160

P

partner ecosystem 57
password database security 191
Payment Card Industry Data Security
    Standard (PCI-DSS) 10
permissions
  managing, without over-privilege 157
persistent state data 193
personally identifiable information (PII) 97
pilot light strategy 205
pipeline run 37
platform-agnostic IaC 15

platform as a service (PaaS) model 23

platform tools 139

policy-as-code framework 38

Poly-cloud 33

ports 354

prescriptive guidance 45

preventative guardrails 146

principle of least privilege

access requirements 161

applying 160

identity and access management
tools, leveraging 161

logging, implementing 164

monitoring, implementing 164

Multi-Factor Authentication
(MFA), implementing 162

regular audits of permissions 162

role-based access control (RBAC) 161

temporary and fine-grained
access, using 163

user education and training 164

**proactive defense and continuous
compliance 171**

proactive guardrails 87

benefits 87

proactive monitoring 171, 395

continuous compliance validation 172

external audits 173

ongoing security assessments 171

proactive security culture, building 173

security processes, automating 172

proactive security culture

building 173

process transformation 60

product backlog 371

product owner 371

product transformation 60

professional service partner 57

provider downtime, preparing 308

multi-cloud architecture 309

offsite backup in, other cloud/
hybrid solutions 309

third-party redundancy 309

trade offs 310

publish and subscribe pattern 41

pull requests (PRs) 18, 95

Q

quality assurance (QA) 149

quality controls 37

quality of service (QoS) 242

R

randomness 209

real-time monitoring 396

real-time transactions

monitoring, significance 266, 267

recovery 35

automating 21

testing 22

recovery point objective (RPO) 21, 204, 293

**recovery time objective
(RTO) 21, 205, 293, 294**

relational databases 216

reliability 37

remediation controls 87

**replicating on-prem security
controls 327, 328**

request for proposal (RFP) 368

request for quote (RFQ) 368

resilience 18, 20, 21, 46

**responsible, accountable, consulted,
and informed (RACI) model
25, 85, 88, 89, 379**

reusable artifacts 47

R models, for cloud migration strategies

refactor 42

rehosting 42

relocate 42

replatforming 42

repurchasing 42

retain 42

retire 43

roadmap 384

adjusting 390

migration plan 385, 386

role-based access control (RBAC) 10

rolling deployments 204

Route 53 Resolver 240

runbooks and documentation update 299

best practices 301, 302

documentation, automating 300

maintaining 299

Standard Operating Procedures (SOPs) 300

S

sandboxes 15

sandpits 15

scalability 22

security 189, 200

security and compliance 167

automation 169

compliance frameworks 168

importance 168

improvements 167

proactive security culture, building 170

wrapping up 170

Security Assertion Markup Language (SAML) 193

security information and event management (SIEM) tools 10

security logging 164

self-sufficient teams 152

champions 155

team topology 153, 154

trifecta leadership 152, 153

T-shaped engineer 155

serverless databases 218, 219

serverless functions

chaining 198

service catalog 40

service control policy (SCP) 145

service-level agreements (SLAs) 19, 203, 242, 395

service-level objectives (SLOs) 203

service meshes 6

service-oriented architecture (SOA) 4

session affinity 193

shared responsibility model 174, 329

across AWS 175

across Azure 175, 176

across GCP 176

cloud provider proof of compliance 179

cloud providers responsibilities 174

customers responsibilities 174

misconceptions 178

misconceptions, addressing 174

misconfigurations 179

shift left approach 13, 35, 97

benefits 97

shift left effect, on development team 149

development, as iterative process 149

feedback 151

security, building 152

shared ownership, of output 150

test first, code later 149

short-lived session tokens 193

siloed model 136

siloed release models 200

siloing 33

Simple Queue Service (SQS) 5, 199

Simple Storage Service (S3) 5, 194

single-purpose function 197

single sign-on (SSO) 10

site reliability engineering (SRE) 145

skill gap 40, 331

  closing 332, 333

slow cloud up-ramp 40

smart logging 262

  example 263, 264

software as a service (SaaS) 6, 36

software bill of materials (SBoM) 201

software composition analysis (SCA) 13

software-defined networking (SDN) 251

  case study 252, 253

  examples 252

  networking mindset changes,
    with cloud native 252

software delivery life cycle (SDLC) 200

software development life cycle
  (SDLC) 7, 112

software vendor

  selecting, considerations 58

software vendor partnership 58

solutions architect (SA) 59

Squad Model 152

stakeholder alignment 378

  challenges 380-384

  required people, identifying 379, 380

  stakeholder management considerations 378

stakeholders 324

  engagement, in cloud adoption 325, 326

  technical considerations 326, 327

Standard Operating Procedures (SOPs) 300

state as a service 195

state assertion pattern 193

stateful processes 192

stateless cloud paradigm 194

stateless server 193, 194

statement of work (SoW) 50

static application security
  testing (SAST) 138

  tools 13

static credentials 165

storage tiers

  archive 220

  cold 220

  hot 220

strangler fig pattern 189, 390

strategic anti-patterns 359

strategic aspects 34

strategic partnerships 55

strategy

  defining 39

  guardrail examples, throughout SDLC 37, 38

  holistic end-to-end view, across SDLC 38

strategy foundations

  defining 36, 37

  people 36

  process 37

  technology 37

  vision 36

strawman

  aspects 44

structured data corruptions 222

subject matter experts (SMEs) 57, 363

supply chain security 180

  challenges 180

  examples 182

  supply chain risks, avoiding 181

supporting data 194

synchronous, versus synchronous traffic 249

  monolithic connectivity, addressing 250, 251

  strongly consistent to eventually
    consistent systems 250

synthetic data

  creating 222

  working with 221, 222

T

tagging 102

  benefits 102

  poor tagging practices, consequences 104

  syntax 107

  taxonomy 106

tagging values 107

tag keys 106

  application identifier 106

  business domain 106

  business owner 106

  cost center 106

  level of detail 106

  portfolio name 106

  service identifier 106

  technical owner 106

tags 102

target state 361

team empowerment 137, 138

technical account manager 59

technical and soft skills

  balancing 333, 334

technical debt 35

technology anti-patterns 360

technology objectives and principles

  buy-in 35

  collaboration 35

  defining 35

  objectives, addressing 35

  principles, defining 35

  stakeholder engagement, continuing 36

  stakeholder management 35

technology transformation 60

telemetry 200

Terraform 36

test-driven development (TDD) 149, 336

  green 336

  red 336

  refactor 336

testing anti-patterns 335

  coverage badge tests 336

  implementation details, testing 337

  intermittently failing tests 338

  multistage tests 340

  never-failing tests 336

  tests, with side effects or
    coupled tests 338, 339

testing honeycomb 350

testing, in cloud

  versus, testing for cloud 350, 351

The 12 Factor App

  URL 142

threat model 201

threat modeling 166

tight coupling 200

time-to-market 35

time to recovery (TTR) 390

timing leaks 191

token lifetimes 193

top-down approach 33

top-down strategy trap 33

total cost of ownership (TCO) 23

traditional testing paradigm 349

traffic segregation (QoS)

  best practices 243

  fintech case study 242

  key considerations, for backup link 244

  risks of failing 242, 243

  undermining 242

transient state data 193

transition architectures

  elements 386

Transport Layer Security (TLS) 190
  certificate management 64
treatment plan 40
trifecta leadership 152
T-shaped engineer 155
Turing test 4
two-pizza team 82
  advantages 82
  topology 13

U

unified observability
  tools, adopting to handle hybrid
    workloads 266
unit tests 345
unstructured data corruptions 223
untagged resources 104
  in AWS 104
  in Azure 105
  in GCP 105
User Acceptance Testing (UAT) 285
user stories 371

V

value stream map 32
vendor lock-in 33
verifiable state representation 193
virtualization 4
Virtual Machine Scale Sets 195
virtual machines (VMs) 4
virtual networks (VNets) 259
virtual private clouds (VPCs) 201, 232
VMWare 42
vulnerability scans and penetration tests 171

W

Wardley Mapping 34
warm recovery 205
web application firewalls (WAFs) 91, 145
Well-Architected Framework 62

Y

you build it, you run it mentality 13

Z

Zero Trust 327
  application patterns 256
  cloud native example 258
  in cloud native, versus on-premises
    environments 257
  key principles 257, 258
  network defense, in depth versus
    flat networks 259, 260
Zero Trust Architecture (ZTA) framework 7
zero-trust authentication and
  authorization 201

packtpub.com

Subscribe to our online digital library for full access to over 7,000 books and videos, as well as industry leading tools to help you plan your personal development and advance your career. For more information, please visit our website.

Why subscribe?

- Spend less time learning and more time coding with practical eBooks and Videos from over 4,000 industry professionals

- Improve your learning with Skill Plans built especially for you

- Get a free eBook or video every month

- Fully searchable for easy access to vital information

- Copy and paste, print, and bookmark content

Did you know that Packt offers eBook versions of every book published, with PDF and ePub files available? You can upgrade to the eBook version at packtpub.com and as a print book customer, you are entitled to a discount on the eBook copy. Get in touch with us at customercare@packtpub.com for more details.

At www.packtpub.com, you can also read a collection of free technical articles, sign up for a range of free newsletters, and receive exclusive discounts and offers on Packt books and eBooks.

Other Books You May Enjoy

If you enjoyed this book, you may be interested in these other books by Packt:

Platform Engineering for Architects

Max Körbächer, Andreas Grabner, Hilliary Lipsig

ISBN: 978-1-83620-359-9

- Make informed decisions aligned with your organization's platform needs
- Identify missing platform capabilities and manage that technical debt effectively
- Develop critical user journeys to enhance platform functionality
- Define platform purpose, principles, and key performance indicators
- Use data-driven insights to guide product decisions
- Design and implement platform reference and target architectures

Continuous Testing, Quality, Security, and Feedback

Marc Hornbeek

ISBN: 978-1-83546-224-9

- Ensure continuous testing, quality, security, and feedback in DevOps, DevSecOps, and SRE practices

- Apply capability maturity models, set goals, conduct discoveries, and set benchmarks for digital transformations

- Implement and assess continuous improvement strategies with various tools and frameworks

- Avoid pitfalls and enhance user experience with gap assessments, value stream management, and roadmaps

- Adhere to proven engineering practices for software delivery and operations

- Stay on top of emerging trends in AI/ML and continuous improvement

Packt is searching for authors like you

If you're interested in becoming an author for Packt, please visit `authors.packtpub.com` and apply today. We have worked with thousands of developers and tech professionals, just like you, to help them share their insight with the global tech community. You can make a general application, apply for a specific hot topic that we are recruiting an author for, or submit your own idea.

Share Your Thoughts

Now you've finished *Cloud Native Anti-Patterns*, we'd love to hear your thoughts! Scan the QR code below to go straight to the Amazon review page for this book and share your feedback or leave a review on the site that you purchased it from.

`https://packt.link/r/1836200595`

Your review is important to us and the tech community and will help us make sure we're delivering excellent quality content.